Essays Contributing to an Understanding of Contemporary Life

America, Changing . . .

Edited by

Patrick Gleeson

San Francisco State College

Charles E. Merrill Publishing Company
Columbus, Ohio
A Bell and Howell Company

Library of Congress Catalog Number: 68-17414

2 3 4 5 6 7 8 9 10 — 72 71 70 69 68

Printed in the United States of America

INTRODUCTION

What is America like in the sixties? *Life* magazine might respond to this question with a photo essay emphasizing the variety of American experience: teenagers skiing down California sanddunes on one page, hippies and a New York happening on the next, and so on. From this and more like it in newspapers and mass circulation magazines one could conclude that contemporary American life is interesting and somehow ongoing, if unpredictable.

But reality is more than the total of discrete events, and in order to understand our environment adequately we need to know about something other than the apparently unrelated incidents that are newsworthy. Behind the single event are interrelated conditions and processes, often in astoundingly far-reaching and complex patterns. It is not only that for want of a shoe the horse was lost, then the fight and finally the war; how did the shoe happen to be wanting in the first place? and why *horses?*

At one time or another we all have difficulty seeing how one social phenomenon relates to another, particularly in instances where we sense, however dimly, that a thorough analysis might threaten our own world view. The white urbanite is angry and confused by the apparently sudden violence of an insurrection in the Negro ghetto, whether in his own city or not, and may retaliate by voting against a local open housing ordinance. In doing so does he see himself *causing* further unrest? Does he see his action as the consequence of his unfamiliarity with black American culture and that as a consequence of the explicit or *de facto* segregation of the schools of his youth? Few are so wise.

To what extent has his subsequent action been determined for him by the media? The newspaper and television coverage although apparently objective has significantly contributed to his view of the matter by presenting a detailed account of *incidents* without saying much about the history of the ghetto or of present living conditions there. Yet the jamming of two families into a three-room flat with a monthly rental as much as fifty per cent higher than the rental for a similar flat outside the ghetto area is as much a "fact" as the television film of a rioter throwing a bottle through the window. The *relation* between these two phenomena is as real as anything photographable, but it is often introduced afterward as a relatively minor matter—"background," or subjective opinion. This journalistic emphasis on action rather than condition has produced among us a crisis mentality: we are alert to *acute* situations but tend not to see fully the significant *chronic* conditions which underlie them.

Commenting on this inability to become sufficiently concerned with social phenomena soon enough to deal with them before they are critical, some writers have implied that we need to make up our minds to look at things differently—that as a matter of social justice we must. This may be true, but the decision is not only moral. We also need to know *how* to view things differently. This is frequently the more difficult task. In *Patterns of Discovery* N. R. Hanson considers Galileo's 1604 formulation of the law regarding the increase in the velocity of falling bodies, namely that the velocity is proportional to the distance of its fall. Physics students will recognize that this early formulation is wrong. The correct form of the law, that velocity is proportional not to distance but time, came to Galileo only in 1632, nearly thirty years later. Since in the abstract distance seems as likely a coordinate as time, how did Galileo err? Because, Hanson writes, "The thinking of scientists in this period ran along geometrical rails; it was constituted of ideas of spatial relations. A 'time co-ordinate' would have had little significance for these natural philosophers, as little as would a 'fragrance' or a 'beauty' co-ordinate." In this light it is really more surprising that Galileo was able to break through his conceptual limitations at all; his greatness consists largely in just that ability. Similarly, we find it difficult to reassess our interpretation of reality not only because we have various stakes in it, but because it is nearly impossible to see that there is an interpretation involved at all, that reality would possibly be construed another way.

Where does reality end and interpretation begin? Journalists frequently distinguish between objective reportage and subjective commentary. In this view there is an irreducible core of fact surrounded by a potentially vast body of opinion, much of it conflicting. In the example above, the motion picture of the rioter throwing a bottle is seen to be a fact, "reality" itself, while the explanation, that economic and social circumstances determined largely by the white community have somehow contributed to the act, is "opinion." Although we frequently distinguish between "mere" and "informed" opinion in order to indicate whether or not we find it compatible with "fact," even informed opinion has, for most of us, quite different status from fact itself.

This view takes insufficient account of the selections involved in arriving at facts. If the motion picture image is "factual," then so is it that a certain image was photographed, edited, and screened while another image was not. This selection of one image over another *is* interpretation, i. e., it consists of many value judgments as to what is newsworthy, what is consistent with the general nature of the insurrection and hence representative, and so forth. It is also the case that the image presented has no meaning until it is *read,* that is, until someone relates it in some way to other material. The material we relate it to, and the way we relate may not be strictly controllable but they are nevertheless selected. It would be more accurate to say that facts are phenomena selected in a less voluntary and more intuitive way than opinion, while opinion is phenomena we feel we have selected voluntarily or that others may have reasonably selected and arranged differently. What we call "reality" then is that core of interpretation which we do not feel free to change.

That different groups see different realities is itself a valuable discovery. The American linguist Benjamin Whorf has pointed out that among speakers of one language certain concepts are almost completely obligatory—one cannot speak without subscribing to them—which in another language have no status at all. Even such conceptions as time, movement, and matter are not universal, and, indeed, whole cultures have existed quite satisfactorily without one or more of these conceptions as we know them. This seems almost incredible to us; we are inclined to think that even if these basic conceptions were never written or uttered they must have existed mentally all the same. In the Hopi Indian language, however, time and space are a single concept, and speakers of Hopi find it just as incredible that although in our language we speak of time and space separately we do not mentally integrate them as they "really" are. Again, as Whorf points out, the language of the Nootkas consists wholly of what we call "verbs." Yet life among these once wealthy Vancouver Island Indians was unimpaired in its materiality; nor could the Nootkas have imagined that in some other language there could be another class of words, "persons, places, and things," or that they could have any real use.

II

We have been considering that even the reality of a single event consists of too many interrelated phenomena to be grasped entirely. Instead we have interpretations which include or are included by others and which we feel more or less free to change.

The essays in this book offer more interpretations, frequently conflicting, which seem to me to deal effectively with the conditions and processes underlying critical social areas: youth, the city, the culture of an economy of abundance, Negro rights, and the social consequences of automation. Within these topics I have selected these rather than other essays for several reasons. In some cases the viewpoints represented are often disregarded or reported with bias by the press. In two or three instances what is written has been a seminal statement or has had enough effect already to give it the continuing relevance of an historical document (Dr. King's letter is the notable instance). More often though I selected those essays which take into account those far-reaching interrelations which, I suggested earlier, are frequently overlooked by the mass media. The first essay, Bruno Bettelheim's "Problem of Generations" is the broadest short discussion of the subject I know of. Breadth has not always been my criterion, however. The last essay, written by an acquaintance, strikes me as cranky and partial. Still it is the best statement of that viewpoint I know of. Between there are others which I consider brilliant (Raymond Williams' "Prelude to Alienation"), admirable (Mario Savio's "Certain Things That Happened at Berkeley"), and wrong (Richard Weaver's "Image of Culture").

Regardless of the viewpoint presented, each essay deserves, I am convinced, more than *evaluation.* No one would deny that one must, as Auden writes, "distinguish between odd and even numbers." But the best use of this book includes evaluation, the estimation from a given standpoint, perhaps *change*, the assumption of a new standpoint, and most important, *understanding.*

If we become so occupied deciding whether a tree is graceful or not according to certain standards we may never see how graceful the tree *is*—how it conforms perfectly to its own standards. The tree, remember, expresses itself perfectly, as nothing else can. Similarly with these essays. We should not spend so much time evaluating them we forget what they *are*. It is useful to decide whether LeRoi Jones' view of Black Nationalism is reasonable, but it is even more useful to infer from his essay why he thinks that way, and what probable effect that way of thinking may have on others. It is also interesting to decide whether Norbert Wiener ("Some Moral and Technical Consequences of Automation") or Arthur Samuel ("Some . . . Consequences: A Refutation") is right, but it is even more important to know that two such opposing views are held by knowledgeable observers of this segment of contemporary culture, and to try to understand why such opposition is possible.

Contents

Sources

The sources of the articles contained in this volume include the following:

Youth: Change and Challenge, edited by Erik H. Erikson
Atlantic Monthly
Dissent
Scientific American
Literary and Philosophical Essays, by Jean-Paul Sartre
The Antioch Review
Understanding Media: The Extensions of Man, by Marshall McLuhan
Man and the Modern City, edited by Elizabeth Green
Organization Man, by William H. Whyte, Jr.
The Affluent Society, by John Kenneth Galbraith
Like a Conquered Province, by Paul Goodman
Industrial Relations: A Journal of Economy and Society
The Guaranteed Income, by Robert Theobald
One-Dimensional Man, by Herbert Marcuse
The American Scholar
A Prophetic Minority, by Jack Newfield
Berkeley: The New Student Revolt, by Hal Draper
National Review
Contact
Daedalus
Visions of Order, by Richard Weaver
Why We Can't Wait, by Martin Luther King, Jr.
Home, by LeRoi Jones
The Negro Mood
Diogenes
Science in the Cause of Man, by Gerard Piel
Science
Man on Earth, by S.P.R. Charter

1

Youth

The Problem of Generations

Bruno Bettelheim

What strikes the psychologist forcefully when he surveys the available literature on adolescence and youth is that, if the amount of discussion were indicative, then all or nearly all problems of youth would appear to be those of the adolescent male. True, the more serious authors nod in the direction of female adolescence and recognize that it creates problems, too. But having done so, they turn so exclusively to the problems of the male adolescent that the net impression remains: female adolescence, if it exists at all, does not create problems equally worthy of the sociologist's or the psychologist's interest.

But whether we view adolescent development from a sociological or a psychological viewpoint, the problems confronting boys and girls should be parallel. The reassertion of sexual desires on reaching physical maturity is typical of both sexes, as are the psychological problems of repressing or satisfying these drives; of postponing the consummation of some and of sublimating the rest. So also, in modern times, are the social and psychological problems of achieving self-identity on a more mature basis, and of finding one's place in society.

Is it really so much easier for the adolescent girl to find her self-identity as a woman and her place in society, than for the boy to gain his as a man? True, Erikson describes cases of negative identity in women, but most of his writings on adolescence concern males, and other recent students of the problem such as Friedenberg and Goodman deal almost wholly with male youth.[1] Though Freud's original work was based on the study of hysteria in females, and though he devoted much thought to their difficulties in achieving sexual maturity, a problem typical of middle-class youth, his later writings centered mainly on the development of the male. In another context I have discussed how, in regard to puberty rites, nearly all psychoanalytic interest centers on boys, neglecting the far-reaching meaning the rites have for both boys and girls in achieving sexual maturity and adult status.[2]

Since I, too, have had to rely on available sources, and since they are so much richer in content and more abundant than any one man's observations can be, my discussion too will be weighted toward male youth; but at least I wish to acknowledge this deficiency in my remarks, and try to rectify it in part. I venture to say that those who conceived of this issue of *Daedalus* were caught in much the same predicament, since a careful reading of the suggestions they kindly offered me permits a consideration of the feminine only by stretching the points they detailed. Yet there must be a reason why the male adolescent and his problems dominate public attention and that of the scholarly expert.

Perhaps my particular topic allows for a first approximation as to why this is so: I was asked to discuss the problem of the generations from the psychologist's point of view. Unfortunately I shall have to transgress heavily into the field of sociology, since in my opinion the problem of generations is at best a psychosocial one, and can never be dealt with on a purely psychological basis.

It may be that the problem of generations is what gives us adults so much trouble, and not the problems of adolescence or youth; and this is why, when we concern ourselves with the problem of youth in our society, it is that of male youth. If delinquency worries us, it is chiefly male delinquency, though to their families and themselves, female delinquents are at least as great a problem.

For the same reason we are concerned with Johnny's not learning to read, or not getting enough science and math, as if reading problems were foreign to Jane, or as if she were automatically good at math and science. And if not, it is thought to matter little, since the number of female contributors to the sciences is relatively negligible. But such an evaluation of women's potential is both shortsighted and wasteful. Despite all the obstacles to women's higher education in the physical sciences, it was a young woman who did pioneering work in radioactivity, a development in physics which eventually led to the present clamor for more science education in our schools.

Since it is adults who conduct the studies and write the articles, and since these adults are predominantly male, they write most of where the shoe pinches them—that is, in regard to the problem of generations. They are neglectful of where the shoe hurts the young—that is, with the problem of sexual maturity and with finding one's place in society. True, each of these is well recognized as problematic, but especially so where they coincide with what is bothersome to adults, the relation of the generations to each other. They are neglected where they trouble adults less, as in the female.

I hasten to add that this respite in regard to the girls' part in the problem of generations is fast disappearing. I submit that already it creates more emotional hardship than that of the males, which at least is officially recognized. Why, then, is the problem of generations so much more acute in the male than in the female?

To put it crassly: the self-identity, and even more the self-realization of the young man, implies to a large degree his replacing the preceding generation. In order to come into his own, the old man (or whoever stands in his place) must move over; or, in the folklore of my native Austria, he must move into the old people's quarters (*Ausgedinge*). This happens as soon as the son is ready to take over the farm, and with it, all other prerogatives including the main building: the farmhouse.

Such ascendancy of youth over old age proceeds smoothly, at the right age and in the correct form, if it tallies with the survival needs of the entire family and with the facts of biology, in short, if it takes place in concordance with nature and nurture. The well-being of the farm family depended on a vigorous male being in charge at least of the farming, if not also of the family. For centuries most men lived on farms tilled by small landholders or serf-tenants, or else made a living as small artisans or shopkeepers. In those times economic success and often mere survival depended on the physical strength and skill of the head of the family. So it seemed "natural" that as the father's vigor declined, a son just reaching the prime of his strength and mental abilities should take over.

When this was so, and since the father's life was meaningful, that of the son who at first helped him and then followed in his footsteps was automatically meaningful, too. An old Chinese proverb summed things up: "He who has sons cannot long remain poor; he who has none cannot remain rich." This was something both fathers and sons understood. The son growing up was secure in everyone's knowledge that he added substantially to the economic well-being of the family. Seeing also that his contributions increased in importance as he approached maturity and the peak of his physical strength, just as his father was declining in vigor, he had no need to worry about his work achievement (as would now come through more indirect employment on the labor market) and whether it supported his claim to have reached manhood.

Such an easy succession of the generations, even in times past, was mainly an "ideal" solution to the changing of the guards. But actuality often approached this ideal; and if not, the biological realities made it seem like the given order of things, since production depended so largely on the male's prowess.

True, even when the level of technology was so low that physical strength counted most, one's experience and skill, the know-how of work and of life, had to be added to strength to succeed; but all one's experience and knowledge were of little avail without physical strength, because it alone powered the economic process. There was no point, therefore, in a selfish holding on to knowledge or even to property rights, because they were only theoretical if they could bring no return, once physical power had failed.

While there were always some old men who held on beyond reason, along with other conflicts of interest and generations, these were clearly men smitten with blindness or carried away by unreasonable emotions. An intelligent self-interest in both old and young still required a transition of power and privilege at the point when physical decline set in among the aging and manhood was gained by the young. An old man might stand in the way of his sons, but his fate was then ordained. Thus O'Neill's Ephraim Cabot is unwilling to recognize his son's contribution; but when the son walks off, not with the farm but with his father's young wife, the father ends up in possession of a farm that he alone cannot tend to.

It is when physical strength is no longer essential for survival or economic success that the biological process of aging as well as of maturing no longer, of necessity, conditions the taking over of the dominant position by youth. What once formed the "ideal" solution, because conditioned by the nature of man, suddenly turns into an arbitrary "ideal" without any necessary or natural basis. Such an ideal soon becomes hard to put into practice, and eventually even ceases to be an ideal.[3]

Even before modern times, wherever physical strength was not essential to survival because the life-assuring labor was performed by others, the problem of generations was acute. This was true, for example, of former ruling classes, and later on of the upper middle classes. It was also true in the Greece of Alcibiades and in Catiline's Rome. Whenever there was no natural order to the ascendancy of the generations, problems arose between them similar to those that are now typical for all in a machine age, when almost nobody's survival depends on physical strength.

If the young man's coming into his place as head of the living unit is not thus assured by the natural order of things, if he cannot be sure that the dominant position will be his at a foreseeable and not too distant moment, then he cannot wait for it in good grace. Then he must fight for it, for both his rights and his obligations, and the sooner the better, because only both in their combination make for the realm of the mature man.

If such a transition does not occur smoothly, is not accepted as natural and inevitable by both partners, then the older generation is likely to view the younger with suspicion, and justifiably so, because youth taking over is no longer necessary and natural. Why should the older generation voluntarily abdicate if it has nothing to gain by it and loses nothing by holding on?

Many if not most adults have an emotional need for children and enjoy bringing them up. It is such a truism that children for their part need their parents for physical and emotional survival that I mention it only to round out the picture. Once childhood is past, however, the picture changes. At certain times in history the older generation had an emotional need to see its way of life continued by the coming generations. This was particularly true when the parent generation had begun a work it could not complete and which it felt would remain pointless if uncompleted, be it the clearing of the land or the raising of a cathedral. Yet the more we came to doubt that things would continue in the old ways, that we were toiling for eternity, the less emotional need was felt by the older generation for the next one to continue what it so auspiciously had begun.

With the advent of modern technology and mass society, only very few have so intimate a feeling for their life's work, such a personal investment in it, that they need to see it continued by others. Short of such a desire, the older generation has little psychological need for youth. If youth tends to move away and build a life very different from that of the old folk, whom they only sporadically remember or visit on special occasions, then even the hope for emotional comfort from youth becomes unrealistic. While youth may still have some emotional and economic need for parents, most parents have little emotional need, and very few an economic one, for a youth striving to be free of its elders. It is because parents still have an emotional need for children, but not for an independent youth, that they often show strenuous resistance when youth fights for its independence. It is also what makes them so critical of certain exaggerations or passing effects of youth's battle for self-realization.

Such resentment and ambivalence about youth's striking out on its own matters little if youth can readily remove itself from the impact. The development of youngsters who went West or ran away to sea was not hampered by adult criticism of their ventures, though their development to full emotional maturity may have known other vagaries. But if youth stays at home or close to home and still fights for its independence from those it depends on, both sides show an emotional deficit.

The resultant scarring of personality in a delinquent youth, for example, is recognized by society as serious. The misanthropic nagging and dissatisfaction of his elders are less well recognized as the price they pay for the conflict. Hamlet thus has his counterpart in King Lear, who, unwilling to make room for youth, tries instead to put reins on the younger generation and to saddle it with a burden of gratitude. It is poetic justice that Cordelia, willing to serve age by foregoing the right of youth to a life of its own, suffers destruction, too.

In the psychoanalytic literature certain aspects of the problem of youth are traced back to a revival and a more violent acting out of the oedipal situation in adolescence. And it is true; something akin to the oedipal situation may be found among the children of most known societies. Specific variations will depend on who is head of the family and to what degree; the character of the persons who minister to the child; how large or small the family is; and how intense or weak is the emotional attachment of specific family members to one another and to the child. But the same cannot be said for the repetition of oedipal conflicts in adolescence.

The girl who marries at fifteen or sixteen and soon thereafter has children of her own is not likely to be beset by a repetition of her oedipal longings for her father or by any fierce competition with her mother for his emotions. As suggested earlier, the repetition of the oedipal conflict is not an issue of nature but depends very much on the structure of family and society.

Only a youth who is kept (or keeps himself) economically and emotionally dependent on the older generation will experience the repetition of the conflict that psychoanalysts observe so frequently nowadays among middle-class adolescents. To cite Hamlet again as the most familiar instance of a revived oedipal conflict in youth—if Hamlet, like Fortinbras, had fought for a kingdom across the sea instead of wishing to inherit his father's place, no tragedy would have taken place; but because he wished to take over from a generation unwilling to yield, rather than to find and win a world of his own, the old oedipal feelings were reactivated and led to the tragedy that destroyed them all. If Hamlet had known for sure what he wished to achieve on his own in life, he could not have been pressed into becoming the avenger of his father. For Hamlet's father, like Lear, put a private burden on his child's too weak shoulders.

Here, then, is another aspect of the conflict of generations: the parent who sees his child's main task in life as the duty to execute his will or to justify his existence (which is different from a parent's devotion to an unfinished labor which the child, on his own, later wishes to bring to fruition). The son who does not revolt when he is expected to devote his life only or mainly to achieving what the parent could not, usually perishes as Hamlet did.

In the present-day world with its tamer middle-class society, we find that the conflicts between a youth either afraid of or prevented from coming into its own and an older generation unwilling or unable to give way, are no less tragic though played out in more muted tones. It follows that whenever society is so organized that youth remains dependent on the older generation, because of the duration of the educational process or for other reasons, and this older generation is not ready to step aside economically, politically or emotionally, a psychological impasse is created which may then be aggravated by unresolved oedipal conflicts.

Here it might be well to remind ourselves that no oedipal situation would exist if the parents were not deeply involved with their child. The revival of the oedipal conflict in adolescence is often due to a parents' wish or need to remain as important to his child in adolescence as he was during infancy.

I venture to guess that many more (particularly middle-class) youths come to grief nowadays because of their parents' insistence that the former justify them as parents than because of any revived oedipal desire for their mothers or fathers. (This again is different from youth's independent wish to prove its own worth and not the worth of a parent.) One form of such an insistence is the overt and covert pressure on youth to provide the parents with what was lacking in their own lives. The mother's pressure on her daughter to live out vicariously her unfulfilled daydreams of popularity or to make a notable marriage can effectively block the girl's efforts to find self-realization in ways that are genuine to her. Often it is both parents who expect their sons to excell in athletics and who take for granted their right to assume that their child will do better than they did.

Nowadays it is usually both middle-class parents who put pressure on youth of both sexes to enter the prestige colleges; this pressure is reinforced by a parallel one from the schools and the general public. I have found those parents most insistent and most unreasonable in such demands who never went to college themselves or never graduated.[4] Many a college youngster needs to ward off this undue attempt to run his life as his parents or teachers want, and longs to carve his own way. He decides that the only way to manage this is to drink, do poorly in college, or flunk out. That is not his original desire; he acts out of a necessity to prove himself master of his own fate.

All this is only part of an attitude that expects American children to do better than their parents, and often, seen objectively, the task is even quite feasible; but to children and adolescents the demand seems emotionally impossible, because it comes at a time when their opinion of their parents' achievements is unrealistically high. Contrary to all psychoanalytic writings that teach clearly how the child and adolescent is overawed by his parents' power and wisdom, both society and his parents continue to expect the emotionally impossible of youth. Off-hand, I can recall no single statement in which consideration of what is expected of high school and college youth is directly linked to the achievement of the youth's parents. While we are more than ready to praise the self-made man, we are reluctant to apply the correlate of such praise: to recognize how difficult it is to outdo one's parents.

True, many youngsters end up doing better than their parents, either socially, economically, or intellectually; but I wonder how the score would show up on a balance sheet that also took account of emotional well-being. A vast number have risen in this way, but then they have hardly been able to manage life, even with the help of a psychoanalyst. If we consider, in evaluating those who do better in life than their parents, not only the externals but also the inner life, perhaps the picture of success that emerges would give us food for second thoughts.

To put the burden of surpassing one's parents on the relations between parent and child leads of necessity to unresolvable conflicts. If youth succeeds, it emasculates the parent. As a result, youth cannot feel successful—partly out of guilt, and partly because he cannot be sure if it was he or his parent who wanted him to succeed. That is, he cannot be sure who it is that truly structures his life.

As for the older generation, the conflict shows many faces. It may take the form of contempt if youth does not fight back (they are weak) or of hostile anxiety if it does (they are delinquent). And if youth has serious doubts about whether it will ever succeed, it must still either rebel or submit in cowardly fashion, or else find some devious (neurotic) way to sidetrack the issue. (To be neither son nor man avoids the fight altogether and hurts the father most, as when the son is a "beat.") Hence the eternal historic and dramatic predicament of the crown prince: if he submits to his father's superannuated clinging to office, he will be a weakling when he finally inherits the throne. If he rejects a role of empty waiting, he must head the revolt against his father.

But what about the girl? Must her mother abdicate for her to come into her own? Not as long as her psychosocial identity resides in childbearing and homemaking. The older generation may stand in her husband's way of realizing his independence, but as long as she accepts that her independence as a social being rests on his, the older generation may stand in her husband's way but it does not stand in hers. Her mother does not need to move over for her to be herself. On the contrary, the mother's having reached an age when childbearing is no longer possible or becoming makes it obvious to one and all who is now in ascendance, and no fight between the generations is needed to settle the issue. (Some modern mothers who cannot accept their gray hair and fading looks, and with it their sexual decline, create a problem for their daughters similar to that of the boy's.)

But what if the girl's psychosocial identity ceases to reside in childbearing and homemaking, or exclusively so? Until the industrial era, as Veblen saw, woman's social identity was "essentially and normally a vicarious one," an expression of the man's life at second remove. And so long as she remained (of necessity) a drudge, she accepted this ancillary role and was largely at peace with her lot. But the less this became true, the more her problems of identity and self-realization were compounded. By now, the female adolescent struggles not only with having to decide whether her place is in the home or in society at large, or in both, but to what degree and with what justification.

Thus the problems of youth have become nearly the same for both sexes; the sexual difference counts for less, because the conflicts of growing up are so much more psychosocial than sexual.

This, I believe, is one of the reasons why psychoanalysis is so often ineffective in adolescence—not because the sexual pressures are so great, and they are great, but because psychoanalysis, which is so well able to help with problems of sex and repression and personal self-realization, does not help with the problem of social self-realization. Or, to put it differently, pitting a helpful authority (the analyst) against repressive authority figures still leaves the adolescent under the sway of some adult authority which he needs to replace with his own. Or, to put it yet differently: psychoanalysis is devised for and effective in helping persons with their intrapersonal difficulties; hence it tends to approach all problems as such. But the problem of the generations is an interpersonal difficulty. Therefore, to deal with it as if it were intrapersonal only complicates matters instead of simplifying them, and makes resolving them less likely.

Of course, this also is true only for Western middle class society. How the problem of generations can differ in different cultures may be illustrated by a controversy between American and Japanese psychoanalysts: in Japan the psychoanalyst's task was seen to consist in helping the young individual to give up his search for self-identity; his self-realization was to be sought not in individuation but in accepting his place within the family in the traditional subservient position of the son toward his father. Thus a Japanese patient "as he approached the successful conclusion of his treatment said, 'During my vacation my mother told me on one occasion that I was now pleasing my father better again.' The psychoanalyst, in reviewing the changes in the patient's personality, says, 'His psychic state is now as harmonious a one as can ever be reached by human beings' i.e., in accordance with the national mores and aspirations of Japan."[5]

Most serious writers on the problem of youth have recognized that youth's present difficulties in Western society are closely related to changed social and economic conditions and to the ensuing difficulty for youth in finding self-realization in work. As Goodman observes: "It's hard to grow up when there isn't enough man's work," and he continues, "To produce necessary food and shelter is man's work. During most of economic history most men have done this drudging work, secure that it was justified and worthy of a man to do it, though often feeling that the social conditions under which they did it were not worthy of a man, thinking, 'It's better to die than to live so hard'—

but they worked on. . . . Security is always first; but in normal conditions a large part of security comes from knowing your contribution is useful, and the rest from knowing it's uniquely yours: they need you."[6]

Just as in this country an earlier generation needed youth because the economic security of the family depended on its contribution, so in Russia today youth is needed because only it can carry on the task of creating the new and better society; and in Africa because only it can move society from tribal confusion toward modern democracy. If the generations thus need each other, they can live together successfully, and the problem of their succession, though not negligible, can be mastered successfully. Under such conditions youth and age need each other not only for their economic but even more for their moral survival. This makes youth secure—if not in its position, at least in its self-respect. But how does the parent in modern society need the next generation? Certainly not for economic reasons any more, and what little expectation a parent may have had that his children would support him in old age becomes superflous with greater social security. More crucially, the status-quo mood of the older generation suggests no need for youth to create a much different or radically better world.

In many respects youth has suddenly turned from being the older generation's greatest economic asset into its greatest economic liability. Witness the expense of rearing and educating youth for some twenty or more years, with no economic return to be expected. Youth still poses emotional problems to the preceding generation, as of old. But in past generations these emotional problems were, so to speak, incidental or subservient to economic necessity. What at best was once the frosting on the cake must now serve as both solid food and trimmings—and this will never work.

Thus the economic roles, obligations, and rewards are no longer clearly defined between the generations, if not turned upside down. Therefore, another aspect of the relation between the generations looms ever larger, in a balance sheet of interaction that is no longer economic but largely emotional. Modern man, insecure because he no longer feels needed for his work contribution or for self-preservation (the automatic machines do things so much better and faster), is also insecure as a parent. He wonders how well he has discharged that other great function of man, the continuation of his species.

At this point modern youth becomes the dreaded avenging angel of his parents, since he holds the power to prove his parents' success or failure as parents; and this counts so much more now, since his parents' economic success is no longer so important in a society of abundance. Youth itself, feeling insecure because of its marginal position in a society that no longer depends on it for economic survival, is tempted to use the one power this reversal between the generations has conferred on it: to be accuser and judge of the parents' success or failure as parents.

How new is all this? It is very hard to compare one age with another. But the Alcibiades or Catiline of antiquity would not have had their followings if the problem of youth having to test itself against an older generation had not existed in those times; nor do Plato's indictments of what he saw as obstreperous youth sound very different from those leveled at our young people today. I may be the victim of those distortions of perspective that make things distant seem far smaller than those looming in the foreground.

Whether this is error in judgment or not, the fact remains that the present problems of Western youth in finding self-definition, and with it security, seem more complex than those of other generations. I say Western youth because, while Russia appears to have its equivalent of the Teddy boys and while Israel does not seem altogether happy with all aspects of Kibbutz-reared youth, the problems there seem different not only in quantity but also in quality. The main differnce lies not so much in the particular tasks society sets for its younger generation but in how clearly the latter realize that only they, the generation of the future, can achieve these tasks.

This difference is critical, for, contrary to some people's opinion, youth does not create its own cause for which it is ready to fight. All it can do is to embrace causes developed by mature men. But youth can only do this successfully if the older men are satisfied with providing the ideals and do not also wish to lead the active battle for reaching them. Or, to put it differently, a youth expected to fight for his personal place in a society of well-defined direction is not lost but on his way. A youth expected to create a new but not yet delineated society finds himself a rebel without a cause. Only when each group has its own important tasks, when one without the other cannot succeed, when age provides the direction but youth the leadership and the fighting manpower, is it clearly understood that whether the battle is won or lost depends on youth's fulfilling its all-important share of the total struggle.

As to who is to provide meaningful work for youth, I believe the answer is that nobody can do that for another. This is why I believe that the well-meant discussions and advice as to what industry should do to make factory work more meaningful has the problem all wrong. Nobody can make life or work more meaningful for others. Nor do most tasks have an absolute significance, not even the growing of food.

On our own plains, for example, stand acres of corn cribs filled to overflowing, while youth continues to leave rural America in droves. Yet its first response to the contemplated Peace Corps for underdeveloped areas was electric. This was the more striking since American farms are now largely mechanized (it is clean work), while the very goals of the Peace Corps include the mechanization of agriculture wherever it is still largely manual (which is "dirty" work). So it is not the work task (growing food) which attracts or repels youth, but the clear evidence that "they need you."[7]

Yet when it became apparent that to join the Peace Corps candidates had to be screened, take examinations, and then be assigned tasks, enthusiasm faltered. It was not initially aroused by the chance to enter one more rat race of competitive examinations nor by the prospect of being sent where the managers of the Corps wanted them to go. They did not want to be emissaries, even of their country. They had jumped at the chance to go where they were needed and to prove how well they could do. They hoped to develop themselves while helping others to develop their country. When it became clear that they were expected to represent something else (in this case American goodwill abroad), they lost interest and, of the many who initially applied, few presented themselves for the scheduled examinations. A chance to act on their own fervor caused a stir; but faced with one more competition, they might as well continue the college rat race for suburbia.

True, a society of plenty can tempt people to waste their time by filling it with empty entertainment or meaningless comfort, or to strive for the wherewithal to do so. But no one need fall for this temptation nor can even the best TV programs make life more meaningful for viewers. At best they can provide the raw material which the individual can then forge into a meaningful life.

Just as freedom and democracy cannot be handed down but have to be fought for, just as knowledge cannot be poured into the heads of our students but only situations created that induce them to seek it, so too industry cannot make work more meaningful for the worker. Only he can first find out what kind of work may be meaningful to him, and then go out and seek it, or at least a reasonable compromise between what is personally meaningful work and what jobs are available to him. I think those who complain that work is not more meaningful are in the wrong, too. What is wrong is that more people do not strive to find meaning in their lives; if they did, they would radically alter our economy and with it our working conditions.

Thus the older generation never has provided meaningful work or life for youth. All they have striven for was a deeper meaning in their own lives, and when they did that, segments of youth could at least follow their lead. It was the mature Marx, not the adolescent, who created Marxism, which then provided the basis for meaningful effort by a whole generation of youth. It was not the youthful but the mature Roosevelt who stimulated another generation of youth to find meaning in life through social improvement and through efforts to reorganize society.

Surely, we too give lip-service to the conviction that man's best hope is the next generation, but this hope does not seem very strong or attractive if we of the older generation do not pursue it with equal vigor. Neither our conviction that the West is declining nor our fear that atomic destruction will wipe man from the earth, realistic as each may well be, offers much hope for assertive self-realization, now or ever. If I cannot feel myself full of vitality because of my hopes for a life in the future, if the world I am about to create will not be better than that of my fathers, better not to live in this world, better to retire from it or feel alive in the moment, no matter what price I must pay in the future. So reasons the criminal delinquent who seeks a moment of heightened self-assertion in the anxious excitement of the criminal act, or through the kick he finds in his drugs.

As one delinquent youngster complained, "You can't live, if there's nothing to push against." What he meant is that you cannot test your own worth, your own strength and vitality, the very things you feel most dubious about as an adolescent, when all you can push against is a vacuum, or an adult society more than ready to give way, to act more youthful than even befits youth. Without something definite to push against, youth feels lost. Many causes are embraced by youth, not for the cause itself, but because in fighting for it, its strength can be tested against something. Hence youth favors causes that run against the established order, even an ultra-conservative cause, because nothing is quite so safe a testing ground as the well-established order.

In Germany today, delinquent youth is often spoken of as the half strong (*die Halbstarken*). They are half strong because for them the older generation and its values mean the Hitler generation. But the ideas and values of those elders proved deficient in all important respects, while the generation of the fathers was cut down by heavy German losses during the war. Hence youth could not test itself against them and remained only half strong.

In the United States a very dissimilar but parallel process took place. The depression led to serious doubts about the values and ideas of the older generations as to the merits of a free enterprise society. The response of the older generation was frequently an inner abdication of the truly parental role. Since that generation felt it had embraced the false goddess of material success, they relinquished being mentors of the next generation and tried instead to be their pals, if not also their peers. They did not, however, give up wanting their children to give meaning to their own now emptier lives. While German fathers were either absent, or died in the war, or were morally destroyed by becoming Hitler's servants, many middle-class American parents simply abdicated their parental function but still wanted their parenthood proved successful by their children's achievements in life.

In terms of generations, then, the question that haunts every young person is: am I as good, as much a man as my father? as much a woman as my mother? This is something to measure up against, to find out if one has it in him to push things a bit further than the parents were able to do. But if the question has to be: am I as much a man as my father should have been, as my mother wants me to be? Or in reverse, and hence even more void of direction, the anxious question: am I the girl my father does not want me to be? Then the person is lost, without guideposts in his struggle to find out what kind of person he is and what kind of a person he wishes to be, as compared with the generation of his parents.

Where is youth to go? How is it to shape itself and its relation to the older generation, the image it must either want to emulate or to supersede with a better one? If I am not mistaken, it is in Jack Kerouac's *On the Road* that two beat characters have the following conversation: "We got to go and never stop till we get there," says the first. The other wonders, "Where are we going, man?" and the answer is, "I don't know, but we gotta go."

These two young men are not in flight from society. They seek a goal—that much is clear. Otherwise, the first would not say they must go until they get there, nor would the second ask where they are going. If they were merely in flight, the first might have said they must go and never stop, and the question of destination would not have come up. More than that, they are in a great hurry to get started toward their goal; but this goal is elusive, and so they are people lost in their search, so lost that they no longer know which direction to take. Worse, they doubt that there is any direction. Therefore, their search for only an unknown goal becomes empty roaming. As long as they are on their way, they feel alive. If they stop, they fear to die.

Therefore, any and all kinds of spurious activities will do, to keep from recognizing how lost they are.

Why is this goal eluding modern young man in search of himself? If manhood, if the good life in the good community, is the goal of adolescence, then the goal is clear, and with it the direction and the path. But what if existing manhood is viewed as empty, static, obsolescent? Then becoming a man is death, and manhood marks the death of adolescence, not its fulfillment. The bouyancy of youth is fed by the conviction of a full life to come, one in which all great things are theoretically attainable. But one cannot believe in the good life to come when the goal is suburbia. One cannot realize one's values by climbing the ladder of the business community, nor prove one's manhood on the greens of the country club; neither can one settle into security in an insecure world.

If there is no certainty of fulfillment, then it is better not to give up the promise of youth with its uncertainty, its lack of definite commitment. Youth at least offers a chance to escape the premature death of rigidity or the anxious confusion of a life that is disgraceful when it is without direction. Neither rigidity nor a confused running in many directions at once (and running after status or money are only the worst among nondirections) is an attractive goal for the young man trying to emerge from his state of uncommittedness into one of inner stability. Better to be committed to such uncommittedness than to commit oneself to spending the rest of one's life as a hollow man.

One's fathers (at least, the best of them) did a good job of showing the young how hollow a life they had built. Let this be a warning not to join them in the waste lands. Better not to enter this land of walking shadows, of immaturity posing as maturity. Better to assert defensively one's uncommitted immaturity, one's remaining poised at the threshold of a life one does not wish to enter. It is the romantic position, but alas, the position of a generation which has little belief in the romance of a better world, a generation whose dreams are not to be striven for but subjected to analysis.

I have said that the present difficulties of youth are related to changed economic and social conditions, and to how much harder it has grown for youth to find its fulfillment in work. In this respect the fate of the girl can be even harder than the boy's. It is impressed on her from an early age that her main fulfillment will come with marriage and children, but her education has nevertheless been the same as that of boys, who are expected to realize themselves mainly through work and achievement in society. To make matters worse, the years in college or even graduate school have further prepared the female elite to seek self-realization in work, while society at large continues to stress that they must find it in motherhood.

Only very occasionally, for boys, is fatherhood added like an afterthought as part of their self-image as mature men. And nowhere, to the best of my knowledge, or only most incidentally, is the complementary image of being a husband even dimly outlined. Yet it should be obvious that women will not find fulfillment in being wives if their partners do not see being a husband as essential to their own self-realization.

True, not long ago there was a time when work around the house was hard, and it could and did proceed in conjunction with raising children and creating a home. But if modern labor-saving devices are relieving women of the most backbreaking work, they have also done away with the satisfactions it yielded. For girls, too, if machines do it better and faster, it is hard to grow up if there's not enough woman's work to be done. Buying ready-to-wear clothes for her family is a vicarious act. It reflects only her husband's ability to provide the money to buy them, but no unique or essential labors of her own. Since the same is nearly as true for cooking and the home arts, what remain, apart from child-rearing, are the most stultifying tasks—dusting, making beds, washing dishes. And beyond that lie mainly the refinements of homemaking, or what Veblen termed an occupation of ceremonial futility.

Many of the young woman's free-time activities are equally futile. I do not refer only to gardening, which replaces the conspicuous embroidery of an earlier age, or to the bridge circle or country-club life designed to help her husband toward his own type of ceremonial futility. I refer also to much that passes, unexamined, as more valuable pastimes, such as the PTA or the League of Women Voters. When used to cover up a vacuum of truly significant activities, of serious involvement, even these lose the genuine satisfactions they could otherwise confer. For, as Veblen also observed, "Woman is endowed with her share—which there is reason to believe is more than an even share—of the instinct of workmanship, to which futility of life or of expenditure is obnoxious," and such an impulse, when denied expression, leaves them "touched with a sense of grievance too vivid to leave them at rest."

But if a girl tries to fulfill her instinct for workmanship, she is subject to pressures not directed at boys. Many young men show little interest in marriage, even through their early thirties, and are allowed to go their way. At worst, a man may come in for gentle nagging at home, and his friends may tease him about it; but in the final analysis they accept his wish to postpone getting married and founding a family; they tacitly acknowledge that he is not ready yet, that he needs more time to find himself in his work life before he can settle down to family life. Such men are often popular, both in married and unmarried circles, and feel no adverse effect on their sense of accomplishment. In brief, a man is considered a failure if he does not support himself, does not achieve in work, but his marital status little affects people's estimate of him.

All this is very different for the girl. A woman, no matter how gifted or successful in her work life, is judged a failure if she does not marry fairly soon. From adolescence on, therefore, the pressure to marry interferes with her ability to find self-realization in her own personal way. Discrimination usually begins in youth, when there is some indulgence for the boy's nonconformity or *revolt* because he must "sow his wild oats"; much less tolerance is accorded the girl who seeks to find herself through such a period of nonconformity.

Many a college boy goes through a crisis of identity during his first years away from home, after exposure to many new ideas. Later, in his last years at college, he may suddenly throw himself into his studies, trying to find new identity in his work achievement. Many a girl finds herself in a parallel position; but then she suddenly realizes that with her new dedication to hard work and study, she is failing to compete in the marriage market. Knowing that she wants to have a family one day, and fearing that with her present singleminded absorption it may slip through her fingers, she stops herself dead in her tracks; or worse, she cannot make up her mind which she really wants, and may lose out on both means of self-realization, if marriage has become the only possibility.

Nor is it only the college girl who suddenly kills her excitement about biochemistry because she realizes she is passing up desirable dates. The noncollege girl goes through a similar experience. She too is caught in the realization that society insists she can only find self-realization through an early marriage. So she gives up her tentative new interests as impractical and buckles down to a course in beauty culture or secretarial work. Later, as the young wife of a skilled or unskilled worker, she is exactly as restless and bewildered as the college girl who gave up biochemistry to achieve married life in the suburbs. Neither girl can understand why, though now a success in the eyes of others, all the meaning of life is evading her. This meaning she now looks for in the task of bringing her children up right, which means finding vicarious satisfaction in their lives, with all the consequences discussed earlier.

Here the worker's wife is perhaps the worst off, because she lacks even the secondary gains of her suburban counterpart. Many such women, uprooted too often, no longer try to fill their emptiness with family gossip or church activities, but try to find, if not meaning, at least some escape from emptiness through a job. Unfortunately, it is rarely the kind of work that gives meaning to their lives; but at least it provides association with equals and is preferred to the drudgery of homemaking.

Yet it is not only the instinct for workmanship which is too often frustrated in the modern young woman; frequently it is also her sexual instinct. While sexual difficulties are neither a recent curse of youth, nor restricted to one sex alone, the American attitude toward sex and the educational system have here, too, burdened female youth more than male youth.

Early in this article I referred to the puberty rites of preliterate societies. These elaborate rituals mark the reaching of sexual maturity and assure the initiates of their new adult status. In most of these societies sex was never at all secret nor was pregenital sex experience forbidden. The child learned what sex was all about as he grew up, watching older persons and animals in intercourse. In farming societies, the fecundity of animals is always a central economic issue, so if adult sex is no longer open, at least animal procreation in all its ramifications is still freely observed and discussed in most parts of the world.

Not so in American middle-class society; and what observations are available to the growing child are shrouded in secrecy, if not in embarrassment or outright shame. We all know that shame and embarrassment about the normal bodily functions make sex experiences difficult for much of modern youth. But compensatory efforts to make of sex relations more than they can ever be are equally confounding. I am speaking of the many literary descriptions of intercourse as an earth-shaking event (for example, Hemingway's description in *For Whom the Bell Tolls*). Obviously, one's own sexual experiences, however rewarding, have no such cosmic effect and hence do not seem to come up to par.[8]

Laurence Wylie describes how, in a large segment of the French middle classes, the adolescent boy receives his training in lovemaking from an older woman and then in turn initiates a girl younger than himself in the art he has learned. There is much more than simple experience involved in this way of teaching sex to an inexperienced young man. His very inexperience makes him attractive to the mature woman. In the typical American pattern, ignorance is supposed to be the best teacher of the ignorant in sexual matters. But here the young man's inexperience makes him feel clumsy and insecure in seducing his girl, who, as likely as not, had to seduce him into becoming the seducer in the first place.

American middle-class youth learns about sex in the back seat of a car, or during a slightly drunken party, or because there was nothing better to do to kill boredom (read: sexual frustration and anxiety). The first sexual experience often leaves ineffaceable impressions, marred by a total lack of experience on either side. Both partners feeling anxious and insecure, neither one can offer encouragement to the other, nor can they take comfort from the accomplished sex act, since they cannot be sure that they did it well, all comparisons lacking.

To use Wylie's example again, the young Frenchman not only knows that his inexperience makes him sexually attractive, he also receives the accolade of the person from whom it counts most: an experienced woman has found him not only sexually attractive but from her rich experience (based on comparisons) she has also assured him that he is a manly lover indeed. Thus, secure in his masculinity, he in due course will be sexually attracted by a young girl's inexperience, rather than frightened by it, as his American counterpart usually is. She, feeling that her innocence, or at least her inexperience, makes her attractive, will not feel clumsy because of it, and he, encouraged by previous experience, will feel himself well able to satisfy his girl sexually.[9] Feeling sure that he can satisfy her, she will feel she has satisfied him.

This, of course, is comparing a French "ideal" type of introduction to sex with an American "ideal" type. In actuality, there are as many variations in France as in the United States in the ways youth is introduced to sex. Still, the French way is as typical there as the other is of middle class youth in America. What goes far beyond a mere paradigm of sex behavior in the two countries is the way youth is prepared for the expected sexual role. In France, as in many other lands, both boy and girl from early childhood on are prepared, the first to take the more dominant, the other the more yielding role, not only in sex but also in the family.

In earlier times there have been societies, or at least subsocieties, in which the woman was dominant in the home and even in intimate relations. This situation may still be found in certain segments of the

French middle classes, and it used to be characteristic of some orthodox Jewish groups. It seems that successful family life can be organized on such a basis as long as the man's dominance in his sphere is clearly recognized and never challenged by women. The man's sphere is usually the work life, be it in the professions, in business, or politics.

In the orthodox Jewish groups referred to, the man's unquestioned superiority in the all-important religious sphere permitted both to accept gladly the wife's dominance in running the home and often also the shop. With the areas of dominance thus clearly marked out, the wife could be dominant in her sphere without extending it to running her husband's life or her children's. Though such a woman was dominant in the home, no "mom-ism" resulted. Secure in her sphere, it did not occur to her to challenge the man's. More importantly, she did not expect her husband to be dominant at home or in business. Therefore, she was not disappointed in what she expected of him, and hence she did not need to make up for it by nagging him or dominating her children.[10] The woman who engages in "mom-ism" and wishes to "wear the pants" does not act out of an original desire to go her husband one better, but in defense and retaliation.

Certainly, our educational system does not prepare the girl to play the more dominant role in the home sphere, nor the more surrendering role, either in sex or other areas of experience. Instead, she is raised in contradiction. On the one hand, she is told that to be feminine means to be yielding, to be courted, and that this is the desirable norm for a woman. She certainly cannot, for example, ask a boy for a date, nor pay the expenses of a date, though in some circles she may sometimes "go dutch."[11]

Contrary to such passivity (waiting to be asked out), where it counts most emotionally, she is taught in school not only to think but also to act for herself. What she is not taught, either at home or in our educational system, is the emotional counterpart of the facts of life: that men and women are neither wholly equal nor by any means opposite sexes, but are complementary; that neither things that are equal nor those that are opposite can be complementary. More importantly, she is not taught wherein men and women are alike—in their talents, aspirations, and emotional needs—and where they are not. From her educationally reinforced but unexamined notion of an equality of the sexes, arise many of the girl's difficulties in her sex relations. For without clearly understanding her own nature, she does not know where and when to be "feminine" and where and when to be "equal."[12]

For example, in societies in which technology has not yet affected the social conditions of women or their expectations, her sexual life is in far less conflict than in ours. It is still sufficient for her if her lover or husband enjoys sex with her. Since she feels that his enjoyment proves her a good woman, nothing stands in her way of enjoying herself; and, not worrying about whether she is frigid or has an orgastic experience, as likely as not she experiences orgasm. He, not obliged by older tradition or by any newer understanding to provide her with an orgastic experience, can enjoy himself, experience orgasm, and thus help her to experience it herself.

In our own society, the male youth needs as much as ever to have his virility attested by his sexual partner, and the female youth has a parallel need. But by now, the boy also needs to have his girl prove him a man by her so-called "orgastic experience," and the girl is even worse off. She not only has to prove him a man by making him experience orgasm; she must also prove her femininity by the same experience, because otherwise she must fear she is frigid. Sexual intercourse cannot often stand up to such complex emotional demands of proving so many things in addition to being enjoyable.

To compound it all, the girl has grown conditioned by all her previous experience in school and college to performing with males on equal grounds, but not on how to complement them.[13] She cannot suddenly learn this in bed. She, trying to make sure that the man has an orgastic experience, and also wondering if she will be able to have one herself, gets so worried that she can truly experience neither, and ends up pretending. In order to prove their manhood or womanhood, the act is now burdened by their having to prove their potency to themselves and to each other, if not also to make the earth shake. Sex becomes another competition of who can make whom have an orgastic experience, and they cannot give up their self-centered needs in the act. The result is that they are unable to enjoy either their mutual desire or the forgetting of self in the experience.

If sexual relations are often less than satisfactory, and if female youth has put work achievement behind her, what is left for the girl by way of self-realization? With home-making now less challenging or satisfying, the children become a concentrated target of the young woman's energies. Here at least, if she starts out feeling less experienced than her mother, she feels considerably more sophisticated. Her world is no longer, as in an older generation, confined to her children, her kitchen, and the church. For years, through the period of her schooling, and perhaps later in a professional occupation, she has worked hard to enlarge her horizon, intellectually and emotionally. Motherhood was depicted to her, and she looked forward to it, as another tremendous, enlarging experience. Yet in reality it forces her to give up most of her old interests, and, unless she is fascinated by the minute developments of the infant, no new and different enrichment is on the horizon. Thus the new world of experience fails to materialize just at the moment when the old enriching experiences are closed, because the infant demands her concentrated attention.

All this is particularly acute with the first child, because the second and third child provide additional content in the mother's life while she cares for the newcomer. I am convinced she will have to find a solution to this problem. It might mean creating something akin to the extended family, through which some societies solved the problem; this meant entrusting part of infant care to the older children or sharing it with relatives. Another solution would be the care of young children by professional people while the mother pursues her individual interests, at least, for part of her time.

In any case, the young mother is now doubly disadvantaged. She cannot find fulfillment in her wifely and motherly role, because she lacks a partner who can complement her in tasks that cannot be mastered alone, or at least not in an emotionally satisfying way. In addition, she is in conflict between her old traditional role and the new image of self-fulfillment through work to which all her schooling has directed her. Or, to put it differently, she is torn between the image of her vicarious role in society as mother and housewife and the self-directed image of herself that developed before marriage. Together, these conflicts are often enough to sour her on motherhood, which she could otherwise fully enjoy.

Resentful in many cases that her husband enjoys what to her seems a fuller life, she tries either to force him to share motherhood with her (which he cannot do without damage to his emotional well-being) or she expects marriage itself to compensate for the frustrated work aspects of her self-realization (which marriage cannot do). Hence she may also sour on her marriage.

The fact that female youth does not react in open conflict with a society that forces her into such an impossible predicament has to do with the actual and socially fostered difference between the sexes. The male delinquent will engage mainly in aggressive acts such as the destruction of property or other forms of aggressive violence; in the "beat," this may be turned inwards, as in the destructive neglect of his own body. In adolescence the female counterpart of violence is sex delinquency, which is less apt to bring the girl into conflict with society.

Yet again this behavior is more often socially imposed than biologically inherent. Many girls who feel "unfeminine" in terms of Hollywood fostered attitudes become sex delinquents to prove they are feminine, or at least to deny that they are not. The nondelinquent, more adult female youth may take things out on her husband and children in less obvious but equally destructive nagging, in a general dissatisfaction that drives her husband to try to achieve for her what only she can achieve for herself.

Others have come to recognize that the problem is largely theirs and are groping for reasonable solutions. Like Negro youth in America, they find themselves a minority with certain psychological advantages. If the majority of young American males can choose their occupations freely but long for more purpose to their labors, the minorities among youth are still fighting with a purpose. Once they do achieve the freedom to pursue self-chosen goals, then the current problems of youth will be no different for boys than for girls, white or Negro.

The elections of 1960 brought an upsurge of purpose, at least in a segment of our population who felt that the new administration had a place for their aspirations, might give them scope to create a better world. This was true for both youth and adult, but youth would not have believed it, if their elders had not shown that their hopes seemed to be justified. As one colleague of mine put it while observing changes on the campus of his university: These students who for years have been rebels without a cause were for the most part too sensible even to rebel. But when they first started to work for Stevenson, and then for Kennedy, and ever since the latter's election, they became dedicated workers for a better future. Yet these, as I say, were only a small segment. The vast majority of the young, like the vast majority of the old, still lacking a direction, seek harder than ever for an empty comfort. This, they hope, may enable them to forget that they have no purpose beyond it, and, as it fails, their search for more of the same becomes increasingly frantic and empty.

Many visitors to Russia, and not only educators, have been struck by how well-behaved Russian children are to their parents, and their parents to them. This mutual respect is entirely different in texture from either fear or the uneasy camaraderie sought by so many parents in our society, where the parent sees his task as that of play companion rather than mentor to the young. Perhaps the explanation lies in what Russian educators have to say about this remarkable difference. They claim that "the good behavior of the children is the result of the clarity and agreement on the part of all teachers [and all adults, we might add] as to their expectations from the children," expectations based on a strong sense of common purpose to create a better social system than has ever existed.[14] Now these for the most part are the children of the people who are still trying to create a new and better society for all, and not of the ruling elite, who already enjoy most of the new advantages. That is why "delinquent" tendencies are found more readily among children of the elite.

Yet even the common purpose of creating a better world, while assuring youth its importance in creating it, is not enough in itself to permit all who seek it to realize themselves. There must be added the clear conception of the usefulness of one's labor; and even then there will always be some who must travel an individual pathway not provided by society, for testing their manhood and worth.

Modern American society has virtually cut off such avenues inside the framework of that society. (Some young people seek them in foreign countries; witness the past attraction of the Spanish Civil War and the current appeal of the Cuban upheaval and of the new African countries.) No longer is there an open frontier for escape from the oppressive feeling that one cannot prove oneself within a rigidly stratified society. Where is a modern Ishmael to roam? Though he may feel like "methodically knocking off people's hats," he cannot run away to sea because life there is now as regulated and devoid of chances for self-realization as on land. Prevented from knocking people's hats off, or hauled into court or to the psychiatrist for trying to, he feels he has no "substitute for pistol and ball," and may end up using them.

I have said before that for youth to come into his own means to a large degree his replacing the older generation, and that, whether the transition is smooth or hard-won, youth is still on its way. Thus the problem of the generations, when it goes wrong, may be characterized by saying that, whenever the older generation has lost its bearings, the younger generation is lost with it. The positive alternatives of emulation or revolt are then replaced by the lost quality of neither.

And this, I am afraid, is the situation in which large segments of American youth find themselves. They are unhappy when they settle down to continue in a pattern of life that their parents have arranged for them, because they know it to be an empty one. But they find it pointless to rebel, as do those others who, sensing emptiness in the lives prepared for them, fight against it but do not know what to fight for.

Old age is happiest when it can take youth up to the threshold of the good and the new and, like the mythical father of the West, point out the Promised Land to its children, saying: you and only you in a hard fight will have to make this your own; because what is handed down to you, what you have not won for yourselves, is never truly your own.

Youth, on the other hand, is happiest when it feels it is fighting to reach goals that were conceived of but not realized by the generation before them. What the older generation then urgently wished for itself, but had to acknowledge as the hope of the future—this is the legacy of youth. That the preceding generation wished to create such a better world makes it a worthy standard for youth. To come closer to achieving it through its own efforts proves to youth that it is gaining its own rich maturity.

REFERENCES

1. Erik H. Erikson, *Identity and the Life Cycle,* New York: International Universities Press, 1959. Edgar Z. Friedenberg, *The Vanishing Adolescent,* Boston: Beacon Press, 1959. Paul Goodman, *Growing Up Absurd,* New York: Random House, 1960.

2. Bruno Bettelheim, *Symbolic Wounds,* Glencoe, Illinois: The Free Press, 1954.

3. Still, we are not yet far removed from it in our deeper feelings about what makes the secure order of things. Witness the feeling of relief, in the last election, when both parties offered young and vigorous candidates for a position being vacated by an old and tired man. Though there is no doubt that millions loved and venerated the old man more than either young candidate, the feeling was prevalent that age had to step aside in favor of youth for the good of the commonweal.

4. Similarly, I know of no Latin scholar who has bought a copy of *Winnie Ille Pooh* for his children; but tens of thousands who never studied Latin have bought the book for their children and have expected them to enjoy it and to acquire an understanding of Latin culture from it. Actually, such a translation is at best a sophomoric prank; taken seriously, it should be obvious on whom the joke is played.

5. J. C. Moloney, "Understanding the Paradox of Japanese Psychoanalysis," *International Journal of Psychoanalysis,* 1953, *34:* 291-303. He also quotes a statement from the *Tokyo Journal of Psychoanalysis* asserting that the task of psychoanalysis is so to strengthen the ego that it can and will respond to the demands of the superego. Those demands in turn are viewed as basically the demands of the emperor, since he represents the all-embracing ethos of his nation.

6. P. Goodman, *op. cit.*

7. A crude index of how far we are from understanding the goals of youth lies in the fact that some United States agricultural extension agents working with 4-H clubs were recently sponsoring a new scheme for keeping youth on the farm: rousing their interest in the care and breeding of race horses!

8. One may also wonder about the success of *Hiroshima, mon Amour* among the intelligentsia. This is a film in which a love affair is significant not because of what it means to the two partners, or of what they find in each other, but because it is played out against a perspective of world history: the German occupation of France and the bombing of Hiroshima. If the earth has to shake or world history to look on before a love affair can be meaningful for the partners, youth

must find itself in awkward straits in its love relations. (I have discussed other difficulties many Americans encounter in finding meaning in their intimate relations in *The Informed Heart,* The Free Press, 1960.)

9. This has been described in Strauss's *Rosenkavalier.*

10. Things changed when such families left the ghettoes and entered modern technological societies. Once the religious sphere lost in importance, while the work sphere grew tremendously important, there were commensurate upheavals in the balance within the family.

11. I can only mention in passing what would call for lengthy discussion: how a society of relative abundance has changed the dating and mating patterns. In other societies it was well known that the greatest attention one could show the courted person was to devote time and attention to him or her. In our society, in which the phrase "time is money" is more than a slogan, money must often make up for time; a boy's car or the money he can spend on his date now replaces the time and attention spent in being with her.

    It is not simply that money is made to make up for emotional dedication, which it can never do; it is also made to prove virility, if not even orgastic potency, for which it is equally unsuitable. Many men who doubt their masculinity and virility try to quiet their fears through their social or economic success. Falsely equating virility with beating the other guy in competition, they must come out on top at all costs. But when success is sought not for itself but to make up for something that is missing, it cannot even be enjoyed for what it is, since it cannot make up for what it is not.

    The counterpart of such a situation is found in a wife who feels thwarted in her hope for a virile man who can truly make her feel and be a woman. Heedlessly, she spends his money and eggs him on to achieve further status, since these have to make up to her for what they never can, her empty feeling of being a failure as a woman.

    But all this comes later in life. It is not yet a problem of youth unless they have been exposed to it in their parents. Similarly, they cannot take their teachers as images to copy, if teachers in their sphere strive for academic success much as members of the business community use money and the status it confers.

12. There is a corresponding confusion in the way we look upon initiative in women, for not all "active" women are unfeminine. Women who strive to "wear the pants" do so for defensive and neurotic reasons, just as the very need to be dominant, whether in man or in woman, is due to thwarted desires, if not also to a thwarted personality. Quite different is the striving to achieve for a purpose, for, like men, some women strive to realize their inner potentials—quite outside any context of competing with other men, other women, or any standard of measurement except their own wish to work toward a purpose. Until we distinguish clearly between the two, we shall continue to hold back, by labeling "unfeminine" those girls who seek to further their own natural growth and development.

13. Things would not be so bad if the competition were only with persons. To compete with somebody one knows well keeps competition in the human dimension and leads to personal jealousies, hopes and disappointments. But much of the competition where it counts most (merit scholarships, college boards) involves not just a person but rather competing with one's whole age group. It is a competitiveness in the abstract, not against another person, but for a score on a test. As if this were not bad enough, competitions other than for grades and scholastic achievement have entered our educational system. All too often, at the same "educational" place where youngsters compete for grades, they are also competing for dates and a marriage partner.

14. B. Spock, "Russian Children," *Ladies' Home Journal,* October 1960.

Youth: Fidelity and Diversity

Erik H. Erikson

The subject of this paper is a certain strength inherent in the age of youth. I call it the sense of and the capacity for Fidelity. To do justice to this theme, I would have to account for the strengths (I call them basic virtues, in the older sense of the word) arising in the stages of life which precede and follow youth. Only in this way could I hope to indicate the place of youth in the evolutionary scheme of the human life cycle, only in this way make plausible the fact that the virtue Fidelity could not develop earlier in life and must not, in the crises of youth, fail its time of ascendance. Obviously, however, such an accounting would demand more than space allows. I must refer the reader to a footnote,[1] which can do no more than list the virtues of which Fidelity is one, and point to publications offering a rationale of the evolutionary scheme from which they all emerge. We can take only a brief look at the stage of life which immediately precedes youth, the school age, and then turn to youth itself.

The school age, which intervenes between childhood and youth, finds the child, previously dominated by the experience of play, ready, willing, and able to apply himself to the rudimentary skills required, eventually wielding the tools and weapons, the symbols and concepts, of his culture. Also, it finds him eager to realize actual roles (previously play-acted) which promise him an eventual identity within the specializations of his culture's technology. However, the stage by stage acquisition during individual childhood of each of man's evolutionary gains leaves the mark of infantile experience on his proudest achievements. The play age bequeaths to all methodical pursuits a quality of grandiose delusion; and the school age leaves man with a naive acceptance of "what works."

As the child makes methods his own, he also permits accepted methods to make him their own. To consider as good only what works, and to feel accepted only if things work, to manage and to be managed, can become his dominant delight and value. And since technological specialization is an intrinsic part of the human horde's or tribe's or culture's system and world image, man's pride in the tools that work with materials and animals extends to the weapons which work against other humans as well as against other species. That this can awaken a cold cunning as well as an unmeasured ferocity rare in the animal world is, of course, due to a combination of developments. Among these we will be most concerned (because it comes to the fore during youth) with man's need to combine technological pride with a sense of identity: a double sense of personal selfsameness slowly accrued from infantile experiences and of shared sameness experienced in encounters with a widening part of the community.

This need too is an evolutionary necessity as yet to be understood and influenced by planning: for men—not being a natural species any more, and not a mankind as yet—need to feel that they are of some special kind (tribe or nation, class or caste, family, occupation, or type), whose insignia they will wear with vanity and conviction, and defend (along with the economic claims they have staked out for their kind) against the foreign, the inimical, the not-so-human kinds. Thus it comes about that they can use all their proud skills and methods most systematically against other men, even in the most advanced state of rationality and civilization, with the conviction that they could not morally afford not to do so.

It is not our purpose, however, to dwell on the easy perversion and corruptibility of man's morality, but to determine what those core virtues are which—at this stage of psychosocial evolution—need our concerted attention and ethical support; for antimoralists as well as moralists easily overlook the bases in human nature for a strong ethics. As indicated, Fidelity is that virtue and quality of adolescent ego strength which belongs to man's evolutionary heritage, but which —like all the basic virtues—can arise only in the interplay of a life stage with the individuals and the social forces of a true community.

The evidence in young lives of the search for something and somebody to be true to is seen in a variety of pursuits more or less sanctioned by society. It is often hidden in a bewildering combination of shifting devotion and sudden perversity, sometimes more devotedly perverse, sometimes more perversely devoted. Yet, in all youth's seeming shiftiness, a seeking after some durability in change can be detected, whether in the accuracy of scientific and technical method or in the sincerity of conviction; in the veracity of historical and fictional accounts or the fairness of the rules of the game; in the authenticity of artistic production (and the high fidelity of reproduction) or in the genuineness of personalities and the reliability of commitments. This search is easily misunderstood, and often it is only dimly perceived by the individual himself, because youth, always set to grasp both diversity in principle and principle in diversity, must often test extremes before settling on a considered course. These extremes, particularly in times of ideological confusion and widespread marginality of identity, may include not only rebellious but also deviant, delinquent, and self-destructive tendencies. However, all this can be in the nature of a moratorium, a period of delay, in which to test the rock-bottom of some truth before committing the powers of body and mind to a segment of the existing (or a coming) order. "Loyal" and "legal" have the same root, linguistically and psychologically; for legal commitment is an unsafe burden unless shouldered with a sense of sovereign choice and experienced as loyalty. To develop that sense is a joint task of the consistency of individual life history and the ethical potency of the historical process.

Let a great tragic play tell us something of the elemental nature of the crisis man encounters here. If it is a prince's crisis, let us not forget that the "leading families" of heaven and history at one time personified man's pride and tragic failure. Prince Hamlet is in his twenties, some say early, some late. We will say he is in the middle of his third decade, a youth no longer young and about to forfeit his moratorium. We find him in a tragic conflict in which he cannot make the one step demanded simultaneously by his age and his sex, his education, and his historical responsibility.

If we want to make Shakespeare's insight into one of "the ages of man" explicit, we know that such an endeavor seems reprehensible to the students of drama, if undertaken by a trained psychologist. Everybody else (how could he do otherwise?) interprets Shakespeare in the light of some prevailing if naive psychology. I will not try to solve the riddle of Hamlet's inscrutable nature, because his inscrutability is his nature. I feel sufficiently warned by Shakespeare himself, who lets Polonius speak like the caricature of a psychiatrist:

> And I do think—or else this brain of mine
> Hunts not the trail of policy so sure
> as it has us'd to do—that I have found
> The very cause of Hamlet's lunacy.

Hamlet's decision to play insane is a secret which the audience shares with him from the start, without their ever getting rid of the feeling that he is on the verge of slipping into the state he pretends. "His madness," says T. S. Eliot, "is less than madness, and more than feigned."

If Hamlet's madness is more than feigned, it appears to be aggravated at least fivefold: by habitual melancholy, an introverted personality, Danishness, an acute state of mourning, and love. All this makes a regression to the Oedipus complex, postulated by Ernest Jones as the main theme of this as of other great tragedies, entirely plausible.[2] This would mean that Hamlet cannot forgive his mother's recent illegitimate betrayal, because he had not been able as a child to forgive her for having betrayed him quite legitimately with his father; but, at the same time, he is unable to avenge his father's recent murder, because as a child he had himself betrayed him in phantasy and wished him out of the way. Thus he forever postpones—until he ruins the innocent with the guilty—his uncle's execution, which alone would free the ghost of his beloved father from the fate of being,

> doomed for a certain term to walk the night
> and for the day confined to fast in fires.

No audience, however, can escape the feeling that he is a man of superior conscience, advanced beyond the legal concepts of his time, consumed by his own past and by that of his society.

One further suggestion is inescapable, that Hamlet displays some of the playwright's and the actor's personality: for where others lead men and change the course of history, he reflectively moves characters about on the stage (the play within the play); in brief, where others act, he play-acts. And indeed, Hamlet may well stand, historically speaking, for an abortive leader, a still-born rebel.

We shall return to this in another context. In the meantime, all that has been stated can only support a biographic view which concentrates on Hamlet's age and status as a young intellectual of his time: for did he not recently return from studies at Wittenberg, the hotbed of humanist corruption, his time's counterpart to Sophist Athens (and today's existentialist centers of learning)?

There are five young men in the play, all Hamlet's age mates, and all sure (or even overdefined) in their identities as dutiful sons, courtiers, and future leaders. But they are all drawn into the moral swamp of infidelity, which seeps into the fiber of all those who owe allegiance to "rotten" Denmark, drawn by the multiple intrigue which Hamlet hopes to defeat with his own intrigue: the play within the play.

Hamlet's world, then, is one of diffuse realities and fidelities. Only through the play within the play and through the madness within the insanity, does Hamlet, the actor within the play-actor, reveal the identity within the pretended identities—and the superior fidelity in the fatal pretense.

His estrangement is one of identity diffusion. His estrangement from existence itself is expressed in the famous soliloquy. He is estranged from being human and from being a man: "Man delights me not; no, nor woman either"; and estranged from love and procreation: "I say we will have no more marriage." He is estranged from the ways of his country, "though I am native here and to the manner born"; and much like our "alienated" youth, he is estranged from and describes as "alienated" the overstandardized man of his day, who "only got the tune of time and outward habit of encounter."

Yet Hamlet's single-minded and tragically doomed search for Fidelity breaks through all this. Here is the essence of the historical Hamlet, that ancient model who was a hero on the folk stage for centuries before Shakespeare modernized and eternalized him:[3]

> He was loth to be thought prone to lying about any matter, and wished to be held a stranger to any falsehood; and accordingly he mingled craft and candor in such a wise that, though his words did not lack truth, yet there was nothing to betoken the truth and to betray how far his keenness went.

It accords with the general diffusion of truth in Hamlet that this central theme is announced in the old fool's message to his son:

> *Polonius:* This above all: to thine own self be true
> And it must follow, as the night the day,
> Thou canst not then be false to any man.

Yet it is also the central theme of Hamlet's most passionate pronouncements, which make his madness but an adjunct to his greatness. He abhors conventional sham, and advocates genuineness of feeling:

> Seems, madam! Nay, it is; I know not "seems."
> 'Tis not alone my inky cloak, good mother,
> Nor customary suits of solemn black,
> Nor windy suspiration of forc'd breath,
> No, nor the fruitful river in the eye,
> Nor the dejected havior of the visage,
> Together with all forms, moods, shapes of grief
> That can denote me truly. These indeed seem,
> For they are actions that a man might play:
> But I have that within which passes show;
> These but the trappings and the suits of woe.

He searches for what only an elite will really understand—"honest method":

> I heard thee speak me a speech once but it was never acted; or, if it was, not above once; for the play I remember, pleased not the million. . . ! it was (as I received it, and others, whose judgments cried in the top of mine) an excellent play, well digested and in the scenes, set down with as much modesty and cunning. I remember one said there were no sallets in the lines to make the matter savoury, nor no matter in the phrase that might indict the author of affection; but called it an honest method.

He fanatically insists on purity of form and fidelity of reproduction:

> . . . let your discretion be your tutor. Suit the action to the word, the word to the action, with this special observance, that you o'erstep not the modesty of nature; for anything so overdone is from the purpose of playing whose end, both at the first and now, was, and is to hold, as 'twere, the mirror up to nature, to show virtue her own image and the very age and body of time his own form and pressure.

And finally, the eager (and overeager) acknowledgment of genuine character in his friend:

> Since my dear soul was mistress of her choice
> And could of men distinguish, her election
> Hath sealed thee for herself; for thou hast been

As one in suffering all, that suffers nothing,
A man that fortune buffets and rewards
Hast ta'en with equal thanks; and bless'd are those
Whose blood and judgement are so co-mingled
That they are not a pipe for fortune's finger
To sound what stop she please. Give me that man
That is not passion's slave, and I will wear him
in my heart's core, ay in my heart of heart,
As I do thee. Something too much of this.

This, then, is the Hamlet with Hamlet. It fits the combined play-actor, the intellectual, the youth, and the neurotic that his words are his better deeds, that he can say clearly what he cannot live, and that his fidelity must bring doom to those he loves: for what he accomplishes at the end is what he tried to avoid, even as he realizes what we would call his negative identity in becoming exactly what his own ethical sense could not tolerate: a mad revenger. Thus do inner reality and historical actuality conspire to deny tragic man the positive identity for which he seems exquisitely chosen. Of course, the audience all along has sensed in Hamlet's very sincerity an element of deadliness. At the end he gives his "dying voice" to his counter-player on the historical stage, victorious young Fortinbras, who in turn insists on having him,

. . . born like a soldier to the stage
For he was likely, had he been put on,
To have prov'd most royal.

The ceremonial fanfares, blaring and hollow, announce the end of this singular youth. He is confirmed by his chosen peers, with the royal insignia of his birth. A special person, intensely human, is buried—a member of his special kind.

To be a special kind, we have said, is an important element in the human need for personal and collective identities—all, in a sense, pseudospecies. They have found a transitory fulfillment in man's greatest moments of cultural identity and civilized perfection, and each such tradition of identity and perfection has highlighted what man could be, could he be all these at one time. The utopia of our own era predicts that man will be one species in one world, with a universal identity to replace the illusory superidentities which have divided him, and with an international ethics replacing all moral systems of superstition, repression, and suppression. Whatever the political arrangement that will further this utopia, we can only point to the schedule of human strengths which potentially emerge with the stages of life and indicate their interdependence on the structure of communal life. In youth, ego strength emerges from the mutual confirmation of individual and community, in the sense that society recognizes the young individual as a bearer of fresh energy and that the individual so confirmed recognizes society as a living process which inspires loyalty as it receives it, maintains allegiance as it attracts it, honors confidence as it demands it.

Let us go back, then, to the origins of that combination of drivenness and disciplined energy, of irrationality and courageous capability which belong to the best discussed and the most puzzling phenomena of the life cycle. The puzzle, we must grant throughout, is in the essence of the phenomenon. For the unity of the personality must be unique to be united, and the functioning of each new generation unpredictable to fulfill its function.

Of the three sources of new energy, physical growth is the most easily measured and systematically exercised, although its contribution to the aggressive drives is little understood. The youthful powers of comprehension and cognition can be experimentally studied and with planning applied to apprenticeship and study, but their relation to ideological imagination is less well known. Finally, the long delayed genital maturation is a source of untold energy, but also of a drivenness accompanied by intrinsic frustration.

When maturing in his physical capacity for procreation, the human youth is as yet unable to love in that binding manner which only two identities can offer each other; nor to care consistently enough to sustain parenthood. The two sexes, of course, differ greatly in these respects, and so do individuals, while societies provide different opportunities and sanctions within which individuals must fend for their potentials—and for their potency. But what I have called a psychosocial moratorium, of some form and duration between the advent of genital maturity and the onset of responsible adulthood, seems to be built into the schedule of human development. Like all the moratoria in man's developmental schedules, the delay of adulthood can be prolonged and intensified to a forceful and fateful degree; thus it accounts for very special human achievements and also for the very special weaknesses in such achievements. For, whatever the partial satisfactions and partial abstinences that characterize premarital sex life in various cultures—whether the pleasure and pride of forceful genital activity without commitment, or of erotic states without genital consummation, or of disciplined and devoted delay—ego development uses the psychosexual powers of adolescence for enhancing a sense of style and identity. Here, too, man is never an animal: even where a society furthers the genital closeness of the sexes, it does so in a stylized manner. On the other hand, the sex act, biologically speaking, is the procreative act, and there is an element of psychobiological dissatisfaction in any sexual situation not favorable in the long run to procreative consummation and care—a dissatisfaction which can be tolerated by otherwise healthy people, as all partial abstinences can be borne: for a certain period, under conditions otherwise favorable to the aims of identity formation. In the woman, no doubt, this dissatisfaction plays a much greater role, owing to her deeper engagement, physiologically and emotionally, in the sex act as the first step in a procreative commitment of which her monthly cycle is a regular bodily and emotive reminder.

The various hindrances to a full consummation of adolescent genital maturation have many deep consequences for man which pose an important problem for future planning. Best known is the regressive revival of that earlier stage of psychosexuality which preceded even the emotionally quiet first school years, that is, the infantile genital and locomotor stage, with its tendency toward autoerotic manipulation, grandiose phantasy, and vigorous play.[4] But in youth, auto-erotism, grandiosity, and playfulness are all immensely amplified by genital potency and locomotor maturation, and are vastly complicated by what we will presently describe as the youthful mind's new historical perspective.

The most widespread expression of the discontented search of youth is the craving for locomotion, whether expressed in a general "being on the go," "tearing after something," or "running around"; or in locomotion proper, as in vigorous work, in absorbing sports, in rapt dancing, in shiftless *Wanderschaft,* and in the employment and misuse of speedy animals and machines. But it also finds expression through participation in the movements of the day (whether the riots of a local commotion or the parades and campaigns of major ideological forces), if they only appeal to the need for feeling "moved" and for feeling essential in moving something along toward an open future. It is clear that societies offer any number of ritual combinations of ideological perspective and vigorous movement (dance, sports, parades, demonstrations, riots) to harness youth in the service of their historical aims; and that where societies fail to do so, these patterns will seek their own combinations, in small groups occupied with serious games, good-natured foolishness, cruel prankishness, and delinquent warfare. In no other stage of the life cycle, then, are the promise of finding oneself and the threat of losing oneself so closely allied.

In connection with locomotion, we must mention two great industrial developments; the motor engine and the motion picture. The motor engine, of course, is the very heart and symbol of our technology and its mastery, the aim and aspiration of much of modern youth. In connection with immature youth, however, it must be understood that both motor car and motion pictures offer to those so inclined passive locomotion with an intoxicating delusion of being intensely active. The prevalence of car thefts and motor accidents among juveniles is much decried (although it is taking the public a long time to understand that a theft is an appropriation for the sake of gainful possession), while automobiles more often than not are stolen by the young in search of a kind of automotive intoxication, which may literally run away with car and youngster. Yet, while vastly inflating a sense of motor omnipotence, the need for active locomotion often remains unfulfilled. Motion pictures especially offer the onlooker, who sits, as it were, with the engine of his emotions racing, fast and furious motion in an artificially widened visual field, interspersed with close-ups of violence and sexual possession—and all this without making the slightest demand on intelligence, imagination, or effort. I am pointing here to a widespread imbalance in adolescent experience, because I think it explains new kinds of adolescent outbursts and points to new necessities of mastery. The danger involved is greatly balanced in that part of youth which can take active charge of technical development, manages to learn, and to identify with the ingeniousness of invention, the improvement of production and the care of machinery, and is thus offered a new and unlimited application of youthful capacities. Where youth is underprivileged in such technical experience, it must explode in riotous motion; where it is ungifted, it will feel estranged from the modern world, until technology and nontechnical intelligence have come to a certain convergence.

The cognitive gifts developing during the first half of the second decade add a powerful tool to the tasks of youth. J. Piaget calls the gains in cognition made toward the middle teens, the achievement of "formal operations."[5] This means that the youth can now operate on hypothetical propositions, can think of possible variables and potential relations, and think of them in thought alone, independent of certain concrete checks previously necessary. As Jerome S. Bruner puts it, the child now can "conjure up systematically the full range of alternative possibilities that could exist at any given time."[6] Such cognitive orientation forms not a contrast but a complement to the need of the young person to develop a sense of identity, for, from among all possible and imaginable relations, he must make a series of ever narrowing selections of personal, occupational, sexual, and ideological commitments.

Here again diversity and fidelity are polarized: they make each other significant and keep each other alive. Fidelity without a sense of diversity can become an obsession and a bore; diversity without a sense of fidelity, an empty relativism.

The sense of ego identity, then, becomes more necessary (and more problematical) wherever a wide range of possible identities is envisaged. Identity is a term used in our day with faddish ease; at this point, I can only indicate how very complicated the real article is.[7] For ego identity is partially conscious and largely unconscious. It is a psychological process reflecting social processes; but with sociological means it can be seen as a social process reflecting psychological processes; it meets its crisis in adolescence, but has grown throughout childhood and continues to re-emerge in the crises of later years. The overriding meaning of it all, then, is the creation of a sense of sameness, a unity of personality now felt by the individual and recognized by others as having consistency in time—of being, as it were, an irreversible historical fact.

The prime danger of this age, therefore, is identity confusion, which can express itself in excessively prolonged moratoria (Hamlet offers an exalted example); in repeated impulsive attempts to end the moratorium with sudden choices, that is, to play with historical possibilities, and then to deny that some irreversible commitment has already taken place; and sometimes also in severe regressive pathology, which we will illustrate presently. The dominant issue of this, as of any other stage, therefore, is that of the active, the selective, ego being in charge and being enabled to be in charge by a social structure which grants a given age group the place it needs—and in which it is needed.

In a letter to Oliver Wendell Holmes, William James speaks of wanting to "rebaptize himself" in their friendship—and this one word says much of what is involved in the radical direction of the social awareness and the social needs of youth. From the middle of the second decade, the capacity to think and the power to imagine reach beyond the persons and personalities in which youth can immerse itself so deeply. Youth loves and hates in people what they "stand for" and chooses them for a significant encounter involving issues that often, indeed, are bigger than you and I. We have heard Hamlet's declaration of love to his friend Horatio, a declaration quickly broken off—"something too much here." It is a new reality, then, for which the individual wishes to be reborn, with and by those whom he chooses as his new ancestors and his genuine contemporaries.

This mutual selection, while frequently associated with, and therefore interpreted as a rebellion against or withdrawal from, the childhood environment, is an expression of a truly new perspective which I have already called "historical"—in one of those loose uses of an ancient and overspecialized word which sometimes become necessary in making new meanings specific. I mean by "historical perspective" something which every human being newly develops during adolescence. It is a sense of the irreversibility of significant events and an often urgent need to understand fully and quickly what kind of happenings in reality and in thought determine others, and why. As we have seen, psychologists such as Piaget recognize in youth the capacity to appreciate that any process can be understood when it is retraced in its steps and thus reversed in thought. Yet it is no contradiction to say that he who comes to understand such a reversal also realizes that in reality, among all the events that can be thought of, a few will determine and narrow one another with historical fatality, whether (in the human instance) deservedly or undeservedly, intentionally or unintentionally.

Youth, therefore, is sensitive to any suggestion that it may be hopelessly determined by what went before in life histories or in history. Psychosocially speaking, this would mean that irreversible childhood identifications would deprive an individual of an identity of his own; historically, that invested powers should prevent a group from realizing its composite historical identity. For these reasons, youth often rejects parents and authorities and wishes to belittle them as inconsequential; it is in search of individuals and movements who claim, or seem to claim, that they can predict what is irreversible, thus getting ahead of the future—which means, reversing it. This in turn accounts for the acceptance by youth of mythologies and ideologies predicting the course of the universe or the historical trend; for even intelligent and practical youth can be glad to have the larger framework settled, so that it can devote itself to the details which it can manage, once it knows (or is convincingly told) what they stand for and where it stands. Thus, "true" ideologies are verified by history—for a time; for, if they can inspire youth, youth will make the predicted history come more than true.

By pointing to what, in the mind of youth, people "stand for," I did not mean to overemphasize the ideological explicitness in the meaning of individuals to youth. The selection of meaningful individuals can take place in the framework of pointed practicalities such as schooling or job selection, as well as in religious and ideological fellowship; while the methods of selection can range from banal amenity and enmity to dangerous play with the borderlines of sanity and legality. But the occasions have in common a mutual sizing up and a mutual plea for being recognized as individuals who can be more than they seem to be, and whose potentials are needed by the order that is or will be. The representatives of the adult world thus involved may be advocates and practitioners of technical accuracy, of a method of scientific inquiry, of a convincing rendition of truth, of a code of fairness, of a standard of artistic veracity, or of a way of personal genuineness. They become representatives of an elite in the eyes of the young, quite independently of whether or not they are also viewed thus in the eyes of the family, the public, or the police. The choice can be dangerous, but to some youths the danger is a necessary ingredient of the experiment. Elemental things are dangerous; and if youth could not overcommit itself to danger, it could not commit itself to the survival of genuine values—one of the primary steering mechanisms of psychosocial evolution. The elemental fact is that only when fidelity has found its field of manifestation is the human as good as, say, the nestling in nature, which is ready to rely on its own wings and to take its adult place in the ecological order.

If in human adolescence this field of manifestation is alternately one of devoted conformism and of extreme deviancy, of rededication and of rebellion, we must remember the necessity for man to react (and to react most intensively in his youth) to the diversity of conditions. In the setting of psychosocial evolution, we can ascribe a long-range meaning to the idiosyncratic individualist and to the rebel as well as to the conformist, albeit under different historical conditions. For healthy individualism and devoted deviancy contain an indignation in the service of a wholeness that is to be restored, without which psychosocial evolution would be doomed. Thus, human adaptation has its loyal deviants, its rebels, who refuse to adjust to what so often is called, with an apologetic and fatalistic misuse of a once good phrase, "the human condition."

Loyal deviancy and identity formation in extraordinary individuals are often associated with neurotic and psychotic symptoms, or at least with a prolonged moratorium of relative isolation, in which all the estrangements of adolescence are suffered. In *Young Man Luther* I have attempted to put the suffering of a great young man into the context of his greatness and his historic position.[8]

It is not our purpose, however, to discuss what to many youths is the most urgent question, and yet to us the most difficult to answer, namely, the relation of special giftedness and neurosis; rather, we must characterize the specific nature of adolescent psychopathology, or, even more narrowly, indicate the relevance of the issue of fidelity to the psychopathology of youth.

In the classical case of this age group, Freud's first published encounter with an eighteen-year-old girl suffering from "*petite hystérie* with the commonest of all . . . symptoms," it is interesting to recall that at the end of treatment Freud was puzzled as to "what kind of help" the girl wanted from him. He had communicated to her his interpretation of the structure of her neurotic disorder, an interpretation which became the central theme of his classical publication on the psychosexual factors in the development of hysteria.[9] Freud's clinical reports, however, remain astonishingly fresh over the decades, and today his case history clearly reveals the psychosocial centering of the girl's story in matters of fidelity. In fact, one might say, without seriously overdoing it, that three words characterize her social history: sexual infidelity on the part of some of the most important adults in her life; the perfidy of her father's denial of his friend's sexual acts, which were in fact the precipitating cause of the girl's illness; and a strange tendency on the part of all the adults around the girl to make her a confidante in any number of matters, without having enough confidence in her to acknowledge the truths relevant to her illness.

Freud, of course, focused on other matters, opening up, with the concentration of a psychosurgeon, the symbolic meaning of her symptoms and their history; but, as always, he reported relevant data on the periphery of his interests. Thus, among the matters which somewhat puzzled him, he reports that the patient was "almost beside herself at the idea of its being supposed that she had merely fancied" the conditions which had made her sick; and that she was kept "anxiously trying to make sure whether I was being quite straightforward with her"—or perfidious like her father. When at the end she left analyst and analysis "in order to confront the adults around her with the secrets she knew," Freud considered this an act of revenge on them, and on him; and within the outlines of his interpretation, this partial interpretation stands. Nevertheless, as we can now see, there was more to this insistence on the historical truth than the denial of an inner truth—and this especially in an adolescent. For, the question as to what confirms them irreversibly as a truthful or a cheating, a sick or a rebellious type is paramount in the minds of adolescents; and the further question, whether or not they were right in not accepting the conditions which made them sick, is as important to them as the insight into the structure of their sickness can ever be. In other words, they insist that the meaning of their sickness find recognition within a reformulation of the historical truth as revealed in their own insights and distortions, and not according to the terms of the environment which wishes them to be "brought to reason" (as Dora's father had put it, when he brought her to Freud).

No doubt, Dora by then was a hysteric, and the meaning of her symptoms was psychosexual; but the sexual nature of her disturbance and of the precipitating events should not blind us to the fact that other perfidies, familial and communal, cause adolescents to regress in a variety of ways to a variety of earlier stages.

Only when adolescence is reached does the capacity for such clear regression and symptom formation occur: only when the historical function of the mind is consolidated can significant repressions become marked enough to cause consistent symptom formation and deformation of character. The depth of regression determines the nature of the pathology and points to the therapy to be employed. However, there is a pathognomic picture which all sick youth have in common and which is clearly discernible in Freud's description of Dora's total state. This picture is characterized first of all by a denial of the historical flux of time, and by an attempt to challenge retrospectively, while retesting in the present all parental premises before new trust is invested in the (emancipated) future.

The sick adolescent thus gradually stops extending experimental feelers toward the future; his moratorium of illness becomes an end in itself and thus ceases to be a moratorium (Dora suffered from a "*taedium vitae* which was probably not entirely genuine," Freud wrote). It is for this reason that death and suicide can be at this time such a spurious preoccupation—one leading unpredictably to suicide (and to murder)—for death would conclude the life history before it joins others in inexorable commitment (Dora's parents found "a letter in which she took leave of them because she could no longer endure life. Her father . . . guessed that the girl had no serious suicidal intentions.") There is also a social isolation which excludes all sense of solidarity and can lead to a snobbish isolation which finds companions but no friends (Dora "tried to avoid social intercourse," was "distant" and "unfriendly"). The energy of repudiation which accompanies the first steps of an identity formation (and in some youngsters can lead to the sudden impulse to annihilate) is in neurotics turned against the self ("Dora was satisfied neither with herself nor with her family").

A repudiated self in turn cannot offer loyalty, and, of course, fears the fusion of love or of sexual encounters. The work inhibition often connected with this picture (Dora suffered from "fatigue and lack of concentration") is really a career inhibition, in the sense that every exertion of skill or method is suspected of binding the individual to the role and the status suggested by the activity; thus, again, any moratorium is spoiled. Where fragmentary identities are formed, they are highly self-conscious and are immediately put to a test (thus Dora obviously defeated her wish to be a woman intellectual). This identity consciousness is a strange mixture of superiority, almost a megalomania ("I am a majority of one," one of my patients said), with which the patient tries to convince himself that he is really too good for his community or his period of history, while he is equally convinced of being nobody.

We have sketched the most obvious social symptoms of adolescent psychopathology, in part to indicate that, besides the complicated structure of specific symptoms, there is in the picture presented of each stage an expression of the dominant psychosocial issue, so open that one sometimes wonders whether the patient lies by telling the simple truth or tells the truth when he seems most obviously to lie.

The sketch presented, however, also serves as a comparison of the isolated adolescent sufferer with those youths who try to solve their doubt in their elders by joining deviant cliques and gangs. Freud found that "psychoneuroses are, so to speak, the negative of perversions,"[10] which means that neurotics suffer under the repression of tendencies which perverts try to "live out." This has a counterpart in the fact that isolated sufferers try to solve by withdrawal what the joiners of deviant cliques and gangs attempt to solve by conspiracy.

If we now turn to this form of adolescent pathology, the denial of the irreversibility of historical time appears to be expressed in a clique's or a gang's delusion of being an organization with a tradition and an ethics all its own. The pseudo-historical character of such societies is expressed in such names as "The Navahos," "The Saints," or "The Edwardians"; while their provocation is countered by society (remember the Pachucos of the war years) with a mixture of impotent rage wherever murderous excess does actually occur, and with a phobic overconcern followed by vicious suppression wherever these "secret societies" are really no more than fads lacking any organized purpose. Their pseudo-societal character reveals itself in their social parasitism, and their pseudo-rebellion in the conformism actually governing their habits. Yet the seemingly unassailable inner sense of callous rightness is no doubt due to an inner realignment of motivations, which can best be understood by briefly comparing the torment of the isolated youngster with the temporary gains derived by the joiner from the mere fact that he has been taken into a pseudo-society. The time diffusion attending the isolate's inability to envisage a career is "cured" by his attention to "jobs"—theft, destruction, fights, murder, or acts of perversion or addiction, conceived on the spur of the moment and executed forthwith. This "job" orientation also takes care of the work inhibition, because the clique and the gang are always "busy," even if they just "hang around." Their lack of any readiness to wince under shaming or accusation is often considered the mark of a total personal perdition, while in fact it is a trademark, an insignia of the "species" to which the youngster (mostly marginal in economic and ethnic respects) would rather belong than to a society which is eager to confirm him as a criminal and then promises to rehabilitate him as an ex-criminal.

As to the isolate's tortured feelings of bisexuality or of an immature need for love, the young joiner in social pathology, by joining, has made a clear decision: he is male with a vengeance, she, a female without sentimentality; or they are both perverts. In either case, they can eliminate the procreative function of genitality altogether and can make a pseudo-culture of what is left. By the same token, they will acknowledge authority only in the form chosen in the act of joining, repudiating the rest of the social world, where the isolate repudiates existence as such and, with it, himself.

The importance of these comparative considerations, which have been stated in greater detail elsewhere, lie in the impotent craving of the isolated sufferer to be true to himself, and in that of the joiner, to be true to a group and to its insignia and codes. By this I do not mean to deny that the one is sick (as his physical and mental symptoms attest), nor that the other can be on the way to becoming a criminal, as his more and more irreversible acts and choices attest. Both theory and therapy, however, lack the proper leverage, if the need for (receiving and giving) fidelity is not understood, and especially if instead the young deviant is confirmed by every act of the correctional or therapeutic authorities as a future criminal or a lifelong patient.

In Dora's case, I have tried to indicate the phenomenology of this need. As to young delinquents, I can only quote again one of those rare newspaper reports which convey enough of a story to show the elements involved. Kai T. Erikson and I have used this example as an introduction to our article "The Confirmation of the Delinquent."[11]

JUDGE IMPOSES ROAD GANG TERM FOR BACK TALK

> *Wilmington, N. D.* (UP)—A "smart alecky" youth who wore pegged trousers and a flattop haircut began six months on a road gang today for talking back to the wrong judge.
>
> Michael A. Jones, 20, of Wilmington, was fined $25 and costs in Judge Edwin Jay Roberts Jr.'s superior court for reckless operation of an automobile. But he just didn't leave well enough alone.
>
> "I understand how it was, with your pegged trousers and flattop haircut," Roberts said in assessing the fine. "You go on like this and I predict in five years you'll be in prison."
>
> When Jones walked over to pay his fine, he overheard Probation Officer Gideon Smith tell the judge how much trouble the "smart alecky" young offender had been.
>
> "I just want you to know I'm not a thief," interrupted Jones to the judge.
>
> The judge's voice boomed to the court clerk: "Change that judgment to six months on the roads."

I quote the story here to add the interpretation that the judge in this case (neither judge nor case differs from a host of others) took it as an affront to the dignity of authority what may have also been a desperate "historical" denial, an attempt to claim that a truly antisocial identity had not yet been formed, and that there was enough discrimination and potential fidelity left to be made something of by somebody who cared to do so. But instead, what the young man and the judge made of it was likely, of course, to seal the irreversibility and confirm the doom. I say "was likely to," because I do not know what happened in this case; we do know, however, the high recidivity of criminality in the young who, during the years of identity formation, are forced by society into intimate contact with criminals.

Finally, it cannot be overlooked that at times political undergrounds of all kinds can and do make use of the need for fidelity as well as the store of wrath in those deprived in their need by their families or their societies. Here social rejuvenation can make use of and redeem social pathology, even as in individuals special giftedness can be related to and redeem neurosis. These are matters too weighty to be discussed briefly and, at any rate, our concern has been with the fact that the psychopathology of youth suggests a consideration of the same issues which we found operative in the evolutionary and developmental aspects of this stage of life.

To summarize: Fidelity, when fully matured, is the strength of disciplined devotion. It is gained in the involvement of youth in such experiences as reveal the essence of the era they are to join—as the beneficiaries of its tradition, as the practitioners and innovators of its technology, as renewers of its ethical strength, as rebels bent on the destruction of the outlived, and as deviants with deviant commitments. This, at least, is the potential of youth in psychosocial evolution; and while this may sound like a rationalization endorsing any high-sounding self-delusion in youth, any self-indulgence masquerading as devotion, or any righteous excuse for blind destruction, it makes intelligible the tremendous waste attending this as any other mechanism of human adaptation, especially if its excesses meet with more moral condemnation than ethical guidance. On the other hand, our understanding of these processes is not furthered by the "clinical" reduction of adolescent phenomena to their infantile antecedents and to an underlying dichotomy of drive and conscience. Adolescent development comprises a new set of identification processes, both with significant persons and with ideological forces, which give importance to individual life by relating it to a living community and to ongoing history, and by counterpointing the newly won individual identity with some communal solidarity.

In youth, then, the life history intersects with history: here individuals are confirmed in their identities, societies regenerated in their life style. This process also implies a fateful survival of adolescent modes of thinking in man's historical and ideological perspectives.

Historical processes, of course, have already entered the individual's core in childhood. Both ideal and evil images and the moral prototypes guiding parental administrations originate in the past struggles of contending cultural and national "species," which also color fairytale and family lore, superstition and gossip, and the simple lessons of early verbal training. Historians on the whole make little of this; they describe the visible emergence and the contest of autonomous historical ideas, unconcerned with the fact that these ideas reach down into the lives of generations and re-emerge through the daily awakening and training of historical consciousness in young individuals.

It is youth, then, which begins to develop that sense of historical irreversibility which can lead to what we may call acute historical estrangement. This lies behind the fervent quest for a sure meaning in individual life history and in collective history, and behind the questioning of the laws of relevancy which bind datum and principle, event and movement. But it is also, alas, behind the bland carelessness of that youth which denies its own vital need to develop and cultivate a historical consciousness—and conscience.

To enter history, each generation of youth must find an identity consonant with its own childhood and consonant with an ideological promise in the perceptible historical process. But in youth the tables of childhood dependence begin slowly to turn: no longer is it merely for the old to teach the young the meaning of life, whether individual or collective. It is the young who, by their responses and actions, tell the old whether life as represented by the old and as presented to the young has meaning; and it is the young who carry in them the power to confirm those who confirm them and, joining the issues, to renew and to regenerate, or to reform and to rebel.

I will not at this point review the institutions which participate in creating the retrospective and the prospective mythology offering historical orientation to youth: obviously, the mythmakers of religion and politics, the arts and the sciences, the stage and fiction—all contribute to the historical logic preached to youth more or less consciously, more or less responsibly. And today we must add, at least in the United States, psychiatry; and all over the world, the press, which forces the leaders to make history in the open and to accept reportorial distortion as a major historical factor.

I have spoken of Hamlet as an abortive ideological leader. His drama combines all the elements of which successful ideological leaders are made: they are the postadolescents who make out of the very contradictions of adolescence the polarities of their charisma. Individuals with an uncommon depth of conflict, they also have uncanny gifts, and often uncanny luck with which they offer to the crisis of a generation the solution of their own crisis—always, as Woodrow Wilson put it, being "in love with activity on a large scale," always feeling that their one life must be made to count in the lives of all, always convinced that what they felt as adolescents was a curse, a fall, an earthquake, a thunderbolt, in short, a revelation to be shared with their generation and with many to come. Their humble claim to being chosen does not preclude a wish to universal power. "Fifty years from now," wrote Kierkegaard in the journal of his spiritual soliloquy, "the whole world will read my diary." He sensed, no doubt, that the impending dominance of mass ideologies would bring to the fore his cure for the individual soul, existentialism. We must study the question (I have approached it in my study of young Luther) of what ideological leaders do to history—whether they first aspire to power and then face spiritual qualms, or first face spiritual perdition and then seek universal influence. Their answers often manage to subsume under the heading of a more embracing identity all that ails man, especially young man, at critical times: danger from new weapons and from natural forces aggravated by man's misuse of nature; anxiety from sources within the life-history typical for the time; and existential dread of the ego's limitations, magnified in times of disintegrating superidentities and intensified in adolescence.

But does it not take a special and, come to think of it, a strange sense of calling, to dare and to care to give such inclusive answers? Is it not probable and in fact demonstrable that among the most passionate ideologists there are unreconstructed adolescents, transmitting to their ideas the proud moment of their transient ego recovery, of their temporary victory over the forces of existence and history, but also the pathology of their deepest isolation, the defensiveness of their forever adolescing egos—and their fear of the calm of adulthood? "To live beyond forty," says Dostoevsky's underground diarist, "is bad taste." It warrants study, both historical and psychological, to see how some of the most influential leaders have turned away from parenthood, only to despair in middle age of the issue of their leadership as well.

It is clear that today the ideological needs of all but intellectual youth of the humanist tradition are beginning to be taken care of by a subordination of ideology to technology: what works, on the grandest scale, is good. It is to be hoped that the worst implications of this trend have outlived themselves already in fascism. Yet in the technological superidentity, the American dream and the Marxist revolution also meet. If their competition can be halted before mutual annihilation, it is just possible that a new mankind, seeing that it can now build and destroy anything it wishes, will focus its intelligence (feminine as well as masculine) on the ethical question concerning the workings of human generations—beyond products, powers, and ideas. Ideologies in the past have contained an ethical corrective, but ethics must eventually transcend ideology as well as technology: the great question will be and already is, what man, on ethical grounds and without moralistic self-destruction, must decide *not* to do, even though he could make it work—for a while.

Moralities sooner or later outlive themselves, ethics never: this is what the need for identity and for fidelity, reborn with each generation, seems to point to. Morality in the moralistic sense can be shown by modern means of inquiry to be predicated on superstitions and irrational inner mechanisms which ever again undermine the ethical fiber of generations; but morality is expendable only where ethics prevail. This is the wisdom that the words of many languages have tried to tell man. He has tenaciously clung to the words, even though he has understood them only vaguely, and in his actions has disregarded or perverted them completely. But there is much in ancient wisdom which can now become knowledge.

As in the near future peoples of different tribal and national pasts join what must become the identity of one mankind, they can find an initial common language only in the workings of science and technology. This in turn may well help them to make transparent the superstitions of their traditional moralities and may even permit them to advance rapidly through a historical period during which they must put a vain superidentity of neonationalism in the place of their much exploited historical identity weakness. But they must also look beyond the major ideologies of the now "established" world, offered them as ceremonial masks to frighten and to attract them. The overriding issue is the creation not of a new ideology but of a universal ethics growing out of a universal technological civilization. This can be advanced only by men and women who are neither ideological youths nor moralistic old men, but who know that from generation to generation the test of what you produce is in the *care* it inspires. If there is any chance at all, it is in a world more challenging, more workable, and more venerable than all myths, retrospective or prospective: it is in historical reality, at last ethically cared for.

REFERENCES

1. Virtue once connoted "inherent strength" and "active quality." In this sense, I consider the following basic virtues (essential to, if not identical with, ego strength) to be anchored in the successive stages of life: Hope, in infancy; Will and Purpose, in the play age; Skill in the school age; Fidelity, in youth; Love, in young adulthood; Care, in adulthood; Wisdom, in old age. For an evolutionary and genetic rationale of this concept of the life cycle, see the writer's "The Roots of Virtue," in *The Humanist Frame,* Sir Julian Huxley, ed. London: Allen and Unwin, 1961; New York: Harper and Brothers, 1961; For a more detailed exposition, see the writer's forthcoming book, *Life Cycle and Community,* in which the other stages of development are treated in chapters analogous to the one presented here.

2. Ernest Jones, *Hamlet and Oedipus.* New York: Doubleday, Anchor, 1949.

3. Saxo Grammaticus, *Danish History,* translated by Elton, 1894 (quoted in Jones, *op. cit.,* pp. 163-164.

4. The classical psychoanalytic works concerned with psychosexuality and the ego defenses of youth are: Sigmund Freud, *Three Essays on the Theory of Sexuality,* standard edition, (London, The Hogarth Press, 1953), vol. 7; and Anna Freud, *The Ego and the Mechanisms of Defence,* New York, International Universities

Press, 1946. For the writer's views, see his *Childhood and Society*. New York: W. W. Norton, 1950.

5. B. Inhelder and J. Piaget, *The Growth of Logical Thinking from Childhood to Adolescence*. New York: Basic Books, 1958.
6. Jerome S. Bruner, *The Process of Education*. Cambridge: Harvard University Press, 1960.
7. See the writer's "The Problem of Ego-Identity" in *Identity and the Life Cycle: Psychological Issues* (New York: International Universities Press, 1959), vol. I, no. 1.
8. *Young Man Luther*. New York: W. W. Norton, 1958; London: Faber and Faber, 1959.
9. Sigmund Freud, *Fragment of an Analysis of a Case of Hysteria*, standard edition (London: The Hogarth Press, 1953), vol. 7.
10. *Ibid.*, p. 50.
11. Erik H. Erikson and Kai T. Erickson, "The Confirmation of the Delinquent," *The Chicago Review*, Winter 1957, *10:* 15-23.

Where Is the College Generation Headed?

David Riesman

The conflict of the generations is neither a new nor a particularly American story, but it is perhaps exacerbated by the self-consciousness and the partial segregation of teen-age culture, to such an extent that both old and young are exceptionally vulnerable to their mutual criticisms. I do not care to add to the complacency of my agemates who, from their clubs, pulpits, and other rostrums, attack the alleged "softness" of the young, whom they have themselves brought up, while failing to see the difficulties young people face today precisely because the manifest hardships with which earlier Americans coped have been, for millions, attenuated. These hardships cannot be artificially restored, at least for people over twelve; however, I believe that college students are now beginning to find new ways to become active politically, and hence responsible humanly.

It is easy to underestimate the importance of this in America, where students until recently did not play the role in politics that they do in Latin America, Turkey, Korea, or Japan. For, the cadres of the

Reprinted from *Atlantic Monthly,* April, 1961 by permission of the author.

disinherited who once helped power political change in this country are diminished in numbers and even more diminished in leadership, now that nearly every bright, motivated boy gets funneled into college if he wants to go. Thus, our expanding colleges absorb increasingly large fractions of the available idealism and dynamism of our society. And at the same time, as I shall try to show, many students are not attracted by the traditional goals of commercial or professional ambition; the best of them have no love for the status quo. Rejecting careerism, they often choose familism instead. But shaken out of this, either by the open discrimination felt by Negroes or the subtler dissatisfaction with contemporary life felt by whites, they comprise a privileged minority, ignorant of its strength, yet capable of change.

College students today often act as if they believed that work in large organizations, and beyond that, work in general, could not be basically satisfying (or, at times, even honest), but is primarily a way to earn a living, to find a place in the social order, and to meet nice or not-so-nice people. This is a conclusion which is partly projected upon the occupational scene as the result of their experience with the curriculum in college and university, and also as the result of experience with college and university as organizations which are viewed as bureaucratic, monolithic, and unchangeable by many students.

I do not think it is the primary task of education to prepare students for their later occupational roles, or, indeed, any narrowly specialized roles, nor to teach them to enjoy work regardless of its quality and meaning. Rather, the relation of education to later life should be a dialectical and critical one. If, however, one result of going to college is to become alienated from work per se and defeatist about the possibility of altering one's relation to it, then it seems to me one ought to re-examine academic institutions themselves and see whether anything in them, or in one's own attitudes, or in both might be changed.

In the spring of 1955, several hundred interviews were done (at the behest of *Time* magazine) with seniors at twenty colleges throughout the country, most of them colleges of distinction. The seniors were supposed to be reasonably representative, but what this was taken to mean and how it was applied at different colleges and universities varied greatly. A good many student leaders were chosen, a good many bright people, but hardly any women were included (a questionnaire circulated by *Mademoiselle* gave me somewhat comparable data concerning college women). When I first examined the interviews, and now again when I have once more gone over them, I have been struck by what appears to be a not quite conscious ambivalence toward work in large organizations. Nevertheless, the majority are planning to enter large organizations in pursuit of their careers: big corporations, big governments, big law offices, and so on. Only a few seek independence in their work, either in terms of old fashioned ideals of entrepreneurship or in terms of the desire to become a foreign correspondent, to enter politics, or to follow some other individualistic or exotic calling. (Moreover, hardly anyone expresses resentment against his prospective army service on the ground that the army is a large organization; there is no eagerness for service, but rather resignation to it as one of the givens of life.)

And yet, when these young people are asked about their lives outside of work, a very different picture emerges. There, bigness and scale are definitely not valued. Only a tiny fraction want to head for the metropolis, even if their careers might make such a location convenient. They want the suburbs—not later, after some bachelor independence in the big city, but now, on graduation. The great majority either are already married or plan to get married soon (even if there is no special one in mind at the moment); they plan to start having children at once and to begin building a community-centered life in the suburbs. They envisage a two-car, but usually not a two-career, family, in which the prospective wife will be active in the parent-teacher association, with assistance from the husband, and in which both spouses will concern themselves with a manageable bit of real estate in a suburban neighborhood in which they can at once be active and hope to make a difference. It does not occur to them that they might be gifted and energetic enough to make a difference even in a big city. Rather, they want to be able to work through a face-to-face group—the postcollegiate fraternity of the small suburbs.

Correspondingly, the very emphasis on family life, which is one of the striking and, in so many ways, attractive qualities of young people today, is an implicit rejection of large organization. The suburban family, with its garden, its barbecue, its lack of privacy in the open-plan house, is itself a manifesto of decentralization, even though it makes use of centralized services such as television, clinics, chain stores, and *House Beautiful.* The wish to build a nest, even if a somewhat transient one, is a striking feature of the interviews, in contrast with the wish to build a fortune or a career, which might have dominated some comparable interviews a generation earlier.

This pattern—the acceptance of large organizations, combined with tacit and uncrystallized resistance to them—appears not only in the respondents' emphasis on the family but also in what they say about their plans and attitudes toward their future work. I get a sense from the material, and from other comparable data, of a certain withdrawal of emotional adherence from work. To be sure, it has become fashionable to speak of one's work or other activities in deprecatory terms and to adopt a pose of relative indifference to the larger goals of an organization. In an era of political, economic, and cultural salesmanship, such deprecation is a way of guarding against being exploited for ends outside one's self. It is as if one had constantly to conduct psychological warfare against an outside enemy. But, as in any such process, students become to some extent the victims of their own defenses. They come to believe that work cannot really be worth doing for its own sake, whether or not it is done on behalf of a large, impersonal organization. They fear overcommitment to their work even while they are at the workplace. In the course of getting rid of earlier collegiate or rah-rah enthusiasm, these young people have come to feel that work is not worth even their part-time devotion, and perhaps that nothing, except the family, deserves their wholehearted allegiance.

We see the same attitudes, of course, among the junior echelons now engaged in work. One hears them talk of their benevolent company as "a mink-lined rat trap," or speak of "the rat race," or refer to fights over principles as "ruckuses" or "blowups"—if somebody cares, he is said to "blow his top." In a number of business novels, of which *The Man in the Gray Flannel Suit* is representative, it is taken for granted that a sensible fellow, and, indeed, an honest one, will prefer suburban domesticity and a quiet niche to ulcerous competition for large business stakes, despite the view from the top and the interesting climb.

Attitudes such as these are of course an aspect of a general cultural shift, not confined to students and not confined to those who seek employment in large organizations; similar attitudes turn up in some measure even among those who, studiously avoiding such organizations, look for a professional career in which they hope to be their own masters. Scholars, for example, are not immune to distaste for their work, nor are architects or physicians. But, while I do not intend to imply that a life without any boredom is conceivable, except for a very stupid person, still, I think we are witnessing a silent revolution against work on the part of even those relatively privileged groups who have been free to choose their work and to exercise some freedom in the doing of it. This reflects, in part, the fact that much work is meaningless per se, save as a source of income, prestige, and sociability, but it also indicates, as I have already implied, that people too readily accept their work as it comes, without the hope of making it more meaningful.

Not all large organizations are alike, despite the sorts of institutional similarities investigated by sociologists, and, of course, not all positions in them are alike. Many, although their top executives clamor for creativity and independence of mind, largely manage to process these qualities out of "their" people in the lower ranks. Others stockpile talent and expect it to keep as gold keeps at Fort Knox. Still others make products or provide services which are either antisocial or useless. But here and there one finds companies which face real and not contrived problems and apply to them an intelligence which is often remarkably disinterested and, in the best sense of the term, "academic." Young people in search of challenge and development would do well to seek out such relatively productive climates, rather than to assume offhand that these (as is true of so many brand-name products) are all alike except for the advertising and the label. And this search is necessary precisely because many of the motives which impelled work in the older generation have fortunately become attenuated, motives such as money for its own sake, power, and fame—goals, that is, whose emptiness became evident with their attainment. Our industrial and commercial plant no longer "needs" such compulsive attachments to work, which are based not on any genuine creative impulse but on the drying up of other alternatives and on the pressure of extrinsic standards of value.

There is a further issue concerning work in large organizations where, again, differentiation is required. I refer to the conception that work in organizations requires surrender of independence of judgment, if not of integrity. When I was in college, there was a prevalent feeling among the more sensitive that this was true only of business and commercial organizations, not of governmental or philanthropic ones, and young men debated whether they would enter Wall Street and make money, or enter government or teaching and be saved. This dichotomy has in large measure vanished, although traces of it do survive among the less cynical. For instance, I have known many graduate students in social psychology who believe that if they teach. they can be honest, but that if they work in market research, they will serve manipulation and corruption and will have no power over their own work. Such judgments oversimplify the ethical dilemmas of any calling and are, in addition, snobbish; one can find hucksterism (often hypocritically veiled) among academic people in search of reputations, grants, and promotions, as well as among market researchers and other businessmen.

Indeed, I am inclined to think that, at present, many observant young people do not need to be persuaded of this; many are actually overpersuaded to the point of believing that every occupation is a racket and that at best some of the racketeers are less pious about it than others. And this, I suspect, is one of the reasons they tend to withdraw emotional allegiance from their work—with the impression that they have no control over it anyway, that all is in the hands of the mysterious men upstairs who run the show. If there is greater wisdom in their belief that all occupations, like all forms of power, are corrupting in some degree, there is also greater resignation, greater passivity and fatalism.

Where are such attitudes learned and confirmed? Even at some of the leading colleges, the more intellectual colleges, the colleges which produce literary magazines, the relation of students to the curriculum has a certain alienated quality, in the sense that the students do not believe they have any control over their own education.

In the last few years I have visited a number of colleges of high quality, colleges which turn out eminent professional men, scholars, and scientists, and I have made it my business to talk with students informally, to read their student newspapers and, where possible, student council reports. At a number of these institutions, the livelier students complain of the educational fare they are getting, of the very little contact the curriculum makes with the problems that are meaningful to them. Sometimes they feel that opportunities for a civilized and intellectual life on campus are wanting—for example, that there are few inviting places to study or to talk, that social pressures in dormitories force any intellectual life out of the group setting, that student publications are either dominated by the school administration or devoted to campus news and trivia, that the bookstore is inadequate, or that the library is geared to meet research needs rather than to attract undergraduate browsers. They often feel that they have no access to the faculty for other then merely routine matters. Sometimes students complain about the prerequisites of a department, which serve its monopolistic aims or protect its mediocre teachers from boycott rather than serve any defensible pedagogic aims.

Yet, when I ask such students what they have done about these things, they are surprised at the very thought that they could do anything. They think I am joking when I suggest that, if things came to the worst, they could picket! They think I am wholly unrealistic when I say that many on the faculty might welcome student initiative in revising the curriculum, or that it might be possible to raise modest sums of money among alumni or others to bring visiting lecturers or poets to the campus, or to furnish commodious rooms for interest-group meetings. When I tell them that the Harvard house plan came about in considerable measure because of the report of a student council committee in 1926 which caught the attention of the philanthropist Edward Harkness, they shrug. That must have been a golden era, they say; nothing like that could happen now. Of course, as long as they think that, they will conduct themselves accordingly.

Why is it that students, often so precocious about many things—about each other, about sex, about their families, and occasionally even about national and world affairs—are comparatively inattentive to what concerns them as closely as does their curriculum?

For one thing, it seems to me that students do not want to believe that their activities might make a difference, because, in a way, they profit from their lack of commitment to what they are doing. I do not mean that they are not industrious students; they go through the required motions of working, but they seldom get really involved with the content of their courses. It is here that the better, more conscientious students sabotage their own education and restrict production; true enough, they turn out the credits and the grades, but they do not believe that it really matters in any fundamental sense what they think and feel.

When I have discussed this with students, they have often told me that it doesn't pay to be too interested in anything, because then one is tempted to spend too much time on it, at the expense of that optimal distribution of effort which will produce the best grades—and after all, they do have to get into medical school, keep their scholarship, and "please the old man." Now, I am convinced that grades contaminate education—they are a kind of currency which, like money, gets in the way of students' discovering their intellectual interests—but here, too, the students in their realism are being somewhat unrealistic. They assume, for one thing, that it is hopeless to try to alter the curriculum so that it might penalize them less for serious interest in one topic at the expense of others, or so that there might be more emphasis on reading and discussion and more opportunity for independent thinking. And here, also, the students have a distorted image of what will actually make an impression on their teachers either now or later. On this point, I have some evidence to back me up.

After I had tried in vain for some time to persuade graduate students at Chicago that they could be more independent in their course and thesis work without any heroism, any martyrdom, there was a thesis done by a student which documented my arguments. The student went around to the departments and asked them which students in recent years they had recommended for jobs or advanced training or fellowships and which they had not. Then he interviewed some of these students in various categories of faculty blessing or disapproval, looked at their grades, and so on. He concluded that those students frequently fared best who were not too obedient, who did not get an undiluted, uncomplicated, straight-A record. (The straight-A students, in fact, sometimes slipped away without anyone's noticing.)

The students who were most successful were a bit rebellious, a bit offbeat, though not entirely "goof-offs"; these were the students likely to appeal to a faculty member who had not entirely repressed a rebelliousness of his own that had led him to be a teacher in the first place, a faculty member who was looking for signs of life, even if they gave him a bit of trouble at times. To be sure, such a student had to do well in something to earn this response, but he was often better off to have written a brilliant paper or two than to have divided his time as an investment banker his money, among a variety of subjects. Those students who were the most self-consciously opportunistic and realistic in allocating their time and emotion were in fact sacrificing themselves unprofitably, suffering not only now, during the studies which they regarded as an anteroom to life, but later on as well.

Now, not all departments at Chicago were alike in this matter; some gave more play to defiance and deviation than others. Moreover, this study encompassed only the social science departments. No doubt departments and institutions differ very much in this respect. But that is just the point I want to emphasize; by concluding prematurely that all organizations are alike, that all demand the same kinds of conformity, students not only surrender the chance to experience an atmosphere that is freer and more conducive to their own development but perpetuate a myth that then controls their passage through jobs in later life. If the University of Chicago or even one's department itself cannot be changed from below, how can one expect to change General Motors, or *Look* magazine, or the big hospitals of San Francisco? And if that is so, then why not settle for the fringe benefits, for a position of moderate respectability and adequate, if not dazzling, salary?

At work here is a characteristic social pattern in which individuals, hesitant to reveal feelings they have scarcely voiced to themselves, are misled about what in effect could be done if they expressed themselves, thereby discovering others who might share their views. (Sociologists refer to this process as "pluralistic ignorance.") Leadership, of course, whether in politics or in other affairs, often serves to help a group change its apparent mood to conform to its actual or potential but repressed views, but leadership also may, and frequently does, serve to continue enforcing the repression. Even in a large organization, radical and what were previously regarded as "impossible" changes come about almost instantaneously once people discover that views they had previously regarded as unacceptable or idiosyncratic are in fact widely shared.

The students know that there are many decisions out of their conceivable control, decisions upon which their lives and fortunes truly depend. But what I am contending is that this truth, this insight, is overgeneralized, and that, being believed, it becomes more and more "true." Not only do we fail to spot those instances in which intervention might change things quite substantially, but we fail to develop the competence and the confidence in ourselves that are necessary to any large endeavor. In that sense, despite our precociousness, we fail to grow up; we remain the children of organization, not the masters of it.

For Americans, there is something paradoxical about this development. Americans in the past have not been overimpressed by mechanical achievements. Workers in a steel mill are not awed by any large rollers, and we take for granted that we are not awed by any large physical construction made by our hands and brains. Contrary to the prevalent impression abroad that we are slaves to our machines, we are actually relatively uninvolved with them, and we surely do not feel dominated by them. But it seems to be different with the organizational machines. These are as much the product of our thinking and our imagination as any technological feat; yet, as Erich Fromm has said, we worship like idolaters the product we have created, an image not of stone but of other images.

It is a commonplace observation that in organizational life we use arguments to convince others which we think will appeal to them, even though they do not convince us. We try to persuade people to behave justly to Negroes because "discrimination makes the United States look bad in the Cold War," as if that were why we ourselves behaved decently. Or we persuade businessmen to give money to colleges for all sorts of public relations reasons, playing on their fear of radicalism or federal control or whatnot, whereas we ourselves devote our lives to education for quite different reasons. All arguments of this nature have two qualities: they patronize the other person and they perpetuate "pluralistic ignorance." It can be contended that there may be occasions when we must appeal to others as they are, not as we should like them to be; when there is not time for idealism. But, in our realism, we often make mistakes about what others will actually respond to, and we sacrifice the integrity and clarity of our argument to our false image of what will go over. The result: we conclude that one cannot be honest while working for an organization, that one can be honest only when one is at home with one's family in the suburbs.

There is another result as well; namely, that we often end up in doubt as to what we ourselves think. We come to believe what we say to others and thus become "more sincere" in the subjective sense, but at the price of becoming still more confused as to what is actually so: we are the first victims of our own propaganda. No wonder we end up without emotional ties to what we do, for it is no longer we who do it, but some limited part of ourselves, playing a role. Not recognizing that we in some measure have done this to ourselves, we attribute to organizations the power and the primacy we have lost. And then, as I have said, we strike back, not directly, but by a kind of emotional attrition in which we lend to our work willingness without enthusiasm, conscientiousness without creativity.

I am sure that many college students who are not only serious but dedicated know this as well as I do. Such students have managed to make college serve their purposes and have in this way gained some rational confidence that they will be able to do the same in the organizations they will enter later, whether these are universities, business concerns, or the many voluntary organizations through which we Americans carry out much of our communal work. What I have principally sought to do in these remarks is to encourage greater and more differentiated realism than many young people already possess, a realism which does not take for granted the social structures which seem so impressive but which looks for the points of leverage where one's own effort, joined to that of others similarly freed from mythology, might make a difference. In many situations, there is more leeway than students think, and college is a good place to find this out.

Three years later, I have naturally asked myself to what extent the foregoing remarks still strike me as true. I had in 1955 and 1957 paid very brief visits to several of the Southern Negro colleges that have since been in the forefront of sit-in demonstrations; at that time they seemed to me, as to some of their own faculty members, acquiescent and cautious, preparing students to enter the army uncomplainingly, the "Black Bourgeoisie" unthinkingly. Of course, the students were aware of the struggles over integration, but for them the issues remained somewhat abstract, particularly as many of them had chosen the shelter of a segregated college, as in their prospective occupations —teaching, the ministry, Negro business—many would choose the still segregated occupations.

As so often, appearances were deceptive; some of these students carried out the first sit-ins and refused to become daunted or disorganized when either their own pressured administrations or reactive whites sought to end the picketing and protests; a brave few, in active civil disobedience, have chosen jail rather than bail. Relatively immune to the economic boycotts that can hamstring their parents, and free, too, of the traditional Negro leadership in their communities, they have discovered their organizational powers and talents. This has been bracing and highly educative.

Meanwhile, among white students in the North, sympathetic picketing of the chain stores was rapidly organized, and many campuses had their first taste of political life in twenty years. The young people I have been describing are markedly tolerant; in the 1955 interviews, hardly any exhibited bigotry (at the Southern universities many said that once the old folks are gone, the race problem will die with them). Moreover, tolerance appears to them a virtue that is civic and personal, tied into one's own immediate human reactions and relations; to be tolerant to classmates, one does not have to fight city hall, though one may sometimes have to fight alumni guardians of the more collegiate fraternities.

Furthermore, the simplicity of the race issue, the near lack of rational or civilized defense of segregation and discrimination, allows Northern students to extrapolate public activity on the basis of private decency, without feeling themselves to be involved in "politics" or in ideology. True, the planned picketing has involved these highly individualistic students in more organization and decision making than appeals to most of them; the term "politician" is as much one of contempt on the better campuses as it is generally in American life. Even so, many students have discovered, though less dramatically than the Southern Negro students, that they are capable of action in areas outside the usual complaints about library hours, dormitory food, and parking, and that even such seemingly large outfits as Woolworth's are not invulnerable.

So, too, there have recently been some energetic student actions in the area of curriculum. In the spring of 1958, students at the University of Wisconsin submitted a petition to the administration requesting more challenge and stimulation in their courses and in their educational program generally. During the same period, undergraduates at Chicago mobilized to defend the general education program against attempts to subordinate it to the requirements of the graduate departments. A group of students at Wesleyan last year arranged a series of discussions on education, geared to the problems and opportunities faced by a liberal arts college; apparently the students helped influence curricular change. While, in some instances, students could graduate before realizing that what they did had any impact, others learned from their experiences that institutions are man-made and subject to change.

It is understandably seldom that such sporadic and ad hoc actions have been carried over into political controversies on the national scene. There have been occasional protests against compulsory ROTC, based as much on the unintellectual waste of time of the programs as on any explicit antimilitarist views. The student political party (Slate) at Berkeley was a factor in last year's protest against the Un-American Activities Committee hearings in San Francisco—a brave protest, since many students fear it will go on their records in an FBI dossier. And, increasingly, the issues of peace and disarmament have found a student audience. Students are picketing weekly on Boston Common under the auspices of the Committee for a Sane Nuclear Policy and are encountering, as they did to only a minor degree in picketing the chain stores, violent and jeering attacks as Reds or yellow appeasers. Challenge at Michigan and Yale, Concern at Ohio Wesleyan, Tocsin at Harvard are among the groups that have sprung up to discuss peace and other political questions. Only a very small minority are involved—but then only a small minority were involved in the supposedly activist 1930s. Probably some of these organizations will last only for the college lifetimes of a handful of committed students.

Indeed, the very fact that academic values have triumphed on many campuses puts heavy competition in the way of all extracurricular activity, including politics. I recall one student who recently felt he had to choose between active participation in organizing a student chapter of SANE and writing a senior distinction thesis; he believed that if he did not do the latter, he would not get into graduate school (not an unrealistic fear) and would jeopardize his whole career (in my judgment, a less realistic fear). Perhaps more important, the professors have taught, especially the better students, that all questions are complex, all ideologies suspect, and all larger passions fanatical; the fear of being naïve prevents many young people from feeling confidence in any action or reaction. (Some of these same adults then criticize the students for apathy!) Questions of foreign policy and disarmament *are* complex—in a way that the race question is not—and students have in the past feared to take a position that expert or "classified" knowledge might explode. Once they begin, however, these same academic values lead them to a seriousness illustrated by the Tocsin students, who have organized seminars on technical problems of disarmament and, as the phrase goes, "done their homework" in Kahn, Kissinger, King-Hall, the *Bulletin of the Atomic Scientists,* and so on.

The long-buried idealism of many gifted and sensitive students has come out most strongly, however, in their response to President Kennedy's proposal of a Peace Corps. It is exciting to watch a group of them examining in detail what American students might contribute to secondary education in Nigeria and what qualities of judgment, self-reliance, pertinacity, and technique such students would need to be of real help. I have seen students who seemed, even in their own eyes, cool customers, ready to ride the organizational escalator, discover in themselves unexpected resources of dedication when beckoned by a chance to serve in an underdeveloped country. To be sure, such service appears to many students as quite unpolitical, outside the polemical orbit of American domestic struggles; and one could argue that there are escapist elements in this choice, this interpretation. But one has to start somewhere, and when one is emerging from privatism, the first movements are apt to be tentative.

We must still ask whether there will be any carry-over from these campus stirrings into the attitudes that college graduates take toward their work: will they continue to regard it as mere "bread," needful for existence, but not a locus either for defining the self or changing the world? If one is apathetic about one's work, it is hard to prevent this apathy from spreading to other areas, even to those on which one had originally thought to build one's life: domesticity, the arts, and personal relations. But, conversely, the vitality and sense for relevant accomplishment that students may gain in college should spread to their academic work and thence to their lifework. For, in the more selective colleges at present, as I have already indicated, there is very little left of the collegiate or teen-ager high jinks of the former *jeunesse dorée*; it is in the high schools now that these ersatz values reign. Thus, college is already, not always happily, an aspect of adult life, not simply a playful preparation, and experience there is no longer compartmentalized as a childish thing.

The Image of the Adolescent Minority

Edgar Z. Friedenberg

In our society there are two kinds of minority status. One of these I will call the "hot-blooded" minorities, whose archetypical image is that of the Negro or Latin. *In the United States, "Teen-agers" are treated as a "hot-blooded" minority.* Then, there are the "long-suffering minorities," whose archetype is the Jew, but which also, I should say, includes women. Try, for a second, to picture a Jewish "teen-ager," and you may sense a tendency for the image to grate. "Teen-agers" err on the hot side; they talk jive, drive hot-rods and become juvenile delinquents. Young Jews talk volubly, play the violin, and go to medical school, though never on Saturday.

The minority group is a special American institution, created by the interaction between a history and an ideology which are not to be duplicated elsewhere. Minority status has little to do with size or proportion. In a democracy, a dominant social group is called a majority and a part of its dominance consists in the power to arrange appropriate manifestations of public support; while a subordinate group is, by the logic of political morality, a minority. The minority stereo-

Reprinted from *Dissent,* Spring 1963, by permission of the publisher.

type, though affected by the actual characteristics of the minority group, develops to fit the purposes and expresses the anxieties of the dominant social group. It serves as a slimy coating over the sharp realities of cultural difference, protecting the social organism until the irritant can be absorbed.

Now, when one is dealing with a group that actually is genetically or culturally different from the dominant social group, this is perhaps to be expected. It is neither desirable nor inevitable, for xenophobia is neither desirable nor inevitable; but it is not surprising.

What is surprising is that the sons and daughters of the *dominant* adult group should be treated as a minority group merely because of their age. Their papers are in order and they speak the language adequately. In any society, to be sure, the young occupy a subordinate or probationary status while under tutelage for adult life. But a minority group is not merely subordinate; it is not under tutelage. It is in the process of being denatured; of becoming, under social stress, something more acceptable to the dominant society, but essentially different from what its own growth and experience would lead to. Most beasts recognize their own kind. Primitive peoples may initiate their youth; we insist that ours be naturalized, though it is what is most natural about them that disturbs adults almost.

The court of naturalization is the public school. A high school diploma is a certificate of legitimacy, not of competence. A youth needs one today in order to hold a job that will permit even minimal participation in the dominant society. Yet our laws governing school attendance do not deal with education. They are not *licensing* laws, requiring attendance until a certain defined minimum competence, presumed essential for adult life, has been demonstrated. They are not *contractual,* they offer no remedy for failure of the school to provide services of a minimum quality. A juvenile may not legally withdraw from school even if he can establish that it is substandard or that he is being ill-treated there. If he does, as many do, for just these reasons, he becomes *prima facie* an offender; for, in cold fact, the compulsory attendance law guarantees him nothing, not even the services of qualified teachers. It merely defines, in terms of age alone, a particular group as subject to legal restrictions not applicable to other persons.

Second-Class Citizen

Legally, the adolescent comes pretty close to having no basic rights at all. The state generally retains the final right even to strip him of his minority status. He has no right to *demand* the particular protection of *either* due process or the juvenile administrative procedure—the state decides. We have had several cases in the past few years of boys sixteen and under being sentenced to death by the full apparatus of formal criminal law, who would not have been permitted to claim its protection had they been accused of theft or disorderly conduct. Each of these executions has so far been forestalled by various legal procedures, but none in such a way as to establish the right of a juvenile to be tried as a juvenile; though he long ago lost his claim to be treated as an adult.

In the most formal sense, then, the adolescent is one of our second class citizens. But the informal aspects of minority status are also imputed to him. The "teen-ager," like the Latin or Negro, is seen as joyous, playful, lazy, and irresponsible, with brutality lurking just below the surface and ready to break out into violence.* All these groups are seen as childish and excitable, imprudent and improvident, sexually aggressive, and dangerous, but possessed of superb and sustained power to satisfy sexual demands. *West Side Story* is not much like *Romeo and Juliet;* but it is a great deal like *Porgy and Bess.*

The fantasy underlying this stereotype, then, is erotic; and its subject is male. The "hot-blooded" minorities are always represented by a masculine stereotype; nobody asks "Would you want your *son* to marry a Negro?" In each case, also, little counter-stereotypes, repulsively pallid in contrast to the alluring violence and conflict of the central scene, are held out enticingly by the dominant culture; the conscientious "teener" sold by Pat Boone to soothe adults while the kids themselves buy *Mad* and *Catcher;* the boy whose Italian immigrant mother sees to it that he wears a clean shirt to school every day on his way to the Governor's mansion; *Uncle Tom.* In the rectilinear planning of Jonesville these are set aside conspicuously as Public Squares, but at dusk they are little frequented.

---

* A very bad—indeed, vicious—but remarkably ambivalent reenactment of the entire fantasy on which the minority-status of the teen-ager is based can be seen in the recent movie *13 West St.* Here, the legal impotence of the "teen-ager" is taken absolutely for granted, and sadistic hostility of adults against him, though deplored is condoned and accepted as natural. Occasional efforts are made to counterbalance the, in my judgment, pornographic picture of a brutal teen-age gang by presenting "good" teen-agers unjustly suspected, and decent police trying to resist sadistic pressure from the gang's victim, who drives one of its members to suicide. But despite this, the picture ends with a scene of the gang's victim—a virile-type rocket scientist —beating the leader of the gang with his cane and attempting to drown the boy in a swimming pool—which the police dismiss as excusable under the circumstances. A Honolulu paper, at least, described this scene of attempted murder as "an old-fashioned caning that had the audience cheering in its seats."

One need hardly labor the point that what the dominant society seeks to control by imposing "hot-blooded" minority status is not the actual aggressiveness and sexuality of the Negro, the Latin, or the JD, but its own wish for what the British working classes used to call "a nice game of slap and tickle," on the unimpeachable assumption that a little of what you fancy does you good. This, the well-lighted Public Squares cannot afford; the community is proud of them, but they are such stuff as only the driest dreams are made of. These are not the dreams that are wanted. In my experience, it is just not possible to discuss adolescence with a group of American adults without being forced onto the topic of juvenile delinquency. Partly this is an expression of legitimate concern, but partly it is because only the JD has any emotional vividness for them.

I would ascribe the success of *West Side Story* to the functional equivalence in the minds of adults between adolescence, delinquency, and aggressive sexuality. Many who saw the show must have wondered, as I did, why there were no Negroes in it—one of the best things about Juvenile Delinquency is that, at least, it is integrated. Hollywood, doubtless, was as usual reluctant to show a member of an enfranchised minority group in an unfavorable light. But there was also a rather sound artistic reason. Putting a real Negro boy in *West Side Story* would have been like scoring the second movement of the *Pastorale* for an eagle rather than flute. The provocative, surly, sexy dancing kids who come to a bad end are not meant realistically. Efforts to use real street-adolescents in *West Side Story* had to be abandoned; they didn't know how to act. What was depicted here was neither Negro nor white nor really delinquent, but a comfortably vulgar middle-class dream of a "hot-blooded" minority. In dreams a single symbolic boy can represent them all; let the symbol turn real and the dreamer wakes up screaming.

Adolescents are treated as a "hot-blooded" minority, then, because they seem so good at slap-and-tickle. But a number of interesting implications flow from this. Slap-and-tickle implies sexual vigor and attractiveness, warmth and aggression, salted with enough conventional perversity to lend spice to a long dull existence. Such perversity is a kind of exuberant overflow from the mainstream of sexuality, not a diversion of it. It is joyous excess and bounty; extravagant foreplay in the well-worn marriage-bed; the generosity of impulse that leads the champion lover of the high school to prance around the shower-room snapping a towel on the buttocks of his team-mates three hours before a hot date, just to remind them that life can be beautiful.

Experience Repressed

When a society sees impulsiveness and sexual exuberance as minority characteristics which unsuit the individual for membership until he is successfully naturalized, it is in pretty bad shape. Adolescents, loved, respected, taught to accept, enjoy, and discipline their feelings, grow up. "Teen-agers" don't; they pass. Then, in middle-age, they have the same trouble with their former self that many ethnics do. They hate and fear the kinds of spontaneity that remind them of what they have abandoned, and they hate themselves for having joined forces with and having come to resemble their oppressors.* This is the vicious spiral by which "hot-blooded" minority status maintains itself. I am convinced that it is also the source of the specific hostility—and sometimes sentimentality—that adolescents arouse in adults. The processes involved have been dealt with in detail by Daniel Boorstin, Leslie Fiedler, Paul Goodman, and especially Ernest Schachtel.** Their effect is to starve out, through silence and misrepresentation, the capacity to have genuine and strongly felt experience, and to replace it by the conventional symbols that serve as the common currency of daily life.

Experience repressed in adolescence does not, of course, result in amnesia, as does the repression of childhood exprience; it leaves no temporal gaps in the memory. This makes it more dangerous, because the adult is then quite unaware that his memory is incomplete, that the most significant components of feeling have been lost or driven out. We at least know that we no longer know what we felt as children. But an adolescent boy who asks his father how he felt on the first night he spent in barracks or with a woman will be told what the father now thinks he felt because he ought to have; and this is very dangerous nonsense indeed.

Whether in childhood or in adolescence, the same quality of experience is starved out or repressed. It is still the spontaneous, vivid and immediate that is most feared, and feared the more because so much is desired. But there is a difference in focus and emphasis because in

---

* Cf. Abraham Kardiner and Lionel Ovesey's classic, *The Mark of Oppression* (New York: Norton, 1951), for a fascinating study of these dynamics among American Negroes.

** Daniel Boorstin, *The Image*. New York: Atheneum, 1962; Leslie Fiedler, "The Fear of the Impulsive Life." *WFMT Perspective,* October, 1961, pp. 4-9; Paul Goodman, *Growing Up Absurd*. New York: Random House, 1960, p. 38; Ernest Schachtel, "On Memory and Childhood Amnesia." Widely anthologized, cf. the author's *Metamorphosis*. New York: Basic Books, 1959, pp. 279-322.

adolescence spontaneity can lead to much more serious consequences.

This, perhaps, is the crux of the matter; since it begins to explain why our kind of society should be so easily plunged into conflict by "hot-blooded" minorities in general and adolescent boys in particular. We are consequence-oriented and future-oriented. Among us, to prefer present delights is a sign of either low or high status, and both are feared. Schachtel makes it clear how we go about building this kind of character in the child—by making it difficult for him to notice his delights when he has them, and obliterating the language in which he might recall them joyfully later. This prepares the ground against the subsequent assault of adolescence. But it is a strong assault, and if adolescence wins, the future hangs in the balance.

The Adolescent Girl

In this assault, adolescent boys play a very different role from adolescent girls; and are dealt with unconsciously by totally different dynamics. Adolescent girls are not seen as members of a "hot-blooded" minority, and to this fact may be traced some interesting paradoxes in our perception of the total phenomenon of adolescence.

Many critics of the current literature on adolscence—Bruno Bettelheim* perhaps most cogently—have pointed out that most contemporary writing about adolescents ignores the adolescent girl almost completely. Bettelheim specifically mentions Goodman and myself; the best novels about adolescents of the past decade or so have been, I think there would be fair agreement, Salinger's *The Catcher in the Rye,* John Knowles' *A Separate Peace,* and Colin MacInnes' less well known but superb *Absolute Beginners.* All these have adolescent boys as heroes. Yet, as Bettelheim points out, the adolescent girl is as important as the adolescent boy, and her actual plight in society is just as severe; her opportunities are even more limited and her growth into a mature woman as effectively discouraged. Why has she not aroused more interest?

There are demonstrable reasons for the prominence of the adolescent boy in our culture. Conventionally, it is he who threatens the virtue of our daughters and the integrity of our automobiles. There are so many more ways to get hung up on a boy. "Teen-agers," too, may be all right; but would you want your daughter to marry one? When she doesn't know anything about him except how she feels—

* In "Adolescence and the Conflict of Generations," *Daedalus,* Winter, 1962, p. 68.

and what does that matter when they are both too young to know what they are doing; when he may never have the makings of an executive, or she of an executive's wife?

For this last consideration, paradoxically, also makes the *boy,* rather than the girl, the focus of anxiety. He alone bears the terrible burden of parental aspirations; it is his capacity for spontaneous commitment that endangers the opportunity of adults to live vicariously the life they never managed to live personally.

Holden, Finny, and the unnamed narrator of *Absolute Beginners,* are adolescent boys who do not pass; who retain their minority status, their spontaneous feelings, their power to act out and act up. They go prancing to their destinies. But what destiny can we imagine for them? We leave Holden in a mental hospital, being adjusted to reality; and Finny dead of the horror of learning that his best friend, Gene, had unconsciously contrived the accident that broke up his beautifully articulated body. The Absolute Beginner, a happier boy in a less tense society, fares better; he has had more real contact with other human beings, including a very satisfactory father, and by this time there is such a thing as a "teen-ager," little as it is, for him to be. On this basis the Beginner can identify himself; the marvelous book ends as he rushes out onto the tarmac at London Airport, bursting through the customs barrier, to stand at the foot of the gangway and greet a plane-load of astonished immigrants by crying, "Here I am! Meet your first teen-ager."

Political Disinterest

There are still enough Finnys and Holdens running around free to give me much joy and some hope, and they are flexible enough to come to their own terms with reality. But the system is against them, and they know it well. Why then, do they not try to change it? Why are none of these novels of adolescence political novels? Why have their heroes no political interests at all? In this respect, fiction is true to American life; American adolescents are notably free from political interests. I must maintain this despite the recent advances of SANE kids and Freedom Riders; for, though I love and honor them for their courage and devotion, the causes they fight for are not what I would call political. No controversy over basic policy is involved, because nobody advocates atomic disaster or racial persecution. The kids' opponents are merely in favor of the kind of American society that these evils flourish in, and the youngsters do not challenge the system itself, though they are appalled by its consequences.

Yet could they, as adolescents, be political? I don't think so; and I don't know that I would be pleased if they were. American politics is a cold-blooded business indeed. Personal clarity and commitment are not wanted in it and not furthered by it. I do not think this is necessarily true of all politics; but it becomes true when the basic economic and social assumptions are as irrational as ours.

Political effectiveness in our time requires just the kind of caginess, pseudo-realism, and stereotyping of thought and feeling; the same submergence of spontaneity to the exigencies of collective action, that mark the ruin of adolescence. Adolescents are, inherently, anti-mass; they take things personally. Sexuality, itself, has this power to resolve relationships into the immediate and interpersonal. As a symbol the cocky adolescent boy stands, a little like Luther, an obstacle to compromise and accommodation. Such symbols stick in the mind, though the reality can usually be handled. With occasional spectacular failures we do manage to assimilate the "teen-age" minority; the kids learn not to get fresh; they get smart, they dry up. We are left then, like the Macbeths, with the memory of an earlier fidelity. But Lady Macbeth was less resourceful than ourselves; she knew next to nothing about industrial solvents. Where she had only perfume we have oil.

The Girl as Woman

This is how we use the boy, but what about the girl? I have already asserted that, since she is not perceived as a member of the "hot-blooded" minority she cannot take his place in the unconscious, which is apt to turn very nasty if it is fobbed off with the wrong sex. Is she then simply not much involved by our psychodynamics, or is she actively repressed? Is she omitted from our fantasies or excluded from them?

It may seem very strange that I should find her so inconspicuous. Her image gets so much publicity. Drum-majorettes and cheerleaders are ubiquitous; *Playboy* provides businessmen with a new *playmate* each month. Nymphets are a public institution.

Exactly, and they serve a useful public function. American males are certainly anxious to project a heterosexual public image, and even more anxious to believe in it themselves. None of us, surely, wishes to feel obligated to hang himself out of respect for the United States Senate; it is, as Yum-Yum remarked to Nanki-Poo, such a stuffy death. I am not questioning our sincerity; the essence of my point is that in what we call maturity we feel what we are supposed to feel, and nothing else. But I am questioning the depth and significance of our interest in the cover or pin-up girl. Her patrons are concerned to experience their own masculinity; they are not much interested in her: I reject the celebration of "babes" in song and story as evidence that we have adolescent girls much on our minds; if we did we wouldn't think of them as "babes." I think, indeed, that in contrast to the boy, of whom we are hyperaware, we repress our awareness of the girl. She is not just omitted, she is excluded.

The adolescent heroine in current fiction is not interpreted in the same way as the adolescent hero, even when the parallel is quite close. Her adolescence is treated as less crucial; she is off-handedly accepted as a woman already. This is true even when the author struggles against it. *Lolita,* for example, is every bit as much a tragic heroine of adolescence as Holden is a hero—she isn't as nice a girl as he is a boy, but they are both victims of the same kind of corruption in adult society and the same absence of any real opportunity to grow up to be themselves. Lolita's failure is the classic failure of identity in adolescence; and Humbert knows this and accepts responsibility for it; this is the crime he expiates. But this is not the way Lolita—the character, not the book—is generally received. Unlike Holden, she has no cult and is not vouchsafed any dignity. It is thought to be comical that, at fourteen, she is already a whore.

A parallel example is to be found in Rumer Godden's *The Greengage Summer.* Here the story is explicitly about Joss's growing up. The author's emphasis is on the way her angry betrayal of her lover marks the end of her childhood; her feelings are now too strong and confused, and too serious in their consequences, to be handled with childish irresponsibility; she can no longer claim the exemptions of childhood. But what the movie presented, it seemed to me, was almost entirely an account of her rise to sexual power; Joss had become a Babe at last.

One reason that we do not take adolescent growth seriously in girls is that we do not much care what happens to people unless it has economic consequences: what would Holden ever be, since he never even graduates from high school; who would hire him? He has a problem. Lolita could always be a waitress or something, what more could she expect? Since we define adulthood almost exclusively in economic terms, we obviously cannot concern ourselves as much about the growth of those members of society who are subject from birth to restricted economic opportunity. But so, of course, are the members of the "hot-blooded" minorities; though we find their hot-bloodedness so exciting that we remain aware of them anyway.

But girls, like Jews, are not supposed to fight back; we expect them, instead, to insinuate themselves coyly into the roles available. In our society, there are such lovely things for them to be. They can take care of other people and clean up after them. Women can becomes wives and mothers; Jews can become kindly old Rabbis and philosophers and even psychoanalysts and lovable comic essayists. They can become powers behind the power; a fine old law firm runs on the brains of its anonymous young Jews just as a husband's best asset is his loyal and unobtrusive wife. A Jewish girl can become a Jewish Mother, and this is a role which even Plato would have called essential.

Effects of Discrimination

Clearly, this kind of discrimination is quite different from that experienced by the "hot-blooded" minorities; and must be based on a very different image in the minds of those who practice it and must have a different impact upon them. Particularly, in the case of the adolescent, the effect on the adult of practicing these two kinds of discrimination will be different. The adolescent boy must be altered to fit middle-class adult roles, and when he has been he becomes a much less vital creature. But the girl is merely squandered, and this wastage will continue all her life. Since adolescence is, for boy and girl alike, the time of life in which the self must be established, the girl suffers as much from being wasted as the boy does from being cut down; there has recently been, for example, a number of tragic suicides reported among adolescent girls, though suicide generally is far less common among females. But from the point of view of the dominant society nothing special is done to the female in adolescence—the same squeeze continues throughout life, even though this is when it hurts most.

The guilts we retain for our treatments of "hot-blooded" and "long-suffering" minorities therefore affect us in contrasting ways. For the boy we suffer angry, paranoid remorse, as if he were Billy the Kid, or Budd. We had to do our duty, but how can we ever forget him? But we do not attack the girl; we only neglect her and leave her to wither gradually through an unfulfilled life; and the best defense against this sort of guilt is selective inattention. We just don't see her; instead, we see a caricature, not brutalized, as in the case of the boy, to justify our own brutality; but sentimentalized, roseate, to reassure us that we have done her no harm, and that she is well contented. Look: she even has her own telephone, with what is left of the boy dangling from the other end of the line.

A Lonely Ride

This is the fantasy; the reality is very different, but it is bad enough to be a "Teen-ager." The adolescent is now the only totally disfranchised minority group in the country. In America, no minority has ever gotten any respect or consistently decent treatment until it began to acquire political power. The vote comes before anything else. This is obviously true of the Negro at the present time; his recent advances have all been made under—sometimes reluctant—Federal auspices because, nationally, Negroes vote, and Northern Negroes are able to cast a ballot on which their buffeted Southern rural fellows may be pulled to firmer political ground. This is what makes it impossible to stop Freedom Rides; just as the comparative militance of the Catholic Church in proceeding toward integration in Louisiana may have less to do with Louisiana than Nigeria, which is in grave danger of falling into the hands of Black Muslims. People generally sympathetic with adolescents sometimes say, "Well, it really isn't fair; if they're old enough to be drafted, they're old enough to vote," which is about as naive as it is possible to get.

Can the status of the "teen-ager" be improved? Only, presumably, through increased political effectiveness. Yet, it is precisely here that a crucial dilemma arises. For the aspirations of the adolescent minority are completely different from those of other minorities. All the others are struggling to obtain what the adolescent is struggling to avoid. They seek and welcome the conventional American middle-class status that has been partially or totally barred to them. But this is what the adolescent is left with if he gives in and goes along.

In the recent and very moving CORE film, *Freedom Ride,* one of the heroic group who suffered beatings and imprisonment for their efforts to end segregation says, as nearly as I can recall, "If the road to feedom leads through the jails of the South, then that's the road I'll take." It may be the road to freedom; but it is the road to suburbia too. You can't tell which the people are headed for until they are nearly there; but all our past ethnic groups have settled for suburbia, and the people who live there bear witness that freedom is somewhere else.

I am not sure there *is* a road to freedom in America. Not enough people want to go there; the last I can recall was H. D. Thoreau, and he went on foot, through the woods, alone. This still may be the only way to get there. For those with plenty of guts, compassion, and dedication to social justice, who nevertheless dislike walking alone through the woods, or feel it to be a Quixotic extravagance, a freedom ride is a noble enterprise. Compared to them, the individual boy or girl on a solitary journey must seem an anachronism. Such a youngster has very little place in our way of life. And of all the criticisms that might be directed against that way of life, this is the harshest.

2
The City

The Origin and Evolution of Cities

Gideon Sjoberg

Men began to live in cities some 5,500 years ago. . . . however, the proportion of the human population concentrated in cities did not begin to increase significantly until about 100 years ago. These facts raise two questions that this article proposes to answer. First, what factors brought about the origin of cities? Second, through what evolutionary stages did cities pass before the modern epoch of urbanization? The answers to these questions are intimately related to three major levels of human organization, each of which is characterized by its own technological, economic, social and political patterns. The least complex of the three—the "folk society"—is preurban and even preliterate; it consists typically of small numbers of people, gathered in self-sufficient homogeneous groups, with their energies wholly (or almost wholly) absorbed by the quest for food. Under such conditions there is little or no surplus of food; consequently the folk society permits little or no specialization of labor or distinction of class.

Although some folk societies still exist today, similar human groups began the slow process of evolving into more complex societies millenniums ago, through settlement in villages and through advances in technology and organizational structure. This gave rise to the second level of organization: civilized preindustrial, or "feudal," society. Here there is a surplus of food because of the selective cultivation of grains—high in yield, rich in biological energy and suited to long-term storage—and often also because of the practice of animal husbandry. The food surplus permits both the specialization of labor and the kind of class structure that can, for instance, provide the leadership and command the manpower to develop and maintain extensive irrigation systems (which in turn make possible further increases in the food supply). Most preindustrial societies possess metallurgy, the plow and the wheel—devices, or the means of creating devices, that multiply both the production and the distribution of agricultural surpluses.

Two other elements of prime importance characterize the civilized pre-industrial stage of organization. One is writing: not only the simple keeping of accounts but also the recording of historical events, law, literature and religious beliefs. Literacy, however, is usually confined to a leisured elite. The other element is that this stage of organization has only a few sources of energy other than the muscles of men and livestock; the later preindustrial societies harnessed the force of the wind to sail the seas and grind grain and also made use of water power.

It was in the context of this second type of society that the world's first cities developed. Although preindustrial cities still survive, the modern industrial city is associated with a third level of complexity in human organization, a level characterized by mass literacy, a fluid class system and, most important, the tremendous technological breakthrough to new sources of inanimate energy that produced and still sustains the industrial revolution. Viewed against the background of this three-tiered structure, the first emergence of cities at the level of civilized preindustrial society can be more easily understood.

Two factors in addition to technological advance beyond the folk-society level were needed for cities to emerge. One was a special type of social organization by means of which the agricultural surplus produced by technological advance could be collected, stored and distributed. The same apparatus could also organize the labor force needed for large-scale construction, such as public buildings, city walls and irrigation systems. A social organization of this kind requires a variety of full-time specialists directed by a ruling elite. The latter, although few in number, must command sufficient political power—reinforced by an ideology, usually religious in character—to ensure that the peasantry periodically relinquishes a substantial part of the agricultural yield in order to support the city dwellers. The second factor required was a favorable environment, providing not only fertile soil for the peasants but also a water supply adequate for both agriculture and urban consumption. Such conditions exist in geologically mature mid-latitude river valleys, and it was in such broad alluvial regions that the world's earliest cities arose.

What is a city? It is a community of substantial size and population density that shelters a variety of nonagricultural specialists, including a literate elite. I emphasize the role of literacy as an ingredient of urban life for good reasons. Even though writing systems took centuries to evolve, their presence or absence serves as a convenient means for distinguishing between genuinely urban communities and others that in spite of their large size and dense population must be considered quasi-urban or nonurban. This is because once a community achieves or otherwise acquires the technological advance we call writing, a major transformation in the social order occurs; with a written tradition rather than an oral one it is possible to create more complex administrative and legal systems and more rigorous systems of thought. Writing is indispensable to the development of mathematics, astronomy and the other sciences; its existence thus implies the emergence of a number of significant specializations within the social order.

As far as is known, the world's first cities took shape around 3500 B.C. in the Fertile Crescent, the eastern segment of which includes Mesopotamia: the valleys of the Tigris and the Euphrates. Not only were the soil and water supply there suitable; the region was a crossroads that facilitated repeated contacts among peoples of divergent cultures for thousands of years. The resulting mixture of alien and indigenous crafts and skills must have made its own contribution to the evolution of the first true cities out of the village settlements in lower Mesopotamia. These were primarily in Sumer but also to some extent in Akkad, a little to the north. Some—such as Eridu, Erech, Lagash and Kish—are more familiar to archaeologists than to others; Ur, a later city, is more widely known.

These early cities were much alike; for one thing, they had a similar technological base. Wheat and barley were the cereal crops, bronze was the metal, oxen pulled plows and there were wheeled vehicles.

Moreover, the city's leader was both king and high priest; the peasants' tribute to the city god was stored in the temple granaries. Luxury goods recovered from royal tombs and temples attest the existence of skilled artisans, and the importation of precious metals and gems from well beyond the borders of Mesopotamia bespeaks a class of merchant-traders. Population sizes can only be guessed in the face of such unknowns as the average number of residents per household and the extent of each city's zone of influence. The excavator of Ur, Sir Leonard Woolley, estimates that soon after 2000 B.C. the city proper housed 34,000 people; in my opinion, however, it seems unlikely that, at least in the earlier periods, even the larger of these cities contained more than 5,000 to 10,000 people, including part-time farmers on the cities' outskirts.

The valley of the Nile, not too far from Mesopotamia, was also a region of early urbanization. To judge from Egyptian writings of a later time, there may have been urban communities in the Nile delta by 3100 B.C. Whether the Egyptian concept of city living had "diffused" from Mesopotamia or was independently invented (and perhaps even earlier than in Mesopotamia) is a matter of scholarly debate; in any case the initial stages of Egyptian urban life may yet be discovered deep in the silt of the delta, where scientific excavation is only now being undertaken.

Urban communities—Diffused or independently invented—spread widely during the third and second millenniums B.C. By about 2500 B.C. the cities of Mohenjo-Daro and Harappa were flourishing in the valley of the Indus River in what is now Pakistan. Within another 1,000 years at the most the middle reaches of the Yellow River in China supported urban settlements. A capital city of the Shang Dynasty (about 1500 B.C.) was uncovered near Anyang before World War II; current archaeological investigations by the Chinese may well prove that city life was actually established in ancient China several centuries earlier.

The probability that the first cities of Egypt were later than those of Sumer and the certainty that those of the Indus and Yellow rivers are later lends weight to the argument that the concept of urban living diffused to these areas from Mesopotamia. Be this as it may, none will deny that in each case the indigenous population contributed uniquely to the development of the cities in its own area.

In contrast to the situation in the Old World, it appears certain that diffusion played an insignificant role or none at all in the creation of the pre-Columbian cities of the New World. The peoples of Mesoamerica—notably the Maya, the Zapotecs, the Mixtecs and the Aztecs

—evidently developed urban communities on a major scale, the exact extent of which is only now being revealed by current investigations. Until quite recently, for example, many New World archaeologists doubted that the Maya had ever possessed cities; it was the fashion to charactrize their impressive ruins as ceremonial centers visited periodically by the members of a scattered rural population. It is now clear, however, that many such centers were genuine cities. At the Maya site of Tikal in Guatemala some 3,000 structures have been located in an area of 6.2 square miles; only 10 percent of them are major ceremonial buildings. Extrapolating on the basis of test excavations of more than 100 of these lesser structures, about two-thirds of them appear to have been dwellings. If only half the present-day average household figure for the region (5.6 members) is applied to Tikal, its population would have been more than 5,000. At another major Maya site—Dzibilchaltun in Yucatán—a survey of less than half of the total area has revealed more than 8,500 structures. Teotihuacán, the largest urban site in the region of modern Mexico City, may have had a population of 100,000 during the first millennium A.D.

Although only a few examples of writing have been identified at Teotihuacán, it is reasonable to assume that writing was known; there were literate peoples elsewhere in Mesoamerica at the time. By the same token, the achievements of the Maya in such realms as mathematics and astronomy would have forced the conclusion that they were an urban people even in the absence of supporting archaeological evidence. Their invention of the concept of zero (evidently earlier than the Hindus' parallel feat) and their remarkably precise calculation of the length of the solar year would surely have been impossible if their literate elite had been scattered about the countryside in villages rather than concentrated in urban centers where a cross-fertilization of ideas could take place.

Mesoamerica was by no means the only area of large, dense communities in the New World; they also existed in the Andean region. A culture such as the Inca, however, cannot be classified as truly urban. In spite of—perhaps because of—their possession of a mnemonic means of keeping inventories (an assemblage of knotted cords called a quipu) the Incas lacked any conventionalized set of graphic symbols for representing speech or any concepts other than numbers and certain broad classes of items. As a result they were denied such key structural elements of an urban community as a literate elite and a written heritage of law, religion and history. Although the Incas could claim major military, architectural and engineering triumphs and apparently were on the verge of achieving a civilized order, they were still quasi-urban at the time of the European conquest, much like the Dahomey, Ashanti and Yoruba peoples of Africa.

The New World teaches us two lessons. In Mesoamerica cities were created without animal husbandry, the wheel and an extensive alluvial setting. One reason for this is maize, a superior grain crop that produced a substantial food surplus with relatively little effort and thus compensated for the limited tools and nonriverine environment. In the Andean region imposing feats of engineering and an extensive division of labor were not enough, in the absence of writing, to give rise to a truly urban society.

In spite of considerable cultural diversity among the inhabitants of the Near East, the Orient and the New World, the early cities in all these regions had a number of organizational forms in common. The dominant pattern was theocracy—the king and the high priest were one. The elite had their chief residences in the city; moreover, they and their retainers and servants congregated mainly in the city's center. This center was the prestige area, where the most imposing religious and government buildings were located. Such a concentration had dual value: in an era when communications and transport were rudimentary, propinquity enhanced interaction among the elite; at the same time it gave the ruling class maximum protection from external attack.

At a greater distance from this urban nucleus were the shops and dwellings of artisans—masons, carpenters, smiths, jewelers, potters—many of whom served the elite. The division of labor into crafts, apparent in the earliest cities, became more complex with the passage of time. Artisan groups, some of which even in early times may have belonged to specific ethnic minorities, tended to establish themselves in special quarters or streets. Such has been characteristic of preindustrial cities in all cultural settings, from the earliest times to the present day. The poorest urbanites lived on the outskirts of the city, as did part-time or full-time farmers; their scattered dwellings finally blended into open countryside.

From its inception the city, as a residence of specialists, has been a continuing source of innovation. Indeed, the very emergence of cities greatly accelerated social and cultural change; to borrow a term from the late British archaeologist V. Gordon Childe, we can properly regard the "urban revolution" as being equal in significance to the agricultural revolution that preceded it and the industrial revolution that followed it. The city acted as a promoter of change in several ways. Many of the early cities arose on major transportation routes;

new ideas and inventions flowed into them quite naturally. The mere fact that a large number of specialists were concentrated in a small area encouraged innovation, not only in technology but also in religious, philosophical and scientific thought. At the same time cities could be strong bulwarks of tradition. Some—for example Jerusalem and Benares—have become sacred in the eyes of the populace; in spite of repeated destruction Jerusalem has retained this status for more than two millenniums.

The course of urban evolution can be correctly interpreted only in relation to the parallel evolution of technology and social organization (especially political organization); these are not just prerequisites to urban life but the basis for its development. As centres of innovation cities provided a fertile setting for continued technological advances; these gains made possible the further expansion of cities. Advanced technology in turn depended on the increasingly complex division of labor, particularly in the political sphere. As an example, the early urban communities of Sumer were mere city-states with restricted hinterlands, but eventually trade and commerce extended over a much broader area, enabling these cities to draw on the human and material resources of a far wider and more diverse region and even bringing about the birth of new cities. The early empires of the Iron Age—for instance the Achaemenid Empire of Persia, established early in the sixth century B.C., and the Han Empire of China, established in the third century B.C.—far surpassed in scope any of the Bronze Age. And as empires became larger the size and grandeur of their cities increased. In fact, as Childe has observed, urbanization spread more rapidly during the first five centuries of the Iron Age than it had in all 15 centuries of the Bronze Age.

In the sixth and fifth centuries B.C. the Persians expanded their empire into western Turkestan and created a number of cities, often by building on existing villages. In this expansion Toprakala, Merv and Marakanda (part of which was later the site of Samarkand) moved toward urban status. So too in India, at the close of the fourth century B.C., the Mauryas in the north spread their empire to the previously nonurban south and into Ceylon, giving impetus to the birth of cities such as Ajanta and Kanchi. Under the Ch'in and Han dynasties, between the third century B.C., and the third century A.D., city life took hold in most of what was then China and beyond, particularly to the south and west. The "Great Silk Road" extending from China to Turkestan became studded with such oasis cities as Suchow, Khotan and Kashgar; Nanking and Canton seem to have attained urban status at this time, as did the settlement that was eventually to become Peking.

At the other end of the Eurasian land mass the Phoenicians began toward the end of the second millennium B.C. to spread westward and to revive or establish urban life along the northern coast of Africa and in Spain. These coastal traders had by then developed a considerable knowledge of shipbuilding; this, combined with their far-reaching commercial ties and power of arms, made the Phoenicians lords of the Mediterranean for a time. Some centuries later the Greeks followed a rather similar course. Their city-states—actually in a sense small empires—created or rebuilt numerous urban outposts along the Mediterranean shore from Asia Minor to Spain and France, and eastward to the most distant coast of the Black Sea. The empire that did the most to diffuse city life into the previously nonurban regions of the West—France, Britain, the Low Countries, Germany west of the Rhine, central and even eastern Europe—was of course Rome.

Empires are effective disseminators of urban forms because they have to build cities with which to maintain military supremacy in conquered regions. The city strongholds, in turn, require an administrative apparatus in order to tap the resources of the conquered area and encourage the commerce needed both to support the military garrison and to enhance the wealth of the homeland. Even when a new city began as a purely commercial outpost, as was the case under the Phoenicians, some military and administrative support was necessary if it was to survive and function effectively in alien territory.

There is a significant relation between the rise and fall of empires and the rise and fall of cities; in a real sense history is the study of urban graveyards. The capitals of many former empires are today little more than ghostly outlines that only hint at a glorious past. Such was the fate of Babylon and Nineveh, Susa in Persia, Seleucia in Mesopotamia and Vijayanagar in India. Yet there are exceptions. Some cities have managed to survive over long periods of time by attaching themselves first to one empire and then to another. Athens, for example, did not decline after the collapse of Greek power; it was able to attach itself to the Roman Empire, which subsidized Athens as a center of learning. Once Rome fell, however, both the population and the prestige of Athens dwindled steadily; it was little more than a town until the rise of modern Greece in the 19th century. On the other hand, nearby Byzantium, a city-state of minor importance under Roman rule, not only became the capital of the Eastern Roman Empire and its successor, the Ottoman Empire, but as Istanbul remains a major city to this day.

In the light of the recurrent rise and decline of cities in so many areas of the world, one may ask just how urban life has been able to persist and why the skills of technology and social organization required for city-building were not lost. The answer is that the knowledge was maintained within the framework of empires—by means of written records and oral transmission by various specialists. Moreover, all empires have added to their store of skills relating to urban development as a result of diffusion—including the migration of specialists—from other civilized areas. At the same time various civilized or uncivilized subjects within empires have either been purposely educated by their conquerors or have otherwise gained access to the body of urban lore. The result on occasion is that the subjects challenge the power of the dominant ruling group.

The rise and fall of the Roman Empire provides a highly instructive case study that illuminates several relations between the life-span of cities and the formation and decline of empires. The Romans themselves took many elements of their civilization from the Etruscans, the Greeks and other civilized peoples who came under their sway. After Rome's northward expansion in western Europe and the proliferation of Roman cities in regions inhabitated by so-called "barbarians"—in this instance preliterate, or "noncivilized," peoples—the Roman leaders were simply unable to staff all the bureaucratic posts with their own citizens. Some of the preliterates had to be trained to occupy such posts both in their own homelands and in the cities on the frontier. This process made it possible for the Romans to exploit the wealth of conquered regions and may have pacified the subjugated groups for a time, but in the long run it engendered serious conflicts. Eventually the Ostrogoths, Vandals, Burgundians and others—having been partially urbanized, having developed a literate elite of their own and having acquired many Roman technological and administrative skills—turned against the imperial power structure and engineered the collapse of Rome and its empire. Nor is this a unique case in history; anologies can be perceived in the modern independence movements of such European colonies as those in Africa.

With the breakup of the Roman Empire, not only did the city of Rome (which at its largest may have had more than 300,000 inhabitants) decline markedly but many borderland cities disappeared or shrank to small towns or villages. The decline was dramatic, but it is too often assumed that after the fall of Rome cities totally disappeared from western Europe. The historian E. Ewig has recently shown that many cities continued to function, particularly in Italy and southern France. Here, as in all civilized societies, the surviving cities were the chief residences and centers of activity for the political and religious elite who commanded the positions of power and privilege that persisted during the so-called Dark Ages.

In spite of Rome's decline many of the techniques and concepts associated with literate traditions in such fields as medicine and astronomy were kept alive; this was done both in the smaller surviving urban communities of Europe and in the eastern regions that had been ruled by the Romans—notably in the cities of the succeeding Eastern Roman Empire. Some of the technology and learning associated with Rome also became the basis for city life in the Arab empires that arose later in the Near East, North Africa, Spain and even central Asia. Indeed, the Byzantine and Arab empires—which had such major intellectual centers as Constantinople, Antioch, Damascus, Cairo and Baghdad—advanced beyond the knowledge inherited from antiquity. The Arabs, for example, took from the Hindus the concept of zero and the decimal system of numerals; by utilizing these concepts in both theory and practice they achieved significant advances over the knowledge that had evolved in the West. Eventually much of the new learning was passed on to Europe, where it helped to build the foundations for the industrial revolution.

In time Europe reestablished extensive commercial contact with the Byzantine and Arab empires; the interchange that followed played a significant role in the resurgence of urban life in southern Europe. The revitalization of trade was closely associated with the formation of several prosperous Italian city-states in the 10th and 11th centuries A.D. Venice and other cities eventually were transformed into small-scale empires whose colonies were scattered over the Mediterranean region—a hinterland from which the home cities were able to extract not only many of their necessities but also luxury items. By A.D. 1000 Venice had forged commercial links with Constantinople and other cities of the Eastern Roman Empire, partly as a result of the activities of the Greek colony in Venice. The Venetians were able to draw both on the knowledge of these resident Greeks and on the practical experience of sea captains and other specialists among them. Such examples make it clear that the Italian city-states were not merely local creations but rather products of a multiplicity of cultural forces.

Beginning at the turn of the 11th century A.D. many European cities managed to win a kind of independence from the rulers of the various principalities and petty kingdoms that surrounded them. Particularly in northern Italy urban communities came to enjoy considerable political autonomy. This provided an even more favorable atmosphere for commerce and encouraged the growth of such urban institutions as craft guilds. The European pattern is quite different from that in most of Asia (for instance in India and China), where the city was never able to attain a measure of autonomy within the broader political structure. At the same time the extent of self-rule enjoyed by the medieval European cities can be exaggerated and often is; by the close of the Middle Ages urban self-rule was already beginning to be lost. It is therefore evident that the political autonomy of medieval cities was only indirectly related to the eventual evolution of the industrial city.

It was the industrial revolution that brought about truly far-reaching changes in city life. In some nations today . . . the vast majority of the inhabitants are city dwellers; nearly 80 percent of the people in the United Kingdom live in cities, as do nearly 70 percent of the people of the U.S. Contrast this with the preindustrial civilized world, in which only a small, socially dominant minority lived in cities. The industrial revolution has also led to fundamental changes in the city's social geography and social organization; the industrial city is marked by a greater fluidity in the class system, the appearance of mass education and mass communications and the shift of some of the elite from the center of the city to its suburban outskirts.

Although there are still insufficient data on the rise of the industrial city—an event that took place sometime between 1750 and 1850—and although scholars disagree over certain steps in the process, the major forces at work in the two or three centuries before the industrial city emerged can be perceived clearly enough. Viewed in the light of Europe's preindustrial urban era, two factors are evident: the expansion of European power into other continents and the development of a technology based on inanimate rather than animate sources of energy. The extension of European trade and exploration (which was to culminate in European colonialism) not only induced the growth of cities in Asia, in parts of nonurban Africa and in the Americas but also helped to raise the standard of living of Europeans themselves and made possible the support of more specialists. Notable among the last was a new occupational group—the scientists. The expansion abroad had helped to shatter the former world view of European scholars; they were now forced to cope with divergent ideas and customs. The discoveries reported by the far-ranging European explorers thus gave added impetus to the advance of science.

The knowledge gained through the application of the scientific method is the one factor above all others that made the modern city possible. This active experimental approach has enabled man to control the forces of nature to an extent undreamed of in the preindustrial era. It is true that in the course of several millenniums the literate elite of the preindustrial cities added significantly to man's store of knowledge in such fields as medicine, astronomy and mathematics, but these scholars generally scorned mundane activities and avoided contact with those whose work was on the practical level. This meant that the scholars' theories were rarely tested and applied in the everyday realm. Moreover, in accordance with prevailing religious thought, man was not to tamper with the natural order or to seek to control it, in either its physical or its social aspect. For example, medical scholars in Greek and Roman cities did not dissect human cadavers; not until the 16th century in Europe did a physician —Andreas Vesalius of Brussels—actually use findings obtained from dissection to revise ancient medical theories.

In the field of engineering, as late as the 17th century most advances were made by artisans who worked more or less on a trial-and-error basis. With the development of the experimental method, however, the learning of the elite became linked with the practical knowledge of the artisan, the barber-surgeon and the like; the result was a dramatic upsurge of knowledge and a fundamental revision of method that has been termed the scientific revolution. Such was the basis of the industrial revolution and the industrial city.

That the first industrial cities appeared in England is hardly fortuitous; England's social structure lacked the rigidity that characterized most of Europe and the rest of the civilized world. The Puritan tradition in England—an ethical system that supports utilitarianism and empiricism—did much to alter earlier views concerning man's place in nature. In England scholars could communicate with artisans more readily than elsewhere in Europe.

The advent of industrialism brought vast improvements in agricultural implements, farming techniques and food preservation, as well as in transportation and communication. Improved water supplies and more effective methods of sewage disposal allowed more people to congregate in cities. Perhaps the key invention was the steam engine, which provided a new and much more bountiful source of energy. Before that time, except for power from wind and water, man had no energy resources other than human and animal muscle. Now the factory system, with its mass production of goods and mechanization of activity, began to take hold. With it emerged a new kind of occupational structure: a structure that depends on highly specialized knowledge and that functions effectively only when the activities of the component occupations are synchronized. This process of industrialization has not only continued unabated to the present day but has actually accelerated with the rise of self-controlling machines.

The evolution of the industrial city was not an unmixed blessing. Historians have argued through many volumes the question of whether the new working class, including many migrants from the countryside, lost or gained economically and socially as the factory system destroyed older social patterns. Today, as industrialization moves inexorably across the globe, it continues to create social problems. Many surviving traditional cities evince in various ways the conflict between their preindustrial past and their industrial future. Nonetheless, the trend is clear: barring nuclear war, the industrial city will become the dominant urban form throughout the world, replacing forever the preindustrial city that was man's first urban creation.

American Cities

Jean-Paul Sartre

For the first few days I was lost. My eyes were not accustomed to the skyscrapers and they did not surprise me; they did not seem like man-made, man-inhabited constructions, but rather like rocks and hills, dead parts of the urban landscape one finds in cities built on a turbulent soil and which you pass without even noticing. At the same time, I was continually and vainly looking for something to catch my attention for a moment—a detail, a square, perhaps, or a public building. I did not yet know that these houses and streets should be seen in the mass.

In order to learn to live in these cities and to like them as Americans do, I had to fly over the immense deserts of the west and south. Our European cities, submerged in human countrysides that have been worked over mile by mile, are continuous. And then we are vaguely aware that far away, across the sea, there is the desert, a myth. For the American, this myth is an everyday reality. We flew for hours

---

between New Orleans and San Francisco, over an earth that was dry and red, clotted with verdigris bushes. Suddenly, a city, a little checkerboard flush with the ground, arose and then, again, the red earth the Savannah, the twisted rocks of the Grand Canyon, and the snows of the Rocky Mountains.

After a few days of this diet, I came to understand that the American city was, originally, a camp in the desert. People from far away, attracted by a mine, a petroleum field or fertile land, arrived one fine day and settled as quickly as possible in a clearing, near a river. They built the vital parts of the town, the bank, the town hall, the church, and then hundreds of one-storey frame houses. The road, if there was one, served as a kind of spinal column to the town, and then streets were marked out like vertebrae, perpendicular to the road. It would be hard to count the American cities that have that kind of parting in the middle.

Nothing has changed since the time of the covered wagons; every year towns are founded in the United States, and they are founded according to the same methods.

Take Fontana, Tennessee, which is situated near one of the great T.V.A. dams. Twelve years ago there were pine-trees growing in the mountain's red soil. As soon as the construction of the dam began, the pines were felled and three towns—two white ones of 3000 and 5000 inhabitants each, and one Negro town—sprang from the soil. The workers live there with their families; four or five years ago, when work was in full swing, one birth was recorded each day. Half of the village looks like a pile-dwellers' community: the houses are of wood, with green roofs, and have been built on piles to avoid dampness. The other half is made of collapsible dwellings, "prefabricated houses". They too are of wood; they are constructed about 500 miles away and loaded onto trucks: a single team of men can set one up within four hours after its arrival. The smallest costs the employer two thousand dollars, and he rents them to his workers for nineteen dollars a month (thirty-one dollars if they are furnished). The interiors, with their mass-produced furniture, central heating, electric lamps, and refrigerators, remind one of ship cabins. Every square inch of these antiseptic little rooms has been utilized; the walls have clothespresses and under the beds there are chests of drawers.

One leaves with a slightly depressed feeling, with the feeling of having seen the careful, small-scale reconstitution of a 1944 flat in the year 3000. The moment one steps outside one sees hundreds of houses, all alike, piled up, squashed against the earth, but retaining in their very form some sort of nomadic look. It looks like a caravan graveyard. The pile-dweller community and the caravan cemetery face one another. Between them a wide road climbs toward the pines. There you have a city, or rather the nucleus of an American city, with all its essential parts. Below is the Woolworth's, higher up the hospital, and at the top, a "mixed" church in which what might be called a minimum service—that is, one valid for all creeds—is conducted.

The striking thing is the lightness, the fragility of these buildings. The village has no weight, it seems barely to rest on the soil; it has not managed to leave a human imprint on the reddish earth and the dark forest; it is a temporary thing. And besides, it will soon take to the road; in two years the dam will be finished, the workers will leave, and the prefabricated houses will be taken down and sent to a Texas oil well or a Georgia cotton plantation, to reconstitute another Fontana, under other skies, with new inhabitants.

This roving village is no exception; in the United States, communities are born as they die—in a day. The Americans have no complaint to make; the main thing is to be able to carry their homes with them. These homes are the collections of objects, furnishings, photographs, and souvenirs belonging to them, that reflect their own image and constitute the inner, living landscape of their dwellings. These are their penates. Like Aeneas, they haul them about everywhere.

The "house" is the shell; it is abandoned on the slightest pretext.

We have workers' communities in France. But they are sedentary, and then they never become real cities; on the contrary, they are the artificial product of neighbouring cities. In America, just as any citizen can theoretically become President, so each Fontana can become Detroit or Minneapolis; all that is needed is a bit of luck. And conversely, Detroit and Minneapolis are Fontanas which have had luck. To take only one example: in 1905 Detroit had a population of 300,000. Its population is now 1,000,000.

The inhabitants of this city are perfectly aware of this luck; they like to recall in their books and films the time when their community was only an outpost. And that is why they pass so easily from city to outpost; they make no distinction between the two. Detroit and Minneapolis, Knoxville and Memphis were *born temporary* and have stayed that way. They will never, of course, take to the road again on the back of a truck. But they remain at the meeting point; they have never reached an internal temperature of solidification.

Things that would not constitute a change of situation for us are, for the American, occasions for real breaks with his past. There are many who, on going off to war, have sold their apartments and everything else, including their suits. What is the point of keeping something that will be outmoded upon their return? Soldiers' wives often reduce their scale of living and go to live more modestly in other neighbourhoods. Thus, sadness and faithfulness to the absent are marked by a removal.

The removals also indicate fluctuations in American fortunes.

It is customary, in the United States, for the fashionable neighbourhoods to slide from the centre to the outskirts of the city; after five years the centre of town is "polluted". If you walk about there, you come upon tumble-down houses that retain a pretentious look beneath their filth; you find a complicated kind of architecture, one-storey frame houses with entrances formed by peristyles supported by columns, gothic chalets, "colonial houses", etc. These were formerly aristocratic homes, now inhabited by the poor. Chicago's lurid Negro section contains some of these Greco-Roman temples; from the outside they still look well. But inside, twelve rat- and louse-plagued Negro families are crowded together in five or six rooms.

At the same time, changes are continually made within the same place. An apartment house is bought to be demolished, and a larger apartment house is built on the same plot. After five years, the new house is sold to a contractor who tears it down to build a third one. The result is that in the States a city is a moving landscape for its inhabitants, whereas our cities are our shells.

In France, one hears only from very old people what a forty-year-old American said to me in Chicago. "When I was young, this whole neighbourhood was taken up by a lake. But this part of the lake was filled in and built over." And a thirty-five-year-old lawyer who was showing me the Negro section said: "I was born here. Then it was a white section and, apart from servants, you would not have seen a Negro in the streets. Now the white people have left and 250,000 Negroes are crowded into their houses."

M. Verdier, the owner of the "City of Paris" department store in San Francisco, witnessed the earthquake and fire that destroyed three quarters of the city. At that time he was a young man; he remembers the disaster perfectly. He watched the reconstruction of the city which still had an Asiatic look around 1913, and then its rapid Americanization. Thus, he has superimposed memories of three San Franciscos.

We Europeans change within changeless cities, and our houses and neighbourhoods outlive us; American cities change faster than their inhabitants do, and it is the inhabitants who outlive the cities.

I am really visiting the United States in wartime; the vast life of the American city has suddenly become petrified; people hardly change their residences any more. But this stagnation is entirely temporary; the cities have been immobilized like the dancer on the film-screen who stays with his foot suspended in air when the film is stopped;

one feels all about one the rising of the sap which will burst open the cities as soon as the war is.ended.

First, there are immediate problems; Chicago's Negro section will have to be rebuilt, for instance. The government had begun this before Pearl Harbour. But the government-built apartment houses barely manage to shelter 7000 people. Now, there are 250,000 to be housed. Then the industrialists want to enlarge and transform their factories; the famous abattoirs of Chicago are going to be completely modernized.

Finally, the average American is obsessed by the image of the "modern house" which is considerably publicized and which will be, so we are told, a hundred times more comfortable than the present dwellings and whose construction in huge quantities certainly has its place in the plans for "industrial conversion" which are now springing up almost everywhere.

When the war is over, America will certainly be seized with a real construction fever. Today the American sees his city objectively; he does not dream of finding it ugly, but thinks it really old. If it were even older, like ours, he could find a social past, a tradition in it. We generally live in our grandfathers' houses. Our streets reflect the customs and ways of past centuries; they tend to filter the present; none of what goes on in the Rue Montorgueil or the Rue Pot-de-Fer is completely of the present. But the thirty-year-old American lives in a house that was built when he was twenty.

These houses that are too young to seem *old* seem merely outdated to them; they lag behind the other tools, the car that can be traded in every two years, the refrigerator or the wireless set. That is why they see their cities without vain sentimentality. They have grown slightly attached to them, as one becomes attached to one's car, but they consider them as instruments, rather than anything else, instruments to be exchanged for more convenient ones.

For us a city is, above all, a past; for them it is mainly a future; what they like in the city is everything it has not yet become and everything it can be.

What are the impressions of a European who arrives in an American city? First, he thinks he has been taken in. He has heard only about skyscrapers; New York and Chicago have been described to him as "upright cities". Now his first feeling is, on the contrary, that the average height of an American city is noticeably smaller than that of a French one. The immense majority of houses have only two storeys. Even in the very large cities, the five-storey apartment house is an exception.

Then he is struck by the lightness of the materials used. In the United States stone is less frequently used than in Europe. The skyscraper consists of a coating of concrete applied to a metal framework, and the other buildings are made of brick or wood. Even in the richest cities and the smartest sections, one often finds frame houses. New Orleans' lovely colonial houses are of wood; many of the pretty chalets belonging to the Hollywood stars and film-directors are made of wood; so are the "California style" cottages in San Francisco. Everywhere you find groups of frame houses crushed between two twenty-storeyed buildings.

The brick houses are the colour of dried blood, or, on the contrary, daubed and smeared with bright yellow, green or raw white.[1] In most of the cities, they are roofless cubes or rectangular parallelepipeds, with severely flat façades. All these houses, hastily constructed and made expressly to be hastily demolished, obviously bear a strange resemblance to Fontana's "prefabricated houses".

The lightness of these jerry-built houses, their loud colours alternating with the sombre red of the bricks, the extraordinary variety of their decorations which does not manage to conceal the uniformity of their patterns, all give one the feeling, when in the middle of the city, of walking through the suburbs of a watering town, like Trouville or Cabourg or La Baule. Only those ephemeral seaside chalets with their pretentious architectural style and their fragility can convey to those of my French readers who have never seen the States an idea of the American apartment house.

To complete the impression, I should also like to add that sometimes one also thinks of an exposition-city, but an obsolescent, dirty one, like those that the years later, in some park, survive the celebration that occasioned them. For these shanties quickly grow dirty, particularly in industrial sections.

Chicago, blackened by its smoke, clouded by the Lake Michigan fog, is a dark and gloomy red. Pittsburgh is more gloomy still. And there is nothing more immediately striking than the contrast between the formidable power, the inexhaustible abundance of what is called the "American Colossus" and the puny insignificance of those little houses that line the widest roads in the world. But on second thought, there is no clearer indication that America is not finished, that her

---

[1] Kisling and Masson have often complained of the fact that the urban landscape of the United States is not very stimulating to painting. I believe this is partly due to the fact that the cities have already been painted. They do not have the hesitant colours of our own cities. What is one to do with these tones which already are art, or artifice at least? All one can do is leave them alone.

ideas and plans, her social structure and her cities have only a strictly temporary reality.

These perfectly straight cities bear no trace of organization. Many of them have the rudimentary structure of a polypary. Los Angeles, in particular, is rather like a big earthworm that might be chopped into twenty pieces without being killed. If you go through this enormous urban cluster, probably the largest in the world, you come upon twenty juxtaposed cities, strictly identical, each with its poor section, its business streets, night-clubs and smart suburb, and you get the impression that a medium-sized urban centre has schizogenetically reproduced itself twenty times.[2]

In America, where the neighbourhoods are added on to each other as the region's prosperity attracts new immigrants, this juxtaposition is the rule. You pass without any transition from a poor street into an aristocratic avenue; a promenade lined with skyscrapers, museums and public monuments and adorned with lawns and trees, suddenly stops short above a smoky station; one frequently discovers at the feet of the largest buildings, along an aristocratic avenue, a "zone" of miserable little kitchen-gardens.

This is due to the fact that these cities that move at a rapid rate are not constructed in order to grow old, but move forward like modern armies, encircling the islands of resistance they are unable to destroy; the past does not manifest itself in them as it does in Europe, through public monuments, but through survivals. The wooden bridge in Chicago which spans a canal two steps away from the world's highest skyscrapers is a survival. The elevated railways, rolling noisily through the central streets of New York and Chicago, supported by great iron pillars and cross-girders, nearly touching the façades of houses on either side, are survivals. They are there simply because no one has taken the time to tear them down, and as a kind of indication of work to be done.

You find this disorder in each individual vista. Nowhere have I seen so many empty lots. Of course they do have a definite function; they are used as car parks. But they break the alignment of the street nonetheless sharply for all that. Suddenly it seems as if a bomb had fallen on three or four houses, reducing them to powder, and as if they had just been swept out: this is a "parking space", two hundred square metres of bare earth with its sole ornament, perhaps, a poster on a big hoarding. Suddenly the city seems unfinished, badly assembled; sud-

---

[2] To convey an idea of this city to the reader, I suggest that he try to imagine, not one Côte d'Azur city, but the entire region between Cannes and Menton.

denly you rediscover the desert and the big empty site: noticeable at Fontana. I remember this Los Angeles landscape in the middle of the city, two modern apartment houses, two white cubes framing an empty lot with the ground torn up—a parking space. A few abandoned-looking cars were parked there. A palm tree grew like a weed between the cars. Down at the bottom there was a steep grassy hill, rather like the fortification mounds we use for garbage disposal. On top of the mound was a frame house, and a little below this a string stretched between two little trees, with multi-coloured washing hanging out to dry. When one turned around the block of houses, the hill disappeared; its other side had been built up, covered with asphalt, streaked with tar roads, and pierced with a magnificent tunnel.

The most striking aspect of the American city is the vertical disorder. These brick shanties are of varying heights; I noted at random during a walk in Detroit the following successive proportions: one storey, two storeys, one storey, one storey, three storeys. You find the same proportions in Albuquerque or San Antonio, at the other end of the country. In depth, above this irregular crenellation, you see apartment houses of all shapes and dimensions, long cases, thick thirty-storeyed boxes with forty windows to a storey. As soon as there is a bit of fog the colours fade away, and only volumes remain—every variety of polyhedron. Between them, you have enormous empty spaces, empty lots cut out in the sky.

In New York, and even in Chicago, the skyscraper is on home ground, and imposes a new order upon the city. But everywhere else it is out of place; the eye is unable to establish any unity between these tall, gawky things and the little houses that run close to the ground; in spite of itself it looks for that line so familiar in European cities, the sky-line, and cannot find it. That is why the European feels at first as though he were travelling through a rocky chaos that resembles a city—something like Montpellier-le-Vieux—rather than a city.

But the European makes a mistake in visiting American cities as one does Paris or Venice; they are not meant to be seen that way. The streets here do not have the same meaning as our streets. In Europe, a street is half-way between the path of communication and the sheltered "public place". It is on a footing with the cafés, as proved by the use of the "terrasses" that spring up on the sidewalks of the cafés in fine weather. Thus it changes its aspect more than a hundred times a day, for the crowd that throngs the European street changes, and men are its primary element. The American street is a piece of highway. It sometimes stretches over many miles. It does not stimulate one to walk. Ours are oblique and twisting, full of bends and secrets. The

American street is a straight line that gives itself away immediately. It contains no mystery. You see the street straight through, from one end to the other no matter what your location in it. And the distances in American cities are too great to permit moving about on foot; in most of them one gets about almost exclusively in cars, on buses and by underground. Sometimes, while going from one appointment to another, I have been carried like a parcel from underground to escalator, from escalator to elevator, from elevator to taxi, from taxi to bus and, again, by metro and elevator, without walking a step.

In certain cities I noticed a real atrophy of the sidewalk. In Los Angeles, for example, on La Cienega, which is lined with bars, theatres, restaurants, antique dealers and private residences, the sidewalks are scarcely more than side-streets that lead customers and guests from the roadway into the house. Lawns have been planted from the façades to the roadway of this luxurious avenue. I followed a narrow path between the lawns for a long time without meeting a living soul, while to my right, cars streaked by on the road; all animation in the street had taken refuge on the high road.

New York and Chicago do not have neighbourhoods, but they do have a neighbourhood life; the American is not familiar with his city; once he is ten "blocks" away from his home, he is lost. This does not mean that there are no crowds in the business streets, but they are crowds that do not linger; people shop or emerge from the Underground to go to their offices.

I rarely saw an occasional Negro day-dreaming before a shop.

Yet one quickly begins to like American cities. Of course they all look alike. And when you arrive at Wichita, Saint Louis or Albuquerque, it is disappointing to realize that, hidden behind these magnificent and promising names, is the same standard checkerboard city with the same red and green traffic lights and the same provincial look. But one gradually learns to tell them apart. Chicago, the noble, lurid city, red as the blood that trickles through its abattoirs, with its canals, the grey water of Lake Michigan and its streets crushed between clumsy and powerful buiildings, in no way resembles San Francisco, city of air, salt and sea, built in the shape of an amphitheatre.

And then one finally comes to like their common element, that temporary look. Our beautiful closed cities, full as eggs, are a bit stifling. Our slanting, winding streets run head on against walls and houses; once you are inside the city, you can no longer see beyond it. In America, these long, straight unobstructed streets carry one's glance, like canals, outside the city. You always see mountains or fields or the sea at the end of them, no matter where you may be.

Frail and temporary, formless and unfinished, they are haunted by the presence of the immense geographical space surrounding them. And precisely because their boulevards are highways, they always seem to be stopping places on the roads. They are not oppressive, they do not close you in; nothing in them is definitive, nothing is arrested. You feel, from your first glance, that your contact with these places is a temporary one; either you will leave them or they will change around you.

Let us beware of exaggerating; I have spent Sundays in the American provinces that were more depressing than Sundays anywhere else; I have seen those suburban "colonial style" inns where, at two dollars a head, middle-class families go to eat shrimp cocktails and turkey with cranberry sauce in silence while listening to the electric organ. One must not forget the heavy boredom that weighs over America.

But these slight cities, still so similar to Fontana and the outposts of the Far West, reveal the other side of the United States: their freedom. Here everyone is free—not to criticize or to reform their customs—but to flee them, to leave for the desert or another city. The cities are open, open to the world, and to the future. This is what gives them their adventurous look and, even in their ugliness and disorder, a touching beauty.

(*Le Figaro,* 1945)

The Three Faces of New York

Daniel Bell

I

In 1956, the Regional Plan Association, a non-profit research agency, asked the Harvard School of Public Administration to conduct an economic and demographic survey of the New York metropolitan region—a 7,000-square-mile, 22-county complex that, with its core, inner ring, and outer ring radiating forty miles out from the Empire State Building, and a population of sixteen million persons, forms the largest urban aggregate in the United States—and to project these economic and demographic trends as far as 1985.

The fruits of the three-year study have been recorded in nine books (one of which has yet to be published), and they constitute the most exhaustive analysis of the region (or of any detailed area of the United State) since the original nine-volume New York Regional Plan studies, which were concluded three decades ago. A single volume, *Metropo-*

Reprinted from *Dissent*, Summer, 1961, by permission of the publisher.

lis 1985, by Raymond Vernon, the director of the survey, interprets the results of the more detailed researches.

Mr. Vernon and most of his associates are economists (with the exception of the historian Oscar Handlin, who did the volume on "The Newcomers," and the political scientist Robert Wood, who is writing the study of local government). They see the growth of cities largely as a function of changes in market patterns, and these, in turn, as a function of resource location, transportation costs, and labor supply. Sociological nuances—such as the thought that New York triumphed over Philadelphia in the early nineteenth-century race for commercial supremacy (the physical port advantages of each were about equal) because the freewheeling traders found the fluid ways of New York more congenial than the already rigidified class structure of Philadelphia; or that the distinctive tempo of New York life in the first decades of the twentieth century reflected the emergence of a fast-moving and new type of manufacturing enterprise, with easy access, high turnover rate, and sudden rises and falls in wealth; or that the remarkable efflorescence of corporate building in New York in the nineteen-fifties was due to prestige rather than to economic need—all are awkwardly suggested, rather than elaborated and explored. Yet no picture of an urban civilization can be complete without such sociological considerations, for, just as good will is often an intangible yet real element in the assets of a business firm, so do status structure, cultural environment, and entertainment resources become inextricable components of the character of a city.

To indicate one example: the expansion of corporate headquarters has given a "new face" to New York, from the unbroken lines of the new glass houses on Park Avenue to the towering high-rental apartment houses along the upper East Side. Yet in the late forties, the talk of the business world was largely about New York's impossibility as a business center, and the need for decentralization. (General Foods moved out to Westchester. Time Inc., which owned the site of the Hotel Marguery, sold it and took an option on land in Rye. Jean-Paul Sartre, commenting sourly on the grid-shadowed streets of midtown New York, predicted that no new office buildings would be erected in New York.) Yet how wrong all this talk was! Since 1947, over 132 new office buildings (86 since 1954) have been put up in Manhattan (Union Carbide, which had bought land in Tarrytown, erected a fifty-story tower on the Marguery site; Time, Inc. built a forty-eight-story building west of Rockefeller Center). Today, 135 of the 500 largest industrial corporations in America have their headquarters in New York. In all, 44,700,500 square feet of office space—or half as much as existed before 1947—has been added to Manhattan since the end of the war.*

Some of this growth has been in response simply to the need for more space, as the administrative ranks of business, reflecting the new complexities of corporate management, expanded. (The labor force as a whole has been growing about one per cent a year; the white-collar force about three per cent a year, in the last two decades.) But equally, as an intangible fact, the convergence of corporations on New York can also be seen as the final stage in the breakup of family capitalism. Where an enterprise has family roots, the prestige and power of the head of the firm are displayed in the town or city where the enterprise has begun, and where the family has its social power. (Alcoa, for example, was on the verge of abandoning Pittsburgh and coming to New York after the war, but Richard Mellon, for family reasons, held the firm back and initiated the move that resulted in the renovation of the "golden triangle.") When the "deracinated" manager "makes it" in the impersonal world of corporate capitalism, he wants other people to know about it, these other people being the tribe of corporate managers; hence the lure of New York.

Such an explanation is admittedly, speculative, and difficult to prove statistically. Yet if one is trying to deal with the forces that shape the character of New York, such speculation is necessary. Otherwise one simply extrapolates existing trends and calls it analysis.

From a different perspective, Mr. Vernon's concluding volume is curiously bloodless, the result of its failure to speculate on the ways in which the admitted defects of the city—broken-down housing, choking traffic, inadequate services—might be remedied, a task the researchers eschewed. Yet if a study is to have any value for policy makers, must it not consider alternative "models" of what New York can be, so that some political steps could be taken to achieve one or another goal? Of all this, more later. Let us take as a useful starting point the fact that the economic life of the area—the kinds of employment, the number of jobs, the distribution of income—is basic to any understanding of the region. What, then, do we know?

---

* Since 1947, two billion dollars in private capital have been expended for construction in Manhattan. Over one billion three hundred million went into office buildings: over six million went for high-rental apartment houses (e.g., Imperial House, at Sixty-eighth Street and Lexington Avenue, where *rentals* are from fifty-five hundred to fourteen thousand dollars a year). Most of the new office construction has been in the midtown area, from Fortieth Street to Fifty-ninth Street; the residential construction has been along the upper East Side.

II

In economic terms, New York is an iceberg. The visible portions are the theaters, art galleries, museums, universities, publishing houses, restaurants, night clubs, *espresso* cafés, smart stores—all the activities that give the city its peculiarly glittering place as the metropolis of America. Yet the base of New York's economic structure is largely unseen. Six and a half million people are employed in the region. Sixty per cent take in each other's wash (i.e. engage in "local-market" activities). Forty per cent—and this is the crucial group—are in the "export trade"; i.e., they produce goods and services sold in the national market; they turn out the added value that sustains the region. The breakdown of the latter group is surprising: New York is usually thought of primarily as a business and finance center, yet two out of every three jobs in its national-market activities are in manufacturing. (New York, in fact, is the largest manufacturing city in the world.) But even here a further distinction has to be made.

If one asks why an enterprise chooses one region rather than another, the answer is that for some, the main need is to be near the supply of raw material; for others, to be close to markets, in order to reduce transport costs; for still others, to be able to draw on a pool of skilled or low-cost labor. The industrial map of nineteenth-century America—the location of heavy industry between the coal deposits of western Pennsylvania and Kentucky, and the iron ore at the end of the Great Lakes, the whole intertwined by the lakes and the Ohio River Valley system—was shaped by these considerations.

New York has offered a peculiarly different attraction. It has not been transport savings or labor costs that have attracted industry, but "external economies," the availability of a pool of specialized facilities and skills that could be shared by firms without their having to carry these items as part of permanent overhead costs. Typically, this has meant that the industries moving to New York tend to be small, fast-moving, risk-taking, and highly competitive in a rough-and-tumble race. In essence, New York is a bazaar in which speed, variety, and specialization are the hallmarks of the services it offers. "For instance," Mr. Vernon points out,

> producers of made-to-order giant turbines and generators are not found in the Region because they operate on production schedules which call for delivery three or four years after the placement of an order. But a high-style dress is sometimes conceived and executed in a fortnight; an advertising brochure may be only hours or days in the making; a lawyer's brief is often printed between midnight and morning.

A dress house, therefore, will need to have immediately available a wide variety of buttons, buckles, embroidery, rhinestones, or other trimmings, without wanting to carry full stocks of these items or machinery for making them; an advertising agency needs a large number of type faces and since it would not be profitable for one firm to have on hand all the specialized fonts that may be called for, smaller printing companies thus find a place for their services.

The moral of all this is that New York exists really because of its fantastic variety of *non-rationalized* enterprises and services, easy to break into because of low capital requirements, but in which survival depends upon ingenuity, "shmearing," cutting a corner, trimming a margin, finding some other way to make a fast buck in the swift race. This is what has given New York its particular beat and distinctive character. It is now changing, but enough survives, as does something of the character of the city's early history, and if New York is now beginning to enter a third phase—that of domination by the large corporate headquarters—the three faces exist as on a palimpsest. To understand New York, one must know all the faces.

III

New York began as a port city. Its large protected harbor, along with the rail-canal system leading to the West, made for important advantages. Point-counterpoint followed with easy economic logic. Frequent ship sailings, the concentration of freight forwarders, insurance specialists, banks to facilitate credit, wholesalers to distribute imports—all these spurred the development of the port. Immigrants poured in, and many of them stayed right in the city. A large floating labor supply, crudely organized, assured a cheap reserve of labor and a quick, profitable turnaround for the ships.

The port gave New York much of its rough nineteenth-century character: the sailor dives along Water Street, the brawling underworld of the Five Points section, the open brothels along Greene Street—features duplicated in every port city of the world, from Marseille to Shanghai. With the growth of the city, the rough spots became localized—along the edges of the piers in Chelsea, around the rim of Red Hook—or they were shoved across the river, to Hoboken and Jersey City. But the port had given New York its initial impetus for growth, and the pattern of "external economies" was duplicated in the city's next epoch.

This second face, which materialized with the emergence of the Jewish community, is the New York of the small enterprise. The archetypal novel of this period is Abraham Cahan's *The Rise of David*

Levinsky, a saga (such novels can only be sagas) of the class that moved from the sweatshops of the lower East Side to the lofts of Seventh Avenue. But if the heart of this economic category has been the dress industry, the same problems turn up in an array of small-unit, single-plant firms—small companies engaged in printing, plastics, electronics, and small-scale machine work. These industries are characterized by uncertainty, by the capacity to make quick-change production shifts, the search for an item or product that will be a sudden hit. Each of these industries depends upon a whole range of auxiliary services. Each manufacturer being, so to speak, a retailer, behind him are the smaller wholesalers who supply his needs. Because decisions have to be made swiftly, there is scarcely any intra-firm hierarchy, little bureaucratization, and usually only a single establishment. (The number of such one-plant firms—averaging about twenty-five employees each—is enormous. In forty-seven industries that are almost entirely single-plant firms, thirty per cent of their national employment is concentrated in New York.) These factors make for an extraordinary reliance on agents, banks, and other finance outfits for survival. Few of these firms have sufficient capital for expansion, and often don't even have enough money to cover current production costs. The commercial banks and factoring corporations thus advance short-term loans or take over accounts receivable as the way of supplying the small companies with cash. Inevitably, the finance agencies achieve a commanding position in the city.

The nature of these enterprises, and the ethnic cast of the men who ran them, made for an extraordinary large middle class in the New York of the last three decades—probably, though no one has ever measured it, the largest middle-class aggregate in any urban center of this country. This bourgeoisie, unlike the traditional small-town Protestant middle class, was quick, sharp, shrewd and, like as not, cynical. And yet, because so many of these businessmen were Jewish, it was a middle class that hungered for culture and self-improvement. The chief contribution of the Jews to the City of New York, as Nathan Glazer noted a few years ago, has been in their role as "consumers of culture." The large symphony orchestras, the theaters, trade-book publishing, the avant-garde magazines, the market for drawings and paintings—all have, as their principal audience and consumer, the Jewish middle class. And this was made possible largely by the entrepreneurial wealth of small-unit firms.

And yet this economic face of New York, which has dominated the city in the past three decades, is changing. One cause of it is the growing rationalization of industry. Consider the radio business, for example: it originated in the New York area because, with its technology untried, its production methods unsettled, its markets uncertain, and its need for sub-contractors crucial, this region, with its vast pool of specialized facilities, offered the most attractive location. As production methods became standardized and markets enlarged, the radio firms grew in size. Increasingly, the critically competitive elements became labor costs and transportation to national markets, rather than production design, and so the industry began moving from New York. Today, the garment industry—the prototype of small entrepreneurial business—is undergoing a small-scale revolution. The recent popularity of casual wear and sports clothes has brought mass-production methods into the industry, to a previously unheard-of extent. An innovation like "section work" in women's clothes, or the breakdown of skill components in actual production, has also spurred the growth of larger business units. And the New York market is losing its share of business.

A second influential factor has been the role of the truck. With the expansion of road transport, industries could begin to separate those operations dependent upon the "bazaar" from those primarily in need of low-paid labor. In the garment industry, therefore, design, cutting, and display are now done in New York, but the actual sewing—the chief labor expense—is farmed out to contractors in the hinterlands of New Jersey, Pennsylvania, and Connecticut. (Similarly, in publishing, book houses and magazines keep their editorial offices in New York, but the printing is done out of town.)

With the decline of these small industries has come a change in the temper of Broadway entertainment. The raucous-toned, vulgar, smart-aleck jokes of a George Jessel, a Myron Cohen, or a Joe E. Lewis reflected the wise-guy quality of the old garment trades. Today, the new sophisticates—raconteurs and satirists like Shelley Berman, Mort Sahl, Elaine May and Mike Nichols—reflect the new face of New York, a white-collar dominance of the large corporation and its advertising-media satellites.

Just why the large corporations keep swarming to New York is not a question economists can answer with their particular logic alone. As Mr. Vernon points out, in manufacturing, "an economic version of the Darwinian principle, feeble and dilute though its effects may be, operates to push industries towards the location which yields the largest return. [But] the central office of a large corporation produces no easily defined product whose costs can be 'priced out' at alternative locations." There are, to be sure, some "external economies" available in New York to the mammoth corporation. Financial institutions like brokerage houses and insurance companies can draw upon many different economic analysts. Corporations with problems ranging in diversity from taxes to advertising commercials can arrange for quick consultations with experts. Yet in the age of the telephone and private company airplanes, distance is less of a barrier to communication than ever before. What draws the rationalized, bureaucratized corporate behemoths to New York is the ancient longing for desire and display. New York is now a new bazaar, with sleek symbols glorifying "Seagram" or "Pan Am" or "Lever Brothers" or "Pepsi-Cola"—the new doges of Park Avenue. It is no longer the ethnic-dominated, nervously swift city of "I Can Get It for You Wholesale." The horizontal axis of New York has shifted from Seventh Avenue to Madison.

One sees this in small ways and large—the mushrooming of chic art galleries, and the cultural dominance of the art world. The New York of the thirties had a "literary" culture. Political and literary magazines, written and edited by the children of immigrant businessmen, dominated the scene. But today, the next generation, which now finds money-making respectable, buys art. It has become a necessary means of achieving cultural cachet. Reading a book is a solitary affair, and one needs like-minded friends to discuss its content. Art, however, is "open"—paintings, particularly large Abstract Expressionist canvases, are attention-getting devices. As a collector, one can acquire a cultural reputation. And, as a result, the art market has boomed. Within one decade, the prices of the best contemporary painters (de Kooning, Rothko, Kline, Baziotes, Gottlieb, Guston) appreciated more than ten times, an arithmetical increase of a hundred per cent per year (something few stocks can match), and even the younger painters (Hartigan, Rivers, Brooks) can now command several thousand dollars for a single painting.

The larger ecological consequences of this shift in axis is the new housing design of the city. Many parts of West End Avenue, once the *haute banlieue* of the garment district, are now transient slums. The upper East Side, once the slum, has become an area of luxury cooperative apartments selling for ten thousand dollars per room. The lower East Side now is a warren of jerry-built public barracks inhabited by Puerto Ricans and old, retired Jewish working people. The suburbs have become bedroom cities for the white-collar salariat of the corporations, and each morning as they push their way into the city, they pass increasing swarms of outward-bound Negro and Puerto Rican workers commuting to the outer ring of the region, where the new, small-manufacturing plastic, electronic, and machine-shop firms have located. And the city center? Now, more than ever, it is a crosshatching of canyoned streets congested by trucks, private cars, buses, taxis, and all the other debris of an industrial civilization. Yet the only "solution" to this congestion is the proposal of the redoubtable Robert Moses for a number of east-west arterial flumes which would bounce the traffic even more violently against itself.

IV

And the future? The authors of the study estimate that the region's population will grow to 16,800,000 by 1965, to 19,000,000 by 1975, and —barring a large migration such as the spectacular Puerto Rican one of the last decade—to 22,000,000 by 1985.

The number of jobs will rise as well, probably to 9,500,000 by the target year—an increase of about forty-five per cent over 1954. But here significant shifts, reflecting forces already in motion, will take place. Port employment will probably decline. New York has already lost the major share of bulk-cargo shipments—coal, grain, iron ore, and petroleum—which can be loaded and unloaded mechanically, in single-boat units. The mechanization of freight-handling, beginning initially with pallets and extending now to fishy-backs—i.e., the hoisting of truck trailers directly onto the ship from pier or railhead—means a decrease in the need for unskilled labor. And competitively, the growth of the St. Lawrence Seaway—through a single great port development on the Great Lakes, as is now being planned along the Indiana dunes below Chicago—may hasten the decline.

Manufacturing will barely manage to hold pace with the growth of the region. But here the internal shifts will be more important than the small growth. The traditional small-unit industries—clothing and printing—will lag, while large increases will occur in metal-product and electrical-machinery manufacturing, reflecting the new technology of the times. The largest growth in jobs will come about in white-collar employment. Financial personnel will grow about eighty-five per cent; business and professional services about seventy per cent; and government jobs more than sixty-five per cent.

These changes can be matched ecologically in the new population distributions, as well. The core boroughs of New York (Manhattan, the Bronx, and Brooklyn) will decline in resident population, and Staten Island will grow. The growth of the inner ring (Nassau County, for example), which has burgeoned in the last decade, will slow down, while the perimeter areas—the only ones still with open space—will show a spectacular jump. ("Counties like Dutchess, Orange, Rockland, and Morris promise to triple or quadruple their populations. Even more significant, because the numbers involved are larger, will be the growth of Suffolk, Monmouth, and Middlesex Counties: in absolute terms, Monmouth is projected as raising in population from 280,000 in 1955 to 1,157,000 in 1985, an almost incredible growth.") Speculators, take notice!

In comparing the magnitude of these new problems with the ineptitude of the public authorities, one begins to despair. Take, first, the problem of transportation. Although the resident population at the core of the city may shrink slightly, half a million new jobs (in business and finance) will be added to Manhattan's central business district by 1985. How will people get there? As Mr. Vernon chastely observes, "The projected magnitudes are large enough to suggest that present and projected facilities will be under a real strain to bear the expansion of daily commuting. Indeed, the projected growth is sufficiently large to permit one to say that public policy in this field may prove a key variable in determining how New York's central business district develops in the future."

The complications arise not only from added numbers but from changing modes of transportation. Fewer people are taking trains, more are taking private cars into the city. In 1948, 3,691,000 persons came into the central business district (defined as Manhattan south of Sixty-first Street), *each day*. Of these, 2,389,000 used public transport, 577,000 came by auto and taxi. In 1956, with the inflow slightly reduced (3,316,000 persons came in each day), 736,000 came by auto or taxi, an *increase* of almost twenty per cent, while the number using public transit had dropped to 1,970,000, a *decrease* of more than 12 per cent. If this trend continues, as seems inevitable, where will all the cars be put? New York City, instead of discouraging cars from coming into the city center, has begun to build a large chain of municipal garages in midtown to accommodate the cars. Surely, such a solution is madness.

The second, and larger problem, particularly for New York City, is housing. What has been done so far has made barely a dent in the mountain of need. In the postwar decade (1948-57), 85,000 new dwelling units were built, housing a total of 500,000 persons. Yet this program has had astonishingly little effect on the way land is used. In Manhattan, Brooklyn, and the Bronx, where "renewal" has made the greatest progress, only 1.4 per cent of the total land area has been utilized. "Even when we add private buildings to public renewal," Mr. Vernon comments, "we find that in these three boroughs . . . only a fraction of 1 per cent of the dwellings were replaced per year." And will this wholly inadequate rate be stepped up in the future? It seems unlikely.

Still another complication is the fading mirage of suburbia. In the last decade, the middle class traded space for time—more open area for the home, as against a longer haul in getting to work. But with the future increases in population, what will happen to residential densities? The suburbs will soon become as choked as the city. The middle class has the choice either of moving still further out—but where? beyond Westport to New Haven, or beyond Princeton to Trenton?—or of surrendering the open suburban spaces, and still have to take the long train ride to the city.

V

What is to be done? Here our academic authors desert us. There are hints here and there of what should be attempted, of the vested interests that must be overcome, of the obstacles involved, but it is all said with innuendo and diminuendo ("Our task here, of course, is not to appraise the desirability of any such measures . . ."). The major fault of these volumes, despite the care that has gone into the gathering of small bits of data, comes of the failure to deal with the economic controllers of New York, and with their intentions. For it has been the decisions of these controllers—the large insurance companies and the banks—that have determined the contours of New York, particularly in building. By granting or withholding mortgage money, by adding size and trimming space, by assessing any project primarily in terms of cost-profit, these financial interests have been the major power centers of New York. (Shortly before his death, Vincent Astor wanted to create an open plaza on Park Avenue at Fifty-third Street, which, combined with the open space in front of Mies van der Rohe's building for Seagram, would have formed a new focal point for the city, similar to Rockefeller Center. But he couldn't get the financing for as much as a narrow tower. The National City Bank, which took over the site, put up a squat building that covers the entire footage.)

One need not look on these men as "villains" (such as the slum landlords of Harlem) who are out merely to exploit the city. Many of them are sincerely concerned with the amenities of life, and express it in such projects as Lincoln Center or the Downtown-Lower Manhattan redevelopment plans. But they are part of a system that assesses costs through a narrow economic calculus, by individual decision units, rather than in terms of social costs and social gains. For example, Erwin Wolfson, who is putting up the giant Pan American building—the sixty-story megalith behind Grand Central Station which will pile forty thousand people into one workplace at the hub of the city—has remarked that the "only" valid argument he heard in opposition to his project was the idea of turning the three-and-a-half-acre site into a plaza. But this was impractical, he said. In terms of an economic calculus, yes; but is it impractical in terms of space and light, a haven for pedestrians, a resting place in the center, an enhancing of light and vista?

Take the more mundane and less utopian question of traffic. The use of midtown-area city streets for private cars represents a subsidy to their owners of twenty feet of public space, at a penalty of waiting time, gas fumes, and other social costs that must be borne by everyone else who works in the area, as well as a financial loss to the rapid-transit networks, whose revenues are thus reduced. Why not bar private cars from midtown? But even this subsidy pales compared with that made to truckers and the industries they serve. Each morning and each evening, midtown streets are all but impassable because of the large forty- and fifty-foot trucks that crowd the streets and back up across the avenues—with the countless burdens of noise, harassment, lost time and other multiple indignities such congestion creates. Why not force all truck loadings to be undertaken before eight in the morning and after seven at night in the midtown district? This would be an added expense to the individual firm, but a social gain for the rest of the community. (It might even cause some firms to bring their production back to New York instead of farming it out; or, if it is proved that such costs would mean competitive disadvantages and a reduction of jobs in New York, one could subsidize these firms by reducing taxes, and thus rents, in the area—and allow them to pay for off-time loading.) Whether utopian or mundane, the point remains that few of these problems are ever explored from any cost calculus other than the individual economic unit, and often in this reckoning, the City of New York (with a Lawrence Gerosa as controller) thinks of itself simply as an economic unit, and has no conception of social costs and gains.

More than this, the city itself has no Master Plan that would allow it to specify priorities and budget ahead for the area as a whole. For example, the City Planning Commission, which has finally introduced a new zoning code to eliminate the present ziggurat style of skyscraper, has no effective control over the Traffic Commission, and no say in the activities of the Port Authority. The behemoth Authority, while a model of service compared with the inefficient city departments, is organized for ends that are now anti-social because of the failure to institute any over-all plan. The Port Authority finances its operations by the floating of bonds, on the basis of credit status, and it now has a vested interest in increasing vehicular traffic through the tunnels and bridges. Meanwhile the basic and obvious need for an integrated rapid-transit system, to link the entire metropolitan region and tie in, as well, the commuter railroads of New Jersey, Long Island, and Connecticut into the New York City subway system, fails to receive any recognition for lack of political and financial support.

But merely to blame the banks, real-estate lobbies, or powerful bureaucratic interests for the chaos of the city is too easy. Where politics is played as a brokerage game, all groups defend private interests against some generalized social desideratum. Take, for example, the postwar decision to deal directly with slum clearance in Manhattan. Any wholesale uprooting, in a city where the vacancy ratio has diminished almost to zero, could result only, as this operation did, in dumping the slum population from one section of the city onto another. Proposals for public housing in the open spaces of Staten Island, where garden-type developments would have been possible, or on the outskirts of the city, or even in the outer ring, were decried—by property owners in these areas, who didn't want Negroes; by Negro politicians in Manhattan, who feared the loss of bloc support through dispersals; by liberals, who felt it was wrong to penalize public-housing residents by increasing the time they travelled to work. So, high-rising, high-density barracks were built on the most expensive land in the world. But if housing is to be subsidized, why shouldn't its beneficiaries pay for this, in part, with travel time—particularly when the social gains would have been greater—in larger rooms and more open space. Slum clearance, as a reform slogan, won the day—but it was a pyrrhic victory.

Clearly no effective plan for New York can be possible in the next twenty-five years (since so many of its problems spill over into the region) as long as the existing helter-skelter of fourteen hundred—yes fourteen hundred—local governments, each with its own decision-making powers about taxes, traffic, schools, parks, housing, sewage, water, police, fire, and other municipal services, continue to exist in the New York metropolitan region. If the New York City economy makes sense only in regional terms, so must the polity. Without such dovetailing, none of the area's fundamental problems—transportation, housing, the port—can be solved. Why, for example, should New York City continue to maintain piers along the lower West Side and the rim of East Side Manhattan, when such piers are inefficient, and the side-street warehouses and the dilapidated wholesale markets that serve them are even more so? Why not rebuild the waterfront areas, with their spectacular abundance of light and vistas, with imaginatively constructed houses and promenades, and locate the cargo piers on the New Jersey side of the Hudson, where freight can more easily connect with trunkline railroads or highways going West or South? The city—needless to say—needs the revenue. But in a properly integrated region, taxes could foot the costs for the whole area. In short, why not begin with a social calculus, and restore the city to its people?

Man and Animal: The City and the Hive

Susanne K. Langer

Within the past five or six decades, the human scene has probably changed more radically than ever before in history. The outward changes in our own setting are already an old story: the disappearance of horse-drawn vehicles, riders, children walking to school, and the advent of the long, low, powerful Thing in their stead; the transformation of the mile-wide farm into a tic-tac-toe of lots, each sprouting a split-level dream home. These are the obvious changes, more apparent in the country than in the city. The great cities have grown greater, brighter, more mechanized, but their basic patterns seem less shaken by the new power and speed in which the long industrial revolution culminates.

The deepest change, however, is really a change in our picture of mankind; and that is most spectacular where mankind is teeming and concentrated—in the city. Our old picture of human life was a picture of local groups, each speaking its mother-tongue, observing some established religion, following its own customs. It might be a civilized

---

From *The Antioch Review,* Vol. XVIII, No. 3, Copyright 1958 by the Antioch Press.

community or a savage tribe, but it had its distinct traditions. And in it were subdivisions, usually families, with their more special local ties and human relations.

Today, natural tribes and isolated communities have all but disappeared. The ease and speed of travel, the swift economic changes that send people in search of new kinds of work, the two wars that swept over all boundaries, have wiped out most of our traditions. The old family structure is tottering. Society tends to break up into new and smaller units—in fact, into its ultimate units, the human individuals that compose it.

This atomization of society is most obvious in a great cosmopolitan city. The city seems to be composed of millions of unrelated individuals, each scrambling for himself, yet each caught in the stream of all the others.

Discerning eyes saw this a hundred years ago, especially in industrial cities, where individuals from far or near came to do what other individuals from far or near had also come to do—each a cog in the new machine. Most of the cogs had no other relation to each other. And ever since this shakeup in society began, a new picture of society has been in the making—the picture of *human masses,* brought together by some outside force, some imposed function, into a superpersonal unit; masses of people, each representing an atom of "manpower" in a new sort of organism, the industrial State.

The idea of the State as a higher organism—the State as a super-individual—is old. But our conception of such a State is new, because our industrial civilization, which begets our atomized society, is new. The old picture was not one of masses driven by some imposed economic power, or any other outside power. The super-individual was a rational being, directed by a mind within it. The guardians of the State, the rulers, were its mind. Plato described the State as "the man writ large." Hobbes, two thousand years later, called it "Leviathan," the great Creature. A city-state like ancient Athens or Sparta might be "a man writ large," but England was too big for that. It was the big fish in the big pond. The mind of Hobbes's fish was perhaps subhuman, but it was still single and sovereign in the organism.

Another couple of centuries later, Rudyard Kipling, faced with a democratic, industrialized civilization, called his allegory of England "The Mother Hive." Here, a common will, dictated by complicated instincts, replaced even Leviathan's mind; each individual was kept in line by the blind forces of the collective life.

The image of the hive has had a great success as an ideal of collaborative social action. Every modern Utopia (except the completely wishful Shangri-La) reflects the beehive ideal. Even a statesman of highest caliber, Jan Smuts, has praised it as a pattern for industrial society.[1] Plato's personified State and Hobbes's sea monster impress us as fantasies, but the hive looks like more than a poetic figure; it seems really to buzz around us.

I think the concept of the State as a collective organism, composed of multitudes of little workers, guided by social forces that none of the little workers can fathom, and accomplishing some greater destiny, is supported by another factor than our mechanized industry; that other factor is a momentous event in our intellectual history: the spread of the theory of evolution.

First biologists, then psychologists, and finally sociologists and moralists have become newly aware that man belongs to the animal kingdom. The impact of the concept of evolution on scientific discovery has been immense, and it has not stopped at laboratory science; it has also produced some less sober and sound inspirations. The concept of continuous animal evolution has made most psychologists belittle the differences between man and his non-human relatives, and led some of them, indeed, to think of *homo sapiens* as just one kind of primate among others, like the others in all essential respects—differing from apes and monkeys not much more than they differ from species to species among themselves. Gradually the notion of the human animal became common currency, questioned only by some religious minds. This in turn has made it natural for social theorists with scientific leanings to model their concepts of human society on animal societies, the ant hill and the beehive.

Perhaps it were well, at this point, to say that I myself stand entirely in the scientific camp. I do not argue against any religious or even vitalistic doctrines; such things are not arguable. I speak not *for,* but *from,* a naturalist's point of view, and anyone who does not share it can make his own reservations in judging what I say.

Despite Man's zoölogical status, which I wholeheartedly accept, there is a deep gulf between the highest animal and the most primitive normal human being: a difference in mentality that is fundamental. It stems from the development of one new process in the human brain—a process that seems to be entirely peculiar to that brain: the use of *symbols for ideas.* By "symbols" I mean all kinds of signs that can be used and understood whether the things they refer to are there or not. The word "symbol" has, unfortunately, many

[1] *Holism and Evolution* (N. Y.: Macmillan Co., 1926).

different meanings for different people. Some people reserve it for mystic signs, like Rosicrucian symbols; some mean by it *significant images,* such as Keats' "Huge cloudy symbols of a high romance"; some use it quite the opposite way and speak of "mere symbols," meaning empty gestures, signs that have lost their meanings; and some, notably logicians, use the term for mathematical signs, marks that constitute a code, a brief, concise language. In their sense, ordinary words are symbols, too. Ordinary language is a symbolism.

When I say that the distinctive function of the human brain is the use of symbols, I mean any and all of these kinds. They are all different from signs that animals use. Animals interpret signs, too, but only as pointers to actual things and events: cues to action or expectation, threats and promises, landmarks and earmarks in the world. Human beings use such signs, too; but above all they use symbols—especially words—to think and talk about things that are neither present nor expected. The words convey *ideas,* that may or may not have counterparts in actuality. This power of thinking *about* things expresses itself in language, imagination, and speculation—the chief products of human mentality that animals do not share.

Language, the most versatile and indispensable of all symbolisms, has put its stamp on all our mental functions, so that I think they always differ from even their closest analogues in animal life. Language has invaded our feeling and dreaming and action, as well as our reasoning, which is really a product of it. The greatest change wrought by language is the increased scope of awareness in speech-gifted beings. An animal's awareness is always of things in its own place and life. In human awareness, the present, actual situation is often the least part. We have not only memories and expectations; we have *a past* in which we locate our memories, and *a future* that vastly over-reaches our own anticipations. Our past is a story, our future a piece of imagination. Likewise our ambient is a place in a wider, symbolically conceived place, the universe. We live in *a world.*

This difference of mentality between man and animal seems to me to make a cleft between them almost as great as the division between animals and plants. There is continuity between the orders, but the division is real nevertheless. Human life differs radically from animal life. By virtue of our incomparably wider awareness, our power of envisagement of things and events beyond any actual perception, we have acquired needs and aims that animals do not have; and even the most savage human society, having to meet those needs and implement those aims, is not really comparable to any animal society. The two may have some analogous functions, but the essential structure must be different, because man and beast live differently in every way.

Probably the profoundest difference between human and animal needs is made by one piece of human awareness, one fact that is not present to animals, because it is never learned in any direct experience: that is our foreknowledge of Death. The fact that we ourselves must die is not a simple and isolated fact. It is built on a wide survey of facts, that discloses the structure of history as a succession of overlapping brief lives, the patterns of youth and age, growth and decline; and above all that, it is built on the logical insight that *one's own life is a case in point.* Only a creature that can think symbolically *about* life can conceive of its own death. Our knowledge of death is part of our knowledge of life.

What, then, do we—all of us—know about life?

Every life that we know is generated from other life. Each living thing springs from some other living thing or things. Its birth is a process of new individuation, in a life-stream whose beginning we do not know.

Individuation is a word we do not often meet. We hear about individuality, sometimes spoken in praise, sometimes as an excuse for being slightly crazy. We hear and read about "the Individual," a being that is forever adjusting, like a problem child, to something called "Society." But how does individuality arise? What makes an individual? A fundamental, biological process of *individuation,* that marks the life of every stock, plant or animal. Life is a series of individuations, and these can be of various sorts, and reach various degrees.

Most people would agree, off-hand, that every creature lives its life and then dies. This might, indeed, be called a truism. But, like some other truisms, it is not true. The lowest forms of life, such as the amoeba, normally (that is, barring accidents) do not die. When they grow very large and might be expected to lay eggs, or in some other way raise a family, they do no such thing: they divide, and make two small ones ready to grow. Well now, where is the old one? It did not die. But it is gone. Its individuation was only an episode in the life of the stock, a phase, a transient form that changed again. Amoebae are individuated in space—they move and feed as independent, whole organisms—but in time they are not self-identical individuals. They do not generate young ones while they themselves grow old; they grow old and *become* young ones.

All the higher animals, however, are final individuations that end in death. They spring from a common stock, but they do not merge back into it. Each one is an end. Somewhere on its way toward death it usually produces a new life to succeed it, but its own story is finished by death.

That is our pattern, too. Each human individual is a culmination of an inestimably long line—its ancestry—and each is destined to die. The living stock is like a palm tree, a trunk composed of its own past leaves. Each leaf springs from the trunk, unfolds, grows, and dies off; its past is incorporated in the trunk, where new life has usually arisen from it. So there constantly are ends, but the stock lives on, and each leaf has that whole life behind it.

The momentous difference between us and our animal cousins is that they do not know they are going to die. Animals spend their lives avoiding death, until it gets them. They do not know it is going to. Neither do they know that they are part of a greater life, but pass on the torch without knowing. Their aim, then, is simply to keep going, to function, to escape trouble, to live from moment to moment in an endless Now.

Our power of symbolic conception has given us each a glimpse of himself as one final individuation from the great human stock. We do not know when or what the end will be, but we know that there will be one. We also envisage a past and future, a stretch of time so vastly longer than any creature's memory, and a world so much richer than any world of sense, that it makes our time in that world seem infinitesimal. This is the price of the great gift of symbolism.

In the face of such uncomfortable prospects (probably conceived long before the dawn of any religious ideas), human beings have evolved aims different from any other creatures. Since we cannot have our fill of existence by going on and on, we want to have *as much life as possible* in our short span. If our individuation must be brief, we want to make it complete; so we are inspired to think, act, dream our desires, create things, express our ideas, and in all sorts of ways make up by concentration what we cannot have by length of days. We seek the greatest possible individuation, or development of personality. In doing this, we have set up a new demand, not for mere continuity of existence, but for *self-realization.* That is a uniquely human aim.

But obviously, the social structure could not arise on this principle alone. Vast numbers of individualists realizing themselves with a vengeance would not make up an ideal society. A small number might try it; there is a place, far away from here, called the Self-Realization Golden World Colony. But most of us have no golden world to colonize. You can only do that south of Los Angeles.

Seriously, however, an ideal is not disposed of by pointing out that it cannot be implemented under existing conditions. It may still be a true ideal; and if it is very important we may have to change the conditions, as we will have to for the ideal of world peace. If complete individuation were really the whole aim of human life, our society would be geared to it much more than it is. It is not the golden world that is wanting, but something else; the complete individualist is notoriously not the happy man, even if good fortune permits his antics.

The fact is that *the greatest possible individuation* is usually taken to mean, "as much as is possible without curtailing the rights of others." But that is not the real measure of how much is possible. The measure is provided in the individual himself, and is as fundamental as his knowledge of death. It is the other part of his insight into nature—his knowledge of life, of the great unbroken stream, the life of the stock from which his individuation stems.

One individual life, however rich, still looks infinitesimal: no matter how much self-realization is concentrated in it, it is a tiny atom—and we don't like to be tiny atoms, not even hydrogen atoms. We need more than fullness of personal life to counter our terrible knowledge of all it implies. And we have more; we have our history, our commitments made for us before we were born, our relatedness to the rest of mankind. The counterpart of individuation from the great life of the stock is our rootedness in that life, our involvement with the whole human race, past and present.

Each person is not only a free, single end, like the green palm leaf that unfolds, grows in a curve of beauty, and dies in its season; he is like the whole palm leaf, the part inside the trunk, too. He is the culmination of his entire ancestry, and *represents* that whole human past. In his brief individuation he is an *expression* of all humanity. That is what makes each person's life sacred and all-important. A single ruined life is the bankruptcy of a long line. This is what I mean by the individual's involvement with all mankind.

All animals are unconsciously involved with their kind. Heredity governs not only their growth, color and form, but their actions, too. They carry their past about with them in everything they do. But they do not know it. They don't need to, because they never could lose it. Their involvement with the greater life of the race is implicit in their limited selfhood.

Our knowledge that life is finite and, in fact, precarious and brief, drives us on to greater individuation than animals attain. Our mental talents have largely freed us from that built-in behavior called instinct. The scope of our imagination gives each of us a separate world, and a separate consciousness, and threatens to break the instinctual ties of brotherhood that make all the herrings swim into one net, and all the geese turn their heads at the same moment. Yet we cannot afford to lose the feeling of involvement with our kind; for if we do, personal life shrinks up to nothingness.

The sense of involvement is our social sense. We have it by nature, originally just as animals do, and just as unconsciously. It is the direct feeling of needing our own kind, caring what happens. Social sense is an instinctive sense of being somehow one with all other people—a feeling that reflects the rootedness of our existence in a human past. Human society rests on this feeling. It is often said to rest on the need of collaboration, or on domination of the weak by the strong, or some other circumstance, but I think such theories deal with its modes, and ignore its deeper structure; at the bottom of it is the feeling of involvement, or social sense. If we lose that, no coercion will hold us to our duties, because they do not feel like commitments; and no achievements will matter, because they are doomed to be snuffed out with the individual, without being laid to account in the continuity of life.

Great individual development, such as human beings are driven by their intellectual insights to seek, does of course always threaten to break the bonds of direct social involvement, that give animal life its happy unconscious continuity. When the strain gets hard, we have social turmoil, anarchy, irresponsibility, and in private lives the sense of loneliness and infinite smallness that lands some people in nihilism and cynicism, and leads others to existentialism or less intellectual cults.

It is then that social philosophers look upon animal societies as models for human society. There is no revolt, no strike, no competition, no anti-anything party, in a beehive. As Kipling, fifty years or more ago, represented his British Utopia that he called the Mother Hive, that ideal State had a completely cooperative economy, an army that went into action without a murmur, each man with the same impulse, the moment an enemy threatened to intrude, and a populace of such tribal solidarity that it would promptly run out any stranger that tried to become established in the State and disrupt its traditions. Any native individual that could not fit into the whole had to be liquidated; the loss was regrettable, but couldn't be helped, and would be made up.

Yet the beehive really has no possible bearing on human affairs; for it owes its harmonious existence to the fact that its members are *incompletely individuated,* even as animals go. None of them perform all of a creature's essential functions: feeding, food-getting, nest-building, mating, and procreating. The queen has to be fed and tended; she has only procreative functions. She doesn't even bring up her own children; they have nurses. The drones are born and reared only as her suitors, and when the romance is finished they are killed, like proper romantic heroes. The building, nursing, food-getting, and fighting are done by sterile females who cannot procreate; amazons who do all their own housework. So there is not only division of labor, but division of organs, functional and physical incompleteness. This direct involvement of each bee with the whole lets the hive function with an organic rhythm that makes its members appear wonderfully socialized. But they are really not socialized at all, any more than the cells in our tissues are socialized; they are associated, by being un-individuated.

That is as far away from a human ideal as one can get. We need, above all, a world in which we can realize our capacities, develop and act as personalities. That means giving up our instinctive patterns of habit and prejudice, our herd-instincts. Yet we need the emotional security of the greater, continuous life—the awareness of our involvement with all mankind. How can we eat that cake, and have it, too?

The same mental talent that makes us need so much individuation, comes to the rescue of our social involvement: I mean the peculiarly human talent of holding ideas in the mind by means of symbols. Human life, even in the simplest forms we know, is shot through and through with *social symbols.* All fantastic beliefs in a Great Ancestor are symbolic of the original and permanent life of the stock from which every individual life stems. The Totem, the Hero, the Sacred Cow, these are the most elementary social symbols. With a maturer view of the world, and the development of religious ideas, the symbolic image of Man is usually taken up into the greater view of a divine world-order and a moral law. We are sons of Adam and daughters of Eve. If Adam and Eve were simply some human couple supposed to have lived in the Near East before it was so difficult, this would be an odd way of speaking; we don't ordinarily refer to our neighbor's children as Mr. Brown's boys and Mrs. Brown's girls. But Adam is Man, and Eve is Woman (the names even mean that): and among us transient little mites, every man is Man, every woman is Woman. That is the source of human dignity, the sense of which has to be upheld at all levels of social life.

Most people have some religious ritual that supports their knowledge of a greater life; but even in purely secular affairs we constantly express our faith in the continuity of human existence. Animals provide lairs or nests for their immediate offspring. Man builds for the future—

often for nothing else; his earliest great buildings were not mansions, but monuments. And not only physical edifices, but above all laws and institutions are intended for the future, and often justified by showing that they have a precedent, or are in accord with the past. They are conveniences of their day, but symbols of more than their day. They are symbols of Society, and of each individual's inalienable membership in Society.

What, then, is the measure of our possible individuation, without loss of social sense? It is the power of social symbolism. We can give up our actual, instinctual involvements with our kind just to the extent that we can replace them by symbolic ones. This is the prime function of social symbols, from a handshake, to the assembly of robed judges in a Supreme Court. In protocol and ritual, in the investment of authority, in sanctions and honors, lies our security against loss of involvement with mankind; in such bonds lies our freedom to be individuals.

It has been said that an animal society, like a beehive, is really an organism, and the separate bees its organic parts. I think this statement requires many reservations, but it contains some truth. The hive is an organic structure, a super-individual, something like an organism. A human city, however, is an *organization.* It is above all a symbolic structure, a mental reality. Its citizens are the whole and only individuals. They are not a "living mass," like a swarm of semi-individuated bees. The model of the hive has brought with it the concept of human masses, to be cared for in times of peace, deployed in times of war, educated for use or sacrificed for the higher good of their state. In the specious analogy of animal and human society, the hive and the city, lies, I think, the basic philosophical fallacy of all totalitarian theory, even the most sincere and idealistic—even the thoroughly noble political thought of Plato.

We are like leaves of the palm tree, each deeply embedded in the tree, a part of the trunk, each opening to the light in a final, separate life. Our world is a human world, organized to implement our highest individuation. There may be ten thousand of us working in one factory. There are several millions of us living in a city like New York. But we are not the Masses: we are the Public.

Road and Paper Routes

Marshall McLuhan

It was not until the advent of the telegraph that messages could travel faster than a messenger. Before this, roads and the written word were closely interrelated. It is only since the telegraph that information has detached itself from such solid commodities as stone and papyrus, much as money had earlier detached itself from hides, bullion, and metals, and has ended as paper. The term "communication" has had an extensive use in connection with roads and bridges, sea routes, rivers, and canals, even before it became transformed into "information movement" in the electric age. Perhaps there is no more suitable way of defining the character of the electric age than by first studying the rise of the idea of transportation as communication, and then the transition of the idea from transport to information by means of electricity. The word "metaphor" is from the Greek *meta* plus *pherein*, to carry across or transport. In this book we are concerned with all forms of transport of goods and information, both as metaphor and

---

exchange. Each form of transport not only carries, but translates and transforms, the sender, the receiver, and the message. The use of any kind of medium or extension of man alters the patterns of interdependence among people, as it alters the ratios among our senses.

It is a persistent theme of this book [*Understanding Media*] that all technologies are extensions of our physical and nervous systems to increase power and speed. Again, unless there were such increases of power and speed, new extensions of ourselves would not occur or would be discarded. For an increase of power or speed in any kind of grouping of any components whatever is itself a disruption that causes a change of organization. The alteration of social groupings, and the formation of new communities, occur with the increased speed of information movement by means of paper messages and road transport. Such speed-up means much more control at much greater distances. Historically, it meant the formation of the Roman Empire and the disruption of the previous city-states of the Greek world. Before the use of papyrus and alphabet created by the incentives for building fast, hard-surface roads, the walled town and the city-state were natural forms that could endure.

Village and city-state essentially are forms that include all human needs and functions. With greater speed and, therefore, greater military control at a distance, the city-state collapsed. Once inclusive and self-contained, its needs and functions were extended in the specialist activities of an empire. Speed-up tends to separate functions, both commercial and political, and acceleration beyond a point in any system becomes disruption and breakdown. So when Arnold Toynbee turns, in *A Study of History*, to a massive documentation of "the breakdowns of civilizations," he begins by saying: "One of the most conspicuous marks of disintegration, as we have already noticed, is . . . when a disintegrating civilisation purchases a reprieve by submitting to forcible political unification in a universal state." Disintegration and reprieve, alike, are the consequence of ever faster movement of information by couriers on excellent roads.

Speed-up creates what some economists refer to as a *center-margin* structure. When this becomes too extensive for the generating and control center, pieces begin to detach themselves and to set up new center-margin systems of their own. The most familiar example is the story of the American colonies of Great Britain. When the thirteen colonies began to develop a considerable social and economic life of their own, they felt the need to become centers themselves, with their own margins. This is the time when the original center may make a more rigorous effort of centralized control of the margins, as, indeed,

Great Britain did. The slowness of sea travel proved altogether inadequate to the maintenance of so extensive an empire on a mere center-margin basis. Land powers can more easily attain a unified center-margin pattern than sea powers. It is the relative slowness of sea travel that inspires sea powers to foster multiple centers by a kind of seeding process. Sea powers thus tend to create centers without margins, and land empires favor the center-margin structure. Electric speeds create centers everywhere. Margins cease to exist on this planet.

Lack of homogeneity in speed of information movement creates diversity of patterns in organization. It is quite predictable, then, that any new means of moving information will alter any power structure whatever. So long as the new means is everywhere available at the same time, there is a possibility that the structure may be changed without breakdown. Where there are great discrepancies in speeds of movement, as between air and road travel or between telephone and typewriter, serious conflicts occur within organizations. The metropolis of our time has become a test case for such discrepancies. If homogeneity of speeds were total, there would be no rebellion and no breakdown. With print, political unity via homogeneity became feasible for the first time. In ancient Rome, however, there was only the light paper manuscript to pierce the opacity, or to reduce the discontinuity, of the tribal villages; and when the paper supplies failed, the roads were vacated, as they were in our own age during gas-rationing. Thus the old city-state returned, and feudalism replaced republicanism.

It seems obvious enough that technical means of speed-up should wipe out the independence of villages and city-states. Whenever speed-up has occurred, the new centralist power always takes action to homogenize as many marginal areas as possible. The process that Rome effected by the phonetic alphabet geared to its paper routes has been occurring in Russia for the last century. Again, from the current example of Africa we can observe how very much visual processing of the human psyche by alphabetic means will be needed before any appreciable degree of homogenized social organization is possible. Much of this visual processing was done in the ancient world by nonliterate technologies, as in Assyria. The phonetic alphabet has no rival, however, as a translator of man out of the closed tribal echo-chamber into the neutral visual world of lineal organization.

The situation of Africa today is complicated by the new electronic technology. Western man is himself being de-Westernized by his own new speed-up, as much as the Africans are being detribalized by our old print and industrial technology. If we understood our own media old and new, these confusions and disruptions could be programmed and synchronized. The very success we enjoy in specializing and separating functions in order to have speed-up, however, is at the same time the cause of inattention and unawareness of the situation. It has ever been thus in the Western world at least. Self-consciousness of the causes and limits of one's own culture seems to threaten the ego structure and is, therefore, avoided. Nietzsche said understanding stops action, and men of action seem to have an intuition of the fact in their shunning the dangers of comprehension.

The point of the matter of speed-up by wheel, road and paper is the extension of power in an ever more homogeneous and uniform space. Thus the real potential of the Roman technology was not realized until printing had given road and wheel a much greater speed than that of the Roman vortex. Yet the speed-up of the electronic age is as disrupting for literate, lineal, and Western man as the Roman paper routes were for tribal villagers. Our speed-up today is not a slow explosion outward from center to margins but an instant implosion and an interfusion of space and functions. Our specialist and fragmented civilization of center-margin structure is suddenly experiencing an instantaneous reassembling of all its mechanized bits into an organic whole. This is the new world of the global village. The village, as Mumford explains in *The City in History,* had achieved a social and institutional extension of all human faculties. Speed-up and city aggregates only served to separate these from one another in more specialist forms. The electronic age cannot sustain the very low gear of a center-margin structure such as we associate with the past two thousand years of the Western world. Nor is this a question of values. If we understood our older media, such as roads and the written word, and if we valued their human effects sufficiently, we could reduce or even eliminate the electronic factor from our lives. Is there an instance of any culture that understood the technology that sustained its structure and was prepared to keep it that way? If so, that would be an instance of values or reasoned preference. The values or preferences that arise from the mere automatic operation of this or that technology in our social lives are not capable of being perpetuated.

In the chapter on the wheel it will be shown that transport without wheels had played a big role before the wheel, some of which was by sledge, over both snow and bogs. Much of it was by pack animal—woman being the first pack animal. Most wheelless transport in the past, however, was by river and by sea, a fact that is today as richly expressed as ever in the location and form of the great cities of the world. Some writers have observed that man's oldest beast of burden was woman, because the male had to be free to run interference for the woman, as ball-carrier, as it were. But that phase belonged to the prewheel stage of transport, when there was only the tractless waste of man the hunter and food-gatherer. Today, when the greatest volume of transport consists in the moving of information, the wheel and the road are undergoing recession and obsolescence; but in the first instance, given the pressure for, and from, wheels, there had to be roads to accommodate them. Settlements had created the impulse for exchange and for the increasing movement of raw material and produce from countryside to processing centers, where there was division of labor and specialist craft skills. Improvement of wheel and road more and more brought the town to the country in a reciprocal spongelike action of give-and-take. It is a process we have seen in this century with the motorcar. Great improvements in roads brought the city more and more to the country. The road became a substitute for the country by the time people began to talk about "taking a spin in the country." With superhighways the road became a wall between man and the country. Then came the stage of the highway as city, a city stretching continuously across the continent, dissolving all earlier cities into the sprawling aggregates that desolate their populations today.

With air transport comes a further disruption of the old town-country complex that had occurred with wheel and road. With the plane the cities began to have the same slender relation to human needs that museums do. They became corridors of showcases echoing the departing forms of industrial assembly lines. The road is, then, used less and less for travel, and more and more for recreation. The traveler now turns to the airways, and thereby ceases to experience the act of traveling. As people used to say that an ocean liner might as well be a hotel in a big city, the jet traveler, whether he is over Tokyo or New York, might just as well be in a cocktail lounge so far as travel experience is concerned. He will begin to travel only after he lands.

Meantime, the countryside, as oriented and fashioned by plane, by highway, and by electric information-gathering, tends to become once more the nomadic trackless area that preceded the wheel. The beatniks gather on the sands to meditate *haiku.*

The principal factors in media impact on existing social forms are acceleration and disruption. Today the acceleration tends to be total, and thus ends space as the main factor in social arrangements. Toynbee sees the acceleration factor as translating the physical into moral problems, pointing to the antique road crowded with dog carts, wagons, and rickshaws as full of minor nuisance, but also minor dangers.

Further, as the forces impelling traffic mount in power, there is no more problem of hauling and carrying, but the physical problem is translated into a psychological one as the annihilation of space permits easy annihilation of travelers as well. This principle applies to all media study. All means of interchange and of human interassociation tend to improve by acceleration. Speed, in turn, accentuates problems of form and structure. The older arrangements had not been made with a view to such speeds, and people begin to sense a draining-away of life values as they try to make the old physical forms adjust to the new and speedier movement. These problems, however, are not new. Julius Caesar's first act upon assuming power was to restrict the night movement of wheeled vehicles in the city of Rome in order to permit sleep. Improved transport in the Renaissance turned the medieval walled towns into slums.

Prior to the considerable diffusion of power through alphabet and papyrus, even the attempts of kings to extend their rule in spatial terms were opposed at home by the priestly bureaucracies. Their complex and unwieldy media of stone inscription made wide-ranging empires appear very dangerous to such static monopolies. The struggles between those who exercised power over the hearts of men and those who sought to control the physical resources of nations were not of one time and place. In the Old Testament, just this kind of struggle is reported in the Book of Samuel (I, viii) when the children of Israel besought Samuel to give them a king. Samuel explained to them the nature of kingly, as opposed to priestly, rule:

> This will be the manner of the King that shall reign over you: he will take your sons, and appoint them unto him for his chariots; and they shall run before his chariots: and he will appoint them unto him for captains of thousands, and captains of fifties; and he will set some to plough his ground, and to reap his harvest, and to make his instruments of war, and the instruments of his chariots. And he will take your daughters to be confectionaries, and to be cooks and to be bakers. And he will take your fields, and your vineyards, and your oliveyards, even the best of them, and give them to his servants.

Paradoxically, the effect of the wheel and of paper in organizing new power structures was not to decentralize but to centralize. A speed-up in communications always enables a central authority to extend its operations to more distant margins. The introduction of alphabet and papyrus meant that many more people had to be trained as scribes and administrators. However, the resulting extension of homogenization and of uniform training did not come into play in the ancient or medieval world to any great degree. It was not really until the mechanization of writing in the Renaissance that intensely unified and centralized power was possible. Since this process is still occurring, it should be easy for us to see that it was in the armies of Egypt and Rome that a kind of democratization by uniform technological education occurred. Careers were then open to talents for those with literate training. In the chapter on the written word we saw how phonetic writing translated tribal man into a visual world and invited him to undertake the visual organization of space. The priestly groups in the temples had been more concerned with the records of the past and with the control of the inner space of the unseen than with outward military conquest. Hence, there was a clash between the priestly monopolizers of knowledge and those who wished to apply it abroad as new conquest and power. (This same clash now recurs between the university and the business world.) It was this kind of rivalry that inspired Ptolemy II to establish the great library at Alexandria as a center of imperial power. The huge staff of civil servants and scribes assigned to many specialist tasks was an antithetic and countervailing force to the Egyptian priesthood. The library could serve the political organization of empire in a way that did not interest the priesthood at all. A not-dissimilar rivalry is developing today between the atomic scientists and those who are mainly concerned with power.

If we realize that the city as center was in the first instance an aggregate of threatened villagers, it is then easier for us to grasp how such harassed companies of refugees might fan out into an empire. The city-state as a form was not a response to peaceful commercial development, but a huddling for security amidst anarchy and dissolution. Thus the Greek city-state was a tribal form of inclusive and integral community, quite unlike the specialist cities that grew up as extensions of Roman military expansion. The Greek city-states eventually disintegrated by the usual action of specialist trading and the separation of functions that Mumford portrays in *The City in History*. The Roman cities began that way—as specialist operations of the central power. The Greek cities ended that way.

If a city undertakes rural trade, it sets up at once a center-margin relation with the rural area in question. That relation involves taking staples and raw produce from the country in exchange for specialist products of the craftsman. If, on the other hand, the same city attempts to engage in overseas trade, it is more natural to "seed" another city center, as the Greeks did, rather than to deal with the overseas area as a specialized margin or raw material supply.

A brief review of the structural changes in the organization of space as they resulted from wheel, road, and papyrus could go as follows: There was first the village, which lacked all of these group extensions of the private physical body. The village, however, was already a form of community different from that of food-gathering hunters and fishers, for villagers may be sedentary and may begin a division of labor and functions. Their being congregated is, itself, a form of acceleration of human activities which provides momentum for further separation and specialization of action. Such are the conditions for the extension of feet-as-wheel to speed production and exchange. These are, also, the conditions that intensify communal conflicts and ruptures that send men huddling into ever larger aggregates, in order to resist the accelerated activities of other communities. The villages are swept up into the city-state by way of resistance and for the purpose of security and protection.

The village had institutionalized all human functions in forms of low intensity. In this mild form everyone could play many roles. Participation was high, and organization was low. This is the formula for stability in any type of organization. Nevertheless, the enlargement of village forms in the city-state called for greater intensity and the inevitable separation of functions to cope with this intensity and competition. The villagers had all participated in the seasonal rituals that in the city became the specialized Greek drama. Mumford feels that "The village measure prevailed in the development of the Greek cities, down to the fourth century . . ." (*The City in History*). It is this extension and translation of the human organs into the village model without loss of corporal unity that Mumford uses as a criterion of excellence for city forms in any time or locale. This biological approach to the man-made environment is sought today once more in the electric age. How strange that the idea of the "human scale" should have seemed quite without appeal during the mechanical centuries.

The natural tendency of the enlarged community of the city is to increase the intensity and accelerate functions of every sort, whether of speech, or crafts, or currency and exchange. This, in turn, implies an inevitable extension of these actions by subdivision or, what is the same thing, new invention. So that even though the city was formed as a kind of protective hide or shield for man, this protective layer was purchased at the cost of maximized struggle within the walls. War games such as those described by Herodotus began as ritual blood baths between the citizenry. Rostrum, law courts, and marketplace all acquired the intense image of divisive competition that is nowadays called "the rat race." Nevertheless, it was amidst such irritations that man produced his greatest inventions as counter-irritants. These inventions were extensions of himself by means of concentrated toil, by which he hoped to neutralize distress. The Greek word *ponos,* or "toil," was a term used by Hippocrates, the father of medicine, to describe the fight of the body in disease. Today this idea is called homeostasis, or equilibrium as a strategy of the staying power of any body. All organizations, but especially biological ones, struggle to remain constant in their inner condition amidst the variations of outer shock and change. The man-made social environment as an extension of man's physical body is no exception. The city, as a form of the body politic, responds to new pressures and irritations by resourceful new extensions—always in the effort to exert staying power, constancy, equilibrium, and *homeostasis.*

The city, having been formed for protection, unexpectedly generated fierce intensities and new hybrid energies from accelerated interplay of functions and knowledge. It burst forth into aggression. The alarm of the village, followed by the resistance of the city, expanded into the exhaustion and inertia of empire. These three stages of the disease and irritation syndrome were felt, by those living through them, as normal physical expressions of counter-irritant recovery from disease.

The third stage of struggle for equilibrium among the forces within the city took the form of empire, or a universal state, that generated the extension of human senses in wheel, road, and alphabet. We can sympathize with those who first saw in these tools a providential means of bringing order to distant areas of turbulence and anarchy. These tools would have seemed a glorious form of "foreign aid," extending the blessings of the center to the barbarian margins. At this moment, for example, we are quite in the dark about the political implications of Telstar. By outering these satellites as extensions of our nervous system, there is an automatic response in all the organs of the body politic of mankind. Such new intensity of proximity imposed by Telstar calls for radical rearrangement of all organs in order to maintain staying power and equilibrium. The teaching and learning process for every child will be affected sooner rather than later. The time factor in every decision of business and finance will acquire new patterns. Among the peoples of the world strange new vortices of power will appear unexpectedly.

The full-blown city coincides with the development of writing—especially of phonetic writing, the specialist form of writing that makes a division between sight and sound. It was with this instrument that Rome was able to reduce the tribal areas to some visual order. The effects of phonetic literacy do not depend upon persuasion or cajolery for their acceptance. This technology for translating the resonating tribal world into Euclidean lineality and visuality is automatic. Roman roads and Roman streets were uniform and repeatable wherever they occurred. There was no adaptation to the contours of local hill or custom. With the decline of papyrus supplies, the wheeled traffic stopped on these roads, too. Deprivation of papyrus, resulting from the Roman loss of Egypt, meant the decline of bureaucracy, and of army organization as well. Thus the medieval world grew up without uniform roads or cities or bureaucracies, and it fought the wheel, as later city forms fought the railways; and as we, today, fight the automobile. For new speed and power are never compatible with existing spatial and social arrangements.

Writing about the new straight avenues of the seventeenth-century cities, Mumford points to a factor that was also present in the Roman city with its wheeled traffic; namely, the need for broad straight avenues to speed military movements, and to express the pomp and circumstance of power. In the Roman world the army was the work force of a mechanized wealth-creating process. By means of soldiers as uniform and replaceable parts, the Roman military machine made and delivered the goods, very much in the manner of industry during the early phases of the industrial revolution. Trade followed the legions. More than that, the legions were the industrial machine, itself; and numerous new cities were like new factories manned by uniformly trained army personnel. With the spread of literacy after printing, the bond between the uniformed soldier and the wealth-making factory hand became less visible. It was obvious enough in Napoleon's armies. Napoleon, with his citizen-armies, was the industrial revolution itself, as it reached areas long protected from it.

The Roman army as a mobile, industrial wealth-making force created in addition a vast consumer public in the Roman towns. Division of labor always creates a separation between producer and consumer, even as it tends to separate the place of work and the living space. Before Roman literate bureaucracy, nothing comparable to the Roman consumer specialists had been seen in the world. This fact was institutionalized in the individual known as "parasite," and in the social institution of the gladiatorial games. (*Panem et circenses.*) The private sponge and the collective sponge, both reaching out for their rations of sensation, achieved a horrible distinctness and clarity that matched the raw power of the predatory army machine.

With the cutting-off of the supplies of papyrus by the Mohammedans, the Mediterranean, long a Roman lake, became a Muslim lake, and the Roman center collapsed. What had been the margins of this center-margin structure became independent centers on a new feudal, structural base. The Roman center collapsed by the fifth century A.D. as wheel, road, and paper dwindled into a ghostly paradigm of former power.

Papyrus never returned. Byzantium, like the medieval centers, relied heavily on parchment, but this was too expensive and scarce a material to speed commerce or even education. It was paper from China, gradually making its way through the Near East to Europe, that accelerated education and commerce steadily from the eleventh century, and provided the basis for "the Renaissance of the twelfth century," popularizing prints and, finally, making printing possible by the fifteenth century.

With the moving of information in printed form, the wheel and the road came into play again after having been in abeyance for a thousand years. In England, pressure from the press brought about hard-surface roads in the eighteenth century, with all the population and industrial rearrangement that entailed. Print, or mechanized writing, introduced a separation and extension of human functions unimaginable even in Roman times. It was only natural, therefore, that greatly increased wheel speeds, both on road and in factory, should be related to the alphabet that had once done a similar job of speed-up and specialization in the ancient world. Speed, at least in its lower reaches of the mechanical order, always operates to separate, to extend, and to amplify functions of the body. Even specialist learning in higher education proceeds by ignoring interrelationships; for such complex awareness slows down the achieving of expertness.

The post roads of England were, for the most part, paid for by the newspapers. The rapid increase of traffic brought in the railway, that accommodated a more specialized form of wheel than the road. The story of modern America that began with the discovery of the white man by the Indians, as a wag has truly said, quickly passed from exploration by canoe to development by railway. For three centuries Europe invested in America for its fish and its furs. The fishing schooner and the canoe preceded the road and the postal route as marks of our North American spatial organization. The European investors in the fur trade naturally did not want the trapping lines overrun by Tom Sawyers and Huck Finns. They fought land surveyors and settlers, like Washington and Jefferson, who simply would not think in terms of mink. Thus the War of Independence was deeply involved in media and staple rivalries. Any new medium, by its acceleration, disrupts the lives and investments of whole communities. It was the railway that raised the art of war to unheard-of intensity, making the American Civil War the first major conflict fought by rail, and causing it to be studied and admired by all European general staffs, who had not yet had an opportunity to use railways for a general blood-letting.

War is never anything less than accelerated technological change. It begins when some notable disequilibrium among existing structures has been brought about by inequality of rates of growth. The very late industrialization and unification of Germany had left her out of the race for staples and colonies for many years. As the Napoleonic wars were technologically a sort of catching-up of France with England, the First World War was itself a major phase of the final industrialization of Germany and America. As Rome had not shown before, and Russia has shown today, militarism is itself the main route of technological education and acceleration for lagging areas.

Almost unanimous enthusiasm for improved routes of land transportation followed the War of 1812. Furthermore, the British blockade of the Atlantic coast had compelled an unprecedented amount of land carriage, thus emphasizing the unsatisfactory character of the highways. War is certainly a form of emphasis that delivers many a telling touch to lagging social attention. However, in the very Hot Peace since the Second War, it is the highways of the mind that have been found inadequate. Many have felt dissatisfaction with our educational methods since Sputnik, in exactly the same spirit that many complained about the highways during the War of 1812.

Now that man has extended his central nervous system by electric technology, the field of battle has shifted to mental image-making-and-breaking, both in war and in business. Until the electric age, higher education had been a privilege and a luxury for the leisured classes; today it has become a necessity for production and survival. Now, when information itself is the main traffic, the need for advanced knowledge presses on the spirits of the most routine-ridden minds. So sudden an upsurge of academic training into the marketplace has in it the quality of classical peripety or reversal, and the result has been a wild guffaw from the gallery and the campus. The hilarity, however, will die down as the Executive Suites are taken over by the Ph.D.s.

For an insight into the ways in which the acceleration of wheel and road and paper rescramble population and settlement patterns, let us glance at some instances provided by Oscar Handlin in his study *Boston's Immigrants.* In 1790, he tells us, Boston was a compact unit with all workers and traders living in sight of each other, so that there was no tendency to section residential areas on a class basis: "But as the town grew, as the outlying districts became more accessible, the people spread out and at the same time were localized in distinctive areas." That one sentence capsulates the theme of this chapter. The sentence can be generalized to include the art of writing: "As knowledge was spread out visually and as it became more accessible in alphabetic form, it was localized and divided into specialties." Up to the point just short of electrification, increase of speed produces division of function, and of social classes, and of knowledge.

At electric speed, however, all that is reversed. Implosion and contraction then replace mechanical explosion and expansion. If the Handlin formula is extended to power, it becomes: "As power grew, and as outlying areas became accessible to power, it was localized in distinctive delegated jobs and functions." This formula is a principle of acceleration at all levels of human organization. It concerns especially those extensions of our physical bodies that appear in wheel and road and paper messages. Now that we have extended not just our physical organs but the nervous system, itself, in electric technology, the principle of specialism and division as a factor of speed no longer applies. When information moves at the speed of signals in the central nervous system, man is confronted with the obsolescence of all earlier forms of acceleration, such as road and rail. What emerges is a total field of inclusive awareness. The old patterns of psychic and social adjustment become irrelevant.

Until the 1820s, Handlin tells us, Bostonians walked to and fro, or used private conveyances. Horse-drawn buses were introduced in 1826, and these speeded up and extended business a great deal. Meantime the speed-up of industry in England had extended business into the rural areas, dislodging many from the land and increasing the rate of immigration. Sea transport of immigrants became lucrative and encouraged a great speed-up of ocean transport. Then the Cunard Line was subsidized by the British government in order to ensure swift contact with the colonies. The railways soon linked into this Cunard service, to convey mail and immigrants inland.

Although America developed a massive service of inland canals and river steamboats, they were not geared to the speeding wheels of the new industrial production. The railroad was needed to cope with mechanized production, as much as to span the great distances of the continent. The steam railroad as an accelerator proved to be one of the most revolutionary of all extensions of our physical bodies, creating a new political centralism and a new kind of urban shape and size. It is to the railroad that the American city owes its abstract grid layout, and the nonorganic separation of production, consumption, and residence. It is the motorcar that scrambled the abstract shape of the industrial town, mixing up its separated functions to a degree that has frustrated and baffled both planner and citizen. It remained for the airplane to complete the confusion by amplifying the mobility of the citizen to the point where urban space as such was irrelevant. Metropolitan space is equally irrelevant for the telephone, the telegraph, the radio, and television. What the town planners call "the human scale" in discussing ideal urban spaces is equally unrelated to these electric forms. Our electric extensions of ourselves simply bypass space and time, and create problems of human involvement and organization for which there is no precedent. We may yet yearn for the simple days of the automobile and the superhighway.

Suburbia Reconsidered: Diversity and the Creative Life

Dorothy Lee

Is the suburb a "paradise regained?" Yes, certainly one image of paradise: the paradise of harp players agreeably getting along with one another; a paradise of lights without shadows, of virtue rather than of vibrant good; a paradise where people do the right, the acceptable, perhaps even what they ought to do. But it is not a paradise which is the "blooming, buzzing confusion" of the senses.

At one time I had thought of the suburb as a good place to bring up my children. There was the country for my children to know, to see, to feel, to incorporate

> . . . the gay
> great happening illimitably earth.

There would be available to them the kind of music I liked, the kind of people I liked, the kind of experience I liked. I did not take my children to a suburb, but I did take them to a homogeneous community in the country, to the edge of the Vassar College campus, near the woods and hills, the brooks, the ponds, the fields, where they could

---

be with deer, and rabbits, and woodchucks, and all the wild growing things. After some years, at tremendous personal expense, and against my children's resistance, I fled from this paradise. I fled, not from the country, but from the filtered experience which I had been providing for my children. We went to where the children could be tempted to join street corner society, where they could see brute poverty, and vice and exultation, and the bewilderment of the rejected immigrant; where they could be exposed to bad English and despicable music. I took them where they could meet taste that had not been labeled good or bad, so that they could make their own decisions about it; where their associates had not been implicitly pre-selected and pre-labeled as desirable.

After a period of disorientation and anguish, my children were all glad of the move. We mourned the loss of the country; we had to get it in the summer alone. But, of course, this loss is not relevant to a discussion of suburbs, because if we had been living in a true suburb the country would have been lost to us in time in any case.

In many respects the culture of the suburbs is only an intensification of the official American culture—the culture implicit in the curricula of the schools of education, expressed in the structure and the teaching of our public school system; the culture underlying all policy-making, and even the appeal we make in our advertising and in the mass-oriented movies produced in Hollywood. It is this culture which the urbanite takes to the suburbs with him and finds there in his children's school. But here the suburb with its relative homogeneity approximates a closed system and intensifies certain aspects of culture.

I would like to consider suburban culture from the following point of view: to what extent does suburban life make it possible for the individual to grow, to maintain inner consistency, to exercise autonomy? What is the range of experience, the variety of society which it offers for the transaction of the self? I should like to discuss the prerequisites for personal growth and strength as offered on the one hand by the city and on the other hand by the suburb.

I shall take up first the subject of the strength of the self. To what extent is the individual enabled and incited to excel, not in a comparative sense, but rather in the sense of exercising all the muscles of his person, intellectual, emotional, physical, with joy and pride? Does suburban living help the individual find and give expression to his own peculiar pattern to the minutest detail, and beyond that, to transcend his potential?

To my mind, one essential for the strengthening of the self is the presence of diversity. The self needs variety of experience directly for its own growth for richer transaction. Diversity is also needed indirectly so that an individual can exercise his powers of perception and discrimination in the area of making a choice, so that in making his own choice he can be an agent in creating his own experience. In fact, I believe that the exercise of one's agency is one way to excellence, and I use "exercise" here in the sense that I exercise my muscles. In the suburbs, diversity is largely absent as compared with the city. David Riesman speaks of this lack of diversity in the paper which he entitles "Suburban Sadness." And I agree with him that this is sad. Sometimes the homogeneity happens without deliberate intent, though people are naturally guided by their own likes. In the case of the establishment of Crestwood Heights, it seems to have been done with deliberation. The authors who in *Crestwood Heights: A Study of the Culture of Suburban Life* describe this pseudonymous community write that the establishment of the suburb was for the purpose of creating "a smaller area in which they and *others like* them" (the italics are added) could agree on a policy.

Now there is a second aspect in which diversity can contribute to, in fact is necessary for, the strength of the self, and that is through making conflict possible. Conflict may be bad when it is overwhelming; but it can evoke an answering strength, and through the exertion of this strength, can mean the growth of the self through experience, an experience which demands the output of all that is available to the self. A lawyer was speaking to me recently about his early years in this country. He arrived from Greece as a boy of eleven and went to live in an industrial city as an immigrant, as a poor boy, as the nephew of a man who owned a pool hall and who employed the little boy as an assistant. He said to me that when finally he managed to go to Princeton, he had deplored this experience of his as poverty stricken. But now, after years of living, thinking, and experience, he sees these early years of conflict as the years which had made it possible for him to grow from strength to strength. This is the kind of experience which a city does provide usually and which is generally not available to the child growing up in the suburb.

In fact official American culture in general tends more and more to view conflict as bad and to eliminate it. Two years ago I was teaching a seminar in which vigorous discussion of freedom was taking place when suddenly a student asked that we agree on a definition of freedom, that we abandon our differences so that we could all be able to state the same thing. Diversity was happily present in this seminar. The members had come from all over the world. But this diversity, the contrapuntal discussion which created the theme in its rich variety of ramifications, threatened the American student's value of "getting along."

Somehow in the official American culture, harmony, the symphonic unification of diversity, has been reinterpreted to mean monotony. In the name of agreement difference is being eliminated—certainly not fostered—giving place to sameness and to agreement as a desired good. There is a trend toward eliminating difference in taste, in values, in standards, in education, in ways of living. And this trend, I believe is at its strongest in the suburb, because here there is a feedback from the relatively homogeneous situation. But in eliminating diversity we deprive ourselves of the opportunity to strengthen ourselves in our own stand, and, in fact, to create our own position. We have little opportunity to learn to respect difference, or knowing the difference, to despise it or reject it according to our own act of decision.

The city at least does offer more diversity. Cities, of course, vary in idiosyncracy and in the degree of differentiation which they offer. Yet, it is in the city that we meet the extremes, the immigrant as well as the old American, the laborer and the president of the corporation. Here is where we encounter the thrill of the refugee who for the first time lays eyes on the Statue of Liberty or sets foot on American soil. It is here that we meet the hardship, the sordidness, as well as the gracious living of the established. Here to some extent existence is not quite filtered for the growing individual. This is not to say that a girl in the city would end up by having a different assortment of friends than she would have had in the suburb. The point I want to make is that in the city she would have arrived possibly at the same kind of friends after having lived through the experience of choice, through perhaps the anguish of rejection and the doubts revolving around selection, and thus would have grown as a person, would have strengthened her own idiosyncratic pattern. In a sense, she would have created her own experience, and she would have been an agent in her own existence.

Yet, whatever the actuality, the ideal of official American culture is that of overcoming differentiation. Agreement is "good," because it is the sign of "getting along." To "get along" is one of the goals of living offered to the growing child in the school, whether in the city or in the suburb. When I analyzed manuals for the teachers of Family Life Education and of Home Economics, I found the emphasis on "getting along" strong in a variety of the situations discussed. These manuals represented suggestions for teachers across the country. In one lesson on Family Relationships, the term "get along" was found to occur seven times. Under the heading of Personality, in the chapters which were actually concerned with teaching the student how to be pleasing to others, "getting along" was also given a high ranking. Getting along means agreement; and as a matter of fact when it was used in connection with one's family relations, it spelled the elimination of diversity, the by-passing of conflict rather than living through conflict or facing the situation of conflict.

Thus agreement is good in itself. It is also good because it is the elimination of conflict. Conversely, conflict must be eliminated in the name of agreement. However, there is another sanction which supports the elimination of conflict. This is the sanction against competition.

The aim of the schools is to teach cooperation; cooperation is seen as good and competition as the enemy of cooperation. Yet competition has been decried without enough reflection and understanding. There is one competition that is seen as leading to a standard of success. There is, however, the other competition, the competition that demands a good and strong antagonist, a respected antagonist so as to make exertion of the self possible. Take a chess player. He needs a strong chess player if he is to play well at all. Or take a tennis player. Not only does he need an antagonist, he also needs a strong one, possibly one stronger than himself, a player who calls forth skill and the strength which cannot emerge without this strong competition. In fact, in my experience, a tennis player prefers to play against a competitor who will defeat him rather than against one who, being weak, will not call for an answering strength and will be defeated as a matter of course.

Now the suburbs are often criticized for the competitive life they offer. But in my opinion it is the other kind of competition, the rivalry within approximate sameness, within a similarity of standards, which rages in the suburbs. The contrapuntal competition which calls forth the hidden forces of the self and helps create a new whole, this is thrown away along with the undesired diversity. Agreement engenders at least a surface placidity. And it often is achieved by means of a Procrustean bed, and—to mix my metaphors—establishes the comfortable, rigid ceiling of the golden mean.

In fact, the exertion itself has ceased to be a value; both exertion and the agency of the self. Writers now deplore the fact that things "happen to us" instead of "our doing them." To my mind, they have reason to do so. I have heard of a suburb in New York where the parents became aware of this and decided they would find some way to get their children to do things for themselves. One of the obvious ways was to have the children walk to school instead of being driven by their parents. But when the parents tried to put this into practice, they found it was impossible. The passivity, the non-exertion, had been built into the suburb. There were no sidewalks anywhere except in the one or two blocks of the shopping district.

I have been speaking of diversity as necessary to the growth of the self in affording situations of choice, in offering an agentival role, and, through providing conflict, in encouraging the exertion which is a dimension of commitment and engagement. In addition to this, diversity in the sense of the "blooming, buzzing confusion" is, I believe, the prime requisite of creativity. The individual must create from the source. He must see the peas roll for himself, to use Fromm's illustration, not depend on someone else's experience. It is imperative that he create his own experience, perceiving his own pattern in the chaos. This, I believe to be true of all creative work. Even in the area of law, according to Charles P. Curtis, the language of law is vague (and I should say deplorably bewildering) so as to give an opportunity to each lawyer to recreate the law for himself in terms of the specific situation. It is certainly true of poetry where "naming an object suppresses three-quarters of the enjoyment of a person about it . . ."; and where "an author knows he will give the reader more only by getting him to do more, to take a larger share in the creation." The unfinished evokes because everything is not organized and on the surface.

Now—if I may continue to generalize—all this is lacking in the suburbs; or, rather, what is offered is just the opposite. The suburbs do name the object for their denizens. Experience is offered, organized, prelabeled, preselected, prefabricated. Stephen Birmingham in his "Commuter's Lament" dreams of going back to New York and "wasting" time doing things like taking a ride on the Staten Island Ferry. He wonders "is it still a nickel" and rushes to say, "don't tell me, I want to find out for myself." This freedom to find out for himself he associates with the city, not with the suburbs. This is the tune that Robert Paul Smith sings in his book *Where Did You Go? Out . . .* when he compares his own growing up in New York with the life of his children in a New York suburb. He says, "My kid went to play soccer the other day. The way you play soccer now is this: You bring home from school a mimeographed schedule for the Saturday morning Soccer League. . . . There are always exactly eleven men on each team, the ball is regulation size, the games are played on a regulation-sized field with regulation-sized soccer balls, and there is a regulation-sized adult referee." In contrast, he describes his own life. "When I was a kid, the way we got to play baseball was this: We . . . grabbed a beat-up fielder's glove, went out on the block and met a friend who had an old first baseman's mitt, a ball, went down the block a little and hollered at the kid who had the bat. . . . We went to the vacant lot and played a game resembling major league baseball, only that it was played with a bat and bases. It was fun. . . . You see it was our game. I think my kid was playing someone else's game."

Of course the father in his own childhood was wasting a lot of time trying to find the bat and ball, rounding up the kids, getting to the vacant lot. In the suburb, there is efficiency, at least in Birmingham's and Smith's description of suburban life. There is no waste of time; and indeed, at least for the commuting fathers, there is no time to waste. When two or three or more hours of commuting are added to the regular day's work, the remaining very few hours of the waking day have to be utilized in an organized and efficient way. Birmingham, in his "Lament," writes of this aspect of suburban life. He says that you can tell the suburbanite by the fact that he drives around in New York. The New Yorker likes to walk because he likes to look around, to smell the smells, to discover what is going on. But then his day is longer; there is more time in it. Perhaps this is why he has not moved to the suburbs. It is not clear here which is the chicken and which is the egg; but I would agree that this stress on efficiency, organization, this battle against wasting time, though a part of official American culture, is perhaps intensified in suburban living. Certainly when I spent three and a half hours on the road commuting, my very few "free" hours had to be rigidly goal-oriented. There was no time to waste on exploration which had not been already mapped and diagrammed and robbed of all creativity.

I must repeat here that this is only an intensification. Throughout our society today there is an emphasis on the streamlined, the efficient. We give our students bibliographies, not so that they may explore, but so that they may save time, so that they may take the shortest route between two points and never have a chance to take a wrong turning and wander around the countryside. In this way they need not "waste" their time looking through poor articles and discovering the inadequacy for themselves, or even in forming their own standards by which to judge a book (and, of course, reading fewer "good" books). We give them a map, not a compass, and quite often we substitute the map for the territory. Now that they have the map, now that they know what other people thought of this book, or of the Renaissance, why should they have to discover for themselves?

A teacher in one of the leading colleges told me how at one time she asked a class in literature to read a book about which they had never heard, and report on it. More than half the class came to her and asked her whether it was a "good book"; because, without knowing this, they did not know how to read it, how to relate to it, what to think of it.

This is the picture I found in the manuals for the teaching of Home Economics which I analyzed in 1954. According to these, the students were to be guided to use even their leisure time with the utmost efficiency. For example, it was suggested that they drive out in the country for a purpose, such as "in order to see the sunset." They were urged to read a book "that had been recommended." They were urged to investigate the radio programs first and then to turn on only the program which had been branded as good. No wandering about, no vagary of the spirit, no sudden exultant discovery of something which had not been approved by a superior beforehand. Here the self is not clearly recognized. It has no validity. Someone outside makes the decisions, clears away the underbrush, smoothes the road, and allows the self to move on only as a zombie, protected against its own mistakes, deprived of its own experience.

This treatment of the self as not significant is seen also, for example, when parents prepare a room for an "eight-year-old boy"; not for John, not for *this* boy. The authors of *Crestwood Heights* speak among other things of the rumpus room and the children's room, "meticulously fitted to what decorators and the furniture trade consider the taste of a child." That is, the child does not create his own room out of the ragged, dreadful bits and treasures that go into the making of his own personal history, the things which eventually produce a room that could be an expression only of his own self and no one else's self.

The Crestwood Heights house in general is described as lacking idiosyncracy. The authors write that it is "reminiscent of a series of department store windows, charmingly arranged, harmoniously matched in color." This statement reminded me of a generalization which a French informant in the Columbia Research Project for Contemporary Cultures said about the French living room, in which one found "the habits, the reminders, the family pictures, the family furniture," a room that grew with the family. This would be a living room uniquely expressing the history, the idiosyncracy of this particular family.

I would say then that for a suburbanite more so than for a city dweller experience comes filtered and preordered. The range of experience has been preselected and highly narrowed. The goal of efficiency is more than elsewhere realized here. And, in the suburb, no less than in the city, the individual is viewed and dealt with as a representative of a category rather than as a person in his own right.

If we are to speak in the language of the existentialist, I would say that all this spells alienation to me. The individual is set on a track which leads and moves him away from encounter with the heterogeneous data of experience. He is provided with a life which does not evoke the exertion of the self, a life which does not call forth commitment. Since experience comes to a large degree prefabricated, the individual is not incited to engage himself in the process of living, to take on his responsibility of choice, and his role as agent. This I believe to be more true of the suburbs than of the city. If suburban life is "paradise regained," it is, to my mind, the wrong kind of paradise.

3

The New Culture

Prelude to Alienation

Raymond Williams

Alienation is now itself an ideology. It is also a category into which many different kinds of experience are directed and in effect lost. Yet the basic emphasis, on an absence or loss of connection or community, remains central to all our thinking. The inquiry that still matters is into the formation of this structure of feeling: an inquiry that can alternatively be imaginative or historical.

One decisive period, for this kind of inquiry, is late eighteenth and early nineteenth-century Europe, when the idea, as we now use it, was shaped. The story of the development through Hegel to Marx is well known. An essentially religious conception of man's alienation from God by the Fall, and of his redemption through Christ, was generalized and transformed into a continuing historical process. The recovery of spiritual connection was then in turn transformed by a translation into human and social processes: the hitherto autonomous realm of spirit, in which both alienation and recovery were to be understood, was seen as a projection and alienation of human ener-

Reprinted from *Dissent,* Summer, 1964, by permission of the publisher.

gies, which could only be recovered by being recognized as human. The emphasis on alienation from God was changed to an emphasis on man's self-alienation, from the world he had made and the society of which he was a member, neither of which he could now recognize. The way of overcoming alienation was then not spiritual but social: a recognition by human process of a human product, which could then be changed by human action. Redemption had become regeneration, and the act of regeneration was social revolution.

To examine this development in detail would be a separate inquiry. But we have been accustomed to think of a Romantic emphasis on spiritual alienation, and then of a revolutionary emphasis on social alienation. If we trace the successive systems this account is reasonable. But the emphasis on alienation as an experience, and a connection of this experience with a pattern of social change, was in fact being made in English romantic literature, independently of the better-known philosophical argument. The eventual result was a characteristic tradition of English social criticism, which may well have had some effect on Marx's concept of social alienation, but which in any case has continued to offer a way of thinking about alienation, and, more generally a still powerful structure of feeling. I draw attention to this work, not to engage in some sterile debate on priorities, but to provide one more case-history of the formation of the idea, to be set beside others and to make more possible a general historical account.

I

For historical reasons, English writers were the first to experience an industrial society. But, equally, they had to negotiate this experience without any of the general ideas which were eventually necessary for an analysis both profound and systematic. It is hardly surprising that their insights were fragmentary. What is more remarkable is that some of these insights, so early, were so deeply revealing. What they experienced, and had to learn to experience, was a social dissolution and the loss of a common world. The description of alienation was then variously made, but in Blake and Wordsworth especially, and then following them in Carlyle, the description was given social connections, which have remained important: precise connections, to new kinds of work, to the metropolis and its new social relations, and to the system of capitalist trade. These connections were built on, in subsequent theory, but equally they were connections of a kind which could never become entirely or even primarily sociological. What was offered was not an account of personal alienation in social terms, or of social alienation in personal terms, but a genuine connection of these processes, into a single process. This has radically affected all subsequent English thinking.

It is particularly necessary to emphasize this unity in Blake. Alienation, evidently, is a major theme in his writing, but it is very easy, in a divided criticism, to take either his sense of social alienation or his sense of spiritual alienation as primary. There is of course the familiar radical dissociation of the self, from Blake's Protestant inheritance:

> My Spectre around me night and day
> Like a Wild Beast guards my way.
> My Emanation far within
> Weeps incessantly for my sin.

Much of Blake's work is concerned with a regeneration in which the unity of the self will be restored, but it is not only that the hiding, guilty self will come back into the world; it is also that the beast outside will be recognized. The regeneration is in any case a wholly human creative act. The spiritual powers have themselves to be redeemed from their long alienation:

> If Gods combine against Man, Setting their
> dominion above
> The Human Form Divine, Thrown down from their
> high Station
> In the Eternal Heavens of Human Imagination,
> buried beneath
> In dark Oblivion with incessant pangs ages
> on ages
> In enmity and war first weaken'd; then in
> stern repentance
> They must renew their brightness, and their
> disorganiz'd functions
> Again reorganize, till they resume the image
> of the human,
> Cooperating in the bliss of Man, obeying his
> Will,
> Servants to the infinite and Eternal of the
> Human Form.

But it is not only the gods who combine against men; it is also human rulers:

> Shall not the King call for Famine from the
> heath,
> Or the Priest for Pestilence from the Fen,

To restrain, to dismay, to thin
The inhabitants of mountain and plain . . .

Shall not the Councellor throw his curb
Of Poverty on the laborious,
To fix the price of labour
To invent allegoric riches? . . .

To turn man from his path,
To restrain the child from the womb,
To cut off the bread from the city,
That the remnant may learn to obey . . .
To teach mortal worms the path
That leads from the gates of the Grave.

This alienation is a conscious social process, related not only to the traditional enemies, the King and the Priest, but to the contemporary conditions of wage labor. It is not only the repression that is noted, but, significantly, the invention of "allegoric riches," the extreme alienation of the laborer's product. And while the repression is social, to teach obedience, it is also total:

That the pride of the heart may fail,
That the lust of the eyes may be quench'd,
That the delicate ear in its infancy
May be dulled, and the nostrils closed up.

The whole natural life of man is stolen from him, by his own political creations. This calculating political system (in which Malthus is as evident as the traditional oppressors) is itself the product of the alienation—the externalization and separation—of reason. Many radicals saw God as an alienation, by projection, of human energies. Blake added to this the alienation, by projection, of reason, which, turning to an external system, then oppressed actual men. Urizen, here, is this projected Reason:

Then left the sons of Urizen the plow and
harrow, the loom,
The hammer and the chisel, and the rule and
compasses,
They forg'd the sword, the chariot of war, the
battle ax,
The trumpet fitted to the battle, and the flute
of summer,
And all the arts of life they chang'd into the
arts of death:

> The hour-glass contemn'd because its simple
> workmanship,
> Was as the workmanship of the plowman, and the
> water wheel
> That raises water into Cisterns broken and
> burn'd in fire
> Because its workmanship was like the workmanship
> of the Shepherd:
> And in their stead, intricate wheels invented, Wheel
> without wheel,
> To perplex youth in their outgoings, and to bind to
> labours
> Of day and night the myriads of Eternity, that they
> might file
> And polish brass and iron hour after hour, laborious
> workmanship,
> Kept ignorant of the use; that they might spend
> the days of wisdom
> In sorrowful drudgery, to obtain a scanty pittance
> of bread,
> In ignorance to view a small portion and think
> that All,
> And call it Demonstration, blind to all the simple
> rules of life.

This remarkable passage can be immediately recognized as a response to the new conditions of industrial work. But we must note also that these are seen as an imposed system, and yet as the actions of men. The limited vision of the industrial worker—alienated from his product, "kept ignorant of the use," "in ignorance to view a small portion and think that All"—is also the limited vision of the system—the "Demonstration"—which has alienated reason from life. The "sorrowful drudgery" and the condition of being "blind to all the simple rules of life" are in this way dependent on each other; the men are oppressed, but by their own creation. What is equally remarkable is that the development of industrialism is seen in the same process as the development of militarism: each is a change from "the arts of life" to "the arts of death."

The new industrial and commercial system was seen, then, as of a piece with a human alienation.

> Where any view of Money exists, Art cannot be
> carried on, but War only.

The whole gamut of alienation—poverty, war, perverted desire—is known in the streets of a city subordinated to trade.

I wander thro' each charter'd street
Near where the charter'd Thames does flow,
And mark in every face I meet
Marks of weakness, marks of woe.

In every cry of every Man,
In every Infant's cry of fear,
In every voice, in every ban,
The mind-forg'd manacles I hear.

How the Chimney-sweeper's cry
Every black'ning Church appals;
And the hapless Soldier's sigh
Runs in blood down Palace walls.

But most thro' midnight streets I hear
How the youthful Harlot's curse
Blasts the new born Infant's tear,
And blights with plagues the marriage hearse.

The "mind-forg'd manacles" and the "charter'd" streets are seen in the same form. To possess himself again, and to possess the city, is then man's common desire. The destruction of false social power is the condition of the recovery of innocence:

The King and the Priest must be tied in a tether
Before two virgins can meet together.

Out of his lost innocence, and through his total experience, man will gain a wisdom which will lead, in the same action, to regeneration and revolution: to recover himself, man must recover brotherhood.

A perfect unity
Cannot exist but from the Universal Brotherhood
of Eden.

Art, as the expression of desire, must fight against trade, which is its alienation, and the human integration is a new society:

The whole business of Man is the Arts, and
All Things Common.

II

Blake's work is, I believe, as well as the earliest the deepest insight into the connections between human and social impoverishment, in the new conditions of industrial capitalism. His revolutionary solution is in many ways wider than anything that succeeded it, for the social revolution and the end of personal alienation are very deeply connected. At the same time, Blake, like every writer of this period, tended to see the new society as a recovery of a lost state. The image of the Fall is dominant, and this made connection with any actual new society difficult. The most common form of this social imagery of the Fall was, in this period, the contrast between country and town, though the idea of a medieval unity and innocence was, in English nineteenth-century thought, to become even more prominent, within the same structure of feeling.

Wordsworth, characteristically, saw alienation most clearly in the modern urban metropolis. Blake's London and Wordsworth's London are equally alienated, but the standpoint is different. The seventh book of Wordsworth's *Prelude—Residence in London*—has been overshadowed by the earlier, more directly autobiographical books. But it is a very remarkable book, if we read it, as we should, for what is seen, rather than for what our predetermined character of Wordsworth happens to see.

The earliest observation is characteristic, to one coming from the country:

> One thought
> Baffled my understanding, how men lived
> Even next-door neighbours, as we say, yet still
> Strangers, and knowing not each other's names.

This is the new kind of anonymous social relationship, and the crowded street, in its now familiar form, is an epitome of it:

> The broad high-way appearance, as it strikes
> On Strangers of all ages, the quick dance
> Of colours, lights and forms, the Babel din,
> The endless stream of men, and moving things,
> From hour to hour the illimitable walk
> Still among streets with clouds and sky above.

The massing of other men in the street changes from a physical to a mental phenomenon: the crowd takes on a kind of absolute, single existence. This movement of mind, so fundamental to the modern imagination, produces a new kind of social relationship, which is more significant than mere anonymity. The conscious individual formulates his relationship with other men as with an undifferentiated mass, and feels at once threatened and hostile:

> The roar continues, till at length
> Escaped as from an enemy, we turn
> Abruptly into some sequester'd nook.

What the individual then sees, in the crowd of others, is not men but social types—images of men—and these are exactly characterized in the "advertisements of giant-size," the "allegoric shapes, female or male," which serve, in this crowded anonymity, to give back to men who have no direct knowledge of each other a generalized image. This is then the way of seeing embodied in a new kind of "Public Show," and the detached individual sees show and spectators—the "many-headed mass"—in comparable forms. Yet within this massing, there is a new kind of display of the self: no longer individuality, of the kind that is socially sustained, but singularity—the extravagance of display within the public emptiness. This is again hostile and competitive:

> All the strife of singularity,
> Lies to the ear, and lies to every sense.

Wordsworth then moves to his most general description of this many sided alienation:

> Foolishness, and madness in parade,
> Though most at home in this their dearest school,
> Are scatter'd everywhere, no rarities,
> Even to the rudest novice of the Schools.
> O Friend! one feeling was there which belong'd
> To this great City, by exclusive right;
> How often in the overflowing Streets,
> Have I gone forward with the Crowd, and said
> Unto myself, the face of every one
> That passes by me is a mystery.
> Thus have I look'd, nor ceas'd to look, oppress'd
> By thoughts of what, and whither, when and how,
> Until the shapes before my eyes became
> A second-sight procession, such as glides
> Over still mountains, or appears in dreams;
> And all the ballast of familiar life,
> The present and the past; hope, fear; all stays,
> All laws of acting, thinking, speaking man
> Went from me, neither knowing me, nor known.

The process which begins in the anonymity of others ends in the anonymity of the self. As other men become a "second-sight procession," it is not only the "ballast of familiar life" that is lost, but also all that makes one's own self human and known: the acting, thinking and speaking of man at once himself and in society. The self is alienated within the whole body of alienated relationships, and the crucial insight here is the connection between seeing others as "the crowd," the masses, and the substantial loss of one's own most general and most individual human identity.

Wordsworth then comes to a memorable image:

> A blind beggar, who, with upright face,
> Stood propp'd against a Wall, upon his Chest
> Wearing a written paper, to explain
> The story of the Man, and who he was.

The combination, in the figure, of the blindness and the identity reduced to a label, is the fact of alienated man. Yet, though Wordsworth has seen it in these precise social conditons, he goes on to generalize it into a permanent human condition:

> It seem'd
> To me that in this Label was a type,
> Or emblem, of the utmost that we know,
> Both of ourselves and of the universe;
> And on the shape of the unmoving man,
> His fixed face and sightless eyes, I look'd
> As if admonish'd from another world.

This significant conclusion is, I would argue, only the last process of alienation. It is this, as a *necessary* blindness, a *necessary absence of* connection, that the mind actually and specifically alienated concludes. The social mystery is projected into a universal mystery, as so often since, under the pressure of this overpowering experience. This structure of feeling—

> such structures as the mind
> Builds for itself

—is now a large part of modern consciousness: the crowd, the masses, the alienated wandering self, the blind and unknowing general condition.

Under the pressure of alienation, delusion is generated. It is this, ironically, that Wordsworth now sees:

> The Wax-work, Clock-work, all the marvellous craft
> Of modern Merlins, wild Beasts, Puppet-shows,
> All out-o'-the-way, far-fetch'd, perverted things,
> All freaks of Nature, all Promethean thoughts
> Of Man.

The "Parliament of Monsters," which is Bartholomew Fair, is now organically related, in this structure of feeling, to the dangerous mob—

> when half the City shall break out
> full of one passion, rage, or fear

—and to a characteristically contemporary vision of the general movement of men:

> as if the whole were one vast Mill,
> . . . vomiting, receiving.

It is this mad rush that lays "the whole creative powers of man asleep," and Wordsworth can conclude:

> Oh, blank confusion! and a type not false
> Of what the mighty City is itself
> To all except a Straggler here and there,
> To the whole Swarm of its inhabitants;
> An undistinguishable world to men,
> The slaves unrespited of low pursuits,
> Living amid the same perpetual flow
> Of trivial objects, melted and reduced
> To one identity, by differences
> That have no law, no meaning and no end;
> Oppression under which even highest minds
> Must labour, whence the strongest are not free.

Thus the alienation, the reduction to the "one identity" of the masses, are seen as social—"what the mighty city is itself," and the men themselves are seen as "slaves unrespited." Yet the structure fixes on the "Swarm," the distinction between "low pursuits" and "highest minds," and, thus, on withdrawal. Wordsworth responds to his own remarkable vision of an alienated social condition with a reaffirmation of the power of his own mind, educated by Nature, to retain order, relation, and composure. There is the way out, he still thinks, from these "self-destroying transitory things" to "composure and ennobling Harmony." His way is from the City to Nature, where the love of humankind can be reaffirmed. He can look back at the City and acknowledge

> that among the multitudes
> . . . oftentimes was seen,
> Affectingly set forth, more than elsewhere
> Is possible, the unity of man.

The human instinct survives, as a potential, and within the vast City there are many "individual sights of courage, and integrity, and truth, and tenderness." The acknowledgments are important, especially the first, but the love of man, the belief in the unity of man, have now been qualified by an act of resignation and withdrawal. Under the pressure of actual alienation, the idea of humanity has been itself abstracted and, set over against the idea of the Swarm, qualified. We need no reminder, now, that the perception of alienation, even as a social fact, can lead either way: to the practice of individual preservation, within a grievous general condition, or to the practice of revolution, which would seek to end the condition. Blake and Wordsworth, this early, point the different ways.

III

The writings we have examined were for the most part completed by 1805. In the subsequent forty years, the experience of alienation is very widely recorded, but I will confine myself here to tracing one line of thought: that which brought together the experience of social isolation and the analysis of a competitive industrial society. The key figure, in England, is Carlyle, who, of course, in his work from the 1820s was influenced by the German tradition in which the main philosophical development of the idea of alienation was taking place. It needs also to be emphasized, however, how much continuity there is, in Carlyle, from Blake and Wordsworth and from the English Romantic structure of feeling in which this kind of unified personal and social criticism was embodied. Carlyle, like Blake, saw a fundamental connection between philosophical mechanism and factual industrialism, and was as insistent on the total effects of this change on the whole substance of man:

> Mechanism has now struck its roots down into man's most intimate, primary sources of conviction; and is thence sending up, over his whole life and activity, innumerable stems—fruit-bearing and poison-bearing.

When he turned to describe alienation, in *Sartor Resartus,* the continuity from Wordsworth is striking:

> Invisible yet impenetrable walls, as of Enchantment, divided me from all living . . . Now, when I look back, it was a strange isolation I then lived in. The men and women around me, even speaking with me, were but Figures; I had, practically, forgotten that they were alive, that they were not merely automatic. In midst of their crowded streets and assemblages, I walked solitary: and (except as it was my own heart, not another's, that I kept devouring) savage also, as the tiger in his jungle.

This, in Carlyle's terminology, is the state of the "Everlasting No," and the emphasis is on a spiritual condition. Yet the transformation, to the "Everlasting Yea," is, significantly, through action:

> Yes here, in this poor, miserable, hampered, despicable Actual, wherein thou even now standest, here or nowhere is thy Ideal: work it out therefrom; and, working, believe, live, be free. Fool! the Ideal is in thyself, the impediment too is in thyself: thy Condition is but the stuff thou art to shape that same Ideal out of . . .

The call is to be "no longer a Chaos, but a World."

It is then not surprising that Carlyle's analysis of the social crisis engulfing industrial England should be in terms of alienation:

> Man has lost the *soul* out of him; and now, after the due period, begins to find the want of it. This is verily the plague-spot; centre of the universal Social Gangrene, threatening all modern things with frightful death. To him that will consider it, here is the stem, with its roots and taproot, with its world-wide upas-boughs and accursed poison-exudations, under which the world lies writhing in atrophy and agony.

In an important sense, this is clearly a metaphysical analysis, but its importance is that it diagnosed the social crisis not in terms of faulty adjustment, as so many liberal thinkers were doing, but as an alienation. Contemporary society is seen as "Unnature," and the first example Carlyle gives of this is the transformation of things to items of selling and exchange. This transformation, which he goes on to call Mammonism, is then the practice of social alienation.

> We for the present, with our Mammon-gospel, have come to strange conclusions. We call it a Society; and go about professing openly the totalest separation, isolation. Our life is not a mutual helpfulness; but rather, cloaked under due laws-of-war, named "fair competition" and so forth, it is a mutual hostility. We have profoundly forgotten everywhere that Cash-payment is not the sole-relation of human beings; we think, nothing doubting, that *it* absolves and liquidates all engagements of man.

He relates this to wage-labor and its degradation of work, with its result that the

> Sons of toil sit enchanted, by the million, in their Poor-Law Bastille, as if this were Nature's Law

and concludes that

> Labour must become a seeing rational giant, with a *soul* in the body of him, and take his place on the throne of things.

It is certainly not surprising to learn that Engels, reading this in *Past and Present,* was sufficiently impressed to write a review for the *Deutsch-Französische Jahrbücher,* which then, in 1843, the young Marx was editing. It was in 1844 that Marx wrote his own first sketch of a socialist theory of alienation.

I am not suggesting that Carlyle was the decisive influence on Marx in this respect, though he was certainly an important influence, in his very individual combination of a philosophical theory of alienation with a critique of capitalist society. I do not think, in any case, that we ought to see all ideas of alienation merely as leading to Marx, and deriving their importance from that fact. I believe that Marx's ability to make a more precise analysis of capitalism, and to relate this to an idea of socialism which was more politically fruitful than anything Carlyle could arrive at, was indeed a major breakthrough. Carlyle's inability to reach this point drove him steadily back into positions which are ultimately reactionary, and this is also generally true of one line (though not the main line, from Carlyle through Ruskin to Morris) of the English Romantic tradition. But, while we acknowledge the great importance of Marx's synthesis, we have also to observe, particularly at the present stage of the tradition deriving from Marx, how much, in detail, the synthesis excluded. It is impossible to read Blake's description of the alienation of human passions without realizing how much is lost in any theory of alienation which practically excludes this substantial personal life. The necessary acknowledgment of social man produced an emphasis which has dangerously diminished the attention of socialists to our whole emotional life, and which at times, even, has hardened into a philistinism, indeed an alienation, of the human passions. Equally, the attention directed by Blake and Wordsworth to the social effects of the city—the anonymous community; of factory work—the fragmentation within the process as well as in the social relations; and to the distortions of human communication, by image-making and advertisement, comes through as still centrally relevant and still theoretically unsatisfied. As we continue to examine, in our own lives, the whole complex of alienation, we shall do well to attend to this prelude.

The Decline of the Protestant Ethic

William H. Whyte, Jr.

Let us go back a moment to the turn of the century. If we pick up the Protestant Ethic as it was then expressed we will find it apparently in full flower. We will also find, however, an ethic that already had been strained by reality. The country had changed. The ethic had not.

Here, in the words of banker Henry Clews as he gave some fatherly advice to Yale students in 1908, is the Protestant Ethic in purest form:

> *Survival of Fittest:* You may start in business, or the professions, with your feet on the bottom rung of the ladder; it rests with you to acquire the strength to climb to the top. You can do so if you have the will and the force to back you. There is always plenty of room at the top. . . . Success comes to the man who tries to compel success to yield to him. Cassius spoke well to Brutus when he said, "The Fault is not in our stars, dear Brutus, that we are underlings, but in our natures."

Thrift: Form the habit as soon as you become a money-earner, or money-maker, of saving a part of your salary, or profits. Put away one dollar out of every ten you earn. The time will come in your lives when, if you have a little money, you can control circumstances; otherwise circumstances will control you. . . .

Note the use of such active words as *climb, force, compel, control.* As stringently as ever before, the Protestant Ethic still counseled struggle against one's environment—the kind of practical, here and now struggle that paid off in material rewards. And spiritually too. The hard-boiled part of the Protestant Ethic was incomplete, of course, without the companion assurance that such success was moral as well as practical. To continue with Mr. Clews:

Under this free system of government, whereby individuals are free to get a living or to pursue wealth as each chooses, the usual result is competition. Obviously, then, competition really means industrial freedom. Thus, anyone may choose his own trade or profession, or, if he does not like it, he may change. He is free to work hard or not; he may make his own bargains and set his price upon his labor or his products. He is free to acquire property to any extent, or to part with it. By dint of greater effort or superior skill, or by intelligence, if he can make better wages, he is free to live better, just as his neighbor is free to follow his example and to learn to excel him in turn. If anyone has a genius for making and managing money, he is free to exercise his genius, just as another is free to handle his tools. . . . If an individual enjoys his money, gained by energy and successful effort, his neighbors are urged to work the harder, that they and their children may have the same enjoyment.

It was an exuberantly optimistic ethic. If everyone could believe that seeking his self-interest automatically improves the lot of all, then the application of hard work should eventually produce a heaven on earth. Some, like the garrulous Mr. Clews, felt it already had.

America is the true field for the human race. It is the hope and the asylum for the oppressed and downtrodden of every clime. It is the inspiring example of America—peerless among the nations of the earth, the brightest star in the political firmament—that is leavening the hard lump of aristocracy and promoting a democratic spirit throughout the world. It is indeed the gem of the ocean to which the world may well offer homage. Here merit is the sole test. Birth is nothing. The fittest survive. Merit is the supreme and only qualification essential to success. Intelligence rules worlds and systems of worlds. It is the dread monarch of illimitable space, and in human society, especially in America, it shines as a diadem on the foreheads of those who stand in the foremost

> ranks of human enterprise. Here only a natural order of nobility is recognized, and its motto, without coat of arms or boast of heraldry, is "Intelligence and integrity."*

Without this ethic capitalism would have been impossible. Whether the Protestant Ethic preceded capitalism, as Max Weber argued, or whether it grew up as a consequence, in either event it provided a degree of unity between the way people wanted to behave and the way they thought they *ought* to behave, and without this ideology, society would have been hostile to the entrepreneur. Without the comfort of the Protestant Ethic, he couldn't have gotten away with his acquisitions—not merely because other people wouldn't have allowed him, but because his own conscience would not have. But now he was fortified by the assurance that he was pursuing his obligation to God, and before long, what for centuries had been looked on as the meanest greed, a rising middle class would interpret as the earthly manifestation of God's will.

But the very industrial revolution which this highly serviceable ethic begot in time began to confound it. The inconsistencies were a long while in making themselves apparent. The nineteenth-century inheritors of the ethic were creating an increasingly collective society but steadfastly they denied the implications of it. In current retrospect the turn of the century seems a golden age of individualism, yet by the 1880s the corporation had already shown the eventual bureaucratic direction it was going to take. As institutions grew in size and became more stratified, they made all too apparent inconsistencies which formerly could be ignored. One of the key assumptions of the Protestant Ethic had been that success was due neither to luck nor to the environment but only to one's natural qualities—if men grew rich it was because they deserved to. But the big organization became a standing taunt to this dream of individual success. Quite obviously to anyone who worked in a big organization, those who survived best were not necessarily the fittest but, in more cases than not, those who by birth and personal connections had the breaks.

As organizations continued to expand, the protestant ethic became more and more divergent from the reality. The Organization was itself creating. The managers steadfastly denied the change, but they, as much as those they led, were affected by it. Today, some still deny the inconsistency or blame it on creeping socialism; for the younger

---

* Henry Clews, *Fifty Years in Wall Street* (New York: Irving Publishing Company, 1908).

generation of managers however, the inconsistencies have become importuning.

Thrift, for example. How can the organization man be thrifty? Other people are thrifty *for* him. He still buys most of his own life insurance, but for the bulk of his rainy-day saving, he gives his proxy to the financial and personnel departments of his organization. In his professional capacity also thrift is becoming a little un-American. The same man who will quote from Benjamin Franklin on thrift for the house organ would be horrified if consumers took these maxims to heart and started putting more money into savings and less into installment purchases. No longer can he afford the luxury of damning the profligacy of the public; not in public, at any rate. He not only has to persuade people to buy more but persuade them out of any guilt feelings they might have for following his advice. Few talents are more commercially sought today than the knack of describing departures from the Protestant Ethic as reaffirmations of it.*

In an advertisement that should go down in social history, the J. Walter Thompson agency has hit the problem of absolution head-on. It quotes Benjamin Franklin on the benefits of spending. "Is not the hope of being one day able to purchase and enjoy luxuries a great spur to labor and industry? . . . May not luxury therefore produce more than it consumes, if, without such a spur, people would be, as they are naturally enough inclined to be, lazy and indolent?" This thought, the ad says, in a meaningful aside, "appears to be a mature afterthought, qualifying his earlier and more familiar writings on the importance of thrift."

"Hard work?" what price capitalism, the question is now so frequently asked, unless we turn our productivity into more leisure, more of the good life? To the organization man this makes abundant sense, and he is as sensitive to the bogy of overwork and ulcers as his forebears were to the bogy of slothfulness. But he is split. He believes in leisure, but so does he believe in the Puritan insistence on hard, self-denying work—and there are, alas, only twenty-four hours a day. How, then, to be "broad gauge"? The "broad-gauge" model we

* Helping in this task is what a good part of "motivation research" is all about. Motivation researcher Dr. Ernest Dichter, in a bulletin to business, says, "We are now confronted with the problem of permitting the average American to feel moral even when he is flirting, even when he is spending, even when he is not saving, even when he is taking two vacations a year and buying a second or third car. One of the basic problems of this prosperity, then, is to give people the sanction and justification to enjoy it and to demonstrate that the hedonistic approach to his life is a moral, not an immoral one."

hear so much about these days is the man who keeps his work separate from leisure and the rest of his life. Any organization man who managed to accomplish this feat wouldn't get very far. He still works hard, in short, but now he has to feel somewhat guilty about it.

Self-reliance? The corporation estates have been expanding so dynamically of late that until about now the management man could suppress the thought that he was a bureaucrat—bureaucrats, as every businessman knew, were those people down in Washington who preferred safety to adventure. Just when the recognition began to dawn, no one can say, but since the war the younger generation of management haven't been talking of self-reliance and adventure with quite the straight face of their elders.

That upward path toward the rainbow of achievement leads smack through the conference room. No matter what name the process is called—permissive management, multiple management, the art of administration—the committee way simply can't be equated with the "rugged" individualism that is supposed to be the business of business. Not for lack of ambition do the younger men dream so moderately; what they lack is the illusion that they will carry on in the great entrepreneurial spirit. Although they cannot bring themselves to use the word bureaucrat, the approved term—the "administrator"—is not signally different in its implications. The man of the future, as junior executives see him, is not the individualist but the man who works through others for others.

Let me pause for a moment to emphasize a necessary distinction. Within business there are still many who cling resolutely to the Protestant Ethic, and some with as much rapacity as drove any nineteenth-century buccaneer. But only rarely are they of The Organization. Save for a small, and spectacular, group of financial operators, most who adhere to the old creed are small businessmen, and to group them as part of the "business community," while convenient, implies a degree of ideological kinship with big business that does not exist.

Out of inertia, the small business is praised as the acorn from which a great oak may grow, the shadow of one man that may lengthen into a large enterprise. Examine businesses with fifty or less employees, however, and it becomes apparent the sentimentality obscures some profound differences. You will find some entrepreneurs in the classic sense—men who develop new products, new appetites, or new systems of distribution—and some of these enterprises may mature into self-perpetuating institutions. But very few.

The great majority of small business firms cannot be placed on any continuum with the corporation. For one thing, they are rarely engaged in primary industry; for the most part they are the laundries, the insurance agencies, the restaurants, the drugstores, the bottling plants, the lumber yards, the automobile dealers. They are vital, to be sure, but essentially they service an economy; they do not create new money within their area and they are dependent ultimately on the business and agriculture that does.

In this dependency they react more as antagonists than allies with the corporation. The corporation, it has become clear, is expansionist—a force for change that is forever a threat to the economics of the small businessman. By instinct he inclines to the monopolistic and the restrictive. When the druggists got the "Fair Trade" laws passed it was not only the manufacturers (and customers) they were rebelling against but the whole mass economy movement of the twentieth century.

The tail wagged the dog in this case and it still often does. That it can, in the face of the growing power of the corporation, illustrates again the dominance mythology can have over reality. Economically, many a small businessman is a counterrevolutionist and the revolution he is fighting is that of the corporation as much as the New or Fair Deal. But the corporation man still clings to the idea that the two are firm allies, and on some particulars, such as fair trade, he often makes policy on this basis when in fact it is against the corporation's interests to do so.

But the revolution is not to be stopped by sentiment. Many anachronisms do remain; in personal income, for example, the corporation man who runs a branch plant on which a whole town depends is lucky to make half the income of the local car dealer or the man with the Coca-Cola franchise. The economy has a way of attending to these discrepancies, however, and the local businessman can smell the future as well as anyone else. The bland young man The Organization sent to town to manage the plant is almost damnably inoffensive; he didn't rent the old place on the hill but a smaller house, he drives an Olds instead of a Caddy, and when he comes to the Thursday luncheons he listens more than he talks. But he's the future just the same.

I have been talking of the impact of organization on the Protestant Ethic; just as important, however, was the intellectual assault. In the great revolt against traditionalism that began around the turn of the century, William James, John Dewey, Charles Beard, Thorstein Veblen, the muckrakers and a host of reformers brought the anachronisms of the Protestant Ethic under relentless fire, and in so doing helped lay the groundwork for the Social Ethic. It would be a long time before organization men would grasp the relevance of these new ideas, and to this day many of the most thoroughgoing pragmatists in business would recoil at being grouped with the intellectuals. (And vice versa.) But the two movements were intimately related. To what degree the intellectuals were a cause of change, or a manifestation, no one can say for certain, but more presciently than those in organization they grasped the antithesis between the old concept of the rational, unbeholden individual and the world one had to live in. They were not rebels against society; what they fought was the denial of society's power, and they provided an intellectual framework that would complement, rather than inhibit, the further growth of big organization.

It is not in the province of this book to go into a diagnosis of the ideas of Dewey and James and the other pragmatists. But there is one point of history I think very much needs making at this time. Many people still look on the decline of the Protestant Ethic as our fall from grace, a detour from Americanism for which we can blame pragmatism, ethical relativism, Freudianism and other such developments. These movements have contributed much to the Social Ethic, and many of their presuppositions are as shaky as those they replaced. To criticize them on this score is in order; to criticize them as having subverted the American temper, however, is highly misleading.

Critics of pragmatism, and followers too, should remember the context of the times in which the pragmatists made their case. The pragmatists' emphasis on social utility may be redundant for today's needs, but when they made their case it was not a time when psychology or adjustment or social living were popular topics but at a time when the weight of conservative opinion denied that there was anything much that needed adjusting. Quite clearly, revolt was in order. The growth of the organization society did demand a recognition that man was not entirely a product of his free will; the country did need an educational plant more responsive to the need of the people. It did need a new breeze, and if there had been no James or no Dewey, some form of pragmatism would probably have been invented anyway. Nonphilosophical Americans sensed that changes were in order too; what the philosophers of pragmatism did was to give them guidance and tell them in intellectually responsible terms that they were right in feeling that way.

Pragmatism's emphasis on the social and the practical, furthermore, was thoroughly in the American tradition. From the beginning, Americans had always been impatient with doctrines and systems; like the Puritans, many came here because of a doctrine, but what they came to was a new environment that required some powerful adapting to, and whenever the doctrine got in the way of practicality, the doctrine lost out. Few people have had such a genius for bending ideals to the demands of the times, and the construction of fundamental theory, theological or scientific, has never excited Americans overmuch. Long before James, *Does it work?* was a respectable question to ask. If impatience at abstract thought was a defect, it was the defect of a virtue, and the virtue, call it what you will, has always been very close to pragmatism as Dewey and James defined it. By defining it they gave it coherence and power at a time when it needed assertion, but the inclination to the practical antedated the philosophy; it was not the product of it.

Reform was everywhere in the air. By the time of the first World War the Protestant Ethic had taken a shellacking from which it would not recover; rugged individualism and hard work had done wonders for the people to whom God in his infinite wisdom, as one put it, had given control of society. But it hadn't done so well for everyone else and now they, as well as the intellectuals, were all too aware of the fact.

The ground, in short, was ready, and though the conservative opinion that drew the fire of the rebels seemed entrenched, the basic temper of the country was so inclined in the other direction that emphasis on the social became the dominant current of U.S. thought. In a great outburst of curiosity, people became fascinated with the discovering of all the environmental pressures on the individual that previous philosophies had denied. As with Freud's discoveries, the findings of such inquiries were deeply disillusioning at first, but with characteristic exuberance Americans found a rainbow. Man might not be perfectible after all, but there was another dream and now at last it seemed practical: the perfectibility of *society*.

Labor, Leisure, and the New Class

John Kenneth Galbraith

In a society of high and increasing affluence there are three plausible tendencies as regards toil. As the production of goods comes to seem less urgent, and as individuals are less urgently in need of income for the purchase of goods, they will work fewer hours or days in the week. Or they will work less hard. Or, as a final possibility, it may be that fewer people will work all the time.

In the last century a drastic decline has occurred in the work week. In 1850 it is estimated to have averaged just under seventy hours, the equivalent of seven ten-hour days a week or roughly six at from six in the morning to six at night. A hundred years later the average was 40.0 hours or five eight-hour days.[1]

From *The Affluent Society* by John Kenneth Galbraith. Reprinted by permission of Houghton Mifflin Company.

[1] J. Frederic Dewhurst and Associates, *America's Needs and Resources,* A New Survey, p. 1053. These figures are the weighted average of agricultural and non-agricultural workers. The average work week in nonagricultural enterprise in 1950 was estimated to be 38.8 hours.

This decline reflects a tacit but unmistakable acceptance of the declining marginal urgency of goods. There is no other explanation. However, such is the hold of production on our minds that this explanation is rarely offered. The importance and rewards of leisure are urged, almost never the unimportance of goods. Or, since production per hour has been increasing as the work week has declined, it is said that we are able to reduce the work because more is produced in less time. No mention is made of the fact that even more would be produced in more time. Or, finally, the decline is related to the feeling that steps must be taken to share the available work as productivity per worker rises. This also implies that the marginal urgency of production is low or negligible, but again the point remains unmade.

A reduction in the work week is an exceedingly plausible reaction to the declining marginal urgency of product. Over the span of man's history, although a phenomenal amount of education, persuasion, indoctrination, and incantation have been devoted to the effort, ordinary people have never been quite persuaded that toil is as agreeable as its alternatives. Thus to take increased well-being partly in the form of more goods and partly in the form of more leisure is unquestionably rational. In addition, the institution of overtime enables the worker to go far to adjust work and income to his own taste and requirements. It breaks with the barbarous uniformity of the weekly wage with its assumption that all families have the same tastes, needs, and requirements. Few things enlarge the liberty of the individual more substantially than to grant him a measure of control over the amount of his income.

Unfortunately in the conventional wisdom the reduction in hours has emerged as the only legitimate response to increasing affluence. This is at least partly because the issue has never been faced in terms of the increasing unimportance of goods. Accordingly, though we have attributed value to leisure, a ban still lies on other courses which seem to be more directly in conflict with established attitudes on productive efficiency. In a society rationally concerned with its own happiness these alternatives have a strong claim to consideration.

II

The first of these is that work can be made easier and more pleasant. The present-day industrial establishment is a greater distance removed from that of the last century or even of twenty-five years ago. This improvement has been the result of a variety of forces—government standards and factory inspection; general technological and architectural advance; the fact that productivity could be often increased by substituting machine power for heavy or repetitive manual labor; the need to compete for a labor force; and union intervention to improve working conditions in addition to wages and hours.

However, except where the improvement contributed to increased productivity, the effort to make work more pleasant has had to support a large burden of proof. It was permissible to seek the elimination of hazardous, unsanitary, unhealthful, or otherwise objectionable conditions of work. The speed-up might be resisted—to a point. But the test was not what was agreeable but what was unhealthful or, at a minimum, excessively fatiguing. The trend toward increased leisure is not reprehensible, but we resist vigorously the notion that a man should work less hard while on the job. Here older attitudes are involved. We are gravely suspicious of any tendency to expend less than the maximum effort, for this has long been a prime economic virtue.

In strict logic there is as much to be said for making work pleasant and agreeable as for shortening hours. On the whole it is probably as important for a wage earner to have pleasant working conditions as a pleasant home. To a degree, he can escape the latter but not the former—though no doubt the line between an agreeable tempo and what is flagrant feather-bedding is difficult to draw. Moreover, it is a commonplace of the industrial scene that the dreariest and most burdensome tasks, requiring as they do a minimum of thought and skill, frequently have the largest numbers of takers. The solution to this problem lies, as we shall see presently, in drying up the supply of crude manpower at the bottom of the ladder. Nonetheless the basic point remains: the case for more leisure is not stronger on purely *prima facie* grounds than the case for making labor-time itself more agreeable. The test, it is worth repeating, is not the effect on productivity. It is not seriously argued that the shorter work week increases productivity—that men produce more in fewer hours than they would in more. Rather it is whether fewer hours are always to be preferred to more but more pleasant ones.

III

The third of the obvious possibilities with increasing affluence is for fewer people to work. This tendency has also been operating for many years although in a remarkably diverse form. Since 1890, when one boy in four and one girl in ten between the ages of ten and fifteen were gainfully employed, large numbers of juveniles have been retired from the labor force and their number now is negligible. At the same time a large number of women have been added. In 1890 19.5 per cent of the female population ten years and over was in the labor force and by 1953 this proportion had risen to 29.7 per cent.[2] However, this change reflects in considerable measure the shift of tasks—food preparation, clothing manufacture, even child-rearing—out of the home. Women who previously performed them have gone along to other work. The woman who takes charge of a day nursery has joined the labor force, as have the women whose children she cares for.

For seventy-five years the proportion of the male population in the labor force has been constant at around seventy-five per cent of those over ten years of age. There are a smaller percentage of the very young and of those over sixty-five, but this has been offset by the increase in population in the ages between twenty and sixty-five where the proportion of workers to the total is very high.[3]

With diminishing marginal urgency of goods it is logical that the first to be spared should be old and young. We have yet, however, to view this tendency consistently and comprehensively. We are able to dispense with the labor of those who have reached retiring age because the goods they add are a low order of urgency, whereas a poor society must extract the last ounce of labor effort from all. But we have ordinarily subjected those who retire to a drastic reduction in income and living standards. Obviously, if the retirement can be afforded because the product is no longer urgent, a satisfactory—meaning for most purposes the customary—living standard can be accorded to the retired employee for the same reason. Similarly we have excluded youngsters from the labor market, partly on the ground that labor at too early an age is unduly painful and injurious to health, and partly to make way for educational opportunity. But while we have felt it possible to dispense with the goods that the youngsters produce, we have yet to provide them, at least in full and satisfactory measure, with the education that their exemption from labor was designed to make possible. If we are affluent enough to dispense with the product of juvenile labor, it again follows that we are affluent enough to provide the education that takes its place.

In addition to releasing the old and young, it may be that we need not use all of the labor force at all times. This possibility was explored in Chapter XVII [of *The Affluent Society*]. If the marginal urgency of goods is low, then so is the urgency of employing the last man or the last million men in the labor force. By allowing ourselves such slack, in turn, we reduce the standards of economic performance to a

[2] *Ibid.*, pp. 726-27.

[3] *Ibid.*, pp. 725-26.

level more nearly consonant with the controls available for its management. And in so widening the band of what is deemed tolerable performance lies our best hope of minimizing the threat of inflation with its further and persistent threat to social balance.

Such a step requires much more adequate provision than now for those who are temporarily unemployed. We have seen, however, that such measures are possible and, indeed, have a vital stabilizing effect. And again such compensation accords with the logic of the situation. If our need for production is of such a low order of urgency that we can afford some unemployment in the interest of stability—a proposition, incidentally, of impeccably conservative antecedents—then we can afford to give those who are unemployed the goods that enable them to sustain their accustomed standard of living. If we don't need what the unemployed do not make, we can obviously afford them what they customarily eat and wear.

IV

However, the greatest prospect that we face—indeed what must now be counted one of the central economic goals of our society—is to eliminate toil as a required economic institution. This is not a utopian vision. We are already well on the way. Only an extraordinarily elaborate exercise in social camouflage has kept us from seeing what has been happening.

Nearly all societies at nearly all times have had a leisure class—a class of persons who were exempt from toil. In modern times and especially in the United States the leisure class, at least in any identifiable phenomenon, has disappeared. To be idle is no longer considered rewarding or even entirely respectable.

But we have barely noticed that the leisure class has been replaced by another and much larger class to which work has none of the older connotation of pain, fatigue, or other mental or physical discomfort. We have failed to appreciate the emergence of this New Class, as it may be simply called, largely as the result of one of the oldest and most effective obfuscations in the field of social science. This is the effort to assert that all work—physical, mental, artistic, or managerial—is essentially the same.

This effort to proclaim the grand homogeneity of work has commanded, for different reasons, the support of remarkably numerous and diverse groups. To economists it has seemed a harmless and, indeed, an indispensable simplification. It has enabled them to deal homogeneously with all of the different kinds of productive effort and to elaborate a general theory of wages applying to all who receive an income for services. Doubts have arisen from time to time, but they have been suppressed or considered to concern special cases.[4] The identity of all classes of labor is one thing on which capitalist and Communist doctrine wholly agree. The president of the corporation is pleased to think that his handsomely appointed office is the scene of the same kind of toil as the assembly line and that only the greater demands in talent and intensity justify his wage differential. The Communist officeholder cannot afford to have it supposed that his labor differs in any significant respect from that of the comrade at the lathe or on the collective farm with whom he is ideologically one. In both societies it serves the democratic conscience of the more favored groups to identify themselves with those who do hard physical labor. A lurking sense of guilt over a more pleasant, agreeable, and remunerative life can often be assuaged by the observation "I am a worker too" or, more audaciously, by the statement that "mental labor is far more taxing than physical labor." Since the man who does physical labor is intellectually disqualified from comparing his toil with that of the brainworker, the proposition is uniquely unassailable.

In fact the differences in what labor means to different people could not be greater. For some, and probably a majority, it remains a stint to be performed. It may be preferable, especially in the context of social attitudes toward production, to doing nothing. Nevertheless it is fatiguing or monotonous or, at a minimum, a source of no particular pleasure. The reward rests not in the task but in the pay.

For others work, as it continues to be called, is an entirely different matter. It is taken for granted that it will be enjoyable. If it is not, this is a source of deep dissatisfaction or frustration. No one regards it as remarkable that the advertising man, tycoon, poet, or professor who suddenly finds his work unrewarding should seek the counsel of a psychiatrist. One insults the business executive or the scientist by suggesting that his principal motivation in life is the pay he receives. Pay is not unimportant. Among other things it is prime index of prestige. Prestige—the respect, regard, and esteem of others—is in turn one of the more important sources of satisfaction associated

---

[4] Marshall defined labor as "any exertion of mind or body undergone partly or wholly with a view to some good other than the pleasure derived directly from the work." (*Principles of Economics*, p. 65.) This definition obviously recognizes a category of individuals for whom work is a reward in itself. However, this group, having been introduced, plays little or no further part in Marshall's analysis. It has played almost no formal role in economic theory since.

with this kind of work. But, in general, those who do this kind of work expect to contribute their best regardless of compensation. They would be disturbed by any suggestion to the contrary.[5]

Such is the labor of the New Class. No aristocrat ever contemplated the loss of feudal privileges with more sorrow than a member of this class would regard his descent into ordinary labor where the reward was only the pay. In the years following World War II a certain number of grade schoolteachers left their posts for substantially higher paid factory work. The action made headlines because it represented an unprecedented desertion of an occupation which was assumed to confer the dignity of the New Class. The college professor, who is more securely a member of the New Class than the schoolteacher, would never contemplate such a change even as an exercise in eccentricity and no matter how inadequate he might consider his income.

In keeping with all past class behavior, the New Class seeks energetically to perpetuate itself. Offspring are not expected to plan their lives in order to make a large amount of money. (Those who go into business are something of an exception at least partly because income, in business, is uniquely an index of prestige.) But from their earliest years the children are carefully indoctrinated in the importance of finding an occupation from which they will derive satisfaction—one which will involve not toil but enjoyment. One of the principal sources of sorrow and frustration in the New Class is the son who fails to make the grade—who drops down into some tedious and unrewarding occupation. The individual who meets with this misfortune—the son of the surgeon who becomes a garage hand—is regarded by the community with pity not unmixed with horror. But the New Class has considerable protective powers. The son of the surgeon rarely does become a garage hand. However inadequate, he can usually manage to survive, perhaps somewhat exiguously, on the edge of his caste. And even if, as a salesman or an investment counselor, he finds little pleasure in his work, he will be expected to assert the contrary in order to affirm his membership in the New Class.

---

[5] We have here an important reason why the income tax, despite high marginal rates and frequent warnings of the damage these may do in imparing incentives, has so far had no visibly deleterious effect. The surtax rates fall almost entirely on members of the New Class. These are people who, by their own claim except when they are talking about the effect of income taxes, are not primarily motivated by money. Hence the tax, which also does not disturb the prestige structure—people are rated by before-tax income—touches no vital incentive. Were high marginal rates to be placed on (say) the overtime income of automobile workers we would expect a substantial withdrawal of effort. Here pay, as an incentive, remains important.

V

The New Class is not exclusive. While virtually no one leaves it, thousands join it every year. Overwhelmingly the qualification is education.[6] Any individual whose adolescent situation is such that sufficient time and money is invested in his preparation, and who has at least the talents to carry him through the formal academic routine, can be a member. There is a hierarchy within the class. The son of the factory worker who becomes an electrical engineer is on the lower edge; his son who does graduate work and becomes a university physicist moves to the higher echelons; but opportunity for education is, in either case, the open sesame.

There can be little question that in the last hundred years, and even in the last few decades, the New Class has increased enormously in size. In early nineteenth-century England or the United States, excluding the leisure class and considering the New Class as a group that lived on what it has carefully called earned income, it consisted only of a handful of educators and clerics, with, in addition, a trifling number of writers, journalists, and artists. In the United States of the eighteen-fifties it could not have numbered more than a few thousand individuals. Now the number whose primary identification is with their job, rather than the income it returns, is undoubtedly in the millions.

Some of the attractiveness of membership in the New Class, to be sure, derives from a vicarious feeling of superiority—another manifestation of class attitudes. However, membership in the class unquestionably has other and more important rewards. Exemption from manual toil; escape from boredom and confining and severe routine; the chance to spend one's life in clean and physically comfortable surroundings; and some opportunity for applying one's thoughts to the day's work, are regarded as unimportant only to those who take them

---

[6] Political capacity is another qualification, and it is of especial importance to those who seek to make their escape after reaching their adult years. The intensity of the campaigns for local political offices—city councilors, school committeemen, sheriffs, and county supervisors—is to be explained by this fact as also is the enduring interest in appointive political office. Those who are already members of the New Class often fail to see how such posts are valued as an *entrée*. They look askance at the competition for such posts between the less well educated members of the community. They fail to realize that such posts provide the greatest opportunity for such individuals and that it is upon such people that we depend for much good (as well as some bad) civic enterprise. The union is another important opportunity for the individual of political capacity. Cf. the interesting sketches by Harvey Swados in *On the Line* (Boston: Atlantic-Little, Brown, 1957).

completely for granted. For these reasons it has been possible to expand the New Class greatly without visibly reducing its attractiveness.

This being so, there is every reason to conclude that the further and rapid expansion of this class should be a major and perhaps next to peaceful survival itself, *the* major social goal of the society. Since education is the operative factor in expanding the class, investment in education, assessed qualitatively as well as quantitatively, becomes very close to being the basic index of social progress. It enables people to realize a dominant aspiration. It is an internally consistent course of development.

Recent experience has shown that the demand for individuals in the occupations generally identified with the New Class increases much more proportionately with increased income and well-being. Were the expansion of the New Class a deliberate objective of the society this, with its emphasis on education and its ultimate effect on intellectual, literary, cultural, and artistic demands, would greatly broaden the opportunities for membership. At the same time the shrinking in the number of those who engage in work *qua* work is something to be regarded not alone with equanimity but with positive approval. For one of the inevitable outlets for the intellectual energies and inventiveness of the New Class will be in finding substitutes for routine and repetitive manual labor. To the extent that such labor is made scarce and more expensive, this tendency will, of course, be accelerated. To minimize the number of people doing such work is the counterpart of the goal of expanding the New Class.

It is a measure of how little we need worry about the danger from reducing the number of people engaged in work *qua* work that, as matters now stand, our concern is not that we will have too few available for toil but too many. We worry lest such technical advances as automation, an already realized dividend of the expansion of the New Class, will proceed so rapidly as to leave a surplus of those who still work. This, indeed, could be the greater danger.

VI

I venture to suggest that the unprofessional reader will find rather reasonable and rational the ideas here offered. Why should men struggle to maximize income when the price is many dull and dark hours of labor? Why especially should they do so as goods become more plentiful and less urgent? Why should they not seek instead to maximize the rewards of all the hours of their days? And since this is the plain and obvious aspiration of a great and growing number of the most perceptive people, why should it not be the central goal of the society? And now to complete the case, we have a design for progress. It is education or, more broadly, investment in human as distinct from material capital.

But in the more sophisticated levels of the conventional wisdom, including, regrettably, some professional economists, any such goal will seem exceedingly undesirable. The production of material goods, urgent or otherwise, is the accepted measure of our progress. Investment in material capital is our basic engine of progress. Both this product and the means for increasing it are measurable and tangible. What is measurable is better. To talk of transferring increasing numbers of people from lives spent mostly in classical toil to lives which, for the most part, are spent pleasantly has less quantitative precision. Since investment in individuals, unlike investment in a blast furnace, provides a product that can be neither seen nor valued, it is inferior. And here the conventional wisdom unleashes its epithet of last resort. Since these achievements are not easily measured, as a goal they are "fuzzy." This is widely deemed to be a fatal condemnation. The precise, to be sure, is usually the old and familiar. Because it is old and familiar it has been defined and measured. Thus does insistence on precision become another of the tautological devices by which the conventional wisdom protects itself. Nor should one doubt its power.

Yet anyone who finds this analysis and these proposals sensible should not be entirely discouraged. We are here in one of the contexts where circumstance has marched far beyond the conventional wisdom. We have seen how general are the efforts to join the New Class and how rapid is its expansion. We are not here establishing a new economic and social goal but identifying one that is already widely if but tacitly accepted. In this situation the conventional wisdom cannot resist indefinitely. The economist of impeccable credentials in the conventional wisdom, who believes that there is no goal in life of comparable urgency with the maximization of total and individual real income, would never think of applying such a standard to himself. In his own life he is an exponent of all the aspirations of the New Class. He educates and indoctrinates his children with but one thing in mind. It is not that they should maximize their income. This is abhorrent. He wants above all that they will have an occupation that is interesting and rewarding. On this he hopes, indeed, that they will take their learned parent as their model.

The Empty Society

Paul Goodman

During Eisenhower's second Administration I wrote a book describing how hard it was for young people to grow up in the corporate institutions of American society. Yet the statistics at that time indicated that most were content to be secure as personnel of big corporations, while a few deviated in impractical and certainly unpolitical ways, like being Beat or delinquent. The system, like its President, operated with a righteous self-satisfaction. There were no signs of its being vulnerable, though a loud chorus of intellectual critics, like myself, were sounding off against it. We were spoil-sports.

Less than ten years later the feeling is different; it turns out that we critics were not altogether unrealistic. The system of institutions is still grander and more computerized, but it seems to have lost its morale. The baronial corporations are making immense amounts of money and are more openly and heavily subsidized by the monarch in Washington. The processing of the young is extended for longer years and its tempo speeded up. More capital and management are exported, interlocking with international capital, and more of the world (including Canada) is brought under American control; when necessary, remarkable military technology is brought to bear. At home there is no political check, for no matter what the currents of opinion, by and large the dominant system wreaks its will, managing the parliamentary machinery to make it look like consensus.

Nevertheless, the feeling of justification is gone. Sometimes we seem to be bulling it through only in order to save face. Enterprises often seem to be expanding simply because the managers cannot think of any other use for energy and resources. The economy is turning into a war economy. There are warnings of ecological disaster, pollution, congestion, poisoning, mental disease, anomie. We have discovered that there is hard-core poverty at home that is not easy to liquidate. And unlike the success of the Marshall Plan in Europe in the forties, it increasingly appears that poverty and unrest in Asia, Africa, and South America are not only not helped by our methods of assistance, they are perhaps made worse. There are flashes of suspicion, like flashes of lightning, that the entire system may be unviable. Influential Senators refer to our foreign policy as "arrogant" and "lawless," but in my opinion our foreign and domestic system is all of a piece and is more innocent and deadly than that: it is mindless and morally insensitive. Its pretended purposes are window-dressing for purposeless expansion and a panicky need to keep things under control.

And now very many young people no longer want to cooperate with such a system. Indeed, a large and rapidly growing number—already more than 5 percent of college students—use language that is openly revolutionary or apocalyptic, as if in their generation they were going to make a French Revolution. More and more often direct civil disobedience seems to make obvious sense. We are exerting more power and feeling less right; what does that mean for the future? I have heard serious people argue for three plausible yet drastically incompatible predictions about America during the next generation, none of them happy.

Some feel, with a kind of Vergilian despair, that the American empire will succeed and will impose for a long time, at home and abroad, its meaningless management and showy style of life. For instance, we will "win" in Vietnam, though such a victory of brute military technology will be a moral disaster. Clubbing together with the other nuclear powers, we will stave off the nuclear war and stop history with a new Congress of Vienna. American democracy will vanish into an establishment of promoters, mandarins, and technicians, though maintaining for a while an image of democracy as in the days of Augustus and Tiberius. And all this is probably the best possible outcome, given the complexities of high technology, urbanization, mass education, and overpopulation.

Others believe, in dismay and horror, that our country is overreaching and is bound for doom; but nothing can be done because policy cannot be influenced. Controlling communications, creating incidents that it then mistakes for history, deceived by its own Intelligence agents, our system is mesmerized. Like the Mikado, Washington is the captive of its military-industrial complex. The way we manage the economy and technology must increase anomie and crime. Since the war economy eats up brains and capital, we will soon be a fifth-rate economic power. With a few setbacks abroad—for instance, when we force a major South American country to become communist—and with the increasing disorder on the streets that is inevitable because our cities are unworkable, there will be a police state. The atom bombs may then go off. Such being the forecast, the part of wisdom is escape, and those who cultivate LSD are on the right track.

Still others hold that Americans are both too decent to succumb to fascism and too spirited to remain impotent clients of a managerial elite. Rather, the tide of protest will continue to rise. The excluded poor are already refusing to remain excluded, and they cannot be included without salutary changes. With the worst will in the world we cannot police the world. The reality is that we are confused. We do not know how to cope with the new technology, the economy of surplus, the fact of One World that makes national boundaries obsolete, the unworkability of traditional democracy. We must invent new forms. To be sure, the present climate of emergency is bad for the social invention and experiment that are indispensable, and there is no doubt that our overcentralized and Establishment methods of organization make everybody stupid from boss to hand. But there is hope in the young. They understand the problem in their bones. Of course they don't know much and their disaffection both from tradition and from the adult world makes it hard for them to learn anything. Nevertheless, we will learn in the inevitable conflict, which hopefully will be mainly nonviolent.

I hold this third view: American society is on a bad course, but there is hope for reconstruction through conflict. It is a wish. The evidence, so far, is stronger for either our empty success or for crackup. My feeling about this is the same as my feeling about the atom bombs. Rationally, I must judge that the bombs are almost certain to go off in this generation; yet I cannot believe that they will go off, for I do not lead my life with that expectation.

Since I have mentioned the bombs, let me stop a moment and make another comparison. Thirty years ago the Jews in Germany believed that Hitler did not mean to exterminate them: "Nobody," they said, "can be that stupid." So they drifted to the gas chambers, finally going even without resistance. Now the nuclear powers continue stockpiling bombs and pouring new billions into missiles, anti-missile missiles, and armed platforms in orbit. You Canadians, like us Americans, do not prevent it. Afterwards, survivors, if there are any, will ask, "How did we let it happen?"

I am eager, as well as honored, to be talking to a Canadian audience, especially to the Canadian young, on the state of American society. You people are not yet so wrongly committed as we: your land is less despoiled, your cities are more manageable, you are not yet so sold on mass-miseducation, you are not in the trap of militarism. A large minority of you are deeply skeptical of American methods and oppose the unquestioned extension of American power. Some of us Americans have always wistfully hoped that you Canadians would teach us a lesson or two, though, to be frank, you have usually let us down.

2. Meaningless Enterprise

In these lectures on our ambiguous position I shall have to talk a good deal about style. To illustrate the current style of American enterprise, let me analyze a small actual incident. It is perfectly typical, banal; no one would raise his eyebrows at it, it is business as usual.

Washington has alloted several billions of dollars to the schools. The schools are not teaching very well, but there is no chance that anybody will upset the applecart and ask if so much doing of lessons is the right way to educate the young altogether. Rather, there is a demand for new "methods" and mechanical equipment, which will disturb nobody, and electronics is the latest thing that every forward-looking local school board must be proud to buy. So to cut in on this melon, electronics corporations like IBM, Xerox, and so on, have hastened to combine with or take over textbook houses. My own publisher, Random House, has been bought by the Radio Corporation of America.

Just now General Electric and Time, Inc., which owns a textbook house, have put nearly $40 million into a joint subsidiary called General Learning. And an editor of *Life* has been relieved of his duties for five weeks in order to prepare a prospectus on the broad educational needs of America and the world, to come up with exciting proposals, so that General Learning can move with purpose into this unfamiliar field. The editor has collected and is boning up on the latest High

Thought on education, and in due course he invites me to lunch, to pick my brains for something new and radical. "The sky," he assures me, "is the limit." (I am known, let me explain, as a severe critic of the school establishment.) "Perhaps," he tells me at lunch, "there *is* no unique place for General Learning. They'll probably end up as prosaic makers of school hardware. But we ought to give it a try."

Consider the premises of this odd situation, where first they have the organization and the technology, and then they try to dream up a use for it. In the eighteenth century Adam Smith thought that one started with the need and only then collected capital to satisfy it. In the nineteenth century there was already a lot of capital to invest, but by and large the market served as a check, to guarantee utility, competence, and relevance. Now, however, the subsidy removes the check of the market and a promotion can expand like weeds in a well-manured field. The competence required is to have a big organization and sales force, and to be *in,* to have the prestige and connections to get the subsidy plausibly. Usually it is good to have some nominal relation to the ostensible function, *e.g.*, a textbook subsidiary related to schooling or *Time-Life* related to, let us say, learning. But indeed, when an expanding corporation becomes *very* grand, it generates an expertise of its own called systems development, applicable to anything. For example, as an expert in systems development, North American Aviation is hired to reform the penal system of California; there is no longer need to demonstrate acquaintance with any particular human function.

Naturally, with the divorce of enterprise from utility and competence, there goes a heavy emphasis on rhetoric and public relations to prove utility and competence. So an editor must be reassigned for five weeks to write a rationale. It is his task to add ideas or talking points to the enterprise, like a wrapper. The personnel of expanding corporations, of course, are busy people and have not had time to think of many concrete ideas; they can, however, phone writers and concerned professionals. Way-out radicals, especially, do a lot of thinking, since they have little practical employment. And since the enterprise is free-floating anyway, it is dandy to include in the prospectus something daring or even meaningful.

In an affluent society that can afford it there is something jolly about such an adventure of the electronics giant, the mighty publisher, the National Science Foundation that has made curriculum studies, and local school boards that want to be in the swim. Somewhere down the line, however, this cabale of decision-makers is going to coerce the time of life of real children and control the activity of classroom teachers. Those who are directly engaged in the human function of learning and teaching have no say in what goes on. This introduces a more sober note. Some of the product of the burst of corporate activity and technological virtuosity will be useful, some not—the pedagogical evidence is mixed and not extensive—but the brute fact is that the children are quite incidental to the massive intervention of the giant combinations.

I have chosen a wry example. But I could have chosen the leader of the American economy, the complex of cars, oil, and roads. This started out at the beginning of the century as a useful enterprise, remarkably suited to American conditions; but it outgrew its proper size perhaps thirty years ago, until now it is destroying both the cities and the countryside, and has been shown to be careless of even elementary safety.

Rather, let me turn abruptly to the Vietnam war, in which we notice the same family traits. Whatever made us embark on this adventure, by now we can define the Vietnam war as a commitment looking for a reason or at least a rationalization. There has been no lack of policy statements, rhetorical gestures, manufactured incidents (it seems), and plain lies (certainly); but as the war has dragged on and grown, all these have proved to be mere talking points. Ringing true, however, has been the fanfare about the superb military technology that we have deployed. The theme is used as a chief morale builder for the troops. In the absence of adequate political reasons, some have even said that the war is largely an occasion for testing new hardware and techniques. It is eerie to hear, in a news broadcast, an airman enthusiastically praising the split-second scheduling of his missions to devastate rice fields. Such appreciation of knowhow is a cheerful American disposition, but it does not do much credit to him as a grown man.

Yet what emerges most strikingly from our thinking about and prosecution of the Vietnam war is, again, the input-output accounting, the systems development, and the purely incidental significance of the human beings involved. The communiqués are concerned mainly with the body count of VC in ratio to our own losses, since there is a theory that in wars of this kind one must attain a kill-ratio of 5 to 1 or 10 to 1. According to various estimates, it costs $50,000 to $250,000 to kill one Vietnamese, hopefully an enemy. Similarly, the bombing of civilians and the destruction of their livelihood occur as if no human beings were involved; they are officially spoken of as unfortunate but incidental. (Indemnity for a dead civilian averages $34.) We claim that we have no imperialist aims in Vietnam—though we are building air bases of some very heavy concrete and steel—but evidently old-fashioned imperialism was preferable, since it tried to keep the subjugated population in existence for taxes and labor.

At home, by the same method of accounting, college students are deferred from the draft because they will be necessary to man the professions and scientific technology, while farm boys, Negroes, and Spanish-speaking Americans are drafted because they are otherwise good for nothing. That is to say, war is regarded not as a dread emergency in which each one does his bit, but as part of the ongoing business of society in which fighting and dying are usual categories of the division of labor. But this is bound to be the case when 20 percent of the Gross National Product is spent on war (using a multiplier of two), when more than half of the gross new investment since 1945 has been in war industry, and when much of higher education and science is devoted to war technology.

The Americans are not a warlike or bloodthirsty people, though violent. The dehumanizing of war is part of a general style of enterprise and control in which human utility and even the existence of particular human beings are simply not a paramount consideration. Great armaments manufacturers have said that they are willing and ready to convert their capital and skill to peaceful production when given the signal; this seems to mean that they are *indifferent* about what they enterprise. Studies of American workmen have shown that they take their moral and esthetic standards not from family, church, friends, or personal interest, but from the organization and style of work at the plant. I think that this explains the present peculiar situation that other nations of the world regard our behavior in the Vietnam war with a kind of horror, whereas Americans sincerely talk as if it were a messy job to be done as efficiently as possible.

This brings us to a broader question: What do we mean by technical efficiency in our system?

3. The Excluding Society

Corporate and bureaucratic societies, whether ruled by priests, mandarins, generals, or business managers, have always tended to diminish the importance of personal needs and human feeling, in the interest of abstractions and systemic necessities. And where there has been no check by strong community ties, effective democracy, or a free market, it has not been rare for the business of society to be largely without utility or common sense. Nevertheless, modern corporate societies that can wield a high technology are liable to a unique temptation: since they do not exploit common labor, they may tend to exclude the majority of human beings altogether, as useless for the needs of the system and therefore as not quite persons.

This has been the steady tendency in America. The aged are ruled out at an earlier age, the young until a later age. We have liquidated most small farmers. There is no place for the poor, *e.g.*, more than twenty million Negroes and Latin Americans, and a rapidly increasing number are certified as insane or otherwise incompetent. These groups already comprise more than a majority of the population. Some authorities say (though others deny) that with full automation most of the rest will also be useless.

There is nothing malevolent or heartless in the exclusion. The tone is not like that of the old exploitative society in which people were thrown out of work during the lows of the business cycle. For humane and political reasons even extraordinary efforts are made to shape the excluded into the dominant style, so they too can belong. Even though the system is going to need only a few percent with elaborate academic training, all the young are subjected to twelve years of schooling and 40 percent go to college. There is every kind of training and social service to upgrade the poor and enable the handicapped to be productive members of society. At high cost of effort and suffering, mentally retarded children must be taught to read, if only "cat" and "rat."

But a frank look shows, I think, that the long schooling is for most a way of keeping the young on ice; the job training is busywork; and the social services turn people into "community dependents" for generations. Much of the anxiety about the "handicapped" and the "underprivileged" is suburban squeamishness that cannot tolerate difference. What is *never* done, however, is to change the rules of the system, to redefine usefulness in terms of how people are, and to shape the dominant style to people. This cannot be done because it would be inefficient and, indeed, degrading, for there is only one right way to exist: Do it our way or else you are not quite a person.

Such self-righteous inflexibility is inevitably self-mesmerizing and self-proving, for other methods and values are not allowed to breathe and prove themselves. Often it would be cheaper to help people to be in their own way or at least to let them be; but anything in a different or outmoded style has "deviant" or "underprivileged" written on it, and no expense is spared to root it out in the name of efficiency. Thus it would have been cheaper to pay the small farmers to stay put if they wished. Anyway, as I shall try to show later, it is not the case in many situations that small farming and local distribution are less efficient than the plantations and national chain grocers that have supplanted them with the connivance of government policy. At present it would be far cheaper to give money directly to the urban poor to design their own lives, rather than to try to make them shape up; it has been estimated that in one area of poverty in New York City, the cost per family in special services is more than $10,000 a year; and anyway, to a candid observer, the culture of poverty is not in many respects inferior to that of the middle class, if it were allowed to be decent, if it were, as Péguy said, *pauvreté* and not *misère.* Again, very many of the young would get a better education and grow up more usefully to themselves and society if the school money were used for real apprenticeships, or even if they were given the money to follow their own interests, ambitions, and even fancies, rather than penning them for lengthening years in increasingly regimented institutions; anyway, many young people could enter many professions without most of the schooling if we changed the rules for licensing and hiring. But none of these simpler and cheaper ways would be "efficient." The clinching proof is that they would be hard to administer.

Also, *are* the people useless? The concept of efficiency is largely, maybe mainly, systemic. It depends on the goals of the system, which may be too narrowly and inflexibly conceived. It depends on the ease of administration, which is finally considered as more important than economic or social costs. And it depends also on the method of calculating costs, which may create a false image of efficiency by ruling out "intangibles" that do not suit the method. This last source of error becomes very important in advanced urban economies where the provision of personal and social services grows rapidly in proportion to hardware and food production and distribution. In providing services, whether giving information, selling, teaching children, admitting to college, assigning jobs, diagnosing illness, serving food, or advising on welfare, standardization and punch cards may seem to fulfill the functions, but they may do so at the expense of frayed nerves, waiting in line, bad mistakes, a physical state less than health, misfitting, and cold soup. In modern conditions, the tailor-made improvisations of fallible but responsive human beings may be increasingly indispensable rather than useless. In the jargon of Frank Riessman, there is a need for "sub-professionals." Yet the mass-production and business-machine style, well adapted to manufacturing hardware and calculating logistics, will decide that people are useless anyway, since they can theoretically be dispensed with. Computers are used not as an adjunct but as a substitute. It is a curious experience to hear a gentleman from the Bureau of the Budget explain the budget of the War on Poverty according to cost-benefit computation. He can demonstrate that the participation of the poor in administering a program is disadvantageous; he can show you the flow chart; he cannot understand why poor people make a fuss on this point. It is useless to explain to him that they do not trust the program (or the director) but would like to get the money for their own purposes.

Abroad, the Americans still engage in plenty of old-fashioned exploitation of human labor, as in Latin America; yet the tendency is again to regard the underdeveloped peoples as not quite persons, and to try to shape them up by (sometimes) generous assistance in our own style. For example, one of the radical ideas of General Learning, the subsidiary of General Electric and Time, Inc., is to concentrate on electronic devices to teach literacy to the masses of children in poor countries; we must export our Great Society. Our enterprisers are eager to build highways and pipelines through the jungle, to multiply bases for our airplanes, and to provide those other items of the American standard of living for which the Western-trained native political leaders have "rising aspirations." Unfortunately, this largesse must often result in disrupting age-old cultures, fomenting tribal wars, inflating prices and wages and reducing decent poverty to starvation, causing the abandonment of farms and disastrous instant urbanization, making dictatorships inevitable and drawing simple peoples into Great Power conflicts. And woe if they do not then shape up, if they want to develop according to their local prejudices, for instance, for land reform. They become an uncontrollable nuisance, surely therefore allied with our enemies, and better dead than Red. In his great speech in Montreal, Secretary of Defense Robert McNamara informed us that since 1958, 87 percent of the very low-income nations and 69 percent of the low-income nations, but only 48 percent of the middle-income nations, have had serious violent disturbances. The cure for it, he said, was development according to the criteria of our cash economy while protected from subversion by our bombers. How to explain to this arithmetically astute man that he is not taking these people seriously as existing?

A startlingly literal application of the principle that our system excludes human beings rather than exploits them is the agreement of all liberals and conservatives that there must be a check on population growth, more especially among backward peoples and the poor at home. We are definitely beyond the need for the labor of the "proletariat" (= "producers of offspring") and the Iron Law of Wages to keep that labor cheap. Yet I am bemused by this unanimous recourse to a biological and mathematical etiology for our social troubles. Probably there *is* a danger of world overpopulation in the foreseeable future.

Certainly with the likelihood of nuclear war there is a danger of world underpopulation. However, until we institute more human ecological, economic, and political arrangements, I doubt that population control is the first order of business; nor would I trust the Americans to set the rules.

4. The Empty Society

In this lecture I have singled out two trends of the dominant organization of American society; its tendency to expand meaninglessly for its own sake, and its tendency to exclude human beings as useless. It is the Empty Society, the obverse face of the Affluent Society. When Adam Smith spoke of the Wealth of Nations, he did not mean anything like this.

Lack of meaning begins to occur when the immensely productive economy overmatures and lives by creating demand instead of meeting it; when the check of the free market gives way to monopolies, subsidies, and captive consumers; when the sense of community vanishes and public goods are neglected and resources despoiled; when there is made-work (or war) to reduce unemployment; and when the measure of economic health is not increasing well-being but abstractions like the Gross National Product and the rate of growth.

Human beings tend to be excluded when a logistic style becomes universally pervasive, so that values and data that cannot be standardized and programmed are disregarded; when function is adjusted to the technology rather than technology to function; when technology is confused with autonomous science, which is a good in itself, rather than being limited by political and moral prudence; when there develops an establishment of managers and experts who license and allot resources, and which deludes itself that it alone knows the only right method and is omnicompetent. Then common folk become docile clients, maintained by sufferance, or they are treated as deviant.

It is evident that, for us, these properties of the empty society are essentially related. If we did not exclude so many as not really persons, we would have to spend more of our substance on worthwhile goods, including subsistence goods, both at home and abroad; we would have to provide a more human environment for children to grow up in; there would be more paths to grow along and more ways of being a person. On the other hand, if we seriously and efficiently tackled the problems of anomie, alienation, riot, pollution, congestion, urban blight, degenerative and mental disease, and so on, we would find ourselves paying more particular attention to persons and neighborhoods, rather than treating them as standard items; we would have a quite different kind of engineering and social science; and we would need all the available human resources.

Certainly we would stop talking presumptuously about the Great Society and find ourselves struggling, in the confusing conditions of modern times, for a decent society.

The chief danger to American society at present, and to the world from American society, is our mindlessness, induced by empty institutions. It is a kind of trance, a self-delusion of formal rightness, that affects both leaders and people. We have all the talking points but less and less content. The Americans are decent folk, generous and fairly compassionate. They are not demented and fanatical, like some other imperial powers of the past and present, but on the contrary rather skeptical and with a sense of humor. They are not properly called arrogant, though they are perhaps presumptuous. But we have lost our horse sense, for which we were once noted. This kind of intelligence was grounded not in history or learning, nor in finesse of sensibility and analysis, but in the habit of making independent judgments and in democratically rubbing shoulders with all kinds and conditions. We have lost it by becoming personnel of a mechanical system and exclusive suburbanites, by getting out of contact with real jobs and real people. We suddenly have developed an Establishment, but our leaders do not have the tradition and self-restraint to come on like an establishment. Thus, we are likely to wreak havoc, not because of greed, ideology, or arrogance, but because of a bright strategy of the theory of games and an impatient conviction that other people aren't quite human.

The Sociology of Leisure: Some Suggestions

Bennett M. Berger

In a world full of newspapers whose headlines daily remind us of the continuing reign of misery and wretchedness in much of the world, and with the persistent cloud of nuclear war hanging over the heads even of the prosperous, the "problem" of leisure is one that we are distinctly privileged to have. Yet the study of leisure is not trivial—far from it. It is, however, worth noting at the outset that leisure assumes the status of a major problem only in a society which has been gripped by a "revolution of rising expectations." Unlike revolutions in underdeveloped countries, our revolution of rising expectations grows out of the demand for psychological as well as material benefits. An affluent society turns its attention to the pursuit of happiness; a well-fed society turns its attention to mental health; a successful society turns its attention to what Daniel Lerner[1] has called "comfort and fun," to personal "fulfillment," that elusive but supposed concomitant of success.

Reprinted from *Industrial Relations A Journal of Economy and Society*, February, 1962, with permission of the journal and the author.

Despite the fact that "the problem of leisure" is already a conventional phrase in the language of the social sciences, the problem had hardly been formulated and the *concept* of leisure has only rarely been directly confronted.[2] To be sure, some problems of leisure may be understood without much attention to the difficulties of conceptualization. Negroes who do not have access to public parks, beaches, theaters, and so on, may be said to have a leisure problem. Culturally deprived persons whose backgrounds handicap them from participation in important voluntary associations, and who are hence deprived of access to sources of power and influence, may also be said by some to have a leisure problem. But these are not situations which are typically referred to as problems of leisure. The phrase, "problem of leisure," also evokes images of the aged rocking in shabby rooms, poor, lonely, unattended, with little to do but wait for death; of adolescents on slum street corners answering with apparently senseless violence the anxious question of "what'll we do tonight?"; of large blocs of a nation's population sitting each evening in darkened living rooms lit only by that blue light from which emanates the irrelevant shadows which people the imaginative life of a society. These images, and the facts which underlie them, are at the core of the concern expressed over the disposition of free time.

Nevertheless, it seems to me that little is contributed to the understanding of these particular problems by conceiving them as problems of leisure. The aged, certainly, have special problems, some of them imposed by sudden retirement, some by the infirmities of age, still others by the breakup of families. Basically, however, these are problems of the aged and can be understood without invoking the unexamined abstraction, leisure. Similarly, problems of adolescents have been intensified or dramatized in recent years by, among other things, their increasingly late entrance into the labor market, by their increasingly early admittance into adolescent status, and by the sight of Negro, Puerto Rican, and other slum youth who are doomed, amid the general prosperity, to an environment of urban blight.

The problems of mass leisure (perhaps best symbolized by the TV narcotic) are inextricably bound up with a technology which renders work progressively more routinized and "easier" (though perhaps not less exhausting), with the purchasing power of large masses of people in the "culture market," and with the consequent rise of enormous "culture industries." In short, each problem of leisure is almost impossible to formulate or to solve without understanding the position of the groups who *have* the problem and the nature of the social and economic changes underlying their problems. More people are presented with more time at various stages of the life cycle than ever before—time when they are free to seek the inner satisfactions which we seem legitimately to expect from leisure. It adds little to our understanding of the difficulties of specific groups to perceive these difficulties as problems of leisure, unless this approach provides clues to aspects of the problem that were previously hidden and aids in the development of a theory of leisure.

Two Traditions in the Discussion of Leisure

Problems are not self-evident. Thus we may raise the empirical question of *to* whom and *for* whom leisure is a problem—for not everybody is concerned about the leisure problems of everybody else. The more familiar social problems of leisure have developed out of the concern *by* specific groups *for* the leisure of other specific groups, and an examination of these groups may cast some light on the conceptual problem of leisure.

Whose leisure is usually a public concern? Certain salient groups may be identified: the aged, children, youth, the unemployed, the handicapped, the ill, and inmates in prisons and mental institutions are groups that come immediately to mind.[3] In general, these groups are relatively unproductive categories of the population; they also often lack many of the basic institutional connections which bind individuals to society. Perhaps most important of all their common characteristics is their vulnerability to public action: in one way or another, these groups tend to be composed of less than fully competent persons. They are dependent, and by virtue of their dependence the disposition of their free time becomes a legitimate concern of those who are responsible for them. Who is responsible, who concerned? The groups seem to be composed primarily of civic officials, certain categories of group workers and social workers, some teachers, clergymen, and people at least to some extent vocationally concerned with the welfare of others. The social problem of leisure in this context seems to be one of providing the dependent groups (to the extent that they are unable to provide for themselves) with opportunities for "wholesome" activities. By keeping them busy and productive and by engaging them in social relations, these activities are expected to give meaning to lives otherwise subject to unusually severe stresses.

The leisure of the masses also gives rise to a good deal of publicly expressed concern. This concern, however, is not typically expressed by the groups I have cited above, but rather by intellectuals or cultural elites, whose concern over mass leisure seems to reflect their fear of the power of the masses in the culture market and the consequent threat to the traditional values of high culture. There are two major ideological approaches to this problem. Conservative intellectuals tend to be pessimistic about the possibilities of elevating popular taste on a mass scale and consequently see the social stratification of culture as inevitable. In their view, cultural elites should tend the garden of high culture and ignore the mass media which, after all, reflect the tastes of the markets they serve.

Liberal and radical intellectuals, on the other hand, tend to accuse the suppliers of mass culture of catering to the lowest levels of popular taste in order to achieve the highest levels of net profit.[4] These intellectuals confer upon the mass media an enormous potential for elevating popular taste, a potential which they argue is not only rarely used but is actually perverted by the commitment of the media to diversion, entertainment, and escape. In other words, they consider the media committed to serve as a distraction from, and compensation for, the presumably drab and monotonous routines of the working lives of the masses. Richard Hoggart, in his description of the decline of English working-class culture, gives precise expression to this view when he says, "The strongest objection to the more trivial popular entertainments is not that they prevent their [consumers] . . . from becoming highbrow, but that they make it harder for people without an intellectual bent to become wise in their own way."[5]

These two types of concern about leisure—that is, the concern of intellectuals and elites over popular taste and mass culture and the concern of more-or-less professional "do-gooders" over the "wholesome" disposition of the free time of relatively vulnerable, dependent groups—are contemporary instances of traditional approaches to leisure which go back a long way and have only rarely complemented one another. One tradition, probably dating from the relatively early stages of industrialization in the West, conceives of leisure as "free time" or time not devoted to paid occupations; leisure activities are viewed primarily as re-creative and restorative; historically the problems involved are associated with the poor, the dependent, or the laboring classes. The much older, classical tradition conceives of leisure in the Greek sense, as "schooling" or cultivation of the self, as a preoccupation with the values of high culture. Historically this tradition has been associated with the functions of aristrocratic, patrician, or leisure classes, since other classes were not culturally important.

To the Greeks, leisure was concerned with those activities that were worthy of a free man, activities we might today call "culture." Politics, debate, philosophy, art, ritual, and athletic contests were activities worthy of a free man because they expressed the moral core of a style of life. Their nobility was not, ideally, compromised or diluted by mere instrumental or productive purposes. "Work" as instrumental or productive activity was regarded as below the dignity of a free man, fit only for slaves and women. Leisure, in this aristocratic usage, is concerned with the maintenance of a style of life expressing the highest values of a culture. There is no problem of leisure because those who have it are bred to it.

What may be called the Protestant or industrial view of leisure is something quite different. When Calvinism sanctified work and industrialism ennobled it, what followed was the separation of work and leisure, the emphasis of economically productive functions as the most significant aspect of life, and the relegation of leisure to the status of spare time—time especially vulnerable to the ministrations of the Devil (witness the depravity of the poor) unless it were used productively to restore or refresh the organism for its primary purpose, work, or for unambiguously "wholesome" purposes such as prayer, Bible reading, or the disciplining of children. With the onset of industrialism, the functions of creating and maintaining the aristocratic values—formerly the avocations of gentlemen of leisure or the preoccupations of men of talent kept as ornaments by aristrocratic families or subsidized by the state—were increasingly taken over by occupational groups whose services were paid for through the market economy.

This brief review of the two traditions of leisure should suggest, above all, that a concept of leisure must be normative. To neither tradition, however different their evaluations of it, is leisure merely neutral time involving neutral activities. For Aristotle, leisure was the aim of life; for the Calvinist divine, it represented a threat to the Protestant virtues. In either case, classical aristrocrat or Protestant preacher, both had clear ideas about the activities to which this time was to be devoted. Where the viability of the Greek idea of leisure rested on slave labor, the Protestant deification of work was supported by the sin of idleness (which to the Greeks was a virtue). The meanings of work and leisure are inextricably related both to each other and to the cultural norms which define their moral place in a social order. A sociological definition which ignores this fact does so at the peril of becoming irrelevant.

Toward a Normative Concept of Leisure

Is there a way of marrying these normative traditions and their associated concerns, thereby creating a unified, value-relevant approach to the sociology of leisure? To some extent, economic development and the spread of political democracy have answered this question for us by bringing the masses onto the stage of history. At the same time, the more severe and ascetic features of Puritanism have been discredited. As citizens, the masses have had human rights and secular dignity conferred on them; as free men they have been invited to participate in "activities worthy of a free man," to pursue happiness and personal fulfillment. And as possessors of discretionary income they have acquired the means to make these goals more than mere formal possibilities.

At the same time, the modern world has witnessed the near disappearance of a leisure class in the classical sense of an aristrocratic group with time completely free of the need to labor productively. Today, practically all of us work and practically all of us have some "free time" beyond the minimum needed to restore or refresh the body for its economic tasks. We are all, at least in principle, compromised Greek citizens carrying the burden of compromised Protestant ethics. The industrial system has created hundreds of thousands of jobs that we feel are degrading,[6] but we are unwilling to do without the wealth which the system creates. We no longer feel that idleness is sinful, but we still retain something of the expectation that work should have moral content and feel rather cheated and slightly betrayed when we discover that moral content has simply disappeared from much industrial work.

It is out of such ambiguous situations that sociologies are made. One would expect a burgeoning sociology of leisure. This is not the case, however. We know a great deal about what people do with their free time, but only a small part of this knowledge has been gathered by students who have undertaken a conscious investigation of leisure. We know, for example, a considerable amount about who participates in what kinds of voluntary associations with what frequency, but the scholars who have done the work do not typically think of themselves as students of leisure. Kinsey studying sex is surely studying leisure. And something like this can be said about studies of mass media impact, juvenile delinquency, family life, and many other fields.[7] Moreover, it seems to me that less has been contributed to a sociological understanding of leisure by studies consciously directed to that end than by good community studies which are only incidentally or peripherally concerned with it. Although books like *Street Corner Society, Elmtown's Youth, Democracy in Jonesville, Middletown, Deep South, Crestwood Heights,* and many others, do not typically deal with the conceptual problem of leisure, they contain not only a wealth of data on free-time activities but data made meaningful through their linkage to a theory of community or class or subculture or whatever the dominant focus of the book in question happens to be.

This theoretical relevance is precisely what is missing from most of the contemporary empirical work in the sociology of leisure. The sociology of leisure today is little else than a reporting of survey data on what selected samples of individuals do with the time in which they are not working and the correlation of these data with conventional demographic variables.[8] There are several important exceptions to this general statement, but they do not alter the melancholy fact that empirical proof that rich people play polo more often than poor people gives us little reason to hope that an incipient sociology of leisure is taking shape. No genuine sociology of leisure is likely to emerge until a body of data is reinforced by a theory of leisure—at the very least by a conceptual understanding of what leisure is.

Leisure has been difficult to conceptualize for two very basic reasons.[9] First, conceptualization in sociology requires the abstraction of a common property or properties from a relatively wide range of events or social behavior. Leisure activities include such a colossally varied assortment of behavior (everything from, say, attendance at the President's Inaugural Ball to—as Louis Kronenberger pointed out—wandering up and down railroad yards collecting the names of Pullman cars and noting them down in a little book) that it has been virtually impossible to conceptualize it on a behavioral basis. Instead, a circumstance of that behavior (that it goes on in time not given over to paid occupations) has typically been made the sole criterion of leisure. Such a definition tells us nothing about the normative content of leisure, nor does it even invite questions about it; it characterizes only the time in which leisure activities occur. Strictly understood, the conventional opposition of work and leisure is a false opposition because these terms characterize different orders of phenomena: leisure is a kind of time, whereas work is a kind of action. Students of leisure, however, do not study time, they study behavior. To contrast work and leisure—and we must contrast them, since they have sociological meaning only vis-à-vis each other—we must conceive of leisure also as a kind of action which, however, is distinguished from work.

The apparently simple characterization of leisure as free time (two of the most complicated words in the language) or unobligated time seems to lead to precisely this kind of distinction: the "free" of free time suggests that leisure activity is voluntary whereas work is constrained. This distinction brings us to the second difficulty with the conceptualization of leisure, because the very idea of free time belongs to a presociological age. If sociology has taught us anything it has taught us that no time is free of normative constraints; what is work for some, is leisure for others, it is said, and of course this is right. Is work work if I love it? Is leisure leisure if I feel it is burdensome or boring? These are the kinds of questions which make students of leisure tear their hair and in despair reach for the operational definition. Any normative distinction between work and leisure as action should be a distinction between the kinds of norms which constrain them or a distinction regarding the extent to which norms have been internalized.

If, sociologically speaking, no time is unconstrained, how can we save leisure as free time from the status of a sociological myth? One way is to invoke Kenneth Burke's famous phrase, "perspective by incongruity," and argue that leisure refers precisely to those activities (or nonactivities) that are *most* constrained by moral norms. Norms may exercise moral force because they are functionally complete (genuine virtue is, after all, its own reward). Or, in some cases, they may have been so thoroughly internalized—so much a matter of conscience and so little a matter of something objectively "out there"—that they are felt as motives or desires freely chosen or as moral responsibilities freely accepted.

This is a way of saying that leisure refers to those activities whose normative content renders them most important to us, those things that we want to do for their own sake or those things that we feel ethically (as distinguished from expediently) constrained to do.[10] *That these activities may empirically be found to occur most frequently in time not devoted to paid occupations is significant primarily as an indication that work has lost much of its moral content*—that work, which was once a calling from God to an earthly place, has become "a job": "it's a living."

This conception of work-leisure is normative. Transcending the usual distinction between work and leisure, it represents a comprehensive cultural ideal; it is, in short, an "ideal type" only imperfectly realized in the actual experience of individuals. At the same time, it is not a moralistic idea; it does not preach the gospel of leisure; it does not regard leisure as an unambiguous good under all circumstances. It is quite probable that certain social functions require predominantly instrumental or expedient motivation; the performance of some essential roles may very well be obstructed by deep moral commitments. But this view of leisure gives us the beginning of a normative concept which can be useful because it invites questions about the conditions under which this comprehensive ideal is attained or approximated, although it does erase the usual distinction between work and leisure.

In place of this distinction, the conception makes possible further distinctions between leisure and such associated terms as rest, relaxation, or recreation, which may not have much moral content; and by suggesting that not everything that one encounters in one's free time qualifies as leisure, it frees the concept from its operational identification with specific forms of, for example, games. But even if the study of leisure turns out to be primarily the study of fun and games, reading and gardening, hunting and fishing, watching and hearing (as I hope it does not), this still suggests only that we are looking away from work, occupations, and careers to find what morally involves the members of our society.

Alienation from Work and the Problem of Leisure

It is perhaps an indication of how far we have come from the great days of the Protestant Ethic that the very characterization of leisure as free time contains a damning judgment on work, for it suggests that what is not leisure is not free, that is, it is for slaves—which is precisely as the Greeks would have had it. But this judgment is a disappointed one because we have not completely lost the expectation that we have some right to moral satisfaction in work; the Protestant Ethic dies hard—values always do—and leaves in us a lingering sense of betrayal when work seems meaningless.

Where work is concerned with wresting food from the earth, creating warmth and shelter for one's family, or even where, in societies undergoing industrialization, it is ideologically envisioned as the collective creation of a bright future (as it is today, for example, in the USSR and China), Protestant ethics have been eminently qualified to confer on such activities profound moral content. But where work is concerned with the manufacture of hoola hoops or mink coats for dogs or refrigerators that never need defrosting or automobiles that almost never need lubrication, and where men trained in English language and literature devote their worklives to the skillful use of the incomplete comparison in order to sell goods, even so versatile an instrument as our traditional value system learns its limitations.[11]

Lest I be misunderstood, I should make it clear that social criticism is not my intent here. The problem of leisure is not created merely by the growth of discretionary income, the reduction in the workweek, the pensioned retirement, and the lengthening span of life, just as alienation in work is not created primarily by the inherent properties of certain jobs.[12] Both problems are created when a value system is rendered apparently incapable of conferring honor on the typical situations which a social system engenders. Where inconsistencies exist between what the social system requires and what the value system prescribes, social problems are created, prominent among which are alienation from work and the problem of leisure, reverse sides of the same coin.

The social system, for example, has created longer adolescence, more years in retirement, and assembly-line jobs, but our value system contains no moral rhetoric with which to confer honor on these phenomena; the 21-year-old college boy is still something considerably less than a man, the aged in impoverished retirement are objects of pity or patronization, and the automobile assembly-line worker is every intellectual's model of alienation from work. Our social system needs and produces "organization men," but the words remain offensive to us; we are all status seekers, but nobody defends status seeking. We don't know how: our value system does not provide us with the moral vocabulary to defend much of the behavior and many of the roles which the social structure requires.

In this respect, the Soviet countries have a bitter lesson to teach us. Soviet cultural rhetoric is offensive to the ears of Western intellectuals because it transparently and grossly attempts to confer moral significance on, and to create heroic images of, precisely those roles and behavior to which the Soviet social system is committed, images which to us are sometimes laughable. The muscled worker raising his sledgehammer above the rubble, the Stakhanovite overproducing his quota, the stocky, fresh-complexioned girl on the tractor, are proper topics for heroic treatment and glorious characterization. The collectivized Horatio Alger morality of Soviet rhetoric confers heroic status on those types of individuals and roles that actually represent the collective purposes of the state.

Consider the strain on our moral vocabulary if it were asked to produce heroic myths of accountants, computer programmers, and personnel executives. We prefer cowboys, detectives, bull fighters, and sports-car racers, because these types embody the virtues which our moral vocabulary is equipped to celebrate: individual achievement, exploits, and prowess. Again, I should make clear that this is *not* a criticism of what we have become and certainly not a celebration of the harmony between Soviet society and culture; it is, rather, an analysis of why we are uneasy about what we have become. A culture which has not learned to honor what it is actually committed to produce creates an uneasy population.[13]

The problems of leisure and of alienation in work, then, are problems created by the inconsistencies between normative and social systems. Two adaptive responses to these problems are typical. The more common response, where certain jobs are not honored, is to withdraw emotion from work, to accept work as something one has to do in order to make possible the things one really cares about. Though the Protestant Ethic is by no means in its grave, there is clearly a growing consensus (more apparent, of course, on the lower levels of the occupational ladder than on the higher) that the major moral satisfactions in life are to be sought through leisure, not work. Or, in my own terms, leisure is to be sought through activities unconnected with occupations. The withdrawal of motivation may thus be replaced, for workers, by emotional involvement in the bowling league, the bridge club, the philatelist society, the golf score, the sports-car rally, or various kinds of spectator activities. For adolescents, there is "youth culture"; for the elderly, Golden Age Clubs.

Another kind of adaptation to alienation from work is much subtler. Manual workers can cope with alienation on the job by the invention of all sorts of factory games and status play. On professional and executive levels, one notes a surprising degree of sophisticated candor about alienation. It is, of course, true that job satisfaction studies[14] generally reveal that professionals and executives are much more satisfied with their jobs than factory workers, but "job satisfaction" does not necessarily tell us much about alienation. In several professional and executive milieux it has become fashionable, almost de rigueur, to be cynical about one's work. The point is that the sophistication and the subtlety of one's cynicism can be highly rewarding, thus creating a situation in which one can be quite alienated from work but quite satisfied with one's job.

The metaphor of the "rat race," so common in highly competitive occupations, suggests that work on higher occupational levels is hardly a sanctified, self-justifying thing. Even in academic life, that former citadel of self-justifying work, the phrase "publish or perish" and the utter cynicism with which scholars (frequently successful ones) typically speak of the mysterious science of grant-getting bear testimony not only to an incipient alienation from work but also to new patterns of sophisticated disaffection, the elegance of which may be granted considerable honor. For these folkways are frequently models of duplicity; functionally, they constitute the conversational equipment to deal with the psychological dimensions of success and failure. The successful contestant in a "rat race" may be all the more highly admired for his success, given the arduous nature of the competition. Thus when successful men characterize their occupational milieu as a "rat race," the characterization may well contain the not-too-well-hidden motive of self-congratulation. When, on the other hand, the characterization is made by the unsuccessful, the metaphor of the "rat race" functions as a "cooling" device;[15] it renders failure honorable, for losing in a race of four-legged rodents is testimony to one's two-legged humanity. To be sure, norms are operating here, and they may account in large part for much of the job satisfaction on higher levels, but these norms bear little resemblance to what we have in mind when we speak of our value system. Sociologists refer to such milieux as "deviant subcultures," and effective participation in them is in itself evidence of one's alienation from the dominant value system as applied to work.

In either case, whether it is the relatively simple alienation so characteristic of assembly-line work in factories or the highly sophisticated kind of alienation we find in the folkways of higher occupations, one thing is clear: the disengagement of self from occupational role not only is more common than it once was but is increasingly regarded as *proper*. Alienation would seem almost complete when one can say with honesty and moral conviction, "I am not what I do; do not judge me by what I do for a living," and when one turns to nonworking life for values and identity.

It may be objected that this analysis ignores important countertendencies in the nature and organization of work. Some cause for optimism regarding the problem of alienation has been sought, for example, in the fact that, of all occupational categories, highly skilled professional and technical occupations show the highest rates of growth. And since job satisfaction tends to be highest in the highly skilled manual classifications and in the nonmanual professional and technical classifications, the future should look somewhat brighter.

While there is clearly some basis for optimism in these occupational trends, there are at the same time several factors latent in them which should considerably temper that optimism. On blue-collar levels, for example, the newest automated types of skills are frequently the kind for which no readily available standards of approbation exist within the peer groups of skilled workers. The skills of a maintenance man in an automated plant, for example, are not the manual skills traditionally accorded honor by blue-collar workers. Moreover, to the extent that progressive refinements in the division of labor represent ever greater specialization of functions, occupational skills tend to become what Wilensky has called "status-invisible": "Ask a 'hindleg toenail remover' what he does and he will tell you he works at Swift's . . . the white-collar 'console operator,' too, will name the company, [but] not the job, because nobody has heard of this latest example of automation."[16] Where such conditions exist, the tendency of highly skilled jobs to command the moral identity of men is compromised; personal ties to work are weakened, and the relevance of working life to nonworking life is obscured.

Regarding professional occupations, bureaucratic organization continues increasingly to define the conditions of professional work. These conditons render such work less and less akin to the traditional model of the liberal professions, with their emphasis on responsibility, personal service, and creativity, and more and more akin to the bureaucratic model of professional and managerial skills organized in a "functionally rational" manner—a type of organization to which traditional professional norms can only be applied with great difficulty. To the extent that such skills can be routinized, managers and professionals, as Wilensky and others have noted, are themselves increasingly subject to "Taylorization," which tends to weaken further a moral commitment to work. Witness the complex, rather panicky response of many teachers to the prospect of automatic teaching devices. There are, of course, professional and technical milieux which are relatively insulated from these tendencies, but to the extent that work is subject to rationalization these will decrease, and unless norms can be found within our value system to celebrate bureaucratization, the withdrawal of motivation and the disengagement of self from work is likely to continue.

As work loses its power to command the moral identifications and loyalties of men, as men look away from work to find moral experience, society loses an important source of normative integration. Widespread belief in the inherent value of work gives economic institutions the power to perform certain necessary integrative functions, and the withdrawal of motivation from work seriously strains the network of bonds which relate the world of work to the world of non-work, and the individual to both.

In such a situation we may expect, if the functionalist view of society as a self-balancing system has any merit, the transfer of functions formerly performed by the institutions of work to the "leisure institutions," and this, it seems to me, is precisely the significance of the enormous increase in attention which the problem of leisure has received in recent years.[17] In much the same sense that functions formerly performed by the family and the church are increasingly shifted to the schools, reluctant and in many respects ill-equipped to handle them, "free time" is increasingly burdened with moral functions formerly performed by the institutions of work. Where public concern over leisure is not merely an attempt by moralistic busy-bodies to impose their own ideas of "wholesome" use of time on others, and where it is not professional or semi-professional mourning over the vulgarity of mass culture, it is a concern with the sources of moral solidarity. For with the weakening of the moral link which binds men to the institutions of work—and religion too—the major institutional sources of social cohesion become problematic.

The Task of a Sociology of Leisure

To my mind, the problem of leisure is a problem of finding, in the norms which exercise constraint in specific situations, the values which command moral identity and assent. The frequent appeals to individuals to use leisure "creatively" and to participate in local community institutions and voluntary associations are not likely to aid much in the solution of the problem because they beg the important questions of whether these activities actually do have moral force and whether the social structure actually does provide access to the goals which the culture recommends. Many of the recommended solutions to the problem of leisure, in short, would be viable only if there were no problem of leisure to begin with. The problem of leisure is exacerbated when men are asked to use their free time for activities beyond their means or for activities whose value they do not recognize.

The problem of leisure is difficult to treat intelligently because it lies in an area that is not amenable to our genius for organized solutions. The problem is a poignant one in a democratic industrial society because it is a Frankenstein's monster: it confronts the society with the spectre of an enormous amount of free time which is created by the society, but over which the society admits that it should, in principle, have little or no conscious influence or control. If leisure is time free of merely instrumental obligations, it is not subject to the criteria of efficiency and hence is immune to the power of rationality and organization. And if the great gift of unbeholden time and discretionary income creates a leisure whose dominant motifs are boredom, violence, and escape, the monster turns on its creator and challenges the viability of the democratic ideal.[18]

But if the values sought through leisure are difficult to find because of changes in the nature and organization of work and the receding horizons of aspiration, they are nevertheless there, both in traditional and in new forms, which is only to say that men have culture. The task of a sociology of leisure is to discover what these values are, the patterns of activity through which they are sought, and the features of social structure which tend to change or sustain them.[19] The sociology of leisure is that part of the sociology of culture which attempts to discover the moral character of a style of life by studying the behavior of groups under conditions where that behavior is least constrained by exclusively instrumental considerations. Increasingly, these conditions are found outside of occupations, and where they are, the "problem" is not too *much* time and money, but too *little*. Leisure styles are created by the kinds of leisure activities that, empirically, tend to cluster together; these are not random, and the sociological analysis of them is the study of how social structure facilitates or obstructs the efforts of men to find in their freest time the moral satisfactions which value systems must provide.

[1] See Daniel Lerner, "Comfort and Fun: Morality in a Nice Society," *American Scholar,* XXVII (Spring, 1958), 153-165.

[2] The classic confrontation is, of course, Johan Huizinga, *Homo Ludens: The Play Element in Culture* (London: Routledge & Paul, 1949). For a Catholic view, see Joseph Pieper, *Leisure, the Basis of Culture* (New York: Pantheon Books, 1952). Though the word "leisure" is hardly mentioned in it, Werner Jaeger's *Paideia: The Ideals of Greek Culture* (New York: Oxford University Press, 1943), is probably the best single source for a classical understanding of leisure. Clement Greenberg, "Work and Leisure Under Industrialism," *Commentary,* XVI (July, 1953), 54-62, is a thoughtful consideration of the impact of industrialization on traditional views of leisure. None of these writings, however, are by sociologists. Almost any of David Riesman's several essays on work and leisure are very helpful in the study of leisure, and Max Kaplan makes a heroic but unsuccessful attempt to conceptualize leisure sociologically in *Leisure in America: A Social Inquiry* (New York: Wiley, 1960), chap. 2. The most promising current work is that outlined by Harold Wilensky in "Work, Careers, and Social Integration," *International Social Science Journal,* XII (Fall, 1960), 543-560.

[3] But not *all* members of these groups. The leisure of rich and prominent aged persons seems not to be a legitimate concern of others. A public or private attempt to help Dwight Eisenhower, Herbert Hoover, Bernard Baruch, or Douglas MacArthur to spend their declining years more "productively" or satisfyingly would probably be regarded as presumptuous.

[4] Bernard Rosenberg and David Manning White, editors, *Mass Culture* (Glencoe, Ill.: Free Press, 1957), contains several examples of both views. For an especially good example of the conservative view, see Edward Shils, "Daydreams and Nightmares: Reflections on the Criticism of Mass Culture," *Sewannee Review,* LXV (Autumn, 1957), 587-608.

[5] *The Uses of Literacy* (London: Chatto and Windus, 1957), p. 276.

[6] Degrading, that is, in terms of the values created by industrialism and which define what men have a legitimate right to expect.

[7] This is typical of the way fields of specialization develop in sociology and, perhaps, in other disciplines too: not because of a rigorously logical division of labor, but rather because of historical accidents in which specific "claims" are laid to certain kinds of data. Sociology's traditional interests in the family and in various aspects of "social disorganization" are due in large measure to the fact that these "fields" had not been claimed by other disciplines at the time sociology formally developed.

[8] Wed to an operational definition of leisure as time not spent in gainful employment, such studies can only rarely get beyond the level of empirical generalization

implicit in simple correlation. Studies of leisure and stratification are good cases in point. See, for example, R. Clyde White, "Social Class Differences in the Use of Leisure," *American Journal of Sociology,* LXI (September, 1955), 145-150; Alfred C. Clarke, "Leisure and Occupational Prestige," *American Sociological Review,* XXI (June, 1956), 301-307; Leonard Reissman, "Class, Leisure, and Social Participation," *American Sociological Review,* XIX (February, 1954), 76-84. Saxon Graham correlates the data from his study with both class and rural-urban residence. See chapter XVIII of his *American Culture* (New York: Harper, 1957). Marjorie Donald and Robert Havighurst relate variations in the meanings attached to leisure to certain demographic variables. See "The Meanings of Leisure," *Social Forces,* XXXVII (May, 1959), 355-360.

[9] That it *is* difficult to conceptualize is implicit in the failure of one recent symposium to come to any agreement on what the term means. See the introductory remarks in Robert W. Kleemeier, editor, *Aging and Leisure* (New York: Oxford University Press, 1961), p. 4. This book is probably the best of the several collections published in recent years on the problems contained in its title, but its utility extends beyond the problems of the aged. Sebastian De Grazia's contribution, "The Uses of Time," presents an enormous amount of data collected for studies under the Twentieth Century Fund; Nelson Foote's chapter, "Methods for the Study of Meaning in Use of Time," carefully reviews the several techniques of data collection in leisure studies. See, in addition, the contributions of Meyersohn, Wilensky, and Gordon.

[10] That one finds it emotionally more difficult to beg off (for phony reasons) from a previously accepted invitation to a party given by a friend, than to call the boss to say one's sick and not coming to work, suggests that leisure obligations are *more* thoroughly internalized than obligations to work. Where this is true (and, of course, it is not under all circumstances), it suggests that free time is *more* obligated precisely because it is "free"; where commitments are voluntary they carry with them a felt responsibility.

[11] Advertising, of course, is the great bête noire of social critics, the very model of organized cynicism. What an interesting study of reactions might be obtained if the writers of pamphlets which are published by the big advertising agencies for distribution to college majors in English and journalism and which describe the satisfactions to be achieved through careers in advertising were confronted with the novels, stories, and nonfiction written by ex-advertising men about life along James Madison's avenue!

[12] See the following three articles which document the increases in leisure time and the money spent on leisure pursuits: Joseph Zeisel, "The Workweek in American Industry, 1850-1956"; Seymour Wolfbein, "The Changing Length of Working Life"; and "30 Billion for Fun," by the editors of *Fortune.* All three articles are reprinted in Eric Larrabee and Rolf Meyersohn, editors, *Mass Leisure* (Glencoe, Ill.: Free Press, 1958). See also, Sebastian De Grazia, "Tomorrow's Good Life," *Teacher's College Record,* LXI, April, 1960, for an argument regarding why such statistics may be misleading; and Ida Craven, "Leisure," in Larrabee and Meyersohn, *op. cit.,* and Harold Wilensky, "The Uneven Distribution of Leisure," *Social Problems,* IX, Summer, 1961, for evidence on the large number of holy days and feast days in the ancient and medieval worlds.

[13] The plethora of television heroes who bear no relation to anyone in real life may not be due to the cynicism of sponsors and network executives. Such people might be only too pleased to present dramatic shows about accountants, IBM technicians, and junior executives, if only writers knew how to write them.

[14] See the very able summary and analysis of these studies by Robert Blauner, "Work Satisfaction and Industrial Trends in Modern Society," in Walter Galenson and Seymour M. Lipset, editors, *Labor and Trade Unionism* (New York: Wiley, 1960).

[15] The expert here is Erving Goffman, "Cooling the Mark Out: Some Aspects of Adaptation to Failure," *Psychiatry,* XV ((November, 1952), 451-463.

[16] Harold Wilensky, "Work, Careers . . . ," p. 19. On the ambiguous status of automated skills, see Robert Blauner, *Freedom in Work and the Diversity of Industrial Environments* (unpublished Ph.D. dissertation, University of California, 1961), chap. V.

[17] Edward Gross assures us that leisure performs important functions in solving all four of the "system problems" of Parsons and his collaborators, but he does not suggest why this discovery was not made until very recently. See Edward Gross, "A Functional Approach to Leisure Analysis," *Social Problems,* IX, Summer, 1961. This issue of *Social Problems* is wholly devoted to articles on leisure.

[18] The great success of the motion picture *Marty*—with its recurrent refrain of "what'll we do tonight?"—suggests the dramatic appeal of the attempt to overcome ennui. Having no ready answer to the question of "what'll we do tonight?" provokes great anxiety because having "nothing to do" is cause for shame in a society burdened by the old view that idleness is vice and the new view that great demands on one's time are evidence of high estate.

[19] What, for example, is it about our social structure that accounts for the transformation of the bowling alley from a haunt of thieves, murderers, and con men, into an eminently respectable place to take the family for an evening of wholesome fun, whereas the poolroom has been unable to lose its unsavory reputation?

The Background to the Guaranteed-Income Concept

Robert Theobald

Social critics often claim that the present need for economic and social reform stems from past failures in economic and social policy. There is, of course, much merit in this contention. It is, however, far more realistic to perceive present problems as resulting not from failures but from the extraordinary success of Western societies in fulfilling their drive for ever greater mastery over nature and, in particular, developing the productive potential that today makes it possible to provide every individual in the rich countries with a decent standard of living while requiring a decreasing amount of toil from the vast majority of the population.[1]

The economic history of the past two hundred years may perhaps most properly be couched—to paraphrase H. G. Wells—in terms of a race between increasing production based on ever more complex and sophisticated technology and man's cultural inventiveness in devising and gaining acceptance of new methods of distributing and using this increasing production. It is surprising, therefore, that the mainstream of economics has only recently become concerned with the problems of balancing the available production with the rights of individuals and institutions to obtain this production. Throughout the nineteenth century it was rather generally accepted by economists that production and purchasing power—effective supply and potential demand—would automatically stay in balance. This assumption, called Say's law after its originator, dominated economic analysis until the great slump of the 1930s.

Innovations in techniques of distributing rights to resources have not, therefore, been based until recent years upon theoretical analysis but rather on pragmatic adjustments to the need to be able to sell what could be produced or to obtain the labor force required for the production of quality goods. The lack of a theoretical basis for changes in techniques of distributing income inevitably led to widespread controversy about the impact and implications of each new measure designed to raise purchasing power or attract workers. Thus Ford's five-dollar day, rapid growth in consumer credit and advertising, social security, and unemployment compensation were, in the past, just as controversial as the guaranteed income is today.

The motivation of Ford in introducing the five-dollar day early in the twentieth century and thus doubling the wages of his workers is still far from clear. Some interpreters argue that his main aim was to increase the number of people who could afford to buy the cars that he was turning out in ever greater numbers. Some have concluded that he was motivated by a desire to obtain a more highly skilled and stable labor force, and some believe he wished to increase the welfare of his workers. It would certainly be unprofitable to re-evaluate Ford's motives at this point in time. It would be equally unprofitable to examine in this essay the implications of the fact that the pattern of income distribution that has resulted from Ford's initiative cannot be reasonably explained in terms of existing economic theory—and indeed destroys its validity.[2] It is important to recognize here only that Ford did introduce a mechanism that made it possible for the wages and salaries of workers to rise in parallel with production. This mechanism has been the chief factor responsible for ensuring that American purchasing power has kept in reasonable balance with American productive power during the last fifty years—with, of course, the exception of the Great Depression.

Two major developments in methods of distributing and using production occurred in the twenties. First, widespread use of consumer credit developed—people were allowed to purchase *before* they had earned the required funds. Second, manufacturers and distributors widened the range and scope of selling activities designed to cultivate new tastes. Despite these efforts, however, potential supply was so far ahead of effective demand by 1929 that the economy collapsed.

It was the Great Depression, which followed this collapse, that led economists to become deeply concerned with the problem of maintaining purchasing power. The change in the thrust of economic analysis is generally and correctly attributed to John Maynard Keynes's book *The General Theory of Employment, Interest and Money*. Nevertheless, it must be noted that there is a good deal of evidence suggesting that the brute facts of the Depression forced politicians to move in the direction of increasing purchasing power before a full economic justification for this step had been found—and indeed even while a large proportion of the economic profession was still opposing this step and calling for decreases in government expenditure. Thus social security and the make-work schemes of the thirties were conceived as a response to social unrest rather than justified on economic grounds as a means of ending the recession through increasing demand.

It is also important to recognize that present developments in economic theorizing, which are generally believed to be an extension of Keynesian analysis, do not adequately reflect the spirit of Keynesian thought—as opposed to his technical conclusions. Keynes's main contribution to theory came when he proved that it was possible for unemployment to persist over long periods because effective demand would not necessarily rise as fast as potential supply. Modern economic theorists grasped this insight and set to work to devise policies that would lead to a sufficiently rapid increase in effective demand to balance increases in potential supply and thus ensure minimum unemployment. However, this is not the *only* policy proposal that can be derived from an interpretation of Keynesian analysis: society could equally well decide that it no longer wished to channel the quasi-totality of its efforts toward the goal of full employment but rather desired to seek a new social order that would allow us to take full advantage of the potential of emerging abundance and our ability to eliminate toil.

Keynes himself quite clearly hoped for the second development, arguing that

> when the accumulation of wealth is no longer of high social importance, there will be great changes in the code of morals. We shall be able to rid ourselves of many of the pseudo-moral principles which have hag-ridden us for two hundred years, by which we have exalted some of the most distasteful of human qualities into the position of the highest

> values. We shall be able to afford to dare to assess the money-motive at its true value. . . . All kinds of social customs and economic practices affecting the distribution of wealth and its rewards and penalties which we now maintain at all costs, however distasteful and unjust they may be in themselves . . . we shall then be free, at last, to discard.[3]

It is quite clear, therefore, that although present policy is justified on the basis of Keynesian analysis, Keynes would, in present conditions, reject many of the policy prescriptions being advanced, for he would hold that they perpetuated the worst of the values of the industrial age.

What methods have economists proposed to ensure that potential supply and effective demand would stay in balance? The first step toward this goal, which was accomplished around the end of the Second World War in almost all Western countries, was the passage of legislation pledging the efforts of governments to ensure that supply and demand would remain in balance and thus provide jobs for all: in the United States this was accomplished by the Employment Act of 1946.

This commitment to a full employment policy through balancing supply and demand has deepened in all Western countries in the years since the Second World War. The United States has undoubtedly been the last country to understand the full implications of this policy approach, but the first five years of the sixties have marked its final acceptance. It is now generally believed, not only by economists but by the vast majority of businessmen, that it is the responsibility of the government to ensure that the economy remains in balance—that the government should aim to balance the economy rather than to balance the budget. As Meno Lovenstein points out in his essay, the government has now essentially taken a commitment to "guarantee the national income" by ensuring that rights to all available productive resources are distributed.

The difference between this approach to the government's responsibility and that current in the nineteenth century, when it was believed that government damaged the operation of the economy whenever it intervened, is so vast as to need no stressing. Unfortunately, economic theory has not yet reexamined all the implications of the shift in approach. For example, if the government is deeply involved in guaranteeing the national income of the whole country, and if, as is inevitable, its interventions affect the pattern of income distribution, what goals should it adopt? Another facet of this problem results from the fact that a large number of people are unable to earn their living because they are too old, too young, too mentally or physically ill.

How should they be provided with incomes and what amount of resources should they receive? Economics has few, if any, answers to these and similar questions.

The problem of providing incomes to those who are too old, too young, or too sick to hold a job is already urgent and is certain to become more so in coming years because of the inevitable shifts in patterns of age distribution. This reality is already causing the emergence of a new consensus that cuts across party lines and interest groups. This consensus is based on a belief that the government has already taken an implied commitment to provide a minimum level of income to all individuals, but that the present mosaic of measures designed to ensure this result is both excessively complex and unduly costly. It is argued that it would therefore be desirable to introduce a single plan that would meet the implied commitment of government as simply and cheaply as possible through the introduction of a guaranteed income floor for all those who either cannot, or should not, earn their living through holding a job.

There should be no need to justify payments to the physically and mentally ill: they cannot work and society should surely provide for them. Some justification, however, is often felt to be required for more adequate payments to the old, for one of the most sanctified of our work myths is that older people both could and should have saved enough to provide for their old age. This is, of course, merely a cynical fiction. Those who are old today worked in an era when their income was necessarily far lower than is paid for jobs demanding a comparable level of skills and application today. They needed to spend a large proportion of their income just to cover their expenses, including the education of their children. They were therefore able to save very little, if anything, whether directly or through insurance schemes. Today's labor force, however, would not be enjoying its present level of income without their hard work and that of earlier generations who had even less to show for their toil. Any fair distribution of the nation's resources should ensure that old people be allowed to share in the wealth they created. Their labor was, in fact, wealth, and it was invested in the national economy at a time when its value was at a premium. Today this group should be collecting their "earned interest."

It will, perhaps, help to put this question in perspective if we recognize that most of those presently being paid social security benefits are receiving more than the actuarial value of their contributions: i.e., they did not pay in enough money to cover the benefits they are receiving. Continuing expansion of the social security system makes it almost certain that it will not become actuarily sound at any point in the future. Thus we have already accepted, on a practical basis, that the old are entitled to a more adequate income than would be theirs on an insurance basis. The next step is to bring the logic of this position into the open and see what more needs to be done.

The question of income distribution among the young poses equally serious problems, for we have not yet been willing to accept the fact that we have extended the principle of parental support of the young far beyond the breaking point. In an agricultural or even an early industrial society, a child was wealth. After a few years of care, the child added to the family income rather than subtracted from it. In addition, the younger generation was expected to support their parents as they grew old. There was, thus, a rough balance between the economic responsibility of the parents and that of the children.

Let us contrast this with the situation today. Because of the demands of the new world in which we live, a child should be educated at least until he is twenty-one and perhaps until he is twenty-five or thirty. Despite the growing number of loans, grants, and scholarships, it is still a fundamental assumption of our society that the primary economic responsibility for the education and support of the child lies with the parent. However, the parent receives little financial return, for by the time the child leaves the educational process he is generally married and feels little obligation for the economic support of his parents. Parents should no longer be expected to underwrite the lengthy educational process that the future society requires of today's and tomorrow's young people. We must recognize that the student is already "working" as relevantly as the man in the factory or the office.

While the idea that we must find new ways of providing income to those who cannot, or should not, hold a job has received increasing support in recent years, the wider concept that *everybody* should receive a guaranteed income as a matter of right is still highly controversial. The proposal for a universal guaranteed income can be justified on the ground that the evolution described in the essays by Robert Davis and Ben Seligman ensures that most types of structured[4] jobs will be taken over, within a relatively brief period, by advanced machinery. This will necessarily be true because, in addition to the often substantial direct economic savings from the use of automatic machinery, machinery also appears more attractive than men for a wide range of noneconomic reasons. Machine systems do not get tired, they can carry out a particular task with a continued precision that cannot be demanded or expected of a human work force; they are incapable of immorality, they do not lie, steal, cheat, or goof off, they do not claim that their rights as human beings are being violated by factory work practices; they are not class-conscious; above all, they are not vocal in their criticism of management and they do not go on strike.

In the relatively near future, therefore, those who need to expand their plant to meet created demand will prefer to buy machines rather than to hire men: the machines they buy will be produced predominantly by other machines. The new machines purchased will be so much more efficient than earlier machinery that large numbers of existing firms using older machinery and thus employing many men will be forced to close down: they will be too inefficient to compete.

The process can be summarized as follows: created demand will lead to purchases of highly efficient and productive machine systems that need few men to control them: i.e., to the installation of cybernation. Thus, in the relatively near future a policy of forcing rapid growth in demand in order to increase employment opportunities will actually lead to the opposite result: it will raise unemployment rather than lower it.

The conclusion that massive unemployment is inevitable is still rejected by most economists and policy-makers, who argue that increases in demand brought about, if necessary, by federal intervention to balance the economy can *always* be large enough to ensure that all the available labor will be used. Unfortunately, however, there is no economic theory or contemporary evidence to support this conclusion. The neoclassical theorizing of the last part of the nineteenth century and the beginning of the twentieth assumed that men and machines would cooperate with each other; today, however, they are competitive. Keynes, who is presently used as the justification for the assertion that demand and supply can be kept in balance, and jobs provided for all, should not be used for this purpose because he excluded from his analysis those very factors that now threaten massive unemployment. "We take as given the existing skill and quantity of available labor, the existing quality and quantity of available equipment, the existing technique. This does not mean that we assume these facts to be constant, but merely that in this place and context, we are not considering or taking into account the effects and consequences of changes in them."[5]

In effect, therefore, economists have no valid theoretical structure to support their contention that unemployment can be avoided by increases in demand. To the non-economist, such a statement will necessarily be shocking, but it is unfortunately valid. Economists, like many social scientists, have generally been far more concerned about theoretical rigor within a given pattern of assumptions than about the validity of the assumptions themselves; the development of theory has proceeded despite the ever decreasing relevance of the assumptions on which it is based. Economic predictions about unemployment rates will not be valid until the analysis from which they are drawn is based on a new and more relevant set of assumptions.

As minimum unemployment cannot be achieved in coming years, fundamental change in the socioeconomic system will be absolutely essential. As we have already seen, our present system is postulated on the belief that every individual who desires a job will be able to find one and that the jobs thus obtained will pay well enough to enable the individual to live with dignity. I am convinced that if we desire to maintain freedom, a guaranteed income will necessarily have to be introduced. In addition, during the period of transition from a scarcity to an abundance socioeconomy, we will have to consider the whole problem of income maintenance for those whose income level is above the minimum income floor in order to allow them to update their education and to minimize hardship when individuals lose their jobs because of further increases in technological sophistication. Although neither this essay nor this book can deal with the issue of income maintenance, it is necessary to stress that the need for an income maintenance program is just as great as the need for a guaranteed income floor.[6]

The economic controversy is not, however, the most important one. Just as Keynes foresaw that the issue of scarcity was not the long-run problem of mankind, he warned us against placing too much emphasis on strictly economic analysis: "Do not let us overestimate the importance of the economic problem, or sacrifice to its supposed necessities other matters of greater and more permanent significance."[7] The real question raised by the coming of cybernation is not whether we *can* provide jobs for everybody, but whether we *should* provide jobs for everybody: the question we need to examine is whether our present policy of providing income rights on the basis of job-holding is the best way to ensure that the urgent work of society will be accomplished.

Most economists, as well as government, management, and union leaders claim that the type of work that now needs to be done and will need to be done in the future can, and should, be turned into jobs for which a wage or salary can then be paid. This is the assumption that is explicitly challenged by those who support the guaranteed income. Jobholding within the increasingly bureaucratic structures whose growth can be expected, given the continuation of the present socioeconomic system, would certainly not be conducive to the self-development of the individual. In addition, and even more importantly, the lack of flexibility inherent in bureaucratic structures makes them unsuitable forms of organization for acting upon, or even perceiving, developments that would benefit the socioeconomic system.

The essayists in the third part of [*The Guaranteed Income*] argue, in effect, that many individuals are perfectly capable of perceiving what needs to be done to develop themselves and their society and that these individuals would act upon this perception if they had the funds that would free them from the necessity of holding a job. A parallel is often made with the ownership of capital: it is claimed that the possession of capital has not led to a general decline in individual and social responsibility and that there is therefore no reason why a guaranteed income should lead to a decline in individual and social responsibility. Comparisons with the dole are rejected; it is suggested that the dole results in degradation partly because it is seen by its recipients as "charity" rather than as a right, and partly because the techniques of distribution used in many areas of the country inevitably sap self-respect and initiative.

For society at large, and especially for those creative individuals now shackled by the absence of a guaranteed source of income, the situation would seem to be analogous to that which obtained at the time of the introduction of limited liability in the nineteenth century. Limited liability was introduced to encourage risk-taking by those investing in companies. The concept of a joint venture was replaced by the concept that a stockholder's liability for company debts no longer put a lien on his total wealth but only on the amount he invested in the company. Limited liability was a precondition for the taking of risks: it did not ensure innovation or risk-taking, but it did make them possible, thus allowing the economy and society to benefit from the self-interested acts of individuals.

A guaranteed income provides the individual with the ability to do what he personally feels to be important. This will allow risk-taking and innovation in areas where the existing and emerging needs of society are not being met by an otherwise efficiently functioning free-enterprise system. The guaranteed income is not mediated through the offices of any other individual or organization within the market system and therefore does not bring with it built-in pressures for the recipient to continue doing what is already being done through the market system.

The guaranteed income therefore involves a major shift in rights and obligations. Today we demand of an individual that he find a job, but we then provide him with the right to "pursue happiness." Tomorrow we will provide him with the right to receive enough resources to live with dignity, and we will demand of him that he develop himself and his society.

The guaranteed-income proposal is based on the fundamental American belief in the right and the ability of the individual to decide what he wishes and ought to do. This is surely the basic meaning of the phrase "private enterprise": that the individual should have the right to obtain enough resources to do what he believes to be important. In the past, the individual could go into business for himself and thus obtain resources. Today all the evidence shows that neither the self-employed businessman nor the small company can compete with the large corporation. The ideal of private enterprise can, therefore, be preserved only if the guaranteed income is introduced.

The guaranteed income will, in fact, lead to the revival of "private enterprise." Once the guaranteed income is available, we can anticipate the organization of what I have called "consentives": productive groups formed by individuals who will come together on a voluntary basis simply because they wish to do so. The goods produced by these consentives will not compete with mass-produced goods available from cybernated firms. The consentive will normally produce the "custom-designed" goods that have been vanishing within the present economy. The consentive would sell in competition with firms paying wages, but its prices would normally be lower because it would need to cover only the costs of materials and other required supplies. Wages and salaries would not need to be met out of income, as the consentive members would be receiving a guaranteed income. The consentive would be market-oriented but not market-supported.

We can anticipate that small market-supported firms will be enabled to survive by transforming themselves into market-oriented consentives. The opposite process will occur as consentives that make significant profits automatically turn into market-supported firms.[8] Thus the guaranteed income would help to bring about a reversal of the present trend toward similarity in type of goods and services, inflexibility in methods of production, and uniformity in productive organization.

At the present time we are committed as a society to the idea that we can and should provide jobs for all. This goal is no longer valid, and we should therefore provide everybody with an absolute right to a guaranteed income. This will, of course, mean that there will be far more unemployment in the future than there is today. We will, however, come to perceive unemployment as favorable rather than unfavorable. The individual and the society fear unemployment today for two reasons: first, because it usually involves the receipt of an inadequate income; second, because it threatens cessation of all activity that seems meaningful and indeed encourages antisocial activities. Once we have provided adequate incomes to all and have introduced the new policies required to develop each individual's potential, unemployment—which will then be redefined as the condition of *not* holding a job—will be seen to be highly desirable, for it will provide the individual with freedom to develop himself and his society.

REFERENCES

1 It is, of course, true that those in the developing countries cannot be provided with a decent standard of living today. But this does not mean, as many argue, that the rich countries should produce everything they can and deliver it to the poor. We should have learned by now that excessive aid can be just as dangerous as too little. We must accept the bitter fact that poverty in the poor countries—opposed to the rich—cannot be abolished in the near future. We must also recognize that we still have no strategy for the elimination of poverty in the underdeveloped countries. For an examination of this subject see: Robert Theobald, "Needed: A New Development Strategy," *International Development Review*, March, 1964.

2 Economic theory claims that each factor of production—land, labor, and capital—will be paid in accordance with its marginal (additional) contribution to production. Throughout the twentieth century, most of the increase in production has resulted from increased sophistication of equipment (i.e. capital) rather than through the harder work or the greater knowledge of the average worker. Thus most of the increase in production should, on the basis of theory, have gone to capital. This does not mean that we should distribute rights to resources by widening the ownership of capital—the proposal made by Lewis Kelso and Mortimer Adler. Rather we need a revision of theory on the basis of new realities of a cybernated era.

3 J. M. Keynes, *Essays in Persuasion* (New York: Harcourt, Brace and Company, 1932), pp. 369-370, "Economic Possibilities for Our Grandchildren."

4 A structured job is one in which the decision-making rules can be set out in advance. While computer theorists agree that the computer can, by definition, take over all structured jobs, they still disagree on the proportion of jobs on the factory floor and in the office which can eventually be structured. Everybody agrees, however, that the process of replacement of men by machines is only beginning.

5 J. M. Keynes, *The General Theory of Employment, Interest and Money* (New York: Harcourt, Brace and Company, 1936), p. 243.

6 Proposals for both a guaranteed income and income maintenance are set out in Part II and the Appendix of my book *Free Men and Free Markets* (Garden City, N.Y.: Doubleday & Company, Inc., 1965).

7 Keynes. *Essays in Persuasion*, p. 373.

8 For a description of these processes see *Free Men and Free Markets*, Chapter 9.

The New Forms of Control

Herbert Marcuse

A comfortable, smooth, reasonable, democratic unfreedom prevails in advanced industrial civilization, a token of technical progress. Indeed, what could be more rational than the suppression of individuality in the mechanization of socially necessary but painful performances; the concentration of individual enterprises in more effective, more productive corporations; the regulation of free competition among unequally equipped economic subjects; the curtailment of prerogatives and national sovereignties which impede the international organization of resources. That this technological order also involves a political and intellectual coordination may be a regrettable and yet promising development.

The rights and liberties which were such vital factors in the origins and earlier stages of industrial society yield to a higher stage of this society: they are losing their traditional rationale and content. Freedom of thought, speech, and conscience were—just as free enterprise,

---

which they served to promote and protect—essentially *critical* ideas, designed to replace an obsolescent material and intellectual culture by a more productive and rational one. Once institutionalized, these rights and liberties shared the fate of the society of which they had become an integral part. The achievement cancels the premises.

To the degree to which freedom from want, the concrete substance of all freedom, is becoming a real possibility, the liberties which pertain to a state of lower productivity are losing their former content. Independence of thought, autonomy, and the right to political opposition are being deprived of their basic critical function in a society which seems increasingly capable of satisfying the needs of the individuals through the way in which it is organized. Such a society may justly demand acceptance of its principles and institutions, and reduce the opposition to the discussion and promotion of alternative policies *within* the status quo. In this respect, it seems to make little difference whether the increasing satisfaction of needs is accomplished by an authoritarian or a non-authoritarian system. Under the conditions of a rising standard of living, non-conformity with the system itself appears to be socially useless, and the more so when it entails tangible economic and political disadvantages and threatens the smooth operation of the whole. Indeed, at least in so far as the necessities of life are involved, there seems to be no reason why the production and distribution of goods and services should proceed through the competitive concurrence of individual liberties.

Freedom of enterprise was from the beginning not altogether a blessing. As the liberty to work or to starve, it spelled toil, insecurity, and fear for the vast majority of the population. If the individual were no longer compelled to prove himself on the market, as a free economic subject, the disappearance of this kind of freedom would be one of the greatest achievements of civilization. The technological processes of mechanization and standardization might release individual energy into a yet uncharted realm of freedom beyond necessity. The very structure of human existence would be altered; the individual would be liberated from the work world's imposing upon him alien needs and alien possibilities. The individual would be free to exert autonomy over a life that would be his own. If the productive apparatus could be organized and directed toward the satisfaction of the vital needs, its control might well be centralized; such control would not prevent individual autonomy, but render it possible.

This is a goal within the capabilities of advanced industrial civilization, the "end" of technological rationality. In actual fact, however, the contrary trend operates: the apparatus imposes its economic and political requirements for defense and expansion on labor time and free time, on the material and intellectual culture. By virtue of the way it has organized its technological base, contemporary industrial society tends to be totalitarian. For "totalitarian" is not only a terroristic political coordination of society, but also a nonterroristic economic-technical coordination which operates through the manipulation of needs by vested interests. It thus precludes the emergence of an effective opposition against the whole. Not only a specific form of government or party rule makes for totalitarianism, but also a specific system of production and distribution which may well be compatible with a "pluralism" of parties, newspapers, "countervailing powers," etc.

Today political power asserts itself through its power over the machine process and over the technical organization of the apparatus. The government of advanced and advancing industrial societies can maintain and secure itself only when it succeeds in mobilizing, organizing, and exploiting the technical, scientific, and mechanical productivity available to industrial civilization. And this productivity mobilizes society as a whole, above and beyond any particular individual or group interests. The brute fact that the machine's physical (only physical?) power surpasses that of the individual, and of any particular group of individuals, makes the machine the most effective political instrument in any society whose basic organization is that of the machine process. But the political trend may be reversed; essentially the power of the machine is only the stored-up and projected power of man. To the extent to which the work world is conceived of as a machine and mechanized accordingly, it becomes the *potential* basis of a new freedom for man.

Contemporary industrial civilization demonstrates that it has reached the stage at which "the free society" can no longer be adequately defined in the traditional terms of economic, political, and intellectual liberties, not because these liberties have become insignificant, but because they are too significant to be confined within the traditional forms. New modes of realization are needed, corresponding to the new capabilities of society.

Such new modes can be indicated only in negative terms because they would amount to the negation of the prevailing modes. Thus economic freedom would mean freedom *from* the economy—from being controlled by economic forces and relationships; freedom from the daily struggle for existence, from earning a living. Political freedom would mean liberation of the individuals *from* politics over which they have no effective control. Similarly, intellectual freedom would mean the restoration of individual thought now absorbed by mass communication and indoctrination, abolition of "public opinion" together with its makers. The unrealistic sound of these propositions is indicative, not of their utopian character, but of the strength of the forces which prevent their realization. The most effective and enduring form of warfare against liberation is the implanting of material and intellectual needs that perpetuate obsolete forms of the struggle for existence.

The intensity, the satisfaction and even the character of human needs, beyond the biological level, have always been preconditioned. Whether or not the possibility of doing or leaving, enjoying or destroying, possessing or rejecting something is seized as a *need* depends on whether or not it can be seen as desirable and necessary for the prevailing societal institutions and interests. In this sense, human needs are historical needs and, to the extent to which the society demands the repressive development of the individual, his needs themselves and their claim for satisfaction are subject to overriding critical standards.

We may distinguish both true and false needs. "False" are those which are superimposed upon the individual by particular social interests in his repression: the needs which perpetuate toil, aggressiveness, misery, and injustice. Their satisfaction might be most gratifying to the individual, but this happiness is not a condition which has to be maintained and protected if it serves to arrest the development of the ability (his own and others) to recognize the disease of the whole and grasp the chances of curing the disease. The result then is euphoria in unhappiness. Most of the prevailing needs to relax, to have fun, to behave and consume in accordance with the advertisements, to love and hate what others love and hate, belong to this category of false needs.

Such needs have a societal content and function which are determined by eternal powers over which the individual has no control; the development and satisfaction of these needs is heteronomous. No matter how much such needs may have become the individual's own, reproduced and fortified by the conditions of his existence; no matter how much he identifies himself with them and finds himself in their satisfaction, they continue to be what they were from the beginning—products of a society whose dominant interest demands repression.

The prevalence of repressive needs is an accomplished fact, accepted in ignorance and defeat, but a fact that must be undone in the interest of the happy individual as well as all those whose misery is the price of his satisfaction. The only needs that have an unqualified claim for satisfaction are the vital ones—nourishment, clothing, lodging at the attainable level of culture. The satisfaction of these needs is the prerequisite for the realization of *all* needs, of the unsublimated as well as the sublimated ones.

For any consciousness and conscience, for any experience which does not accept the prevailing societal interest as the supreme law of thought and behavior, the established universe of needs and satisfactions is a fact to be questioned—questioned in terms of truth and falsehood. These terms are historical throughout, and their objectivity is historical. The judgment of needs and their satisfaction, under the given conditions, involves standards of *priority*—standards which refer to the optimal development of the individual, of all individuals, under the optimal utilization of the material and intellectual resources available to man. The resources are calculable. "Truth" and "falsehood" of needs designate objective conditions to the extent to which the universal satisfaction of vital needs and, beyond it, the progressive alleviation of toil and poverty, are universally valid standards. But as historical standards, they do not only vary according to area and stage of development, they also can be defined only in (greater or lesser) *contradiction* to the prevailing ones. What tribunal can possibly claim the authority of decision?

In the last analysis, the question of what are true and false needs must be answered by the individuals themselves, but only in the last analysis; that is, if and when they are free to give their own answer. As long as they are kept incapable of being autonomous, as long as they are indoctrinated and manipulated (down to their very instincts), their answer to this question cannot be taken as their own. By the same token, however, no tribunal can justly arrogate to itself the right to decide which needs should be developed and satisfied. Any such tribunal is reprehensible, although our revulsion does not do away with the question: how can the people who have been the object of effective and productive domination by themselves create the conditions of freedom?

The more rational, productive, technical, and total the repressive administration of society becomes, the more unimaginable the means and ways by which the administered individuals might break their servitude and seize their own liberation. To be sure, to impose Reason upon an entire society is a paradoxical and scandalous idea—although one might dispute the righteousness of a society which ridicules this idea while making its own population into objects of total administration. All liberation depends on the consciousness of servitude, and the emergence of this consciousness is always hampered by the predominance of needs and satisfactions which, to a great extent, have become the individual's own. The process always replaces one system of preconditioning by another; the optimal goal is the replacement of false needs by true ones, the abandonment of repressive satisfaction.

The distinguishing feature of advanced industrial society is its effective suffocation of those needs which demand liberation—liberation also from that which is tolerable and rewarding and comfortable—while it sustains and absolves the destructive power and repressive function of the affluent society. Here, the social controls exact the overwhelming need for the production and consumption of waste; the need for stupefying work where it is no longer a real necessity; the need for modes of relaxation which soothe and prolong this stupefication; the need for maintaining such deceptive liberties as free competition at administered prices, a free press which censors itself, free choice between brands and gadgets.

Under the rule of a repressive whole, liberty can be made into a powerful instrument of domination. The range of choice open to the individual is not the decisive factor in determining the degree of human freedom, but *what* can be chosen and what *is* chosen by the individual. The criterion for free choice can never be an absolute one, but neither is it entirely relative. Free election of masters does not abolish the masters or the slaves. Free choice among a wide variety of goods and services does not signify freedom if these goods and services sustain social controls over a life of toil and fear—that is, if they sustain alienation. And the spontaneous reproduction of superimposed needs by the individual does not establish autonomy; it only testifies to the efficacy of the controls.

Our insistence on the depth and efficacy of these controls is open to the objection that we overrate greatly the indoctrinating power of the "media," and that by themselves the people would feel and satisfy the needs which are now imposed upon them. The objection misses the point. The preconditioning does not start with the mass production of radio and television and with the centralization of their control. The people enter this stage as preconditioned receptacles of long standing; the decisive difference is in the flattening out of the contrast (or conflict) between the given and the possible, between the satisfied and the unsatisfied needs. Here, the so-called equalization of class distinctions reveals its ideological function. If the worker and his boss enjoy the same television program and visit the same resort places, if the typist is as attractively made up as the daughter of her employer, if the Negro owns a Cadillac, if they all read the same newspaper, then this assimilation indicates not the disappearance of classes, but the extent to which the needs and satisfactions that serve the preservation of the Establishment are shared by the underlying population.

Indeed, in the most highly developed areas of contemporary society, the transplantation of social into individual needs is so effective that the difference between them seems to be purely theoretical. Can one really distinguish between the mass media as instruments of information and entertainment, and as agents of manipulation and indoctrination? Between the automobile as nuisance and as convenience? Between the horrors and the comforts of functional architecture? Between the work for national defense and the work for corporate gain? Between the private pleasure and the commercial and political utility involved in increasing the birth rate?

We are again confronted with one of the most vexing aspects of advanced industrial civilization: the rational character of its irrationality. Its productivity and efficiency, its capacity to increase and spread comforts, to turn waste into need, and destruction into construction, the extent to which this civilization transforms the object world into an extension of man's mind and body makes the very notion of alienation questionable. The people recognize themselves in their commodities; they find their soul in their automobile, hi-fi set, split-level home, kitchen equipment. The very mechanism which ties the individual to his society has changed, and social control is anchored in the new needs which it has produced.

The prevailing forms of social control are technological in a new sense. To be sure, the technical structure and efficacy of the productive and destructive apparatus has been a major instrumentality for subjecting the population to the established social division of labor throughout the modern period. Moreover, such integration has always been accompanied by more obvious forms of compulsion: loss of livelihood, the administration of justice, the police, the armed forces. It still is. But in the contemporary period, the technological controls appear to be the very embodiment of Reason for the benefit of all social groups and interests—to such an extent that all contradiction seems irrational and all counteraction impossible.

No wonder then that, in the most advanced areas of this civilization, the social controls have been introjected to the point where even individual protest is affected at its roots. The intellectual and emotional refusal "to go along" appears neurotic and impotent. This is the socio-psychological aspect of the political event that marks the contemporary period: the passing of the historical forces which, at the preceding stage of industrial society, seemed to represent the possibility of new forms of existence.

But the term "introjection" perhaps no longer describes the way in which the individual by himself reproduces and perpetuates the external controls exercised by his society. Introjection suggests a variety of relatively spontaneous processes by which a Self (Ego) transposes the "outer" into the "inner." Thus introjection implies the existence of an inner dimension distinguished from and even antagonistic to the external exigencies—an individual consciousness and an individual unconscious *apart from* public opinion and behavior.[1] The idea of "inner freedom" here has its reality: it designates the private space in which man may become and remain "himself."

Today this private space has been invaded and whittled down by technological reality. Mass production and mass distribution claim the *entire* individual, and industrial psychology has long since ceased to be confined to the factory. The manifold processes of introjection seem to be ossified in almost mechanical reactions. The result is, not adjustment but *mimesis:* an immediate identification of the individual with *his* society and, through it, with the society as a whole.

This immediate, automatic identification (which may have been characteristic of primitive forms of association) reappears in high industrial civilization; its new "immediacy," however, is the product of a sophisticated, scientific management and organization. In this process, the "inner" dimension of the mind in which opposition to the status quo can take root is whittled down. The loss of this dimension, in which the power of negative thinking—the critical power of Reason—is at home, is the ideological counterpart to the very material process in which advanced industrial society silences and reconciles the opposition. The impact of progress turns Reason into submission to the facts of life, and to the dynamic capability of producing more and bigger facts of the same sort of life. The efficiency of the system blunts the individuals' recognition that it contains no facts which do not communicate the repressive power of the whole. If the individuals find themselves in the things which shape their life, they do so, not by giving, but by accepting the law of things—not the law of physics but the law of their society.

I have just suggested that the concept of alienation seems to become questionable when the individuals identify themselves with the existence which is imposed upon them and have in it their own development and satisfaction. This identification is not illusion but reality. However, the reality constitutes a more progressive stage of alienation. The latter has become entirely objective; the subject which is alienated is swallowed up by its alienated existence. There is only one dimension, and it is everywhere and in all forms. The achievements of progress defy ideological indictment as well as justification; before their tribunal, the "false consciousness" of their rationality becomes the true consciousness.

This absorption of ideology into reality does not, however, signify the "end of ideology." On the contrary, in a specific sense advanced industrial culture is *more* ideological than its predecessor, inasmuch as today the ideology is in the process of production itself.[2] In a provocative form, this proposition reveals the political aspects of the prevailing technological rationality. The productive apparatus and the goods and services which it produces "sell" or impose the social system as a whole. The means of mass transportation and communication, the commodities of lodging, food, and clothing, the irresistible output of the entertainment and information industry carry with them prescribed attitudes and habits, certain intellectual and emotional reactions which bind the consumers more or less pleasantly to the producers and, through the latter, to the whole. The products indoctrinate and manipulate; they promote a false consciousness which is immune against its falsehood. And as these beneficial products become available to more individuals in more social classes, the indoctrination they carry ceases to be publicity; it becomes a way of life. It is a good way of life—much better than before—and as a good way of life, it militates against qualitative change. Thus emerges a pattern of *one-dimensional thought and behavior* in which ideas, aspirations, and objectives that, by their content, transcend the establish universe of discourse and action are either repelled or reduced to terms of this universe. They are redefined by the rationality of the given system and of its quantitative extension.

The trend may be related to a development in scientific method: operationalism in the physical, behaviorism in the social sciences. The common feature is a total empiricism in the treatment of concepts; their meaning is restricted to the representation of particular operations and behavior. The operational point of view is well illustrated by P. W. Bridgman's analysis of the concept of length.[3]

> We evidently know what we mean by length if we can tell what the length of any and every object is, and for the physicist nothing more is required. To find the length of an object, we have to perform certain physical operations. The concept of length is therefore fixed when the operations by which length is measured are fixed: that is, the

concept of length involves as much and nothing more than the set of operations by which length is determined. In general, we mean by any concept nothing more than a set of operations; *the concept is synonymous with the corresponding set of operations.*

Bridgman has seen the wide implications of this mode of thought for the society at large.[4]

To adopt the operational point of view involves much more than a mere restriction of the sense in which we understand 'concept,' but means a far-reaching change in all our habits of thought, in that we shall no longer permit ourselves to use as tools in our thinking concepts of which we cannot give an adequate account in terms of operations.

Bridgman's prediction has come true. The new mode of thought is today the predominant tendency in philosophy, psychology, sociology, and other fields. Many of the most seriously troublesome concepts are being "eliminated" by showing that no adequate account of them in terms of operations or behavior can be given. The radical empiricist onslaught . . . thus provides the methodological justification for debunking of the mind by the intellectuals—a positivism which, in its denial of the transcending elements of Reason, forms the academic counterpart of the socially required behavior.

Outside the academic establishment, the "far-reaching change in all our habits of thought" is more serious. It serves to coordinate ideas and goals with those exacted by the prevailing system, to enclose them in the system, and to repel those which are irreconcilable with the system. The reign of such a one-dimensional reality does not mean that materialism rules, and that the spiritual, metaphysical, and bohemian occupations are petering out. On the contrary, there is a great deal of "Worship together this week," "Why not try God," Zen, existentialism, and beat ways of life, etc. But such modes of protest and transcendence are no longer contradictory to the status quo and no longer negative. They are rather the ceremonial part of practical behaviorism, its harmless negation, and are quickly digested by the status quo as part of its healthy diet.

One-dimensional thought is systematically promoted by the makers of politics and their purveyors of mass information. Their universe of discourse is populated by self-validating hypotheses which, incessantly and monopolistically repeated, become hypnotic definitions or dictations. For example, "free" are the institutions which operate (and are operated on) in the countries of the Free World; other transcending modes of freedom are by definition either anarchism, communism, or propaganda. "Socialistic" are all encroachments on private enterprises not undertaken by private enterprise itself (or by government contracts), such as universal and comprehensive health insurance, or the protection of nature from all too sweeping commercialization, or the establishment of public services which may hurt private profit. This totalitarian logic of accomplished facts has its Eastern counterpart. There, freedom is the way of life instituted by a communist regime, and all other transcending modes of freedom are either capitalistic, or revisionist, or leftist sectarianism. In both camps, non-operational ideas are non-behavioral and subversive. The movement of thought is stopped at barriers which appear as the limits of Reason itself.

Such limitation of thought is certainly not new. Ascending modern rationalism, in its speculative as well as empirical form, shows a striking contrast between extreme critical radicalism in scientific and philosophic method on the one hand, and an uncritical quietism in the attitude toward established and functioning social institutions. Thus Descartes' *ego cogitans* was to leave the "great public bodies" untouched, and Hobbes held that "the present ought always to be preferred, maintained, and accounted best." Kant agreed with Locke in justifying revolution *if and when* it has succeeded in organizing the whole and in preventing subversion.

However, these accommodating concepts of Reason were always contradicted by the evident misery and injustice of the "great public bodies" and the effective, more or less conscious rebellion against them. Societal conditions existed which provoked and permitted real dissociation from the established state of affairs; a private as well as political dimension was present in which dissociation could develop into effective opposition, testing its strength and the validity of its objectives.

With the gradual closing of this dimension by the society, the self-limitation of thought assumes a larger significance. The interrelation between scientific-philosophical and societal processes, between theoretical and practical Reason, asserts itself "behind the back" of the scientists and philosophers. The society bars a whole type of oppositional operations and behavior; consequently, the concepts pertaining to them are rendered illusory or meaningless. Historical transcendence appears as metaphysical transcendence, not acceptable to science and scientific thought. The operational and behavioral point of view, practiced as a "habit of thought" at large, becomes the view of the established universe of discourse and action, needs and aspirations.

The "cunning of Reason" works, as it so often did, in the interest of the powers that be. The insistence on operational and behavioral concepts turns against the efforts to free thought and behavior *from* the given reality and *for* the suppressed alternatives. Theoretical and practical Reason, academic and social behaviorism meet on common ground: that of an advanced society which makes scientific and technical progress into an instrument of domination.

"Progress" is not a neutral term; it moves toward specific ends, and these ends are defined by the possibilities of ameliorating the human condition. Advanced industrial society is approaching the stage where continued progress would demand the radical subversion of the prevailing direction and organization of progress. This stage would be reached when material production (including the necessary services) becomes automated to the extent that all vital needs can be satisfied while necessary labor time is reduced to marginal time. From this point on, technical progress would transcend the realm of necessity, where it served as the instrument of domination and exploitation which thereby limited its rationality; technology would become subject to the free play of faculties in the struggle for the pacification of nature and of society.

Such a state is envisioned in Marx's notion of the "abolition of labor." The term "pacification of existence" seems better suited to designate the historical alternative of a world which—through an international conflict which transforms and suspends the contradictions within the established societies—advances on the brink of global war. "Pacification of existence" means the development of man's struggle with man and with nature, under conditions where the competing needs, desires, and aspirations are no longer organized by vested interests in domination and scarcity—an organization which perpetuates the destructive forms of this struggle.

Today's fight against this historical alternative finds a firm mass basis in the underlying population, and finds its ideology in the rigid orientation of thought and behavior to the given universe of facts. Validated by the accomplishments of science and technology, justified by its growing productivity, the status quo defies all transcendence. Faced with the possibility of pacification on the grounds of its technical and intellectual achievements, the mature industrial society closes itself against this alternative. Operationalism, in theory and practice, becomes the theory and practice of *containment*. Underneath its obvious dynamics, this society is a thoroughly static system of life: self-propelling in its oppressive productivity and in its beneficial coordination. Containment of technical progress goes hand in hand with its growth in the established direction. In spite of the political fetters imposed by the status quo, the more technology appears capable of creating the conditions for pacification, the more are the minds and bodies of man organized against this alternative.

The most advanced areas of industrial society exhibit throughout these two features: a trend toward consummation of technological rationality, and intensive efforts to contain this trend within the established institutions. Here is the internal contradiction of this civilization: the irrational element in its rationality. It is the token of its achievements. The industrial society which makes technology and science its own is organized for the ever-more-effective domination of man and nature, for the ever-more-effective utilization of its resources. It becomes irrational when the success of these efforts opens new dimensions of human realization. Organization for peace is different from organization for war; the institutions which served the struggle for existence cannot serve the pacification of existence. Life as an end is qualitatively different from life as a means.

Such a qualitatively new mode of existence can never be envisaged as the mere by-product of economic and political changes, as the more or less spontaneous effect of the new institutions which constitute the necessary prerequisite. Qualitative change also involves a change in the *technical* basis on which this society rests—one which sustains the economic and political institutions through which the "second nature" of man as an aggressive object of administration is stabilized. The techniques of industrialization are political techniques; as such, they prejudge the possibilities of Reason and Freedom.

To be sure, labor must precede the reduction of labor, and industrialization must precede the development of human needs and satisfactions. But as all freedom depends on the conquest of alien necessity, the realization of freedom depends on the *techniques* of this conquest. The highest productivity of labor can be used for the perpetuation of labor, and the most efficient industrialization can serve the restriction and manipulation of needs.

When this point is reached, domination—in the guise of affluence and liberty—extends to all spheres of private and public existence, integrates all authentic opposition, absorbs all alternatives. Technological rationality reveals its political character as it becomes the great vehicle of better domination, creating a truly totalitarian universe in which society and nature, mind and body are kept in a state of permanent mobilization for the defense of this universe.

[1] The change in the function of the family here plays a decisive role: its "socializing" functions are increasingly taken over by outside groups and media. See my *Eros and Civilization* (Boston: Beacon Press, 1955), p. 96 ff.

[2] Theodor W. Adorno, *Prismen. Kulturkritik and Gesellschaft.* (Frankfurt: Suhrkamp, 1955), p. 24 f.

[3] P. W. Bridgman, *The Logic of Modern Physics* (New York: Macmillan, 1928), p. 5. The operational doctrine has since been refined and qualified. Bridgman himself has extended the concept of "operation" to include the "paper-and-pencil" operations of the theorist (in Philipp J. Frank, *The Validation of Scientific Theories* [Boston: Beacon Press, 1954], Chap. II). The main impetus remains the same: it is "desirable" that the paper-and-pencil operations "be capable of eventual contact, although perhaps indirectly, with instrumental operations."

[4] P. W. Bridgman, *The Logic of Modern Physics,* loc. cit., p. 31.

4

Students and Politics

American Students and the "Political Revival"

Kenneth Kenniston

The apolitical stance of American youth is something of a puzzle. Our liberal political tradition once led us to believe that intelligent political concern went hand in hand with public well-being and education; and yet despite prosperity and the highest level of education in the world, our young men and women remain overwhelmingly uninterested in the state of the nation and the world. Even in a time of "political revival" and "revolt on the campus," the highest estimates of politically active students range around ten percent; while at most colleges, ninety, or ninety-five, or ninety-nine percent of the student body take no active part in any cause or organization that could be called truly political. In other nations—both the highly industrialized and the rapidly developing—a much larger proportion of educated young men and women are involved in political life, actively debate the issues of the day and demonstrate their vigorous approval or disapproval of the trends of the times. In Korea and Turkey, successful revolutions have

---

recently been led by students; in Japan, as in Latin America and Africa, student demonstrations can affect national policy; and even in industrialized Europe, educated youth is more politically conscious and active than in America. It almost appears that affluence and education have a negative effect on political involvement, at least in America.

The puzzle is deepened when we recall the close historical association between rapid social change and a politically active youth. It is an axiom of historical observation that drastic social change puts enormous stresses on the individual, that the aspirations of young people often—indeed usually—outrun the facts of society during such periods, and that a radically altered social scene makes impossible any easy continuity between the generations. All of these factors increase the likelihood that young men and women will attempt to change the society to conform with their own democratic and often radical aspirations. And in this country during the past hundred years we have witnessed precisely the kind of social transformations that elsewhere led to a politically active youth. Beginning with the spurt of industrialization after the Civil War, American society has undergone and continues to undergo deep transformations, no less drastic because they are no longer reflected in the indices of economic output, and no less affecting because we have grown used to them. Yet despite this, American youth is predominantly apolitical, and has been so almost without interruption since the foundation of this nation.

A full explanation of the predominantly apolitical outlook of American youth—as of the active participation in politics of an increasing few—would involve nothing less than a social and psychological history of this nation. Here I can only suggest one or two factors that have played a role in the development of this outlook and then, in the light of these factors, try to assess the meaning and prospects of the recent "revival" of political interest among students.

To understand so current a topic as the campus "political revival" and the inert student masses against which this "revival" takes place, we must take a long step backward to consider some of the factors that distinguish American social development from that of most other nations; for in them, I think, lies the key to understanding the apolitical outlook of today's young. For one, as many commentators on American life have noted, America never had a feudal past to overcome. If we define feudal broadly, so that it includes not only established aristocracies but land- and mine-owning oligarchies and colonial rulers, then there are only a handful of former British colonies that had the same fresh start that we did. Concretely, this has meant that Americans, from the beginning, have lacked clear and obvious targets for rebellion. Young people growing up in this country have, for one hundred and fifty years, found themselves *already* living in a nation whose major public values are still the mottoes of revolution elsewhere—equal rights, equal opportunities, justice under law and so on. Not that these values are always practiced—but at least they are subscribed to almost universally and probably practiced to a greater extent than in many countries. Thus, generations of young Americans awakened to consciousness to find themselves already living in a "post-revolutionary" world. If they remained dissatisfied, impoverished or underprivileged, there were no aristrocrats, land-owners or colonial rulers to rebel against. Instead, Americans have always perceived their chief obstacle as some quality of their own like ignorance, laziness, bad luck or inexperience, chains that could be cast off by effort, by education or, in our own time, by psychotherapy.

A second relevant constant in American life is the anti-ideological bias of American thinking. Even Toqueville commented in the 1830's that Americans' passion for grand ideas was not matched by any parallel passion for translating these ideas into practice. And it has remained true, in general, that ideological speculations in this country have been a kind of game played by intellectuals who themselves often doubted their practicality on a large scale. For example, even though the founders of the utopian communities that dotted the countryside in the 1800's were discontented with the status quo, they did not attempt to change the whole society through revolution or political action as they might have done in an ideological nation like France or Germany. Rather, they withdrew from the wider society to set up their own private utopias. Americans who were explicitly disaffected have rarely attempted political action on a grand scale but have chosen instead for withdrawal, emigration or exemplary self-reform. As a nation, we are not only hostile to the translation of grand schemes into political reality, but, more important, it seldom even occurs to most of us that ideological (or even intellectual) considerations have much to do with the workings of political life.

This characteristic American distrust of grand political schemes, coupled with our fresh start as a nation, has given a peculiar and perhaps unique coloring to Americans' attitudes toward social change. It has meant that the burden of proof has always been on those who opposed or sought to direct the economic and social transformations of the nation. In countries with Establishments, whether of title, education, race or conquest, it has seemed quite natural that the original Establishment or its latter-day successor should seek to direct the changes of the nation's social face. And in such countries, the vestiges of the older "feudal" orders have often served as foci of opposition to the new, the modern and the untried. But in America, lacking such foci and mistrusting social planning, we have consistently preferred to let society run its "natural course," which has in practice meant that the needs of a burgeoning industry have usually been most heeded. To this fact we owe part of our industrial accomplishments and our high standard of living, which could not have been achieved without a people who were convinced that the new, the modern, the "latest" were good, and that what was old and established was "old-fashioned," "obsolete" and "outmoded." Concretely, this has meant that each new product, institution, custom or even value has been eagerly seized by a nation rushing to outgrow its yesterdays and hurrying to enter a future ever brighter than the present. In a word, Americans have been and continue to be on the side of change, and have considered it their obligation to make whatever accommodations were necessary to Progress.

In this continuing context of unopposed, undirected and highly valued social change, the last four generations of Americans have been formed. And, more important, their conceptions of themselves and their tasks as youths have been shaped by social definitions of youth that have been broadly consonant with this context of social change. Such social definitions exist unnoticed in every society, dictating what kinds of behavior are legitimate for youth—and when not legitimate, then expected, and when not expected, then at least comprehended by other members of society as signs of protest, illness or divine favor. A young man or woman who lives within the confines of these definitions is understandable and predictable to his fellows and (even more important to an adolescent) understandable and "normal" to himself; whereas one who deviates from the sheltering confines of such images is considered strange, erratic, weird (in our society, "un-American"), and eventually begins to wonder about his own normality. To "work" in the broader context of society, an image of youth must be broadly consonant with the basic values of the society and, furthermore, it must help the young to grow into adulthood, resolving the peculiar stresses of adolescence in that society and strengthening in each youth an attachment to the tasks that maturity will require.

In a complex and changing society like ours, two basic definitions of youth exist, each with many subvariants. These two images, which I will call youth as *apprenticeship for social mobility* and youth as *youth culture,* are very different in most ways. But both are consistent with American values about social change; both permit the resolution of some of the major problems created by rapid change, and—most relevant to this context—both discourage political activity among the young.

To understand the role played by these definitions of youth, we must consider in more detail the specific directions of social change in this country over the past hundred years or so. And on this point there is a good deal of consensus among historians and sociologists. Put very generally, we are moving from an economy of scarcity to one of relative affluence, from the takeoff point of rapid industrialization to an era of mass consumption, from basic production to service industries. Sociologically, this has meant a relative shift from individual entrepreneurship to bureaucratic corporations limited by government regulation, from the rugged competitiveness of the Protestant Ethic in the last century to the smoother group orientation of the Social Ethic in this century and, on the family front, from the more authoritarian entrepreneurial family to the newer, more team-minded bureaucratic family. And most important for the understanding of youth has been the shift in social character first discussed by Riesman—a shift from an organization of character based on internal standards of personal worth that lead to competitive achievement, from this inner-direction to the newer other-directed character based on sensitivity to the feelings of others and on interpersonal standards of worth.

The heyday of the older entrepreneurial society seems to have occurred in the northern United States during the decades of rapid industrialization following the Civil War; these years saw the transformation of this country from an agrarian into an industrial society. These were decades of very rapid social mobility, of fortunes quickly made and quickly lost in the next panic—a time much like our own when adults found themselves living in a kind of society their own parents had never dreamed of, and hence had not been able to prepare their children for. Comparable periods in Germany and Japan saw the rise of militant youth groups aiming at radical changes in the social organization of the nation; but of course in America there has never been any such movement.

Part of the explanation for the quiescence of American youth undoubtedly lies in the facts I have already mentioned: in America there was no feudal, preindustrial order to block the advancement or frustrate the democratic aspirations of the young; but in Japan and Germany such an order did exist, and did frustrate the dreams of radical youth. But even more important, I think, was the existence in this country of another mythical and to some extent real alternative to politics for youth—rapid social mobility. Horatio Alger is probably the best-known spokesman for this view. Recall the basic plot of his stories: his heroes were poor but honest lads who were befriended by a wealthy older man, a man successful and prosperous *within* the existing social order. The lads, partly by dint of their own drive and energy, but also with large amounts of assistance from the obliging older man, eventually take over the bank or company, marry the older man's lovely, rich daughter and become roaring successes. The presence of the helping older man is crucial here. Horatio Alger implies that if one's parents are inadequate models, others will act in their stead. Indeed Horatio Alger, like the motto, "from rags to riches," positively *urges* the young to abandon their rag-ridden parents and follow other, more modern and successful elders into the new world of riches. Generational discontinuity is of course one of the chief problems of rapid social change, in that parents can seldom serve as exemplars to their children; but here it is made a virtue. The young are told that the remedy for discontent is hard work *within* the existing system, which will reward the deserving according to their industry, ambition and honesty.

Although probably only a few young men took Horatio Alger literally, the general moral of his stories was widely accepted. Youth was defined as an apprenticeship for adulthood; the specific task of youth was to cultivate the many virtues and acquire the few skills needed for success in the upward road ahead. And so long as it remained credible, this definition of youth worked fairly well. It enjoined the young to answer discontent with hard work, to abandon the past willingly for greater goods ahead, and to view their schools and colleges as if they were the Pennsylvania Railroad Station, in Edgar Friedenberg's phrase. The only problem for a young man (although it was not always a small problem) was to locate the right track and stay on it to his destination. Education was above all a matter of memorizing the map and timetable, and getting out as quickly as possible for the main journey ahead. Furthermore, as long as many young men believed in the possibility and desirability of upward mobility and success, this definition of youth assured the society a goodly reserve of eager young men who were determined to abandon the past, quick to learn the techniques of the new society, convinced that it was to their own benefit to work hard, and sustained even in poverty by fantasies of success, luck and a helping hand ahead. And, finally, by transforming potential discontent and unrest into the struggle to get ahead *within* the system, this image of youth effectively prevented political involvement among the young.

But as we all now know, there were not enough kindly and helping bankers to go around, or enough thriving businesses to take over, or enough lovely bosses' daughters to marry. And, more important, American society has changed since Horatio Alger's day, so that its most visible, prestigeful positions are no longer the conspicuous castles of bank presidents and robber barons, but rather the discreetly restrained, steel-and-glass offices of executive vice-presidents, technical advisers, scientists in business and even, occasionally, of a college professor with a government grant. Increasingly in our present society, the older "entrepreneurial" virtues of thrift and determination, grit and gumption, are no longer enough; the newer requirements for prestige are at least a B.A., a certain personal sophistication, specialized technical competence, an acceptable wife and at least a good imitation of a "genuine interest in people." Then, too, the intensity of the drive to success and prestige has itself lessened. In a day of middle-class affluence, the push to escape the poverty and restriction of slum, farm or immigrant background has lessened, and people worry more, and longer, about *how* to live the rich full life with the goods they *already* possess—and even sometimes question whether it is all worth the effort to begin with. Horatio Alger and "from rags to riches" are tokens of a fast-disappearing day; and with them, the image of youth as an apprenticeship for upward mobility is waning too.

The definition of youth that in many places has replaced this older image is harder to pin down, harder even to find an adequate name for. I can only call it, in a cumbersome way, the image of youth as youth culture, and then try to make clear what I mean. The youth culture is the special set of mores, customs, roles and values of youth considered as a distinctive, separate age group. In many primitive societies youth is not so considered; on the contrary, youths are seen either as old children or as young adults, not as members of an age group who—simply because they are adolescents—are expected to behave in a way distinct from both children and adults. But in other societies, especially those like our own where the transition from childhood to adulthood is difficult, late adolescents and early adults are expected to behave in special, idiosyncratic ways that are symptomatic of their age.

In America it is probably best to speak of many youth cultures, rather than one, for under this rubric we must subsume a great many different phenomena: teen-agers, "Joe College" students, youthful beatniks, rock-and-rollers, juvenile delinquents. But, at the same time, all of these distinct cultures have certain common features. Talcott

Parsons lists emphasis on physical attractiveness, irresponsibility, interest in athletics, repudiation of adult things—and to this list I would add other common characteristics, for example, a kind of hedonism of the moment, a reluctance to undertake long-range commitments, a high value placed on sensation, experience and excitement. F. Scott Fitzgerald's picture of Princeton before and after the First War came to epitomize an earlier, "flaming youth" version of youth culture. In our own day, we have more various and contrasting versions, ranging from the black-jacketed delinquent to the oversensitive Catcher in the Rye, from the misunderstood James Dean to the fun-and-football fraternity man. The particular group most relevant to a discussion of student politics is what could be called "elite youth"—that is, those educationally privileged young men and women who correspond in talent and intelligence to the most politically active students in other nations. It is from this group that tomorrow's leaders will most likely be drawn; and these young men and women usually act as pace-setting models to other students. Although such "elite" students are more articulate than most of their contemporaries, they often voice aspirations and ideas implicit in other versions of the youth culture, and a consideration of the most salient views of elite students may serve as summary of the outlooks of other American youth cultures as well.

One of the outstanding characteristics of many young people today is their apparent *lack of deep commitment to adult values.* A large number of young men and women are relatively alienated from their parents' conceptions of the world, disaffiliated from previous ideas of the good life. They often view the adult world with considerable lack of enthusiasm, seeing it as cold, mechanical, impersonal and overspecialized, lacking in qualities of dignity and vitality that might make commitment to it worthwhile. For some, it is very important to be "cool," and "coolness" involves, above all, lack of overt enthusiasm. This is not to say that students are cynical or calculating—indeed, most of them wish there were purposes to which they could wholeheartedly subscribe. When they see such purposes, they usually find them abroad, in the underdeveloped countries, which have become the last frontier and refuge of American idealism. When something like the Peace Corps comes along, a surprising number express a willingness to drop everything and join up. But usually, if they are enthusiastic about anything, it is about their steady girl friend, their role in the college dramatic society, about a piece of music, about a weekend with their friends. Yet the opposite side of the coin is that these same young men and women are surprisingly sane, level-headed and realistic—probably in many ways more "adult" than their parents were at their age. They are never given to fanaticism, indeed they have a sometimes paralyzing awareness of the world's complexity. They are well read and well informed; they are kind and tolerant and decent in their dealings with other people.

Secondly, I am struck with the *lack of rebelliousness* among today's college students. This is in a way surprising, because we are used to thinking that lack of commitment must mean rejection and rebellion. Indeed, in the classical stories of filial rebellion, where the son is in real danger of being forced to become like his father, he does rebel rather than accept this definition of himself. But many young men and women today simply see no possibility of being like their parents; the world of parents is so distant, so different, that it neither tempts nor threatens the young; and therefore rebellion is seldom necessary. On the contrary, many young people show a touching understanding for their parents' often hesitant efforts to counsel and advise them. Parents, too, usually sense, at some level, their own out-of-datedness to their children, and this awareness makes them reluctant to try to impose their own values. The result is a kind of unstated gentleman's agreement between the generations that neither will interfere with the other.

Such an agreement creates new problems, however, and leads directly to another characteristic of many students: their *lack of admired paternal figures.* Our modern literary heroes seldom have fathers at all; or when they do have biological fathers, these are portrayed as weak, ineffectual, absent or otherwise unable to fulfill the traditional psychological role of fathers as exemplars. Take Augie March or Holden Caulfield, consider the heroes of Arthur Miller's and Tennessee Williams' plays, or recall the types played by Jimmie Dean. None of these young men has a father who can act as a model or even as a target of rebellion—nor does he like Horatio Alger's heroes, find an exemplary substitute. Here I think current fiction displays life writ large. One sometimes even hears students lament the fact that their parents give so little authoritative guidance: "If only they would tell me what *they* think I should do." Young men and women want and need models, both positive and negative, and they require older adults who will act as guardians to their identity while it is still fledgling. When such models and guardians are absent, the young feel—and indeed are—cheated.

Another outlook of many students—and here we move closer to politics—is a widespread feeling of *social powerlessness.* This involves politics, to be sure, but it extends far beyond it, to the point where many young people feel helpless to influence or direct any but the most personal and immediate spheres of their lives. The world appears to be a fluid and chaotic place; individuals seem the victims of colossal and impersonal historical forces which can seldom be understood and never controlled.

The most common response to this feeling of social powerlessness is what David Riesman has called *privatism.* Young people generally emphasize and value precisely those areas of life that are farthest from the wider society, and which therefore seem most manageable. Consider the matter of families: most young people want large families, they marry earlier than in the past, they are prepared to work very hard to create happy families, and they often value family closeness far more than meaningful work. Or, similarly, recall the emphasis many youths place on leisure: their eagerness to learn how to spend their leisure to good advantage, to find jobs with good vacations in areas where leisure time can be pleasantly spent. Indeed, I know several young men who anticipate working at their leisure with an intensity that will be quite lacking from their work itself. In both these areas, we see a search for private styles of life that will be predictable and under control.

Closely related to privatism is the *foreshortening of time span.* The most extreme form of this trend is found in the "beat" emphasis on present satisfactions, with an almost total refusal to consider past commitments or future consequences. In far less psychopathic form, a great many young people emphasize pursuits and interests that can be enjoyed for their own sake and in the present. The decline of the Protestant Ethic has brought a virtual disappearance of the idea of a Life Work, of the long-deferred goals and satisfactions of an earlier breed of Americans. Few young men and women have life goals that extend more than a few years ahead; most can see only as far as graduate school; and many drift into, rather than actively or consciously choose, their future careers.

In general, then, many college students have what can be called a *cult of experience,* which stresses, as one student put it, "the maximum possible number of sense experiences." Indeed, part of the fascination of the "beat generation" for college students lies in its unencumbered quest for kicks, for an intensification of private, present experience to almost unbearable degrees. Few students go this far, even though they may ride motorcycles, frequent coffee houses and sport beards. But other types of private experience less asocial than speed, sex and stimulants are sought nonetheless: the enjoyment of nature, the privacy of erotic love, the company of friends—these occupy a similar place in the hierarchy of values.

At best, such a youth culture has important virtues for the individual as for the society, providing what Erik Erikson calls a "psycho-social moratorium," that is, a sanctioned time and place when the young can decide how, where—and even whether—they will fit into society. And, above all, it provides a breathing spell between childhood and adulthood, time to develop a sense of personal identity that will link the problematical individual social and national past with the uncertain future, and, hopefully, will enable the young to develop their own guidelines for commitment and action. Thus, the definition of youth as youth culture helps the young to cope with the stresses and strains created by rapid social change and, at the same time, to do so in a thoroughly apolitical way that will not rock the social or political boat.

The transition from apprenticeship to youth culture is, of course, far from a completed fact. At many colleges, especially those that recruit primarily working-class and lower middle-class students, the apprentices still dominate the scene. And even in so-called elite colleges, some students still view their education as an occupational passport, and resist involvement with both the youth culture and the academic enterprise. Furthermore, as I will suggest below, I think we are witnessing the emergence of yet a third conception of youth, which differs from both apprenticeship and youth culture. So the shift in images of youth is complex and far from complete.

Nor do I want to imply that young men and women are either *simply* apprentices or *simply* youth culturists. To do so would be to leave out what is probably the central fact about most college students—namely, their *ambivalence toward their own youth.* A great deal has been said and written about the ambivalence of older people toward adolescents—the mixture of envy, respect, fear, titillation, exaggeration and hope with which non-youths perennially eye the younger generation. But much less has been said about the ambivalence of the young toward themselves, their fluctuation between a view of themselves as free and reckless participants in the most irresponsible of youth cultures, and the alternate image of themselves as sober and dedicated apprentice citizens. Indeed, a controversy rages between those observers who see American youth as wild and irresponsible, and those who see only the deferential and conformist side of youth.

The point is, I think, that these observers are usually looking at two sides of the very same people, mistaking the part for the whole. Such oversimplification is especially hard to avoid because young people themselves present now one and now another face, all the while maintaining that there is no more than meets the eye. Not that they deliberately deceive older people as to what they are like—on the contrary, when a young man or woman is with representatives of the adult world (teachers, ministers, admissions officers, polltakers) he not only acts like a future citizen of America, he really *feels* that way. And the same youths under other circumstances—when with friends, at Fort Lauderdale or Newport, in campus coffee houses, fraternities and sororities or dormitories—really *feel* like hoods, beatniks, College Joes or Dekes. But in each of these stances some of the same ambivalence exists, despite the frequent insistence of the young (with a characteristic adolescent combination of ambivalence and intolerance for ambivalence) that there is only one side to the coin.

However complex, shifting and ambivalent these definitions of youth, they have in common a fundamental indifference to politics. Indeed, they do more than suggest indifference to politics; they make it virtually abnormal for a young man of standard middle-class background to become passionately involved with national or international issues. Not surprisingly, those few who have violated the implicit prohibition on politics in these images have often come from atypical milieus—usually either from recent European immigrant stock, or from upper-class backgrounds capable of resisting the dominant American mores. And also not surprising is the array of reinforcing and supporting customs that have buttressed the apolitical outlook of American students. Among these buttressing customs two seem to me especially important today: what is usually referred to as campus politics, and what is often called the legacy of McCarthyism. Both of these are commonly misunderstood.

"Campus politics," as most Americans use the term, refers primarily to the intramural politics of American undergraduate life—the quarrels over elections to student legislatures and student judiciary councils, over the role of the dean of women and over that traditionally most vexing of college problems, the hours at women's dormitories. Thus, "campus politician" is a slightly pejorative term for a would-be manipulator of campus factions—and it seldom refers to a young person interested in broader political issues. Indeed, the substantive issues of campus politics seldom resemble the topics of what I will henceforth call "true politics"—that is, active concern with state, national and international issues. But because of similarities in outward form (both have elections, issues, parties, candidates, campaigns and parliaments), campus politics is usually seen as a "training for democracy," as a preparation for political responsibility in later life. In fact, however, I think that campus politics acts as a subtle deterrent to true political activity.

Campus politics usually short-circuits energy from political activity on the broader scene—much as, among adults, passionate arguments about new roads, school bond issues and fluoridation distract attention from more pressing and affecting national and international affairs. Once the energies of young men and women are channeled into such matters as the relationship between fraternity members and non-members, or two a.m. signouts from women's dormitories, they are seldom likely to be rechanneled into broader matters. The topics about which students are concerned are often quite important, but the point is that such intramural politics are often a substitute for, rather than a complement to, truly political interests. This short-circuiting is often abetted by frightened college administrators who distinguish between "on-campus" issues which are deemed within the competence of the young, and "off-campus" issues about which they cannot express themselves publicly. Such a distinction of course merely reinforces the definitions of youth that make it a time for preparation or panty raids, but not for real political interests.

But so-called student politics is a deterrent to true politics for another more important reason: it implicitly suggests that individuals are not capable of making important decisions about the general welfare. To make this point clearer, assume that under the guise of "training for democracy" we were seeking to convince a generation of young Americans that they lacked the wisdom to make policy decisions, and that omnicompetent officials alone possessed this wisdom. It would be hard to find a better system than student politics. We would begin in grade school by gradually giving to students all the minor decisions with which the grownups did not want to be bothered—dances, class elections, crossing streets, bond drives and so on. At the same time, however, we would reserve all of the major decisions for the grown-ups, met in secret council of the Tuesday Teachers' Meeting or in private session of the Board of Regents. To make sure that a complete feeling of incompetence ensued, we would make all student decisions, no matter how trivial, subject to review by some higher adult body. By these techniques, I think we could create in all but the most independent and strong-willed a subtle feeling—perhaps the more effective because never openly stated—that they were incapable of making any but the most trivial decisions, and even these, only if subject to review by higher authority. A generation so trained would feel powerless and helpless with major issues, and would be inclined to leave truly political matters—things that really mattered—in the hands of higher-ups, whether they be Principals, Deans, Pentagons or National Security Councils. In short, campus politics is too often instead of, rather than in addition to, true politics: it subtly convinces students that they are incapable of dealing with the major issues of national welfare and survival that ultimately affect them far more deeply than most campus issues.

Another factor that conspires with our apolitical images of youth—indeed is reinforced by them—is the fear remaining from the McCarthy period. When such fear is mentioned, we usually think of a youth who refuses to take part in some political activity in which he believes lest it "go on his record" and subsequently be "used against him." In fact, however, I think that the fear of later reprisal is small compared to that special American fear of one's own idealism and innocence, against which the "disclosures" of the McCarthy period reverberated. Americans, and especially American men, have always been afraid of being a "sucker," of being "taken in," of being "had" or of being "duped"—of becoming the unwilling and unknowing instrument of another's will. One of the revealing peculiarities of American speech illustrates this fear in a more general context—it is good for a man to make something, but never to be made—whether it be to be made to *do* something, to be made *into* something or, worst of all, simply to *be made.*

Thus, the "disclosures" of the red-baiters, and their world of "unwitting dupes," "front organizations," "inconscient tools," "pseudo-reds," "hapless victims," et cetera, activated a not-too-latent fear in many young Americans that their idealism, tendermindedness, sensitivity or innocence might mislead them into the position of the "sucker." When students give reasons for refusing to sign political petitions with which they fully agree, they usually cite their doubts as to the backers and sponsors of the petition, worrying about the uses to which their names might be put. It is a mistake to assume that these students are really considering future security clearance; rather, in an age of conspiratorial interpretations of history, all but the most resolute or insensitive tremble lest they too become the pawns of conspiracy. Given such nagging doubts, and the impossibility of ever being *sure* about the credentials of any petition, individual or group, inaction is often the safest and easiest course. But by taking this course, young men and women merely confirm that image of youth that deems youthful political activity somehow "un-American."

Given these apolitical images of youth, and the distractions and fears that have supported them, it is not surprising that until recently few lights have broken the political darkness on most American campuses. To be sure, in the thirties there were flickers of left-wing political groups in metropolitan and "elite" colleges, but their total membership was small; and although the students involved were talented and vocal far beyond their numbers, they found few answering voices among the majority of their fellow-students. Further, the ardor of even these students was first channeled into the war and then cooled by the cold war, so that by 1950 left-wing groups had disappeared from most American campuses. The McCarthy period brought no student political protest, although students as a group were far more opposed to indiscriminate red-hunting than the general population. Nor did student organizations like the Young Republicans and Young Democrats constitute real exceptions. Small as these groups were, their claimed membership was swollen by inactive members who joined in search of an extracurricular activity for the nonathletic; and their active membership included a disproportionate number of ex-debaters and future lawyers, including not a few seeking prepolitical apprenticeships and free visitors' passes to the next National Convention.

In the past two years, however, there have been signs of increasing political activity on a number of campuses. And although I should re-emphasize that by foreign standards the students involved are very few in number, they are of interest both for the unprecedented attention they receive and for their possible role as forecasts of things to come. The two most visible new groups are the right-wing organizations usually associated with Young Americans for Freedom (Y.A.F.), and the single-issue groups, usually left-wing, organized around such issues as desegregation, disarmament and loyalty oaths. It is generally agreed that right-wing groups elicit less support from most student bodies than the single-issue groups, and that they are not always spontaneous student creations. But on the basis of very unsystematic acquaintance with such right-wing groups and their literature and with one or two current studies of their membership, I think that they are bringing into political activity a kind of youth who has previously been politically inactive—a type we can call the displaced apprentice.

Such students continue to view college, and youth, in terms of an older apprentice image. At liberal arts colleges, however, they increasingly find no timetable to memorize, no maps of the terrain ahead, but instead a heavy pressure to make a commitment to the youth culture or even the academic enterprise itself. They frequently come from small conservative towns; and their parents' teachings and sacrifices have given them an outlook and a character that would have fit them well for upward mobility in the older, more entrepreneurial society. These students at many liberal arts colleges now find themselves in a minority, viewed with puzzlement by their contemporaries and teachers; furthermore, they usually see that academic rewards and prestige go to the more sensitive searching and interpersonally minded. The broader political scene also affects them: during the Eisenhower Administration, there still seemed a place for the inner-directed in the counsels of state and power; but the Kennedy Administration, with its surrounding phalanxes of college professors, suggests that the days of the old-fashioned entrepreneur are numbered. From several points of view, the displaced apprentice faces the unpleasant alternative of accepting his college's and by extension his society's judgment of him as out-of-date—or else of finding a way to repudiate the values and the people that deem him outmoded.

A group like Y.A.F. seems to provide an answer to some such students. For one, it offers a meeting place with other like-minded young men and women, and a sense of belonging to a group with powerful backers and a conspiratorial air. But more important, the ideology of a group like Y.A.F., which ascetically calls for a return to a purer, harder and tougher America, gives the displaced apprentice a voice for repudiating the soft-minded liberals, college professors, bureaucrats and others who epitomize the newer America in which he is characterologically obsolescent. And, not least of all, belonging to such a group permits a student of conservative backgound to retain and reinforce his loyalty to his parents and home town, and perhaps even to contemplate going home again to run for office on a conservative ticket.

But if the so-called resurgent right can be partly understood in terms of traditional American definitions of youth, the single-issue groups that are more prominent on most college campuses do not fit these definitions. To understand these groups we must posit the emergence of a third American definition of youth, one that is only now beginning to take shape, and one whose future remains uncertain. This new conception of youth, which I will call "academic," has as its distinctive feature a commitment to intellect, to knowledge, to scholarship and the academic enterprise, relatively unheard-of in earlier American college generations. At the same time, it involves considerable generational self-consciousness—awareness of oneself as a member of a distinctive age group rather like the youth culture—and also a basic acceptance of the traditional values of our society: those values that, although not always practiced by parents and elders, are at least preached.

The emergence of the academic image of youth is in part a consequence of the changing complexion of student bodies. As admission standards rise, the caliber of college applicants rises with them, so that more and more students arrive at college well prepared, already committed to the values and vices of the academic community, more genuinely interested in getting an education (if necessary for its own sake), less patient with both vocationalism and fraternities. Most teachers will testify that these students are still in a minority; but they are a growing minority that at some colleges will soon become the majority. Their level of sophistication and awareness is extremely high, probably higher than that of any previous college group; and while they are not immune to the pressures against political commitment in this country, they are at the same time more realistically aware of the importance of national and international issues for their own and their generation's future.

To be sure, the outlooks of such students are not necessarily political. Often their interests are rather narrowly academic; and for some, ascent of the ladders of academic specialization and promotion will merely replace older forms of status-seeking, leaving little time for politics. And when they are politically committed, such academic students are seldom radical or revolutionary; rather, they are interested in basic and unexceptionable American values like peace, equality and freedom. Their differences with their parents are seldom over matters of basic value, but rather over the implementation of these values, as with the Negro students active in the sit-in movement who have shocked older Negro leaders—including their own parents—by trying to achieve in practice the rights that their elders had always affirmed but never dared to demand. And, finally, the distinctive political style of such students is restrained, reflective, cautious, intellectual and even pedantic.

Only some, and perhaps only a few, of the students active in the single-issue groups fit this picture; but there are enough, I think, to color the style of these groups. One sees the restraint of these students in their picketing and petitions rather than protests and parades, in their carefully planned study-and-discussion groups, in their debates at which they give their opponents the platform, and above all in the nonviolence and self-control of the Negro sit-in movement. Such students resist efforts to organize them in the service of some general ideological program, so that attempts of radical groups to capture the student peace movement or the Negro sit-in movement have been remarkably unsuccessful. And the academic style of such students was manifest during the recent Peace March on Washington in their original (if not invariably successful) effort to present carefully studied and reasoned arguments to Congressmen and government officials.

The recent political activity of "academic" students is due to a variety of factors. For one, the number of such students is increasing, so that the reservoir of students intelligently aware of "true politics" has increased. And, for another, the relative success and restraint of the Negro sit-in movement has inspired white students in the North to supporting action which, once begun, was easily redirected into other activities like disarmament and anti-House Un-American Activities Committee groups. But most important has been the change of administration in Washington. Unlike its predecessor, the Kennedy Administration has been solicitous of the good opinion of future voters and responsive to student demonstrations—at least to the extent of "symbolic" pots of coffee, if not to changes in policy. And most crucial to students of academic outlook has been the presence of a number of academic, academically respected men on the President's staff. If the entrepreneurial apprentice found justification for inactivity in the golf-links-and-shooting-brake ethos of the Eisenhower regime, the academic student finds a spur to activity in the Harvard-Senior-Common-Room mentality of Kennedy's immediate entourage. Not even the touch football of the Kennedy Clan, which reminds him uncomfortably of his own lack of athletic prowess, subdues his hopes that his kind may yet have a say in Washington.

But for all of the interest and publicity aroused (and sought) by the new political activists on American campuses, the fact remains that few students are involved, and that most of them are concentrated at a few of the most selective institutions like California, Harvard, Michigan, Antioch, et cetera. The vast majority—at "elite" colleges more than ninety percent and at most colleges probably more than ninety-nine percent—remain uninvolved with true politics beyond perhaps a perfunctory membership in the local branch of the Young Republicans. So in considering the future of student politics, the critical question is whether these "inert masses" are destined to become more active than they have been traditionally.

The future is, of course, something that is determined by men and groups of men. And it follows that the shape of the future is not merely something to be guessed at, but, if we have hopes, something to be molded in accordance with these hopes. There are many, of course, who hope that American youth will remain unconcerned with politics. Political apathy, it is said, prevents the radical youth movements that plague other governments; and in more sophisticated sociological terms, essentially the same argument is phrased in terms of social stability and social solidarity. It is probably apparent by now that my own hopes differ. For one, I see little likelihood of American students ever playing a radical role, much less a revolutionary one, in our society. And, even if they did, it would be far from a calamity, given the almost total absence of radical or fundamental criticism of American society at present. On the contrary, I am more impressed with the dangers of political inactivity, ignorance and helplessness, especially in an era when the future of civilization or of life itself depends on a few words spoken into a red telephone in the Rockies or the Urals. In such a time, the greatest danger is not student ferment but resignation from concern with the shape of the wider world—the delegation of responsibility for survival to experts, weapons specialists, generals and even to Presidents and their academic advisers.

More important, then, than guessing at the future of student politics, is the effort to suggest ways of increasing political involvement and activity on college campuses. And here the academic community seems to be bound to play a major role. I noted earlier that the form and style of the "academic" definition of youth was still indeterminate. Just as the real-life counterparts of Horatio Alger's bankers helped form the concept of apprenticeship, and just as the peer group and mass media helped define the youth culture, so the members of the academic community will have an especially large part in forming the outlooks of the emerging "academic" student, determining among other things the extent to which these students consider political concern and activity appropriate and necessary to their lives.

Here teachers can do a number of things. For one, I think we must increasingly question our traditional American opposition to "ideology." To be sure, everyone is against narrow and blind dogmatism; but if by "ideology" we merely mean a coherent political program that embraces many sectors of society, then common sense dictates an "ideological" approach to politics. All of the recent evidence from the social sciences suggests how difficult it is to deal with single issues in isolation. To deal with only one issue at a time is rather as if the physician agreed to treat only the external symptoms of a disease, or the psychiatrist pledged himself to discuss only the current manifestations of a neurosis. Social and political issues are complex, complexly interrelated; and sometimes the best way to alleviate one problem is to ignore it and start with another. A commitment to a single-issue approach or inflexible opposition to "ideology" is too often a commitment to ineffectuality or opposition to fundamental cure.

Secondly, and at a very different level, far more can be done to encourage students to understand their own position in the world and their role in society. Here I obviously do not mean that students should be lectured about social responsibility and the perversity of privatism. Such preaching would have the opposite effect, if only because privatism is already a kind of *faute de mieux* response, a compensation on the part of young men and women who would quickly seize a beautiful or noble or challenging purpose if they could but find one. Nor do I mean that students should be required to take more courses in political science and international relations. Instead, or in addition, I think that intelligent young people should be encouraged and helped to explore their own positions and places in society, to understand better the conflicts and stresses that beset them, not only as individuals, but as members of a generation, a nation and the twentieth century. Here most colleges do far too little, for those courses that deal with our society and our motivations often deliberately seek to prevent personal involvement, soul-searching and application of knowledge to one's own life—in short, they seek to prevent that participation that alone can give insight. But one can imagine—in fact many of us have seen it happen—that a real awareness of the psychosocial forces that confront their generation can give students a vastly heightened sense of their political responsibilities and powers.

And, finally, teachers must be aware of their growing role not only as imparters of information and techniques to their students, but as personal exemplars. This is a role that most teachers consciously dislike, but students cast their teachers as heroes or villains in the best of times. Even the most anti-intellectual undergraduate finds among his instructors models of ivory-tower withdrawal and narrow pedantry that he determines *not* to emulate. But when society by and large lacks adequate paternal exemplars, students become more inclined to seek them among their teachers. And in the coming years as more and more students arrive in college already committed to academic interests and values, they will be even more likely to search for epitomes of the good (academic) life among their instructors. Less insulated against emulation by a contempt for the "merely academic" and by a loyalty to the youth culture, they will be more inclined to find their teachers worthy unless proved otherwise, and probably more likely to emulate them even when they are not worthy.

All of this means that an increased responsibility (and to most teachers an unwanted one) falls on the academic community in shaping the self-definitions and ideals of youth. The academic community has two mutually exclusive possibilities, which lead to very different outcomes in terms of student politics. One is pedantry—a narrow concentration on subspecialties within fenced-off fields, hostility to general interests, to speculation and to broad commitments. The other I would call intelligence at its best, and it is marked by social and political concern and by openness to the nonacademic world, which is after all the ultimate *raison d'être* of the college and university. Which possibility prevails seems to me very important; for what is ultimately at issue is our own personal survival and the survival of civilization in the world. Not that these issues will be decided by or at American colleges—far from it; but if we are granted so much time, they will be decided in part by young men and women who have attended these colleges. And just as past generations of Americans have patterned themselves on earlier images of youth, so the coming generation will be formed by the conceptions of youth, and life, available to them.

At worst, a narrow academicism of the young could result, made more intolerant and vicious by the fusion of personal ambition and a pseudopatriotism that thinks we can "harness brainpower" to beat the Russians. At best, an academic generation might become a truly intelligent generation, animated by public concern and guided by political understanding. In helping to shape such a concept, the most that teachers can do (and it is a great deal) is to suggest possibilities, to hold open doors, to criticize the false and spurious and support the true—and above all to try to embody in their own lives that humane political concern and openness of social vision that is the mark of true intelligence.

The Beat Generation and the Un-Generation

Jack Newfield

The employers will love this generation. They aren't going to press many grievances. They are going to be easy to handle. There aren't going to be any riots.

—CLARK KERR, 1959

A time-capsule representative of the generation reaching adulthood during the 1950's would have consisted of a subpoena, a blacklist, a television tube, a gray flannel suit, a copy of *Time* magazine with Herman Wouk on the cover, a Lawrence Welk album, an "I like Ike" button, and a blank sheet of paper.

It was a decade during which a senator from Mississippi was able to bully the greatest newspaper in the world; a President's favorite reading was pulp cowboy novels; a Gallup Poll showed that 58 percent of all college students listed *Mad* as their favorite magazine; and an ex-socialist wrote a book called *The End of Ideology.* It was a time when potential poets read Jack Kerouac and potential radicals ran for student council.

It was a decade during which McCarthyism was the most vital political movement in the land, and liberalism, after two decades of creative exertion, had reached a point of pessimistic exhaustion. Many of the older liberal architects of the New Deal and the CIO were comfortably ensconced in labor bureaucracies and academic hierarchies. In the argot of the fight game, the liberals weren't hungry anymore.

McCarthyism had put the liberals on the defensive, making them wonder who had lost China and who had promoted Peress. Moreover, the liberals idea bank was empty. The New Deal had used up all their intellectual capital, and now only slogans were left to cope with the new post-World War II problems of the anti-colonial revolution, the Cold War, nuclear proliferation, and technology and automation.

At the same time radicalism was at its absolute nadir. The Socialist Party was a shell. The cumulative blows of the Korean War, the Rosenbergs' conviction, the Smith Act trials, the Hungarian revolt, and the revelations about Stalin at the 20th Soviet Party Congress wrecked the Communist Party and its apparatus. In 1957 the Labor Youth League, the CP's youth arm, voted to dissolve.

Radicals were driven out of public life and liberals bullied into silence and conformity. *Time* magazine hailed the reconciliation between capitalist America and its intellectuals. The country seemed to be dozing in an easy chair after a great meal, belching intermittently to prove it was not quite asleep.

In its issue of March 9, 1957, at the height of the Silence, *The Nation* devoted an entire issue to reports from sixteen college campuses documenting the extraordinary apathy that afflicted the young. Stanley Kunitz, the poet and English professor at Queens College, wrote:

> However, I must add that when a liberal or speculative voice is heard in the classroom, it is more likely than not to be the professor's, despite whatever caution the years might have taught him. As for the students, they matriculate cautious, wanting above all—so well conditioned are they by the prevailing social climate—to buy security for themselves in the full knowledge that the price is conformity. "Why should we go out on a limb about anything?" one of them remarked in class. "We know what happened to those who did." Another expressed a measure of gratitude towards Senator McCarthy for having taught his generation a valuable lesson: "to keep its mouth shut."

Poet Karl Shapiro, writing from the University of Nebraska, the crucible of the Norris-LaFollette Progressivism, commented:

> Passivity is the last word we expect to use in connection with a generation of students, but that's the only word that applies to the American university student of the last few years.

Perhaps the sharpest evocation of the dead feeling of the 1950's came in an article that appeared in an obscure periodical called *Assay*, published by the University of Washington. It was written by a co-ed named Dorothy Rosebud Doe, and it said in part:

> What we all lack who are under 30, is some guiding passion, some moral vision if you will. We are unable to wind the loose threads of our experience into some larger pattern, and we know it. We write to please this authority or that professor while the universe skids about under our feet. We profess to disbelieve everything partially because, at heart, we do not yet believe in ourselves. What we are facing is a process of re-education, of self-discovery—a painful process, but without it no human being has understood the reason for his short walk across eternity . . . if our revolt seems mild, it is because we have not found anything to promote; deep in the dreams of ourselves in our relation to others, we realize with Yeats that there's more enterprise in walking naked.

Why the 1950's did not provide rebellious, sensitive souls like Dorothy with "some guiding passion" or "anything to promote" is a mystery. Why the New Left didn't emerge then, when there was a virulent right-wing that threatened to become a majority, when there was a series of economic recessions, when there were atrocities like the lynchings of Emmett Till and Mack Charles Parker, and when there was an unthawed Cold War, is an enigma of history. That the New Radicalism flowered *after* the death rattle of McCarthyism and during a period of remarkable prosperity contradicts most theories about the nature of social discontent and rebellion.

My own suspicion is that rebellion explodes not when repression is at its worst, but when it begins to ebb, when the possibility of something better is dimly glimpsed. Both the American and the Hungarian revolutions took place when conditions were beginning to improve. The same is true of the birth of the New Left here. It happened after Khrushchev's visit to America and after the liberal victories in the 1958 congressional elections.

The election of John Kennedy in 1960 probably hastened the flowering of the New Radicalism. In that election the nation chose vitality over torpor, adventure over caution, hope over passivity; and this decision liberated energies bottled up for a decade. If Nixon had won in 1960, I think the earliest protests would have been crushed in a McCarthyite paroxysm and the New Left aborted. Kennedy provided a friendly umbrella for the New Left to grow under, and held up a vision of social idealism, represented by the Peace Corps, which led students to take the logical next step—into SNCC and SDS.

My own undergraduate experience at Hunter College in the Bronx was foreshadowed by a sign I saw during my freshman semester (1956) on the bulletin board in the office of the student newspaper, the *Hunter Arrow*. The sign read bluntly, "Conform or Die."

Hunter was lucky enough during the McCarthy plague to have a liberal Catholic president, Dr. George N. Shuster. But the college had neither the radical tradition of CCNY, Antioch, or Berkeley, nor the rich intellectual tradition of Harvard, Chicago, or Michigan. The students, mostly lower middle class and Jewish, reflected their families and their times. They were fearful and conformist. During my later terms on the *Arrow* we officially banned the use of the word "apathy" because it had been so overworked in shrill editorials of exhortation.

Few of the three thousand undergraduates joined any of the myriad campus clubs and organizations, a lesson absorbed from the "don't sign and don't join" McCarthy experience. We all remembered the State Department employee McCarthy pilloried because of editorials he had written for the *Columbia Spectator* and petitions he had signed twenty-five years before. When speakers like Norman Thomas came to the campus they addressed seventy-five students and hundreds of vacant auditorium seats. At Hunter, politics meant running for student council on an innocuous platform, and dissent meant a vague, emotional yearning for Adlai Stevenson. The life pattern today's campus rebels recoil from in disgust, my classmates deified: marry well and early, don't be a troublemaker, start a career in daddy's business or in a large corporation, and save up for a split-level home in the lily-white suburbs.

The vast majority of my classmates just sat through four years. They didn't challenge any authority, take any risks, or ask any questions. They just memorized "the given," not even complaining when instructors turned them into mindless tape recorders, demanding they recite rather than reason. They seemed genuinely content with the world, and interested only in being rewarded with a painless niche in it. They signed loyalty oaths without complaint in order to receive college loans. When the administration suggested stringent dress regulations on the campus, the student council meekly voted to ratify this infringement on their liberties. When a maverick political science instructor was denied tenure and left, no one protested.* Most of my classmates became teachers, accountants, press agents, housewives, and salesmen.

No public question seemed to touch Hunter's class of '60; not McCarthyism, not Dulles' brinkmanship, not pollution of the atmosphere by nuclear testing, not even the nascent integration movement. They were worse than a Silent Generation or an Un-committed Generation—they were an Un-generation.

They were an Un-generation in the sense that nothing positive distinguished them or set them apart. They were bereft of passions, of dreams, of gods. Even their small, conventional expectations were squeezed out of the same label-less tube. If any single characteristic bound them together it was withdrawal. Not the experimental, alienated withdrawal of the Beats, but a timid, unfeeling withdrawal. They withdrew from conflict and emotion into a false, protective, "cool" detachment. They took up the pose of the jazz buff who dug the "cool jazz" of Brubeck and Getz. They carried around paperbacks by clinical and unfeeling novelists like William Golding and the latest example of *The New Yorker* school of bloodless, overdetailed fiction. And their *Zeitgeist*—J. D. Salinger—stood for a total withdrawal from reality into the womb of childhood, innocence, and mystical Zen. Most of my contemporaries even managed to sustain their withdrawal beyond graduation, drifting off to Europe or going on to take meaningless graduate courses.

There were, I suspect, deeper reasons for the Un-generation's withdrawal than the intimidation by McCarthyism and the collapse of an energizing liberalism. One such reason seems to have been the instructive image of a passive President who withdrew from the world's problems. Just as John Kennedy's celebrated vigor ignited the country's spirit in 1960, I think Eisenhower's inability to deal with segregation, Laos, Eastern Europe, the economy, McCarthy, and the rest created a sense of futility in the country at large.

A second underlying cause of the Silence was the often-forgotten fact that American youth has never been particularly political in the way that Latin American, Asian, and European youth have. There was no dramatic upsurge of youthful radicalism accompanying the Pro-

* By 1961, however, attitudes had changed. Eighty-five percent of the Hunter student body supported a strike against the City University speaker ban, which denied Communists, black nationalists, and others the right to speak on campuses.

gressive movement, the Populists, the abolitionists, or the American Revolution itself. American youth has no tradition of vanguard radicalism. One of the more subtle inspirations to the New Left was, I think, the catalytic role students played in 1960 in overthrowing the reactionary regimes of Menderes in Turkey and Syngman Rhee in Korea.

The last of the deeper reasons for the Silence was probably the traditional banality of the American campus and student-government politics. Until quite recently campus politics were insulated from "outside issues" like war, civil rights, and poverty; they have been a substitute for, rather than a supplement to, the substantive national politics of the country. Indicatively, the FSM had at its core the notion of replacing real issues in the real world for the vacuity of campus politics. Also, I suspect that the traditional style of campus sandbox politics tended to reinforce the feeling of helplessness and futility in coping with the adult world of complex, worldly issues. Campus politics were constructed to prepare Joe College to become a docile Organization Man.

> The psychopath is a rebel without a cause, an agitator without a slogan, a revolutionary without a program: in other words his rebelliousness is aimed to achieve goals satisfactory to himself alone; he is incapable of exertions for the sake of others.
>
> —Dr. Robert Lindner

It was a bone-chilling November night during my junior year at Hunter. The college auditorium was packed tight for a debate on "Is There a Beat Generation?" The combatants were British novelist Kingsley Amis; James Wechsler, the liberal hero of my youth; anthropologist Ashley Montague; and the alleged "King of the Beats," novelist Jack Kerouac. From the start it was clear that much of the leotard and beard-freckled mob (mostly non-Hunter types) had come to cheer the King of the Beats, look over Amis as a possible Angry Young Man, and scorn the committed liberalism of Wechsler as a delusion for squares and do-gooders.

But Kerouac disappointed his disciples. Gulping brandy compulsively, dragging poet Allen Ginsberg out of the wings like a donkey, reciting doggerel about Harpo Marx and clowning with Wechsler's hat, Kerouac seemed more in harmony with the clown spirit of his "beloved Harpo" than with the merchandised image of the creative, adventuristic, iconoclastic Beats.

When asked from the audience to "define the Beat Generation," Kerouac belched drunkenly, "Being Beat goes back to my ancestors, to the rebellious, the weird, the mad. To Laurel and Hardy, to Popeye; to Lamont Cranston, the Shadow, with his insane heh-heh-heh laugh. . . ."

Wechsler, the optimistic liberal, could only respond to Kerouac's premature Camp by sputtering, "I think what you are doing is to try to destroy anybody's instinct to care about this world. . . . There is no valor in the Beats' flight and irresponsibility."

Wechsler, of course, was right, and the irrational, impotent dissent of Kerouac that night at Hunter was a fairly accurate example of the Beat Generation. The Beats were not political or effective, and except for Ginsberg and William Burroughs, not very creative. They were the children of futility. They withdrew from society into an anti-social subculture, instead of challenging and trying to change the society. But with the traditional voices of dissent mute, the Beat Generation became the only option for those in opposition. The Beats may have been rebels without a cause, but theirs was the only rebellion in town.

The Beat Generation was partly a small literary faction that centered around an in-group of friends. Kerouac, who according to critic Seymour Krim "single-handedly created the Beat Generation," was the leader. The more gifted followers included Allen Ginsberg, the Jewish-radical-mystical-homosexual from Paterson, New Jersey; Gregory Corso, whom critic Robert Mazzocco once labeled, "The Shelley of the Mafia;" and William Burroughs, junkie, petty criminal, and dark genius out of the millionaire Burroughs adding-machine family and Harvard, '36.

The Beat movement was also a sociological phenomenon; an underground subsociety that developed about 1953, was mythicized by the Beat novelists and poets, and quickly spawned colonies in North Beach, San Francisco; Venice West, Los Angeles; Greenwich Village, New York; and out-posts in Mexico City, Paris, and Tangiers. Its full-timers ranged from dreamy teen-agers on the bum to maladjusted Korean war veterans to jazzmen, criminals, and peyote-inspired poets. Each weekend its ranks would be swollen with Bronx boys picking up Brooklyn girls on MacDougal Street in the Village. At its periphery Beat just meant sloppy dress, inter-racial dating and poetry read to jazz backgrounds. At its vortex it meant criminality, mainline drug addiction, and mental instability. Lawrence Lipton, the Beats' Boswell, wrote: "One of the things which distinguish the holy barbarians [the Beats] from the respectable poets is their insistence on the non-rational as a way of knowing and a therapy to overcome squareness."

Allen Ginsberg, who saw "the best minds of my generation destroyed by madness," once spent eight months in a mental institution. Later he dedicated his brilliant work, *Howl,* to the institutionalized Carl Solomon. Seymour Krim wrote a chilling essay, "The Insanity Bit," after he "flipped out." And Kerouac was discharged from the Navy as a "schizoid personality."

A study of the San Francisco Beat enclave by psychiatrist Dr. Francis Rigney in the late 1950's showed 60 percent "were so psychotic or crippled by tensions, anxiety and neurosis as to be nonfunctional in the competitive world." In contrast, the several studies released so far made of the student radicals at Berkeley show them to be stable, serious, and of above-average intelligence. The point is that the Beats had to "cop out" of the Rat Race because they couldn't perform; the New Left chooses to reject a society it could easily be successful in.

The Beat Generation was anything but a revolutionary thrust to create a new society. It was as hostile to politics as it was to police and employment agencies. I recall asking one of Hunter's few authentic Beats to join the 1959 Youth March for Integrated Schools, and his laconic response, "You're too enthusiastic, man. Cool it."

The closest the Beats came to politics was to write bad poetry against the Bomb. But even this was more in the nature of self-justification for their own immediate savoring of all experience than a moral or political outcry against the shadow of genocide. Paul Goodman, generally sympathetic to the Beat impulse, pointed out in *Growing Up Absurd* that the Beats were no more against nuclear warfare than "mothers with families or squares who have common sense." And critic George Dennison, in putting down a Beat poem about the Bomb, observed, "The poet seems miffed that people pay attention to the atom bomb instead of to him."

Perhaps because the Beats—as writers and participants—didn't threaten anybody politically, the Beat Generation ended up as a Madison Avenue and Hollywood gimmick. The beatnik joined the plump suburban matron and the jowly business tycoon as a stock cartoon figure; slouched, bearded, and mumbling, "Like, man. . . ." A New York entrepreneur went into business renting out "real live beatniks" at twenty-five dollars per evening, plus carfare. *Playboy Magazine* had a "Beat Playmate of the Month." Hollywood ground out a Grade Z epic called *The Beat Generation* and an artless adaptation of Kerouac's novel, *The Subterraneans.* And the July, 1959, issue of *The Saturday Evening Post* featured a short story by Harriet Frank called,

"Beauty and the Beatnik," whose hero declaims, "Let's face it. I'm a beatnik, through and through. James Jones, Jack Kerouac. They're Dun and Bradstreet compared to me. I'm a real bum."

Still, despite their absurdity and ultimate commercialization, many of the values of the Beats have been absorbed into the broader stream of the New Left. The Beats seem to be a greater influence on the New Radicals than are the 1930's Left.

On many campuses today hipster and bohemian types serve as a sort of *lumpen* proletariat, an easily available army of bodies, ready to participate in any demonstration. But they are generally not the creative and stable leaders of movements; rather the undisciplined followers who get interviewed by cynical television reporters. SNCC's Texas-born Casey Hayden has a point when she says, "The beatniks were—and are—just the Movement without altruism and energy. They are alienated by exactly the same things we are, but they just can't act on their discontent in an effective political way."

Nevertheless, the Beats' mysticism, anarchy, anti-intellectualism, sexual and drug experimentation, hostility to middle-class values, and idealization of the Negro and of voluntary poverty all have clear parallels in the New Left. Moreover, there is a broad area of overlap between the Beats' creative expressions and the cultural tastes of the New Left. Individuals like Bob Dylan, Paul Krassner, and Allen Ginsberg serve as bridges between the two traditions. And within the New Left there is considerable liking for writers like Norman Mailer and Jean Genet; musical rebels like the Beatles and the half-rock'n'roll, half-pornographic Fugs; and for underground filmmakers like Kenneth Anger. Both movements represent a rebellion against Puritanism, hypocrisy, repression, and commercialism. Only the Beats were apolitical, self-indulgent, and a bit mad, while the New Left has a moral vision of a new society and is trying to create it with social activism.

More than anything else, the Beat Generation was a portent, the first wind of a new storm, a coded signal that America's youth was starting to gag on conformity, materialism, and silence. By the end of the 1950's there were not only the subcultures of Beats, but the irreverent satire of Lenny Bruce and Mort Sahl, the stirings of SANE, Martin Luther King's local protests against segregation, and the slow growth of dissident publications like *I. F. Stone's Weekly, The Village Voice,* and *The Realist.*

This subtle new mood, which was to spawn the sit-in movement in 1960, was clearly perceived by Arthur Schlesinger, Jr., in a prophetic essay penned late in 1959 and called, "The New Mood in Politics." Perhaps thinking already of John Kennedy's bid for the Presidency, he wrote:

> At periodic moments in our history, our country has paused on the threshold of a new epoch in our national life, unable for a moment to open the door, but aware that it must advance if it is to preserve its national vitality and identity. One feels that we are approaching such a moment now. . . .
>
> The beginning of a new political epoch is like the breaking of a dam. Problems which have collected in the years of indifference, values which have suffered neglect, energies which have been denied employment—all suddenly tumble as in a hopeless, swirling flood onto an arid plain. . . .

The Beat Generation was the first trickle of the angry flood that is now promising to wash away so many of America's false totems, and cleanse so many of its rotted institutions.

Certain Things That Happened at Berkeley

Mario Savio

There are many things that happened at Berkeley which will not be of interest to people elsewhere, and need not be; it is to be hoped that others will have their own problems to contend with, and will have interesting things of their own to do. Others should not have to get their experience second hand. But there are certain things that happened at Berkeley which it would be useful for people in other places to know about, as an aid in understanding themselves, as help to them in preparing revolts of their own.

There were some things which made the Berkeley revolt peculiarly Berkeley's, but other things made it a revolt among white middle-class youth that could happen at any state university. And it is the second set of factors which will probably be of most importance to people outside Berkeley.

Why did it happen in Berkeley? The important question to ask, rather, is: why did it happen in Berkeley *first?*—because there are

---

several universities in the East and Midwest where, since last semester, little home-grown revolts have flared up.

Asking why it happened in Berkeley first is like asking why Negroes, and not Americans generally, are involved in securing access for all, to the good which America could provide for her people. This may seem strange to those who imagine America to be a virtual paradise except for certain groups, notably Negroes, who have been excluded. But this is a distortion. What oppresses the American Negro community is merely an exaggerated, grotesque version of what oppresses the rest of the country—and this is eminently true of the middle class, despite its affluence. In important ways the situation of students at Berkeley is an exaggerated representation of what is wrong with American higher education.

The forces influencing students at Berkeley—not merely those resulting from participation in the university itself, but also those deriving from student involvement in politics—these forces are likewise exaggerations of the forces to which society subjects other university students in other parts of the country. So probably the reason it could happen here first is this: while the same influences are present elsewhere, there is no university (none that I know of, at all events) where these influences are present in as extreme a form as here in Berkeley.

The influences upon students are of three main kinds: those deriving from personal history; "internal" problems resulting directly from being a student; and "external" problems deriving from after-class political activities. The external influences on students result primarily from involvement in the civil-rights movement, both in the Bay Area and in the South. The internal derive primarily from the style of the factory-like mass miseducation of which Clark Kerr is the leading ideologist. There are many impersonal universities in America; there is probably none more impersonal in its treatment of students than the University of California. There are students at many Northern universities deeply involved in the civil-rights movement; but there probably is no university outside the South where the effect of such involvement has been as great as it has been at Berkeley.

One factor which helps explain the importance of civil rights here is the political character of the Bay Area. This is one of the few places left in the United States where a personal history of involvement in radical politics is not a form of social leprosy. And, of course, there are geographical considerations. The Berkeley campus is very close to the urban problems of Oakland and San Francisco, but not right in either city. On campus it is virtually impossible for the thoughtful to banish social problems from active consideration. Many students here find it impossible not to be in some sense *engagé*. The shame of urban America (just south of campus or across the bay) forces itself upon the conscience of the community. At the same time it is possible to think about political questions by retreating from their immediate, physical, constant presence. Thus, at Columbia or CCNY it is difficult to tell where the city ends and the university begins, whereas at Berkeley there is a clearly demarcated university community, with places where students and faculty members can enjoy a certain sense of retreat and apartness. At Berkeley we are both close enough to gross injustice not to forget; but far enough away, and set well enough apart, so as neither to despair nor simply to merge into the common blight. Furthermore, ours is not a commuter school; the students live here at least part of the year. This makes possible a continuing community such as would be impossible at UCLA for example. This community, with a great deal of internal communication, has been essential to the development of political consciousness. And there is a good deal for the students to communicate to one another. Over ten per cent of the student body has taken part *directly* in civil-rights activity, in the South or in the Bay Area. These three thousand, all of whom have at least walked picket lines, are a leaven for the campus. And many more can be said to have participated vicariously: there is great and widespread interest in what those who "go South" have done and experienced. Of course, there is a natural receptivity for politics at Berkeley simply because this is a state-supported university: a good percentage of the student body comes from lower-middle-class or working-class homes; many who can afford to pay more for an education go, for example, to Stanford.

Now for those problems which have their origin within the university: the tale which follows is strictly true only for undergraduates in their first two years; there are some improvements during the second two years; but only graduate students can expect to be treated tolerably well.

It is surprising at first, after taking a semester of undergraduate courses here—except in the natural sciences or mathematics—to realize how little you have learned. It is alarming at the same time to recognize how much busy work you have done: so many papers hastily thrown together, superficially read by some graduate-student teaching assistant. Even if you want to work carefully, it is difficult to do so in each of five courses, which often have unrealistically long reading lists—courses with little or no logical relationship to one another. Perhaps in the same semester, the student will "take" a superficial survey of all the major (and many minor) principles of biology, *and* a language course a good part of which is spent in a language "laboratory" very poorly integrated into the grammar and reading part of the course, a laboratory which requires its full hour of outside preparation but which benefits the student very little in terms of speaking ability in the foreign language. Perhaps, ironically, the semester's fare will include a sociology course in which you are sure to learn, in inscrutably "scientific" language, just what is so good and only marginally improvable in today's pluralistic, democratic America.

If you are an undergraduate still taking non-major courses, at least one of your subjects will be a "big" lecture in which, with field glasses and some good luck, you should be able, a few times a week, to glimpse that famous profile giving those four- or five-year-old lectures, which have been very conveniently written up for sale by the Fybate Company anyway. The lectures in the flesh will not contain much more than is already in the Fybate notes, and generally no more than will be necessary to do well on the examinations. Naturally, it will be these examinations which determine whether or not you pass the course. Such an education is conceived as something readily quantifiable: 120 units constitute a bachelor's degree. It is rather like the outside world—the "real" world—where values are quantified in terms of the dollar: at the university we use play money, course units. The teacher whom you will have to strain to see while he lectures will be very seldom available for discussion with his students; there is usually an hour set aside, in the course of each week, during which all of the students who want to speak with him will have to arrange to do so. In the face of physical impossibility, there are generally few such brave souls. If more came, it would make little difference; this system is rarely responsive to individual needs. There are too few teachers, and too little time. Indeed, if the professor is one of those really famous scholars of whom the university is understandably proud, then the primary reason there is not enough time for the problems of individual undergraduates is that the bulk of the professor's time (other than the six or eight hours spent in the classroom each week) is devoted to "research" or spent with graduate students. The moral of the piece is: if you want to get an education, you will have to get it yourself. This is true in any case, but it is not usually intended to be true in the sense that getting it yourself means *in spite* of the work at school. There are just too many nonsense hours spent by American students, hours to "do" much as one "does" time in prison.

In the course of one semester, doubtless, there will be several opportunities for each unlucky student to come into contact with the administration of the university. This may be to request an exception from some university requirement. However formal the requirement may be, invariably at least once a semester, the student finds he cannot be excepted, not because the requirement is important but simply because it happens to be a *requirement.* Well, that is a problem common to bureaucracies of various kinds, but one wonders if this is the sort of thing that should be regularly encountered at a university. Yet this ordeal is what a large part of American college-age youth have to endure. We should ask not whether such intellectual cacophony and bureaucratic harassment are appropriate at universities—for certainly they are not—but rather, whether these local "plants" in what Clark Kerr calls the "knowledge industry" deserve the name university at all.

This is a somewhat overdrawn picture of life at Berkeley. The students are aware of meaningful activity going on outside the university. For there is some meaningful activity going on in America today—in the civil-rights movement, certainly. At the same time, but much more dimly, each student is aware of how barren of essential meaning and direction is the activity in which he is primarily involved, as a card-carrying student. I write "each student is aware" but I realize that this is to express more hope than fact. In less than a tenth of the students is this "awareness" a "consciousness." This consciousness of the poverty of one's immediate environment is a difficult thing to come by. In most it must remain a dim awareness. It is far easier to become aware of (and angry at) the victimization of others than to perceive one's own victimization. It is far easier to become angry when others are hurt. This is so for a number of reasons. Fighting for others' rights cannot engender nearly so great a guilt as striking rebelliously at one's own immediate environment. Also, it is simply easier to see the injustice done others—it's "out there." Many of us came to college with what we later acknowledge were rather romantic expectations, perhaps mostly unexpressed at first, about what a delight and adventure learning would be. We really did have unanswered questions searching for words, though to say so sounds almost corny. But once at college we quickly lose much of the romantic vision; although, fortunately, some never give in to the disappointment. Discovering that college is really high school grown up and not significantly more challenging, many console themselves with the realization that it is not much more difficult either.

The revolt began in the fall semester of 1964 as an extension of either vicarious or actual involvement in the struggle for civil rights. It was easy to draw upon this reservoir of outrage at the wrongs done to other people; but such action usually masks the venting, by a more acceptable channel, of outrage at the wrongs done to oneself. I am far from propounding a psychoanalytic theory of politics, yet most people whom I have met who are committed to radical political innovation are people who have experienced a good deal of personal pain, who have felt strong frustration in their own lives. This mechanism made possible the *beginning* of one pint-sized revolution on the Berkeley campus. The university set about denying students access to those facilities and rights on campus which had made possible student involvement in the civil-rights movement in the previous few years. Yet very rapidly the concern of the movement shifted from Mississippi to much closer to home; we soon began doing an awful lot of talking and thinking about the limitations of the university, the "Multiversity," the "knowledge industry"—these metaphors became ever more a part of the rhetoric of the movement. Civil rights was central in our fight because of business-community pressure on the university to crack down on campus-launched campaigns into the surrounding community—which had proven all too effective. University spokesmen have acknowledged that the need to respond to such pressures was the only "justification" for the ban on political activity. Nevertheless, the focus of our attention shifted from our deep concern with the victimization of others to outrage at the injustices done to ourselves. These injustices we came to perceive more and more clearly with each new attack upon us by the university bureaucracy as we sought to secure our own rights to political advocacy. The political consciousness of the Berkeley community has been quickened by this fight. The Berkeley students now demand what hopefully the rest of an oppressed white middle class will some day demand: freedom for all Americans, not just for Negroes!

The New Left and the Old Right

Max Geltman

As the year 1966 was drawing to a close, Professor Charles Susskind of the University of California summed up his opinions of the student demonstrators on the Berkeley campus in these words: "I don't know why they think of themselves as the New Left. Their methods look to me much more like those of the Nazi students whom I saw in the 1930s harassing deans, hounding professors and their families, making public disturbances, and interfering with lectures, until only professors sympathetic to the Nazi cause remained." The professor's comparison of the New Left with the Old Right is not only apt but just.

It is sometimes forgotten that the Hitler youth took to the streets of Berlin in the years immediately preceding 1933 with the cry, "Out with the old crap." For those not too familiar with the inelegant terminology of the youthful Nazis, it should be noted that they got it straight from a letter Karl Marx wrote to his friend Dr. Ludwig Kugelmann. And Marxists today, in instances too numerous to mention, are

From *National Review,* June 13, 1967. Reprinted by permission of *National Review.*

fond of repeating the "same old crap" as if they were words of divine revelation.

But when the Nazis of the Left, the Beefsteak Nazis as they were called—brown on the outside and red on the inside—ranted their cries of "down with theory, only action counts," they were indeed imprinting an ideology all their own with hobnailed boots over the body of the German nation. This ideology was largely an amalgam of racism, nationalism and Marxism, couched in terms of action, action, action. To a large extent mindlessness was its great appeal, but a kind of mindlessness that would lead ultimately to the destruction of the mind itself. But even the most inarticulate conception needs someone to verbalize it for the masses who, in the end, do all the *acting* when the actions are called for. So the "armed barbarians" of Nazism, the Brown Shirt intellectuals, went about finding virtues in the actions of the man in the street—the street fighter, the speechless apostle of the deed—and both Hitler for his movement (National Socialism) and Karl Radek for his (Communism) found him in the person of Leo Schlageter, the primordial martyr of Nazism, killed in a street brawl in Berlin in 1923 and mourned by Hitler and apostrophized by Radek as the symbol of the fallen proletariat.

Later the Schlatgeters—the millions of them, imbued with the theoryless theory of action—would go about knocking the brains out of anyone who stood in their way (on university campus or off) in the march toward the chiliastic apocalypse of the *Now*. Freedom now, they shouted. Action! Speech is dead! We want action now! They got plenty of it during the next two decades.

Protest Against Satiety

But America of the Sixties is not Germany of the Twenties. Here history is merely repeating itself as farce. Our "alienated" student rebels and New Leftists are not rebelling against a nation in poverty —the lib-Left poverty slogans of our day are mostly a matter of demagogy to help a few nerveless politicians to well-paying jobs at the public expense—they are protesting, it would seem, against too much of everything. Too much schooling, too much spending money, too much idleness, too much free entertainment on and off TV, and too much permissiveness in general. What they are seeking is a free ride to power, without the consequences or the responsibility of thinking things through. Thinking is hard work, and they would prefer to have others do it for them. That is why so much of their behavior is motivated by a compulsion for action—not serious involvement. When some of them do try to express themselves it usually comes in halting sentences beginning with "like" and ending with "man." Or they assume a kind of military shorthand to describe their most piddling activities. Here is the way one leading representative of the New Left responded to a discussion of the subject in the over-cerebrated *Partisan Review*, Tom Hayden reporting:

"*Monday:* Staff meeting at 10:00. Mike was supposed to have found bail money for this afternoon in case we have trouble. We didn't." Etcetera.

"*Noon:* Tied up with phone calls to Episcopalian civil rights committee in New York; fund raising always hectic, but the bills get paid. Finally got to 18th Avenue at 2:00 o'clock. Told Mrs. Queen, who lives in a two-room place with no toilet or closet, about the demonstration. Said she'd be there." Etcetera.

"*Four O'Clock:* The people on the other block, Avon Avenue, were in a different situation. They had seen someone from the Traffic Division . . . [This minute-by-minute log of the day's revolutionary activities is concerned with a demonstration—for a traffic light. But let's continue the day's military events and skirmishes.]

"*Eleven O'Clock:* Came back to apartment after eating with Sampson, who was jubilant." (Cause of joy the fact that "the captain from the Fourth Precinct" made a call to the Deputy Mayor, who promised "an immediate 'traffic study' to determine if a traffic light is needed.")

Did I say farce? Of course I did and I meant it. All the more so since Sargent Shriver, another contributor to the *PR* symposium on the "New Radicalism" found it necessary to present his credentials as an intellectual by quoting Gertrude Stein's "It's hard to write poetry in a late age," and ending with the tired old words of the New Left, "Don't get hung up." At the same time—and with an assist from David Riesman—he felt called upon to defend himself and the Peace Corps with the advice to the young that "half of Gandhi" is not enough. I should think it would be too much.

But Mr. Shriver is not really part of the New Left and neither are the other middle-aged and middle-class intellectuals who are drawn to its mystique in a way that is sad, for it is so obviously a ploy to recapture their own lost youth when things were jolly and gay and one was still without responsibility of wife and children and job, and ideas for remolding the world in the image of a utopian socialism had not yet been tarnished by the concentration camps of Stalin and the gas chambers of Hitler. Still some of our Old Left intellectuals can't seem to tear themselves away from the incoherent attractions of the New Left.

MacDougal Street: the World?

Jack Newfield of the *Village Voice*, the middling and middle-aged (by teeny-bopper standards, at least, to which he is partial) voyeur of New Left folkways, is all for the inarticulate mindlessness of the New Left at the same time he finds the articulate mindlessness of Irving Howe rather a bore. Can't fault him much for that. Not because Howe's ideologism isn't more attractive as ideologies go these days, still, as so much antiquated baggage Howe can no more divest himself of his depression-imposed socio-pathologic environment than Newfield of his well-fed Greenwich Village beat. MacDougal Street is all the world for him, and big enough a world for a small revolution in art, manners and life—such as it is—all of it smeared with pizza and pasta sauce, the girls so dirty and the boys so hairy; the art so faky and the protest so perverse that if one took away from them a half-dozen four-letter words they would all become speechless.

Murray Kempton, however, finds the essential mindlessness of both rather stimulating. Like most good word-slingers (and Kempton is better at this than Howe and Newfield), he has an ill-concealed envy for the inarticulate. Oh, if only one didn't have to employ words to earn one's daily bread! Thus he drools with appreciation at the way Stokely Carmichael expresses himself: "I just got into that Bob Moses bag. I had to see what I could down in the place no one else could go." Influenced by this assault on the language, Mr. Kempton concludes his own contribution to the subject in the *New York Review of Books* with a wild disregard for the rules of common sense and grammar, thus: ". . . The tidal fact about the New Left and those of us who are older but still have trouble lying to ourselves is that none of us know what to do." Some of us know. But Kempton doesn't.

Perhaps the ones best equipped to write about the New Left are the young. After all, they ought to know what is troubling them even if they can't quite articulate it as well as their elders. But what is most astonishing in all this pother about the *new* Left is that its authentic heroes and spiritual guides are among the oldest men alive in the world today. Bertrand Russell in his nineties and A. J. Muste in his eighties were (until Muste's death this spring) the sun and the moon around which the juvenile rebels revolved as mere satellites. (The nonagenarian trying desperately to relive his nonage and the octogenarian reveling in a bit of violent glory denied him all his fourscore pacifist years are perhaps explainable in terms of the ravages of time on the human mind. That certain young people in America, and elsewhere, should embrace them as heroes of the *new* is a strange phenomenon indeed.)

Strange Bedfellows

Others in an advanced stage of a disintegrating middle age with whom the New Left sometimes identifies include men like Eric Fromm, who cannot tell fact from fantasy, and Paul Goodman, who *says* things better than he *writes* them. Both of these can be said to be "hung-up" on something they really don't understand. It is possible for this reason that the movement has been better understood by young men of the Right who have written on the theme in depth and with a good deal of insight and intelligence.

Phillip Abbot Luce, himself formerly a dedicated and committed member of the New Left, has published the best book on the subject so far. And David Greenwald, a graduate student at the University of California in Berkeley, has written a fine essay about our youthful rebels in the conservative *Intercollegiate Review*. (I would argue only with Mr. Greenwald's need to compare the antics of the less inhibited members of the New Left with the wild ecstasies of the Dionysian cults of ancient Greece. A parallel closer to hand—although not too close—especially in its mindless-godless manifestations, can be found in the orgiastic fanaticism of such cults as the Ranters in Cromwell's England.)

With all this it should be kept in mind that not all the New Left is as innocent in rebellion against an older generation as some on both sides of the aisle have presumed. Much of it is guided and manipulated by hardcore professionals, ranging all the way from Soviet-loving Bettina Aptheker in California to the American branch of Mao's Red Guards coagulated in the Progressive Labor Party.

Berkeley Dissected

In recent days we have seen that some of the protest at Berkeley with which one could sympathize originally was not quite the innocent rebellion of young people wanting more of an identity than the "multiversity" was prepared to offer. Of course for most of them it was just that. But for certain others, for the professional nonstudent rioter like Mario Savio or the professional Communist on the campus, it was much more than that. For them it was a means to an end, even if Miss Aptheker's ends are not quite the same as Mr. Savio's (whose ends are perhaps not even clear to himself). Now that Dr. Clark Kerr is out as president of the university, Mario is prepared to forgive him his sins, and Bettina is urging her comrades on toward the governor's mansion to strike at the root of power itself, as it were, campus capers being too tame for her in any case.

Leslie Fiedler, a wise old owl of the Old Left, thinks he understands the mindlessness of the New Left's agitation on the campus as simply the desire of some students to call the professor "a fink." But this does not explain the fact that in many instances it was the professor himself, the "fink," who egged the young stalwarts on. What is so pathetic about all this is that this is probably the first generation of rebels in all history which has had its protest virtually underwritten by some of the most sacred institutions of the Establishment—from the Ford Foundation to the *New York Times.* No wonder that some of them who wanted a protest all their own found it in an escape from the real world into the never-never land of the hallucinatory drugs. If only the prevailing liberalism of an older generation had not been so damned tolerant of their activities, hell, man, the protest might have lasted at least until one got his Ph.D. But even this was denied them.

Surely the young have a right to be wrong. But not wrong in the way their fathers were. In this connection, it is a pleasure to read how young Mr. Luce broke from the movement which had entrapped him without once resorting to the kind of "God-that-failed" apologia for his sins that was the custom with the older comrades when they broke with the Soviet myth. Not that such literature of heartache did not influence him. It did. But in closing his book he is capable of a real affirmation, one that his brothers of a generation ago, could not make. Quoting from Supreme Court Justice Holmes that "it is required of a man that he should share the passion and action of his time at peril of being judged not to have lived," Luce adds: "Young people should follow this advice and involve themselves more and more in politics in this country. . . . We are obliged to do better than our parents in governing. . . . But we will never succeed in solving anything if we listen to the Communists, be they young or old." The only thing which he was probably mistaken about was the durability of the movement from which he had just broken. But that is understandable.

The New Left seemed so formidable a force a short time ago. But today it is being written off even by its early sponsors. Only a hard core of turbulent Vietniks, aided and abetted by some old men on and off the campus, still pursue the theme. In California it is possible that Ronald Reagan is in for a spell of deviltry, but this too will dissipate itself as soon as the Clark Kerr affair is forgotten. Meanwhile all that is left to record of New Left victories is the organization of a couple of Chinese-oriented Marxist groups who know Mao as little as they know Marx; Stokely Carmichael's sudden emergence as the leader of an almost all-white, all middle-class Puerto Rican movement demanding independence *now;* a poetry reading in Washington Square, New York, by Allen Ginsberg, who titillated the young ladies in the crowd by calling the President a dirty name; and the formation of the new cult of LSD by its divine inspirator, Timothy Leary. Its major contribution to the culture of the times was a drama in blank verse—more blank than verse, as Dwight Macdonald opined—which told in broken pentameters how the present incumbent in the White House murdered his predecessor with the aid and connivance of the First Lady of the land. No wonder Murray Kempton (friend and partisan of the New Left) concludes his article with a plea for another try. Suddenly assuming the role of mystic he asks that someone sit down and write across the title page of his bright new manuscript the cryptic words "What is to be done?" This is his new hope and his new dream—that someone will *once again* inscribe the same, old, tired monosyllables of Lenin's and then, like a flash, the world will be made new and the millennium of the here and now will be achieved. But when Lenin asked himself "What is to be done?", he knew the answer all along. It seems a pity that the lessons so clearly implicit in the answers applied by the Bolsheviks in their seizure of power (and emulated with a bloody finesse by the Brown Bolsheviks in Germany) have not yet been fully absorbed by otherwise thoughtful people who, for a time, thought to channel the energies of the nation's youth into a mindlessness of action that brought back the horrible memories of the Hitlerite years to a professor at the University of California in Berkeley.

Notes on the Frenzied Right

Irving Howe

I want to begin with a mild protest against the term "radical right" which has recently become popular. It is an unfortunate term and should be dropped for there has long been in America a valuable tradition of democratic radicalism, and I see no reason to cede the word "radical" to either the Birch Society or the Communist Party. More than a linguistic refinement is at stake here; it is a political point of some importance to which I shall return at the end.

The Spectrum of the Far Right

We do not yet have in the United States a coherent and unified reactionary or semi-fascist movement. There is a scattering of groups; no undisputed leader seems yet in sight; uneasy intellectuals float past.

The right-wing organizations have won some limited successes. They have discovered that like American reactionary movements in the past they can call upon a stable potential of support among

From *Contact,* III (June, 1962). Reprinted by permission of Johnson Reprint Corporation, Publishers.

middle-class and wealthy people; they have enjoyed the pleasures of meeting in halls and whipping themselves up with rhetoric and eloquence. The various groups find a common basis in anti-Communism; but this does not prove to be enough for building a political *movement,* it merely provides a useful emotional stance. The right-wing groups are still in the phase of Preliminary Bundling which also means a good deal of preliminary quarreling. They have managed to move beyond the condition of the marginal or crackpot sect, but even in their sum, do not yet constitute a *national* movement. Most of their strength makes itself felt in small towns and suburbs, where they can cajole librarians and intimidate school boards, thereby creating an atmosphere of repression.

Several distinct right-wing tendencies can be observed:

a) *The Suburban Hoodlums.* These, in California, are the Minutemen type. They have no interest in ideas or ideology, not even in politics; they want to relieve the boredom of their lives by doing close-order drill and fingering machine guns. They are not merely like their shirted equivalents of the thirties, urban flotsam and small town jetsam; now the *lumpens* drive Buicks. Primitives of the far right, they are men who simply accept the idea of war, perhaps even yearn for it, and lack the imagination to understand how different an atomic war would be from all previous ones. They really suppose, poor deluded naifs, that if there is an atomic bombing, they will still be alive to "defend" their shelters. Essentially their present conduct releases fantasies of future revenge: if you can't kill a Communist, then at least kill a city slicker trying to escape radiation.

So diseased is our moral atmosphere that the "problem" of "protecting" bomb shelters against urban refugees is debated seriously in the national press, one Catholic priest having even confirmed the moral propriety of shooting "invaders"—that is, fellow-citizens—who might descend upon suburban shelters, and one California county having even issued directives—but this is madness!—on how to take care of pets after an attack.

That such hoodlums are allowed to maintain their "private army" is a scandal: here is one area for clear and obvious political pressures: we should all insist that these gangs be disarmed. In California, to be sure, district attorneys seem more interested in getting Henry Miller's novels banned than in prosecuting fascist militiamen. And how significant it is that when a local Minuteman leader was finally arrested, the charge against him was not that he had set up a private guerrilla band but that he had failed to register with the police as a pervert. Whatever else, one can count on the powers-that-be to hold the line to the bitter end, at least in public, against the specter of sexual deviation; whether they will be as devoted to protecting civil freedoms is another question.

b) *The Enraged Intellectuals.* Clustered about the *National Review* and led by the articulate William Buckley is a group of intellectuals ranging in opinion from sophisticated conservatism to quasi-fascist reaction. Buckley and his friends take a condescending view of the burgeoning right-wing groups; they regard the Birchers and Christian Crusaders as ignorant clods and somewhat comic Bottoms. The *National Review* recently printed an editorial criticizing the Birch Society and trying to teach Robert Welch that there is a difference between "liberal softness" *vis-à-vis* Communism and conscious submission to it. Yet we should not suppose that this preliminary response will necessarily be an abiding one.

For some time now, these intellectuals have been trying to create a respectable ideological grouping on the far right. I would guess that this perspective dooms them to powerlessness for a long time, and that they know it—for their opposition to welfare measures places them in conflict with the desires of a majority of Americans. Partly because they anticipate a fairly long period of being a minority, but for a good many other reasons as well, the right-wing intellectuals believe in the need for a coherent ideology, a total world-view. This creates for them an irksome dilemma: the more they nurture an ideology, the more isolated they are likely to be, while the more they yield to the temptation of pure-and-simple anti-Communism, the more they must forego their pretensions to ideology.

Finally, they cannot abandon their ideological ambitions, first because they are intelligent enough to know the world is not so simple as the right-wing agitators make it seem, second because they see their task as preparing long-range perspectives for the conservatism of tomorrow, and third because they are, by training and ambition, intellectuals who not only want something that resembles serious thought but also, and amusingly, wish to gain the respect of the very liberal and left intellectuals they hope to defeat. This they can hardly do by associating with the candy king of Belmont, Massachusetts.

The right-wing intellectuals are therefore ambivalent in their response to the far-right movements: tempted by the idea of large audiences, perhaps fascinated by visions of power, driven by a half-secret elitist conviction that in talking to boobs a bit of demagogy may be in order, yet holding their troubled noses. They have a problem.

c) *The Frightened Bourgeoisie.* I would surmise that the major social base of the Birch organization is a section of the middle class, suddenly and belatedly stirred into a kind of political consciousness.

Among liberals eager for easy targets, it has become a commonplace to see the Birch Society in terms of paranoia, hysteria, and other syndromes. No doubt true; but not enough. For it is in the nature of any effort to build this kind of semi-fascist vanguard—the secret mover behind many motions—that it must provide an ideology, even a program, of sorts. An ideology, to be sure, can itself be heavily clotted with paranoia, as the Birch ideology is. Yet it needs to be examined on its own terms.

Essentially, the far right constitutes the American war party. The Birchers want two things: preventive war and an authoritarian dictatorship. They believe the country to be surrounded by Communist powers and itself heavily corrupted by Communist agents; hence, democracy, for which they have no use anyway, becomes a luxury no longer to be indulged, while efforts to cope with Communism abroad through political methods are felt to be a liberal illusion or, often enough, a deliberate betrayal. This is a politics of desperation, a politics preparing for Fortress America, in which we, the Last of the Rich, will make a final stand against Communism and all its "disguises." Especially the "disguises," which they hate even more than the thing itself. If one accepts these premises, it more or less follows that welfare legislation should be abolished: the time has come to "cleanse" the nation of its softness. The Birchers are Communists stood on their heads: they too believe in a "final conflict" between authoritarian extremes, they too harbor contempt for modulated thought, they too nourish fantasies of an ultimate apocalypse in which all error will be wiped out.

Together with these rudiments of ideology and politics there are several characteristic styles of Birch thought:

The Principle of Reversal. Like certain literary critics, the Birchers believe nothing is what it seems to be. Everyone is out to fool you—a pathetic reflex of the small-town American discovering that blueberry pie isn't a universal favorite. If Khrushchev says, Hammerskjold must go, it really means they want him to stay. If the Communists oppose foreign aid, it means they want it to continue. Thus the hostile world closes in . . . enemies lurk . . . all of them so experienced in using political ideas against us poor, that is, rich Americans. . . . no one can be trusted . . . the one hope is the bomb and meanwhile, before the deluge, at least the joy of abolishing income taxes . . .

The Principle of Extension. Evil is absolute, and only a few escape it. If there are but a small number of Communists left in the U.S., that's because everyone is tainted—a version of J. Edgar Hoover's First Law of Logic by which the Communist Party is seen as an increasing threat the smaller and weaker it becomes. A socialist is like a Communist; a liberal like a socialist; a moderate conservative, a liberal in disguise; and so this parody of thought continues until we reach . . .

The Principle of Guilt Through Association with One's Own Unconscious. Thus, one far right leader writes: "A lot of people in this country are Communists without knowing it." This parody of original sin, which also suffuses all consciousness, is accompanied by . . .

The Principle of the Excluded Middle. All choices are frozen into extremes, so that the very thought of moderation becomes a source of treason.

To see the Birch Society, or its numerous competitors, as a mere recurrence of McCarthyism would be a mistake.* No doubt, it draws on some of the same emotions and attracts some of the same people that McCarthy did. But in the East, McCarthyism was based primarily on plebian and lower-middle-class sectors of the population—in Boston, for example, on the numerous Irish-Catholic poor. So far as one can tell, the Birch society and its allies seem to attract a segment of the well-to-do, apparently those suburbanites and *nouveaux riches* who are genuinely frightened that Communism, or the income tax, will take away privileges they have recently acquired and barely learned to enjoy.

McCarthyism made no pretense to a program: it was a sheer outbreak of paranoia and *ressentiment,* given clever shape, half spontaneous and half calculated, by a brilliant nut. The right-wing groups have their share of all this too, and continue McCarthy's tradition of attacking not so much the Communists as the conspiracy of those declared guilty of handing over the country to the Communists. Yet it is noteworthy that even among the Birchers there is some effort at developing a coherent political outlook. McCarthy, by contrast, had no sense of the political future: what mattered to him was the immediate sensation, the feeling that sufficient unto each day is the smear thereof. But the Birchers, realizing that they have a long way to go politically and that their survival as a movement depends on more than emotions of fright, do need a political program of sorts. That is why

* The following two paragraphs are taken from my article, "Journey to the End of the Right," *Dissent,* Winter 1962.

one witnesses the astonishing spectacle of right-wing secret "cells" and public "study groups"—shades of the Marxist past!—in which some effort is apparently made toward a serious examination of Communism. And how ironic it is that only the far right has thus far managed to solve the problem of getting people out of their suburban homes and into political activity.

d) *Earnest Folks.* It is to such people, sincerely troubled by the threat of Communism and unable to distinguish between its power abroad and its weakness at home, that Dr. Fred Schwartz and his Christian Anti-Communist Crusade direct their appeal. When he spoke recently at Stanford University, Dr. Schwartz tried hard to use the accents of a reasonable man; indeed, his talk resembled the argument of an intellectual somewhat in the way the chatter of a parrot resembles the conversation of humans.

The appeal of this group lies in its ideological emptiness. Dr. Schwartz offers his followers the surface of his intellectuality together with the relief that in following him they can surrender the burden of thought. For he tells them that his crusade is non-political: just all good anti-Communist folks together. That the idea of an anti-Communist movement without politics is as absurd as a religious congregation without a view concerning the nature of God, does not seem to trouble his people. And since he steadfastly refuses to specify his ideas beyond the single notion, really a slogan, of anti-Communism, he does not run the danger of antagonizing potential followers through disagreements on political particulars.

The Schwartz group can be seen as a "front" for the far right, quite apart from whether this is Dr. Schwartz's conscious intention or not. Its vagueness, its air of good-fellowship, its aura of piety, its mimicry of thought—all ensure the "Crusade" a somewhat larger momentary appeal than, say, the Birchers are likely to command, but also make probable its later disintegration into more closely-defined political tendencies.

Dr. Schwartz's "crusade" reminds one of the "anti-war" front groups cultivated by the Communists in the late thirties. There used to be a gentleman named Dr. Harry F. Ward, an inveterate fellow-traveler, who, when asked about Communist control of his American League Against War and Fascism, would say, "If the Communists are for peace, I'm with them." Now Dr. Schwartz, speaking at Stanford, says, "If the Birchers are against Communism, I'm with them." His version of anti-Communism melts into a shapeless piety, an empty noise, the politics of the all-inclusive zero.

Sources of Support

The following seem to me some of the main sources of support for the far right:

a) *Fear of Disturbance.* Very often, I'd suspect, old-fashioned isolationism turns into new-fashioned reaction. For it has become clear that history can no longer be avoided by Americans, that history will shape and perhaps undo us: so that there follows a kind of collective tantrum against history which comes from a profound wish not to be disturbed. Yet disturbed Americans must be, and even the most narrow-minded Birchers know this. Previously quite unpolitical, many Birchers throw themselves into politics with an energy and desperation characteristic of people who hate and fear politics yet must engage in it. And the tacit revenge they take upon "the enemy" for having forced them into politics is an insistence upon a total blinding solution which finally can mean only war. It may seem a paradox to suggest that the fear of disturbance can lead people into wishing for a holocaust, yet it is precisely of such paradoxes that our life and politics are often comprised.

b) *The Wish to Preserve Privileges.* The Birch and Schwartz movements draw heavily upon upper-middle-class people, many of whom have made their money only recently. Often, too, I'd guess they appeal to prosperous small businessmen. Now it is characteristic of such businessmen to feel threatened by the large corporation, the federal government, everything that is "big," even as they themselves enjoy a certain prosperity. This makes them both defensive and aggressive, irrationally opposed to the programs of government spending and the spread of the war economy on which their well-being often depends. Fighting Communism through a tougher policy abroad and cutting taxes at home—such contradictions are the very stuff of far right politics.

c) *The Frustration of World Politics.* It is quite true that Communism on an international scale is a serious menace to freedom, and the people on the far right respond to this threat with both drama and fantasy. For, as they look upon Communism, nothing seems to work in stopping it; they have fantasies of a "total victory," which will undo recent defeats through one blazing apocalypse; yet it is hard openly to advocate war. What then can be done? Turn inward, punish enemies at home to release frustration caused by the success of enemies abroad. Nor is the far right alone in this respect: it is merely aping and enlarging upon the politics of the Eisenhower era. If you lose China, you put Eugene Dennis in jail, which if not exactly a fair exchange is certainly an understandable token of panic.

d) *The Helpless Might of the Military.* Generals and admirals, ill-prepared for sustained political thought, find themselves impatient with the diplomatic maneuvers which any administration has to employ if it is to avoid a direct plunge into war. Upon their retirement, and sometimes before it, these frustrated generals and admirals form a coterie of the disgruntled which is somewhat like, though not yet nearly so violent as, those military ultras in France who seek to establish a military dictatorship. Their plight is both sad and comic: bombs everywhere and barely a drop of blood to shed. Locked into the impotence of their strength, they can destroy the world—but very little short of that. And so they dream of a fighting posture, of talking tough, of giving the enemy ultimatums, of "cleaning up the mess" in, say, Cuba, little realizing that if that mess were cleaned up through military intervention it would soon lead to a dozen new and worse ones all through South America.

c) *The Legacy of the Cold War.* The right-wing groups did not spring up in a vacuum; the way was prepared for them by political fantasies spawned by the Eisenhower administration. For the far right inherits frustrations that need never have been aroused: John Foster Dulles should never have talked about "rolling back" the Russians in eastern Europe or "unleashing Chiang Kai-shek" in Asia, for he knew that short of war he had no way to do these things. The emotions of the far right can thus be seen as a consequence of a decade of systematic deception and self-deception in American politics, as the legacy of a national existence which avoided serious issues and never squarely confronted the significance of McCarthyism.

The Future of the Right

It has been a commonplace in liberal and radical analysis of the American right to say that, while reactionary groups could make some progress even in times of prosperity and social peace, they could not become a significant national movement until and unless there were a major crisis, a depression, in our domestic economy. This kind of argument rested upon a tacit analogy with the rise of European fascism; it assumed that movements of the far right could take on a truly mass character only if they were in a position to exploit a burning domestic issue.

Yet one wonders whether this is still entirely true. Isn't it possible to foresee a situation something like this: the United States continues to lose ground in the cold war, especially in Asia, Africa, and South America; several key countries like Indonesia, Brazil, and Algeria come under Communist rule; the sense of panic and doom which follows in American society sweeps through every class, igniting the passions not merely of the suburban bourgeoisie but also of the lower classes, who feel that something desperate, something urgent must be done; and then there follows the cry for a strong administration, abandoning liberalism, foreign aid, perhaps even the Atlantic alliance, and transforming this country into an armed fortress that will be ruled by a semi-military authoritarian force, ready to do desperate battle abroad and to scour the land for heretics at home. Is this so impossible? Is it even implausible? I think not. For the first time, then, there arises the possibility of a *mass* reactionary movement even if there is no depression or severe unemployment, even if a measure of prosperity continues. For the first time, that is, one can foresee a large-scale impulse toward irrational authoritarianism based on desperation concerning *foreign* policy. Which is to say, the fortunes of the far right in the United States are closely dependent on those of the Communist movements in the rest of the world.

And this, finally, leads me back to the point I made at the outset. The world in which we live, the world of poverty and desperation evoked by the names of Asia, Africa, and South America, needs radical, democratic radical, measures far bolder than have yet been imagined in Washington. Lacking them, the false radicalism of Communism will take over, and thereby provide the far right in America with its opportunity. That is why we must not grant the far right the term, or idea, of radicalism: it is too precious, too valuable, too necessary in our present world. And that is why I would say about the far right: in their health lie the symptoms of our trouble, and the way to overcome their trouble is to cultivate our social and political health.

5

The New Power of Blackness

The Two Worlds of Race: A Historical View

John Hope Franklin

I

Measured by universal standards the history of the United States is indeed brief. But during the brief span of three and one-half centuries of colonial and national history Americans developed traditions and prejudices which created the two worlds of race in modern America. From the time that Africans were brought as indentured servants to the mainland of English America in 1619, the enormous task of rationalizing and justifying the forced labor of peoples on the basis of racial differences was begun; and even after legal slavery was ended, the notion of racial differences persisted as a basis for maintaining segregation and discrimination. At the same time, the effort to establish a more healthy basis for the new world social order was begun, thus launching the continuing battle between the two worlds of race, on the one hand, and the world of equality and complete human fellowship, on the other.

Reprinted by permission from *Daedalus,* published by the American Academy of Arts and Sciences, Boston, Massachusetts. Vol. 94 (Fall, 1965).

For a century before the American Revolution the status of Negroes in the English colonies had become fixed at a low point that distinguished them from all other persons who had been held in temporary bondage. By the middle of the eighteenth century, laws governing Negroes denied to them certain basic rights that were conceded to others. They were permitted no independence of thought, no opportunity to improve their minds or their talents or to worship freely, no right to marry and enjoy the conventional family relationships, no right to own or dispose of property, and no protection against miscarriages of justice or cruel and unreasonable punishments. They were outside the pale of the laws that protected ordinary humans. In most places they were to be governed, as the South Carolina code of 1712 expressed it, by special laws "as may restrain the disorders, rapines, and inhumanity to which they are naturally prone and inclined. . . ." A separate world for them had been established by law and custom. Its dimensions and the conduct of its inhabitants were determined by those living in a quite different world.

By the time that the colonists took up arms against their mother country in order to secure their independence, the world of Negro slavery had become deeply entrenched and the idea of Negro inferiority well established. But the dilemmas inherent in such a situation were a source of constant embarrassment. "It always appeared a most iniquitous scheme to me," Mrs. John Adams wrote her husband in 1774, "to fight ourselves for what we are daily robbing and plundering from those who have as good a right to freedom as we have." There were others who shared her views, but they were unable to wield much influence. When the fighting began General George Washington issued an order to recruiting officers that they were not to enlist "any deserter from the ministerial army, nor any stroller, negro, or vagabond, or person suspected of being an enemy to the liberty of America nor any under eighteen years of age." In classifying Negroes with the dregs of society, traitors, and children, Washington made it clear that Negroes, slave or free, were not to enjoy the high privilege of fighting for political independence. He would change that order later, but only after it became clear that Negroes were enlisting with the "ministerial army" in droves in order to secure their own freedom. In changing his policy if not his views, Washington availed himself of the services of more than 5,000 Negroes who took up arms against England.[1]

Many Americans besides Mrs. Adams were struck by the inconsistency of their stand during the War for Independence, and they were not averse to making moves to emancipate the slaves. Quakers and other religious groups organized antislavery societies, while numerous individuals manumitted their slaves. In the years following the close of the war most of the states of the East made provisions for the gradual emancipation of slaves. In the South, meanwhile, the anti-slavery societies were unable to effect programs of state-wide emancipation. When the Southerners came to the Constitutional Convention in 1787 they succeeded in winning some representation on the basis of slavery, in securing federal support of the capture and rendition of fugitive slaves, and in preventing the closing of the slave trade before 1808.

Even where the sentiment favoring emancipation was pronounced, it was seldom accompanied by a view that Negroes were the equals of whites and should become a part of one family of Americans. Jefferson, for example, was opposed to slavery; and if he could have had his way, he would have condemned it in the Declaration of Independence. It did not follow, however, that he believed Negroes to be the equals of whites. He did not want to "degrade a whole race of men from the work in the scale of beings which their Creator may *perhaps* have given them. . . . I advance it therefore, as a suspicion only, that the blacks, whether originally a distinct race, or made distinct by time and circumstance, are inferior to the whites in the endowment both of body and mind." It is entirely possible that Jefferson's later association with the extraordinarily able Negro astronomer and mathematician, Benjamin Banneker, resulted in some modification of his views. After reading a copy of Banneker's almanac, Jefferson told him that it was "a document to which your whole race had a right for its justifications against the doubts which have been entertained of them."[2]

In communities such as Philadelphia and New York, where the climate was more favorably disposed to the idea of Negro equality than in Jefferson's Virginia, few concessions were made, except by a limited number of Quakers and their associates. Indeed, the white citizens in the City of Brotherly Love contributed substantially to the perpetuation of two distinct worlds of race. In the 1780's, the white Methodists permitted Negroes to worship with them, provided the Negroes sat in a designated place in the balcony. On one occasion, when the Negro worshippers occupied the front rows of the balcony, from which they had been excluded, the officials pulled them from their knees during prayer and evicted them from the church. Thus, in the early days of the Republic and in the place where the Republic was founded, Negroes had a definite "place" in which they were expected at all times to remain. The white Methodists of New York had much the same attitude toward their Negro fellows. Soon, there were separate Negro churches in these and other communities. Baptists were very much the same. In 1809 thirteen Negro members of a white Baptist church in Philadelphia were dismissed, and they formed a church of their own. Thus, the earliest Negro religious institutions emerged as the result of the rejection by white communicants of their darker fellow worshippers. Soon there would be other institutions—schools, newspapers, benevolent societies—to serve those who lived in a world apart.

Those Americans who conceded the importance of education for Negroes tended to favor some particular type of education that would be in keeping with their lowly station in life. In 1794, for example, the American Convention of Abolition Societies recommended that Negroes be instructed in "those mechanic arts which will keep them most constantly employed and, of course, which will less subject them to idleness and debauchery, and thus prepare them for becoming good citizens of the United States." When Anthony Benezet, a dedicated Pennsylvania abolitionist, died in 1784 his will provided that on the death of his wife the proceeds of his estate should be used to assist in the establishment of a school for Negroes. In 1787 the school of which Benezet had dreamed was opened in Philadelphia, where the pupils studied reading, writing, arithmetic, plain accounts, and sewing.

Americans who were at all interested in the education of Negroes regarded it as both natural and normal that Negroes should receive their training in separate schools. As early as 1773 Newport, Rhode Island, had a colored school, maintained by a society of benevolent clergymen of the Anglican Church. In 1798 a separate private school for Negro children was established in Boston; and two decades later the city opened its first public primary school for the education of Negro children. Meanwhile, New York had established separate schools, the first one opening its doors in 1790. By 1814 there were several such institutions that were generally designated as the New York African Free Schools.[3]

Thus, in the most liberal section of the country, the general view was that Negroes should be kept out of the main stream of American life. They were forced to establish and maintain their own religious institutions, which were frequently followed by the establishment of separate benevolent societies. Likewise, if Negroes were to receive any education, it should be special education provided in separate educational institutions. This principle prevailed in most places in the North throughout the period before the Civil War. In some Massachusetts towns, however, Negroes gained admission to schools that had been maintained for whites. But the School Committee of Boston refused to admit Negroes, arguing that the natural distinction of the races, which "no legislature, no social customs, can efface renders a promiscuous intermingling in the public schools disadvantageous both to them and to the whites." Separate schools remained in Boston until the Massachusetts legislature in 1855 enacted a law providing that in determining the qualifications of students to be admitted to any public school no distinction should be made on account of the race, color, or religious opinion of the applicant.

Meanwhile, in the Southern states, where the vast majority of the Negroes lived, there were no concessions suggesting equal treatment, even among the most liberal elements. One group that would doubtless have regarded itself as liberal on the race question advocated the deportation of Negroes to Africa, especially those who had become free. Since free Negroes "neither enjoyed the immunities of freemen, nor were they subject to the incapacities of slaves," their condition and "unconquerable prejudices" prevented amalgamation with whites, one colonization leader argued. There was, therefore, a "peculiar moral fitness" in restoring them to "the land of their fathers." Men like Henry Clay, Judge Bushrod Washington, and President James Monroe thought that separation—expatriation—was the best thing for Negroes who were or who would become free.[4]

While the colonization scheme was primarily for Negroes who were already free, it won, for a time, a considerable number of sincere enemies of slavery. From the beginning Negroes were bitterly opposed to it, and only infrequently did certain Negro leaders, such as Dr. Martin Delany and the Reverend Henry M. Turner, support the idea. Colonization, however, retained considerable support in the most responsible quarters. As late as the Civil War, President Lincoln urged Congress to adopt a plan to colonize Negroes, as the only workable solution to the race problem in the United States. Whether the advocates of colonization wanted merely to prevent the contamination of slavery by free Negroes or whether they actually regarded it as the just and honorable thing to do, they represented an important element in the population that rejected the idea of the Negro's assimilation into the main stream of American life.

Thus, within fifty years after the Declaration of Independence was written, the institution of slavery, which received only a temporary reversal during the Revolutionary era, contributed greatly to the emergence of the two worlds of race in the United States. The natural rights philosophy appeared to have little effect on those who became committed, more and more, to seeking a rationalization for slavery. The search was apparently so successful that even in areas where slavery was declining, the support for maintaining two worlds of race was strong. Since the Negro church and school emerged in Northern communities where slavery was dying, it may be said that the free society believed almost as strongly in racial separation as it did in racial freedom.

II

The generation preceding the outbreak of the Civil War witnessed the development of a set of defenses of slavery that became the basis for much of the racist doctrine to which some Americans have subscribed from then to the present time. The idea of the inferiority of the Negro enjoyed wide acceptance among Southerners of all classes and among many Northerners. It was an important ingredient in the theory of society promulgated by Southern thinkers and leaders. It was organized into a body of systematic thought by the scientists and social scientists of the South, out of which emerged a doctrine of racial superiority that justified any kind of control over the slave. In 1826 Dr. Thomas Cooper said that he had not the slightest doubt that Negroes were an "inferior variety of the human species; and not capable of the same improvement as the whites." Dr. S. C. Cartwright of the University of Louisiana insisted that the capacities of the Negro adult for learning were equal to those of a white infant; and the Negro could properly perform certain physiological functions only when under the control of white men. Because of the Negro's inferiority, liberty and republican institutions were not only unsuited to his temperament, but actually inimical to his well-being and happiness.

Like racists in other parts of the world, Southerners sought support for their ideology by developing a common bond with the less privileged. The obvious basis was race; and outside the white race there was to be found no favor from God, no honor or respect from man. By the time that Europeans were reading Gobineau's *Inequality of Races*, Southerners were reading Cartwright's *Slavery in the Light of Ethnology*. In admitting all whites into the pseudo-nobility of race, Cartwright won their enthusiastic support in the struggle to preserve the integrity and honor of *the* race. Professor Thomas R. Dew of the College of William and Mary comforted the lower-class whites by indicating that they could identify with the most privileged and affluent of the community. In the South, he said, "no white man feels such inferiority of rank as to be unworthy of association with those around him. Color alone is here the badge of distinction, the true mark of aristocracy, and all who are white are equal in spite of the variety of occupation."[5]

Many Northerners were not without their own racist views and policies in the turbulent decades before the Civil War. Some, as Professor Louis Filler has observed, displayed a hatred of Negroes that gave them a sense of superiority and an outlet for their frustrations. Others cared nothing one way or the other about Negroes and demanded only that they be kept separate.[6] Even some of the abolitionists themselves were ambivalent on the question of Negro equality. More than one antislavery society was agitated by the suggestion that Negroes be invited to join. Some members thought it reasonable for them to attend, but not to be put on an "equality with ourselves." The New York abolitionist, Lewis Tappan, admitted "that when the subject of acting out our profound principles in treating men irrespective of color is discussed heat is always produced."[7]

In the final years before the beginning of the Civil War, the view that the Negro was different, even inferior, was widely held in the United States. Leaders in both major parties subscribed to the view, while the more extreme racists deplored any suggestion that the Negro could ever prosper as a free man. At Peoria, Illinois, in October 1854, Abraham Lincoln asked what stand the opponents of slavery should take regarding Negroes. "Free them, and make them politically and socially, our equals? My own feelings will not admit of this; and if mine would, we well know that those of the great mass of white people will not. Whether this feeling accords with justice and sound judgment, is not the sole question, if indeed, it is any part of it. A universal feeling, whether well or ill founded, cannot be safely disregarded. We cannot, then, make them equals."

The Lincoln statement was forthright, and it doubtless represented the views of most Americans in the 1850's. Most of those who heard him or read his speech were of the same opinion as he. In later years, the Peoria pronouncement would be used by those who sought to detract from Lincoln's reputation as a champion of the rights of the Negro. In 1964, the White Citizens' Councils reprinted portions of the speech in large advertisements in the daily press and insisted that Lincoln shared their views on the desirability of maintaining two distinct worlds of race.

Lincoln could not have overcome the nation's strong predisposition toward racial separation if he had tried. And he did not try very hard. When he called for the enlistment of Negro troops, after issuing the Emancipation Proclamation, he was content not only to set Negroes apart in a unit called "U. S. Colored Troops," but also to have Negro privates receive $10 per month including clothing, while whites of the same rank received $13 per month plus clothing. Only the stubborn refusal of many Negro troops to accept discriminatory pay finally forced Congress to equalize compensation for white and Negro soldiers.[8] The fight for union that became also a fight for freedom never became a fight for equality or for the creation of one racial world.

The Lincoln and Johnson plans for settling the problems of peace and freedom never seriously touched on the concomitant problem of equality. To be sure, in 1864 President Lincoln privately raised with the governor of Louisiana the question of the franchise for a limited number of Negroes, but when the governor ignored the question the President let the matter drop. Johnson raised a similar question in 1866, but he admitted that it was merely to frustrate the design of radical reformers who sought a wider franchise for Negroes. During the two years following Appomattox Southern leaders gave not the slightest consideration to permitting any Negroes, regardless of their service to the Union or their education or their property, to share in the political life of their communities. Not only did every Southern state refuse to permit Negroes to vote, but they also refused to provide Negroes with any of the educational opportunities that they were providing for the whites.

The early practice of political disfranchisement and of exclusion from public educational facilities helped to determine subsequent policies that the South adopted regarding Negroes. While a few leaders raised their voices against these policies and practices, it was Negroes themselves who made the most eloquent attacks on such discriminations. As early as May 1865, a group of North Carolina Negroes told President Johnson that some of them had been soldiers and were doing everything possible to learn how to discharge the higher duties of citizenship. "It seems to us that men who are willing on the field of battle to carry the muskets of the Republic, in the days of peace ought to be permitted to carry the ballots; and certainly we cannot understand the justice of denying the elective franchise to men who have been fighting *for* the country, while it is freely given to men who have just returned from *four* years fighting against it." Such pleas fell on deaf ears, however; and it was not until 1867, when Congress was sufficiently outraged by the inhuman black codes, widespread discriminations in the South, and unspeakable forms of violence against Negroes, that new federal legislation sought to correct the evils of the first period of Reconstruction.

The period that we know as Radical Reconstruction had no significant or permanent effect on the status of the Negro in American life. For a period of time, varying from one year to fifteen or twenty years, some Negroes enjoyed the privileges of voting. They gained political ascendancy in a very few communities only temporarily, and they never even began to achieve the status of a ruling class. They made no meaningful steps toward economic independence or even stability; and in no time at all, because of the pressures of the local community and the neglect of the federal government, they were brought under the complete economic subservience of the old ruling class. Organizations such as the Ku Klux Klan were committed to violent action to keep Negroes "in their place" and, having gained respectability through sponsorship by Confederate generals and the like, they proceeded to wreak havoc in the name of white supremacy and protection of white womanhood.[9]

Meanwhile, various forms of segregation and discrimination, developed in the years before the Civil War in order to degrade the half million free Negroes in the United States, were now applied to the four million Negroes who had become free in 1865. Already the churches and the military were completely segregated. For the most part the schools, even in the North, were separate. In the South segregated schools persisted, even in the places where the radicals made a half-hearted attempt to desegregate them. In 1875 Congress enacted a Civil Rights Act to guarantee the enjoyment of equal rights in carriers and all places of public accommodation and amusement. Even before it became law Northern philanthropists succeeded in forcing the deletion of the provision calling for desegregated schools. Soon, because of the massive resistance in the North as well as in the South and the indifferent manner in which the federal government enforced the law, it soon became a dead letter everywhere. When it was declared unconstitutional by the Supreme Court in 1883, there was universal rejoicing, except among the Negroes, one of whom declared that they had been "baptized in ice water."

Neither the Civil War nor the era of Reconstruction made any significant step toward the permanent elimination of racial barriers. The radicals of the post-Civil War years came no closer to the creation of one racial world than the patriots of the Revolutionary years. When Negroes were, for the first time, enrolled in the standing army of the United States, they were placed in separate Negro units. Most of the liberals of the Reconstruction era called for and worked for separate schools for Negroes. Nowhere was there any extensive effort to involve Negroes in the churches and other social institutions of the dominant group. Whatever remained of the old abolitionist fervor, which can hardly be described as unequivocal on the question of true racial equality, was rapidly disappearing. In its place were the sentiments of the business men who wanted peace at any price. Those having common railroad interests or crop-marketing interests or investment interests could and did extend their hands across sectional lines and joined in the task of working together for the common good. In such an atmosphere the practice was to accept the realities of two separate worlds of race. Some even subscribed to the view that there were significant economic advantages in maintaining the two worlds of race.

III

The post-Reconstruction years witnessed a steady deterioration in the status of Negro Americans. These were the years that Professor Rayford Logan has called the "nadir" of the Negro in American life and thought. They were the years when Americans, weary of the crusade that had, for the most part, ended with the outbreak of the Civil War, displayed almost no interest in helping the Negro to achieve equality. The social Darwinists decried the very notion of equality for Negroes, arguing that the lowly place they occupied was natural and normal. The leading literary journals vied with each other in describing Negroes as lazy, idle, improvident, immoral, and criminal.[10] Thomas Dixon's novels, *The Klansman* and *The Leopard's Spots,* and D. W. Griffith's motion picture, "The Birth of A Nation," helped to give Americans a view of the Negro's role in American history that "proved" that he was unfit for citizenship, to say nothing of equality. The dictum of William Graham Sumner and his followers that "stateways cannot change folkways" convinced many Americans that legislating equality and creating one great society where race was irrelevant was out of the question.

But many Americans believed that they *could* legislate inequality; and they proceeded to do precisely that. Beginning in 1890, one Southern state after another revised the suffrage provisions of its constitution in a manner that made it virtually impossible for Negroes to qualify to vote. The new literacy and "understanding" provisions permitted local registrars to disqualify Negroes while permitting white citizens to qualify. Several states, including Louisiana, North Carolina, and Oklahoma, inserted "grandfather clauses" in their constitutions in order to permit persons, who could not otherwise qualify, to vote if their fathers or grandfathers could vote in 1866. (This was such a flagrant discrimination against Negroes, whose ancestors could not vote in 1866, that the United States Supreme Court in 1915 declared the "grandfather clause" unconstitutional.) Then came the Democratic white primary in 1900 that made it impossible for Negroes to participate in local elections in the South, where, by this time, only the

Democratic party had any appreciable strength. (After more than a generation of assaults on it, the white primary was finally declared unconstitutional in 1944.)

Inequality was legislated in still another way. Beginning in the 1880's, many states, especially but not exclusively in the South, enacted statutes designed to separate the races. After the Civil Rights Act was declared unconstitutional in 1883 state legislatures were emboldened to enact numerous segregation statutes. When the United States Supreme Court, in the case of Plessy *v.* Ferguson, set forth the "separate but equal" doctrine in 1896, the decision provided a new stimulus for laws to separate the races and, of course, to discriminate against Negroes. In time, Negroes and whites were separated in the use of schools, churches, cemeteries, drinking fountains, restaurants, and all places of public accommodation and amusement. One state enacted a law providing for the separate warehousing of books used by white and Negro children. Another required the telephone company to provide separate telephone booths for white and Negro customers. In most communities housing was racially separated by law or practice.[11]

Where there was no legislation requiring segregation, local practices filled the void. Contradictions and inconsistencies seemed not to disturb those who sought to maintain racial distinctions at all costs. It mattered not that one drive-in snack bar served Negroes only on the inside, while its competitor across the street served Negroes only on the outside. Both were committed to making racial distinctions; and in communities where practices and mores had the force of law, the distinction was everything. Such practices were greatly strengthened when, in 1913, the federal government adopted policies that segregated the races in its offices as well as in its eating and rest-room facilities.

By the time of World War I, Negroes and whites in the South and in parts of the North lived in separate worlds, and the apparatus for keeping the worlds separate was elaborate and complex. Negroes were segregated by law in the public schools of the Southern states, while those in the Northern ghettos were sent to predominantly Negro schools, except where their numbers were insufficient. Scores of Negro newspapers sprang up to provide news of Negroes that the white press consistently ignored. Negroes were as unwanted in the white churches as they had been in the late eighteenth century; and Negro churches of virtually every denomination were the answer for a people who had accepted the white man's religion even as the white man rejected his religious fellowship.

Taking note of the fact that they had been omitted from any serious consideration by the white historians, Negroes began in earnest to write the history of their own experiences as Americans. There had been

Negro historians before the Civil War, but none of them had challenged the white historians' efforts to relegate Negroes to a separate, degraded world. In 1882, however, George Washington Williams published his *History of the Negro Race in America* in order to "give the world more correct ideas about the colored people." He wrote, he said, not "as a partisan apologist, but from a love for the truth of history."[12] Soon there were other historical works by Negroes describing their progress and their contributions and arguing that they deserved to be received into the full fellowship of American citizens.

It was in these post-Reconstruction years that some of the most vigorous efforts were made to destroy the two worlds of race. The desperate pleas of Negro historians were merely the more articulate attempts of Negroes to gain complete acceptance in American life. Scores of Negro organizations joined in the struggle to gain protection and recognition of their rights and to eliminate the more sordid practices that characterized the treatment of the Negro world by the white world. Unhappily, the small number of whites who were committed to racial equality dwindled in the post-Reconstruction years, while government at every level showed no interest in eliminating racial separatism. It seemed that Negro voices were indeed crying in the wilderness, but they carried on their attempts to be heard. In 1890 Negroes from twenty-one states and the District of Columbia met in Chicago and organized the Afro-American League of the United States. They called for more equitable distribution of school funds, fair and impartial trial for accused Negroes, resistance "by all legal and reasonable means" to mob and lynch law, and enjoyment of the franchise by all qualified voters. When a group of young Negro intellectuals, led by W. E. B. Du Bois, met at Niagara Falls, Ontario, in 1905, they made a similar call as they launched their Niagara Movement.

However eloquent their pleas, Negroes alone could make no successful assault on the two worlds of race. They needed help—a great deal of help. It was the bloody race riots in the early years of the twentieth century that shocked civic minded and socially conscious whites into answering the Negro's pleas for support. Some whites began to take the view that the existence of two societies whose distinction was based solely on race was inimical to the best interests of the entire nation. Soon, they were taking the initiative and in 1909 organized the National Association for the Advancement of Colored People. They assisted the following year in establishing the National Urban League. White attorneys began to stand with Negroes before the United States Supreme Court to challenge the "grandfather clause," local segregation ordinances, and flagrant miscarriages of justice in which Negroes were the victims. The patterns of attack developed during these years were to become invaluable later. Legal action was soon supplemented by picketing, demonstrating, and boycotting, with telling effect particularly in selected Northern communities.[13]

IV

The two world wars had a profound effect on the status of Negroes in the United States and did much to mount the attack on the two worlds of race. The decade of World War I witnessed a very significant migration of Negroes. They went in large numbers—perhaps a half million—from the rural areas of the South to the towns and cities of the South and North. They were especially attracted to the industrial centers of the North. By the thousands they poured into Pittsburgh, Cleveland, and Chicago. Although many were unable to secure employment, others were successful and achieved a standard of living they could not have imagined only a few years earlier. Northern communities were not altogether friendly and hospitable to the newcomers, but the opportunities for education and the enjoyment of political self-respect were the greatest they had ever seen. Many of them felt that they were entirely justified in their renewed hope that the war would bring about a complete merger of the two worlds of race.

Those who held such high hopes, however, were naive in the extreme. Already the Ku Klux Klan was being revived—this time in the North as well as in the South. Its leaders were determined to develop a broad program to unite "native-born white Christians for concerted action in the preservation of American institutions and the supremacy of the white race." By the time that the war was over, the Klan was in a position to make capital of the racial animosities that had developed during the conflict itself. Racial conflicts had broken out in many places during the war; and before the conference at Versailles was over race riots in the United States had brought about what can accurately be described as the "long, hot summer" of 1919.

If anything, the military operations which aimed to save the world for democracy merely fixed more permanently the racial separation in the United States. Negro soldiers not only constituted entirely separate fighting units in the United States Army, but, once overseas, were assigned to fighting units with the French Army. Negroes who sought service with the United States Marines or the Air Force were rejected, while the Navy relegated them to menial duties. The reaction of many Negroes was bitter, but most of the leaders, including Du Bois, counseled patience and loyalty. They continued to hope that their show of patriotism would win for them a secure place of acceptance as Americans.

Few Negro Americans could have anticipated the wholesale rejection they experienced at the conclusion of World War I. Returning Negro soldiers were lynched by hanging and burning, even while still in their military uniforms. The Klan warned Negroes that they must respect the rights of the white race "in whose country they are permitted to reside." Racial conflicts swept the country, and neither federal nor state governments seemed interested in effective intervention. The worlds of race were growing further apart in the postwar decade. Nothing indicated this more clearly than the growth of the Universal Negro Improvement Association, led by Marcus Garvey. From a mere handful of members at the end of the war, the Garvey movement rapidly became the largest secular Negro group ever organized in the United States. Although few Negroes were interested in settling in Africa—the expressed aim of Garvey—they joined the movement by the hundreds of thousands to indicate their resentment of the racial duality that seemed to them to be the central feature of the American social order.[14]

More realistic and hardheaded were the Negroes who were more determined than ever to engage in the most desperate fight of their lives to destroy racism in the United States. As the editor of the *Crisis* said in 1919, "We return from fighting. We return fighting. Make way for Democracy! We saved it in France, and by the Great Jehovah, we will save it in the U.S.A., or know of the reason why." This was the spirit of what Alain Locke called "The New Negro." He fought the Democratic white primary, made war on the whites who consigned him to the ghetto, attacked racial discrimination in employment, and pressed for legislation to protect his rights. If he was seldom successful during the postwar decade and the depression, he made it quite clear that he was unalterably opposed to the un-American character of the two worlds of race.

Hope for a new assault on racism was kindled by some of the New Deal policies of Franklin D. Roosevelt. As members of the economically disadvantaged group, Negroes benefited from relief and recovery legislation. Most of it, however, recognized the existence of the two worlds of race and accommodated itself to it. Frequently bread lines and soup kitchens were separated on the basis of race. There was segregation in the employment services, while many new agencies recognized and bowed to Jim Crow. Whenever agencies, such as the Farm Security Administration, fought segregation and sought to deal with people on the basis of their needs rather than race they came under the withering fire of the racist critics and seldom escaped alive. Winds of change, however slight, were discernible, and nowhere was this in greater evidence than in the new labor unions. Groups like the Congress of Industrial Organizations, encouraged by the support of the Wagner Labor Relations Act, began to look at manpower resources as a whole and to attack the old racial policies that viewed labor in terms of race.

As World War II approached, Negroes schooled in the experiences of the nineteen-twenties and thirties were unwilling to see the fight against Nazism carried on in the context of an American racist ideology. Some white Americans were likewise uncomfortable in the role of freeing Europe of a racism which still permeated the United States; but it was the Negroes who dramatized American inconsistency by demanding an end to discrimination in employment in defense industries. By threatening to march on Washington in 1941 they forced the President to issue an order forbidding such discrimination. The opposition was loud and strong. Some state governors denounced the order, and some manufacturers skillfully evaded it. But it was a significant step toward the elimination of the two worlds.

During World War II the assault on racism continued. Negroes, more than a million of whom were enlisted in the armed services, bitterly fought discrimination and segregation. The armed services were, for the most part, two quite distinct racial worlds. Some Negro units had white officers, and much of the officer training was desegregated. But it was not until the final months of the war that a deliberate experiment was undertaken to involve Negro and white enlisted men in the same fighting unit. With the success of the experiment and with the warm glow of victory over Nazism as a backdrop, there was greater inclination to recognize the absurdity of maintaining a racially separate military force to protect the freedoms of the country.[15]

During the war there began the greatest migration in the history of Negro Americans. Hundreds of thousands left the South for the industrial centers of the North and West. In those places they met hostility, but they also secured employment in aviation plants, automobile factories, steel mills, and numerous other industries. Their difficulties persisted as they faced problems of housing and adjustment. But they continued to move out of the South in such large numbers that by 1965 one third of the twenty million Negroes in the United States lived in twelve metropolitan centers of the North and West. The ramifications of such large-scale migration were numerous. The concentration of Negroes in communities where they suffered no political disabilities placed in their hands an enormous amount of political power. Consequently, some of them went to the legislatures, to Congress, and to positions on the judiciary. In turn, this won for them political respect as well as legislation that greatly strengthened their position as citizens.

V

Following World War II there was a marked acceleration in the war against the two worlds of race in the United States. In 1944 the Supreme Court ruled against segregation in interstate transportation, and three years later it wrote the final chapter in the war against the Democratic white primary. In 1947 the President's Committee on Civil Rights called for the "elimination of segregation, based on race, color, creed, or national origin, from American life."[16] In the following year President Truman asked Congress to establish a permanent Fair Employment Practices Commission. At the same time he took steps to eliminate segregation in the armed services. These moves on the part of the judicial and executive branches of the federal government by no means destroyed the two worlds of race, but they created a more healthy climate in which the government and others could launch an attack on racial separatism.

The attack was greatly strengthened by the new position of world leadership that the United States assumed at the close of the war. Critics of the United States were quick to point to the inconsistencies of an American position that spoke against racism abroad and countenanced it at home. New nations, brown and black, seemed reluctant to follow the lead of a country that adhered to its policy of maintaining two worlds of race—the one identified with the old colonial ruling powers and the other with the colonies now emerging as independent nations. Responsible leaders in the United States saw the weakness of their position, and some of them made new moves to repair it.

Civic and religious groups, some labor organizations, and many individuals from the white community began to join in the effort to destroy segregation and discrimination in American life. There was no danger, after World War II, that Negroes would ever again stand alone in their fight. The older interracial organizations continued, but they were joined by new ones. In addition to the numerous groups that included racial equality in their over-all programs, there were others that made the creation of one racial world their principal objective. Among them were the Congress of Racial Equality, the Southern Christian Leadership Conference, and the Student Non-Violent Coordinating Committee. Those in existence in the 1950's supported the court action that brought about the decision against segregated schools. The more recent ones have taken the lead in pressing for new legislation and in developing new techniques to be used in the war on segregation.

VI

The most powerful direct force in the maintenance of the two worlds of race has been the state and its political subdivisions. In states and communities where racial separation and discrimination are basic to the way of life, the elected officials invariably pledge themselves to the perpetuation of the duality. Indeed, candidates frequently vie with one another in their effort to occupy the most extreme segregationist position possible on the race question. Appointed officials, including the constabulary and, not infrequently, the teachers and school administrators, become auxiliary guardians of the system of racial separation. In such communities Negroes occupy no policy-making positions, exercise no influence over the determination of policy, and are seldom even on the police force. State and local resources, including tax funds, are at the disposal of those who guard the system of segregation and discrimination; and such funds are used to enforce customs as well as laws and to disseminate information in support of the system.

The white community itself acts as a guardian of the segregated system. Schooled in the specious arguments that assert the supremacy of the white race and fearful that a destruction of the system would be harmful to their own position, they not only "go along" with it but, in many cases, enthusiastically support it. Community sanctions are so powerful, moreover, that the independent citizen who would defy the established order would find himself not only ostracized but, worse, the target of economic and political reprisals.

Within the community many self-appointed guardians of white supremacy have emerged at various times. After the Civil War and after World War I it was the Ku Klux Klan, which has shown surprising strength in recent years. After the desegregation decision of the Supreme Court in 1954 it was the White Citizens' Council, which one Southern editor has called the "uptown Ku Klux Klan." From time to time since 1865, it has been the political demagogue, who has not only made capital by urging his election as a sure way to maintain the system but has also encouraged the less responsible elements of the community to take the law into their own hands.

Violence, so much a part of American history and particularly of Southern history, has been an important factor in maintaining the two worlds of race. Intimidation, terror, lynchings, and riots have, in succession, been the handmaiden of political entities whose officials have been unwilling or unable to put an end to it. Violence drove Negroes from the polls in the 1870's and has kept them away in droves since that time. Lynchings, the spectacular rope and faggot kind or the quiet kind of merely "doing away" with some insubordinate Negro, have served their special purpose in terrorizing whole communities of Negroes. Riots, confined to no section of the country, have demonstrated how explosive the racial situation can be in urban communities burdened with the strain of racial strife.

The heavy hand of history has been a powerful force in the maintenance of a segregated society and, conversely, in the resistance to change. Americans, especially Southerners whose devotion to the past is unmatched by that of any others, have summoned history to support their arguments that age-old practices and institutions cannot be changed overnight, that social practices cannot be changed by legislation. Southerners have argued that desegregation would break down long-established customs and bring instability to a social order that, if left alone, would have no serious racial or social disorders. After all, Southern whites "know" Negroes; and their knowledge has come from many generations of intimate association and observation, they insist.

White Southerners have also summoned history to support them in their resistance to federal legislation designed to secure the civil rights of Negroes. At every level—in local groups, state governments, and in Congress—white Southerners have asserted that federal civil rights legislation is an attempt to turn back the clock to the Reconstruction era, when federal intervention, they claim, imposed a harsh and unjust peace.[17] To make effective their argument, they use such emotion-laden phrases as "military occupation," "Negro rule," and "black-out of honest government." Americans other than Southerners have been frightened by the Southerners' claim that civil rights for Negroes would cause a return to the "evils" of Reconstruction. Insecure in their own knowledge of history, they have accepted the erroneous assertions about the "disaster" of radical rule after the Civil War and the vengeful punishment meted out to the South by the Negro and his white allies. Regardless of the merits of these arguments that seem specious on the face of them—to say nothing of their historical inaccuracy—they have served as effective brakes on the drive to destroy the two worlds of race.

One suspects, however, that racial bigotry has become more expensive in recent years. It is not so easy now as it once was to make political capital out of the race problem, even in the deep South.

Local citizens—farmers, laborers, manufacturers—have become a bit weary of the promises of the demagogue that he will preserve the integrity of the races if he is, at the same time, unable to persuade investors to build factories and bring capital to their communities. Some Southerners, dependent on tourists, are not certain that their vaunted racial pride is so dear, if it keeps visitors away and brings depression to their economy. The cities that see themselves bypassed by a prospective manufacturer because of their reputation in the field of race relations might have some sober second thoughts about the importance of maintaining their two worlds. In a word, the economics of segregation and discrimination is forcing, in some quarters, a reconsideration of the problem.

It must be added that the existence of the two worlds of race has created forces that cause some Negroes to seek its perpetuation. Some Negro institutions, the product of a dual society, have vested interests in the perpetuation of that society. And Negroes who fear the destruction of their own institutions by desegregation are encouraged by white racists to fight for their maintenance. Even where Negroes have a desire to maintain their institutions because of their honest commitment to the merits of cultural pluralism, the desire becomes a strident struggle for survival in the context of racist forces that seek with a vengeance to destroy such institutions. The firing of a few hundred Negro school teachers by a zealous, racially-oriented school board forces some second thoughts on the part of the Negroes regarding the merits of desegregation.

VII

The drive to destroy the two worlds of race has reached a new, dramatic, and somewhat explosive stage in recent years. The forces arrayed in behalf of maintaining these two worlds have been subjected to ceaseless and powerful attacks by the increasing numbers committed to the elimination of racism in American life. Through techniques of demonstrating, picketing, sitting-in, and boycotting they have not only harrassed their foes but marshaled their forces. Realizing that another ingredient was needed, they have pressed for new and better laws and the active support of government. At the local and state levels they began to secure legislation in the 1940's to guarantee the civil rights of all, eliminate discrimination in employment, and achieve decent public and private housing for all.

While it is not possible to measure the influence of public opinion in the drive for equality, it can hardly be denied that over the past five or six years public opinion has shown a marked shift toward vigorous support of the civil rights movement. This can be seen in the manner in which the mass-circulation magazines as well as influential newspapers, even in the South, have stepped up their support of specific measures that have as their objective the elimination of at least the worst features of racism. The discussion of the problem of race over radio and television and the use of these media in reporting newsworthy and dramatic events in the world of race undoubtedly have had some impact. If such activities have not brought about the enactment of civil rights legislation, they have doubtless stimulated the public discussion that culminated in such legislation.

The models of city ordinances and state laws and the increased political influence of civil rights advocates stimulated new action on the federal level. Civil rights acts were passed in 1957, 1960, and 1964—after almost complete federal inactivity in this sphere for more than three quarters of a century. Strong leadership on the part of the executive and favorable judicial interpretations of old as well as new laws have made it clear that the war against the two worlds of race now enjoys the sanction of the law and its interpreters. In many respects this constitutes the most significant development in the struggle against racism in the present century.

The reading of American history over the past two centuries impresses one with the fact that ambivalence on the crucial question of equality has persisted almost from the beginning. If the term "equal rights for all" has not always meant what it appeared to mean, the inconsistencies and the paradoxes have become increasingly apparent. This is not to say that the view that "equal rights for some" has disappeared or has even ceased to be a threat to the concept of real equality. It is to say, however, that the voices supporting inequality, while no less strident, have been significantly weakened by the very force of the numbers and elements now seeking to eliminate the two worlds of race.

REFERENCES

1. Benjamin Quarles, *The Negro in the American Revolution* (Chapel Hill, N. C., 1961), pp. 15-18.

2. John Hope Franklin, *From Slavery to Freedom: A History of American Negroes* (New York, 1956), pp. 156-157.

3. Carter G. Woodson, *The Education of the Negro Prior to 1861* (Washington, D. C., 1919), pp. 93-97.

4. P. J. Staudenraus, *The African Colonization Movement, 1816-1865* (New York, 1961), pp. 22-32.

5. John Hope Franklin, *The Militant South, 1800-1861* (Cambridge, Mass., 1956), pp. 83-86.
6. Louis Filler, *The Crusade Against Slavery, 1830-1860* (New York, 1960), pp. 142-145.
7. Leon F. Litwack, *North of Slavery; The Negro in the Free States, 1790-1860* (Chicago, 1961), pp. 216-217.
8. Benjamin Quarles, *The Negro in the Civil War* (Boston, 1953), p. 200.
9. John Hope Franklin, *Reconstruction After the Civil War* (Chicago, 1961), pp. 154-158.
10. Rayford W. Logan, *The Negro in American Life and Thought: The Nadir, 1877-1901* (New York, 1954), pp. 239-274.
11. John Hope Franklin, "History of Racial Segregation in the United States, *Annals of the Academy of Political and Social Science,* Vol. 304 (March 1956), pp. 1-9.
12. George W. Williams, *History of the Negro Race in America from 1619 to 1880* (New York, 1882), p. x.
13. Franklin, *From Slavery to Freedom,* pp. 437-443.
14. Edmund David Cronon, *Black Moses, The Story of Marcus Garvey and the Universal Negro Improvement Association* (Madison, Wis., 1955), pp. 202-206.
15. Lee Nichols, *Breakthrough on the Color Front* (New York, 1954), pp. 221-226.
16. *To Secure These Rights, The Report of the President's Committee on Civil Rights* (New York, 1947), p. 166.
17. John Hope Franklin, "As For Our History," in Charles G. Sellers (ed.), *The Southerner as American* (Chapel Hill, N. C., 1960), pp. 1-18.

Harlem, My Harlem

Claude Brown

At the age of nine I had already acquired the reputation of being the worst boy in the neighborhood. And in my neighborhood this was no easy accomplishment. My frequent appearance in juvenile court was beginning to bother the judges. By spring of 1946 I had been placed in four juvenile detention centers by the Manhattan Domestic Relations Court. However, during my travels through New York City while truant from school, I had become exceptionally well acquainted with the city subways. As a result, I was usually back on the streets of Harlem within two days, from wherever the court had placed me. A year earlier, I had acquired the habit of staying away from home for several days and nights which occasionally lengthened into weeks. Due to my skill at living in the streets, it would sometimes be many days before my parents learned of my unofficial departure from the places to which I had been confined by the courts.

While roaming the streets at night with one or two other boys who were also afraid to go home or disgusted with home life, I was often

---

Reprinted from *Dissent,* Summer 1961, by permission of the publisher.

arrested for breaking into stores and stealing. I only stole items that I could sell to my private customers or to one of the neighborhood "fences." And I knew a large number of the latter. Among my many customers and associates were prostitutes, pimps, dope peddlers, stick-up artists, professional thieves, and other petty criminals with great ambitions.

My favorite fence was Miss Eileen. She was not the highest paying fence; in fact, there is no such thing. Any thief will tell you, they are all a bunch of crooks. But Miss Eileen had such a nice way of robbing me. She would put her arm around me and beg me in a very sexy tone while she played with my ears. I thought she was the prettiest lady in the world. I think she was the first woman I ever knew who had red hair. Miss Eileen was also something more than a fence, and I would have discovered this much sooner had it not been for my youth. Many times when I came to her house at night she would be in her slip and a new husband would be there. As time went on I heard the older fellows talking about selling Miss Eileen something for a "piece of loving." I too began to dream of the day when I could sell her something for a piece of loving, but to my regret I never got the chance. A year later Miss Eileen went to jail for three years, and when she came out she wasn't as pretty as she used to be. As a result, she changed her "game" to selling drugs. For three years she was very successful in the "horse trade," but gave it up and did seven years for her troubles at the insistence of the Narcotics Bureau. The last time I saw her she was profitably engaged in one of Harlem's more legal vices; the "numbers" racket.

These were the people I admired and wanted to be accepted by. People like Miss Eileen and my other teachers from the streets of Harlem.

By June 1946 I had been expelled from not less than six public schools in New York City, and refused acceptance by as many others. The Board of Education would tolerate my numerous absences from school, and even my fighting with teachers. But they refused to have a boy in the school system who had attempted to push another boy out of a five-story window.

Following a thirty-day psychiatric observation period in Bellevue Hospital, I was ordered out of the state by a juvenile court judge. After enduring what seemed at the time a miserable year on a small farm in South Carolina, I returned to New York. When I arrived in Harlem on August 10, 1947, I was also returning to a familiar way of life. Less than two months later I was standing before Judge Bolyn diligently trying to look pathetic. She appeared to be a woman devoid of any emotions, especially pity. From Judge Bolyn, to whom I am deeply indebted today, I received my first sentence.

My first court sentence was actually not a sentence at all, but a commitment to Wiltwyck School for Boys for an indefinite time.

Wiltwyck is an interracial institution which accepts delinquent boys from eight to twelve, committed by the courts of New York or by social agencies. Only children are considered who can profit by its program of individualized treatment in the regulated and planned environment of a children's community.

Following a two and a half years stay at Wiltwyck, I returned to my dear old Harlem. I was then thirteen. In a few weeks I became uncomfortably aware of not being able to fit in anymore. There were many new vices to learn, but somehow I just could not pick up where I had left off. Having no alternative, however, I set out to reestablish myself in the old community.

Things were somewhat different now. The dope fad had hit New York, and all of my old gang were using heroin. I wanted nothing to do with drugs, but the problem was very disturbing. Either I could continue my relationship with my old cohorts or get in with a younger gang of delinquents, my own age. The younger group was stealing and making much less money than my former partners. I would have chosen my old friends, but I was handicapped by parental restrictions. So I became leader of a gang of fellows mostly my own age. There were many things I could teach them, such as how to pick locks, how to rob a subway slot machine, how to pick a woman's pocketbook, how to bargain with the "fence," and how to roll "pot." Also, I knew how to organize a gang fight and hold a gang together.

I didn't have to steal for money, because Butch, Kidd, and Danny were doing good, "pushing horse," and money was mine for the asking. I think they preferred that I steal it from them. So, that's how I usually got it. Butch, Kidd, and Danny were all at least four years older than I was, and for many years we had all lived in the same tenement building. These guys whom I considered to be "big time," were like older brothers to me. They fought the bigger guys who tried to bully me. It was they who had taught me how to steal, how to live in the streets of Harlem. It was Danny who had taught me most of the street ways. He taught me by cheating me, taking me along on "scores," and showing me my mistakes whenever I lost a fight.

Whenever I lost a fight Danny would always say you should have stabbed that punk. To Danny, everybody was a punk. It was Danny who had first taught me how to use a knife in a street fight. I remember him showing me how to get the knife out of my belt without my opponent seeing it. Danny would say "a cat should never know that you have a knife until he has been cut or stabbed." And this is usually the way it was when he stabbed a guy.

Butch was the most loyal guy I knew, and also the best thief. Butch had taught me how to hitch rides on street cars and buses. He also taught me not to run when I stole something. Butch would never admit that he was the best thief in the neighborhood. He would always say that Sol was the best because Sol had taught him many things about stealing. Sol was much older than Butch and had been stealing much longer, but he had been caught while Butch had not yet been "busted." In my opinion that made Butch the better thief.

Kidd had taught me how to play hookey from school. I was about six years old when I first heard about "hookey" and I pleaded with Kidd to teach me the game. He promised me he would teach me on the first day I went to school. This promise had to wait until the second day, because on the first day my mother took me to get me registered. Once I learned how to play hookey, I seldom went to school, and this often led to staying away from home. I would look in the mailbox and could always tell if there was a card from the school. The yellow truancy card in the mailbox meant that if I went home that night, the razor strop awaited me. When I played hookey I would either go on a stealing tour of the city or sneak into a movie. Kidd had also taught me how to sneak into a movie.

Stealing had become a part of me and I became very adept at this art. After Wiltwyck I felt lost whenever I was not stealing or "rumbling." Perhaps that's why I began to spend more time with my new gang and less time with my old cohorts.

Less than three months after my release, I was arrested for gang fighting, but was released in my mother's custody. Three weeks later I was in a backyard stealing some sheets off a clothes line. Turk, a member of my new gang whom I had become "tight" with, was with me. At my house there were festivities taking place because mama had hit the number. I had to get away from it and when I reached the street, the first person I saw was Turk. He was always ready to do whatever I suggested. Turk's favorite words were "Sonny, what are we gonna do?" That cold night in December, when I said to Turk, let's go steal some sheets, he seemed to be waiting for the suggestion.

When we had been in the backyard for about fifteen minutes, Turk shouted, "Foot it, Sonny!" I stood there waiting to see what he wanted to run from. I didn't see anybody, but after the first shot was fired I decided to run. By the time I reached the top of the stairs leading from the backyard I was feeling unusually tired. But I kept running even after I felt the blood streaming down my leg and realized I had been shot. I panicked and started yelling, "Turk! Turk! I'm shot." I ran into a fish-and-chip joint where I collapsed. As I lay on the floor of the dirty joint, my fear of dying began slowly to diminish.

I found myself wishing that mama would stop jumping up while she cried, because she was shaking the shabby floor and it made me feel the bullet more. I never gave a second thought to Turk's question when he bent over me as I fell to the floor, and asked me if I were going to tell the cops that he was with me. This was all very normal in Harlem where somebody was always getting shot, stabbed, or his throat cut. However, I found it disturbing to have it happen to me. As the pain began to ease up, I started thinking how lucky I was to die this way. I thought about the boy whom I had watched two members of my old gang throw from the roof of a six-story building. I recalled how frightened he looked when they grabbed him, and I recalled his terrified screams as he went over. Yeah, compared to him I was really lucky.

While I lay on the rolling stretcher in Harlem Hospital emergency ward, I thought the police would never stop questioning me. Danny, Butch, and Kidd arrived shortly after I did. First Butch would beg me to tell him who had shot me, then Danny would start while Kidd threatened to kill Turk if I died. They all had their "pieces" and were ready and anxious to shoot somebody. Fortunately, I had not seen whoever it was that shot me, and could tell them no more than I had told the police.

Three weeks after my two week stay in Harlem Hospital, and while the surgeon who had operated on me was still marveling at what he and God had done, I was sent to New York State Training School for Boys at Warwick, New York. I stayed at Warwick for nine months. When I returned to Harlem, I had learned many new ways of crimes. I had also become well acquainted with many of New York City's teenage criminals.

Upon my return to Harlem I no longer cared to steal or partake in gang fights, but I had to steal a few things to show my gang that getting shot had not unnerved me. Two days after I came home, I received my first real pistol, as a coming home gift. After pulling enough scores to get up one hundred dollars, I bought a half pound of pot and went into business. Within two weeks, the word had gotten around that I had the best pot in town. For the next three months—at the end of which I got "busted"—I did a pretty good job of emulating a Harlem "hustler" who was doing good. This included wearing thirty-dollar shoes and giving frequent handouts to old friends who had become junkies. Danny, one of my favorite old tutors in the ways of the street, had now become my favorite junkie; I would always give him a "nickel bill" to get a fix.

Following two more trips to Warwick, I moved out of Harlem and got a job. Most of my spare time was spent in Harlem, taking the ribbing and laughing that my attending evening high school evoked from my old street corner cronies. They laughed for three years. When I entered college there were no more laughs.

Some interesting changes have occurred in Harlem during the past few years. It seems that many of the people who I once thought were merely waiting for something to happen to them, have made things happen. The last time I saw Danny, I could not help but admire him. Danny is making money by the fists full. There is nothing remarkable about a guy making lots of money selling drugs. But in Danny's case the admirable feat was his being able to kick an eight-year drug habit, and then make the stuff work for him. Danny is the only reformed junkie I have ever known to stay reformed for any length of time. And his presence in Harlem is most encouraging to other junkies who dream of kicking their habit and becoming pushers in turn.

I saw Turk yesterday and we talked of his next fight. It was an inspiring experience for me to hear Turk, who has become one of the world's leading heavyweight fighters, explain how he would beat his next opponent. It seems like only yesterday when I was explaining to him the strategy of our next "rumble."

The big changes in Harlem are in the people I know who have changed my sympathy to respect and admiration. If you've ever known a junkie for any length of time you'll understand the struggle he has to go through to get off the poison kick. He can't leave the world entirely, so for him to become master and dispenser of the thing that had ruled him for so long and so destructively is a great achievement. Harlem still has a much greater number of the miserable than any place else I know. This is inspiring also. Where else can one find so many people in such pain and so few crying about it?

The Image of Culture

Richard Weaver

However much opinions of the realities involved may differ, no one can deny that there is widespread discussion of the decline of Western culture. This has been present in philosophical works for more than half a century; the shock of the First World War brought it into more popular organs of discussion, and today one may encounter it, though usually in frivolous forms, in the columns of daily newspapers. That the idea has not merely persisted but has seeped increasingly into the modern consciousness is itself a cultural and social fact of great importance which cannot be overlooked among the signs of the times.

Attempts to dismiss the idea often take the easy route of attributing it to temperamental pessimism or some other condition of the critic. It is alleged that those who say our culture is decaying are those who regularly take an apprehensive view of the future, or they are those who have lost their nerve amid the complexities of an age of transition, or they are those who suffer from nostalgia. The presence of such persons, it is argued, is not peculiar to this age, and hence their warnings are not to be taken as a serious sign that our way of life is deteriorating. The properly constituted man shuns the red-blooded attitude toward things; he goes along with changes because he realizes that change and progress are the law of life and that, although some valued institutions may be disappearing, they will more than be made up for by new ones that are in process of creation. The upholders of this view retort, in brief, that the world instead of growing worse is growing better and that it is really one's civic duty to believe this and to proclaim it.

Thus two largely antithetical views are regularly placed before the public. It is well to see that both of these views are capable of support. One can argue that our culture is in serious decline, and one can argue that it is flourishing and improving. But both arguments cannot be equally valid. Whenever large-scale tendencies are being examined, facts taken from a superficial level and facts taken from a profound one may conflict or point in opposite directions. Like two air masses, one moving at ground level and one moving at a high altitude, they can for awhile pursue opposite courses. If one reads from the top level of phenomena, one may get many signs of assurance which will be contradicted by a look lower down. The real issue in this controversy, then, is one of depth of implication. Yet there can be no implication at all unless one is willing to contemplate an order of human values. The nature and proper end of man are central to any discussion not only of whether a certain culture is weakening, but also of whether such a culture is worth preserving. It is when we look at the depth of implication that we see the real difference between the parties to this argument.

Those who contend that things are going well enough or are improving are found to be nonserious, in the sense of refusing to look at serious things. They glean their data from the novel, or flashy, or transitory sort of development, which often does indicate a sort of vitality, but shows at the same time a lack of direction and a purposelessness. Their data is likely to be the kind that can be quantified in the style of the social scientists or at least of the publicist—so many more people owning record players, so many more books circulating from public libraries, and the like. They ignore the deep sources of tendency which can very easily render nugatory any gains of the above kind. In short, their fact finding is superficial and simplistic, and their claims are made sometimes in strident tone which is itself a demerit to their case.

Moreover, it is certain that some if not many of the defenders of this optimistic position have a vested interest in "progress," or the present trend of things. A continuation of this trend means for them reputation and money, and they fall in with it as supporters who expect to be rewarded. There are many disintegrative processes which are immediately profitable to those engaged in promoting them, and it is human weakness to covet even such ill-gotten rewards. Therefore it is not hypercritical to look closely at the situation of those who argue for the excellence of modernism to see whether they stand to profit in practical ways from these developments. Not only advertising and journalism but considerable areas of education now invite this kind of scrutiny.

When we turn to the other view, we find that it is made up predominantly of persons who are concerned with the nature of man and the problem of value. They are people with definite ideas of right and wrong, possessing the faculty of taste and consciences which can be offended. Furthermore, they usually will be historically informed, with the result that to them novelty is not always originality nor a fresh departure toward a new horizon. If they are conservative, it is because they have learned the truth of the maxim, "The good is hard," and they know how tempting it is to try to circumvent this. It is my observation that these people suffer a great deal, and their suffering is sometimes used to condemn them, as if failure to achieve complacency were an indictable thing. But it is only those who are capable of discrimination and of feelings *against* things who can be the custodians of culture. Accordingly, I am satisfied that T. S. Eliot made a true appraisal of our times in asserting that "our own period is one of decline; that the standards of culture are lower than they were fifty years ago; and that the evidences of this decline are visible in every department of human activity."[1]

Another way of understanding this conflict of opinion is to recognize that the "optimists" have the current rhetoric on their side even while the "pessimists" have the proof. The modern world has a terrific momentum in the direction in which it is going, and many of the words of our everyday vocabulary are terms implicit with approval of modern tendencies. To describe these tendencies in the language that is used most widely is to endorse them, whereas to oppose them is to bring in words that connote half-forgotten beliefs and carry disturbing resonances. Thus the signs and probabilities are with the optimists, and their task of expression is an easy one, since they have so many ready-made terms at hand. They have the rhetorician's advantage of a language in circulation and a set of "prejudices" in the mind of the majority. It is the object of this writing to bring a rhetoric along with a proof to show that the present course of our culture is not occasion for complacency but for criticism and for possible reconstruction. This requires meeting a rhetoric derived from circumstances with one based more on definition and causal analysis.

I anticipate the further objection that all ages are ages of anxiety just because all ages are in some respect ages of transition. Since transition is a passage to the unknown, a degree of apprehensiveness over what is tentative, unformed, and uncertain is natural. There is some truth in this generalization, yet it would be as absurd to say that every period in the history of a culture is equally healthy and fruitful as to say that every period in the life of an individual is equally happy. It would in fact be intellectual and moral skepticism to deny that some periods are distinct as crises, and the troubled consciousness of modern man gives ample ground for believing that ours is such a period.

The need then is great for a revisionist view of what is known as modernism. The mindless approval of everything modern—indeed, of each dissolution of an old pattern—as something better than what preceded it, or acceptance of the Spenglerian thesis of inevitable decay, massive and intellectually serious as this is, does not constitute a true dilemma for the man who wishes to orient himself with reference to the culture of our time. There is the answer of some third alternative, involving basic principles and leading through free will and effort to some creative result. The imagination of the time cannot, at least, leave this possibility unexamined.

One more thing needs to be said about the relation of a critic to his culture. There is an opinion, by no means easy to refute, that culture is like a brotherhood: either you are of it or you are not. If you are of it, you can do something about it to the extent of carrying it on by living according to its prescriptions. If you are not of it, there is nothing you can do about it, except perhaps describe it from a distance while missing the real *Innigkeit*. On this assumption there is no such thing as aiding a culture from the outside or of aiding it consciously in any way. If you belong to it, you live in and by it; if you are outside it, you find the gulf impassable, except to certain superficial contacts. "Culture is culturing," and when a culture has lost its will to live, outside ministrations are of no use.

But in a further view, there is more than one way of being outside a culture. One can be outside it simply in the sense of having been born outside its pale and of having received no nurture through it. People in this position constitute the kind of "foreigners" the Greeks called *barbaroi*—"those speaking a different language." Certainly not to speak the language of a culture, in the figurative sense, is to suffer effective disbarment. These persons are alien, even when they belong to another culture of high development. The man of a different culture has different intellectual and moral bearings, and except in the case of gifted individuals having long periods to assimilate, there is no crossing over, nor any real desire for it. The men of another culture are outsiders, and one expects no more from them than from a friendly stranger, although there is sometimes critical value in an outside view.

There is another type of outsider, however, who may entertain hope of doing something about a culture that is weakening. He is a member of the culture who has to some degree estranged himself from it through study and reflection. He is like the *savant* in society; though in it, he is not wholly of it; he has acquired knowledge and developed habits of thought which enable him to see it in perspective and to gauge it. He has not lost the intuitive understanding which belongs to him as a member, but he has added something to that. A temporary alienation from his culture may be followed by an intense preoccupation with it, but on a more reflective level than that of the typical member. He has become sufficiently aware of what is outside it to see it as a system or an entity. This person may be a kind of doctor of culture; in one way he is crippled by his objectivity, but in another way he is helped to what he must have, a point of view and a consciousness of freedom of movement.

It has been observed, to cite a kind of parallel, that nearly all of the leaders of strong nationalistic movements in the present age were men who had some type of "outside" experience in their rearing or their education. They were men who knew their nations from the inside, but who had also seen them from a vantage point elsewhere. Thus it was with Parnell and Ireland, with Sun Yat-sen and China, with Hitler and Germany, with Gandhi and India. Even Franco is a "Gallego"—not a Spaniard in the true sense. These men had all at one time been far enough removed from their future nations to see what these were, and what they saw engendered in them an urge to define the reality and the consciousness of that nationhood. Although they were "doctors" of nationalism rather than "doctors" of culture, their case shows enough analogy to provide guiding points here. The man who is simply a carrier of his culture may not be armed in the same way to do something about it when it flags. His role may be too much that of simply acting; he can keep in stride, but he cannot coach. For diagnostic and remedial work we may have to turn to those who have in a way mutilated themselves by withdrawal, by a special kind of mental discipline, and by the kind of fixation upon a task which even impedes free cultural participation.[2] We may therefore regard it as no anomaly, but rather as an understandable event, if a person not conspicuously cultured himself should discern what is impairing the health of a culture. Thus it is not the person who has contributed most to a culture who will necessarily have the most useful things to say when the culture shows signs of dissolution.

But what can this person, who is not a paragon of the culture, but who finds himself profoundly stirred by its uneasy situation, actually contribute? From his mixed position he probably can recognize the hostile or disruptive forces. Like the doctor again, he cannot make the object of his attention live, but he can combat those things which would keep it from living. He can point out: this is a disease, this is a poison, this is bad diet. If the inimical conditions are removed and if there is a true vitality, the sufferer should recover. There are, of course, limits of the analogy of a human culture to an organism, yet culture is a creation in the world, and it must obey certain fundamental conditions of existence.

A radical perspective on the subject may even start with the question of whether culture as such is something we ought to cherish and defend. It would be uncritical to assume that the answer has always been affirmative. Now and in the past, culture in the sense meant here has had to meet open and covert hostility. Certain religions have been largely hostile to it; moralists have condemned it as a frivolity or an indulgence; men of business have been impatient with its demands and its "extravagence"; statesmen of a certain type have opposed it as producing "effeminacy." At present there is a fairly widespread feeling that culture "costs too much" in the sense of gratifying certain educated appetites at considerable expense while the masses are deprived. If the friends of culture were to allow the matter to be put to a popular vote, they might still win, but I do not think that the size of the majority would be reassuring. The public of today does not understand clearly either the nature or the role of culture, and general literacy has not helped the situation.

The claim of culture as such to exist is best explained through its genesis. Man is a special creature in the respect that he has to live with two selves. One of these is his existential part, his simple animal being, which breathes and moves and nourishes itself. This is man without qualification or adornment, an organism living in an environment. In this existence he is a very predictable animal—or would be except that the second self can have effects upon his somatic appearance and behavior.

The second self is an image which he somehow evolves from his spirit. It is made up of wishes and hopes, of things transfigured, of imaginations and value ascriptions. It is a picture to which the subjective part of our being necessarily gives a great deal, and hence the danger of trying to read it literally from external facts. A culture expresses itself very extensively through artistic creation, and, as Suzanne Langer has pointed out in her *Problems of Art,* we cannot infer artistic vision from a symptom. That is to say, a mere noting of details without insight and some constructive use of the imagination will not produce an understanding of a culture.

It appears that even the most primitive people have this urge to depict themselves in some fashion. Without the picturization, man feels an unendurable nakedness in the face of his environment and before the questions of life. From such poverty he rescues himself through projections that include the natural environment and whatever is suggested by his spirit regarding the mystery that broods over creation. Look beneath the surface of the most brilliant cultures of history, and you find a hunger and a wonderment, reaching even to a kind of melancholia. Nietzsche has shown how this impelled the Greeks to create their splendid world of illusion in myth and art. Impulses of like kind can be found beneath the efflorescence of Elizabethan England. The more man is impressed with the tragic nature of his lot, the more he dramatizes his relation with the world. A strain of artist in the race causes it to reach out in proportion as its awareness deepens and to throw up great protective creations.

This great yearning of man to *be something* in the imaginative sense, that is, to be something more than he is in the simple existential way or in the reductionist formula of materialism is both universal and proper to him. The latter may be asserted because he is the only creature who asks the question why he is here and who feels thwarted in his self-realization until some kind of answer is produced. This urge to be representative of something higher is an active ingredient of his specific humanity; it has created everything from the necklace of animal teeth with which the primitive adorns his body to the elaborate constructions which the men of high cultures have made to interpret the meaning of life and their mission in it. This is the point at which he departs from the purely utilitarian course and makes of himself a being with significance. It is a refutation of all simplistic histories and psychologies, but it is one of the most verifiable facts about man.

No one has been able to define exactly how a culture integrates and homologizes the ideas and actions of many men over a long period of time any more than how the consciousness gives a thematic continuity to the life of an individual. As far as one can tell, the collective consciousness of the group creates a mode of looking at the world or arrives at some imaginative visual bearing. It "sees" the world metaphorically according to some felt need of the group, and this entails an ordering which denotes dissatisfaction with "things as they are." Of course cultures do respond to differences in what nature has provided, such as the sea, or a kind of terrain, or a hot or cold climate, these having the power to initiate imaginative reactions. But man meets the given part way, and then proceeds with something of his own. So cultures reflect different regions and varying kinds of historical endowment. But the decisive thing is the work of the spirit, which always operates positively by transfiguring and excluding. It is of the essence of culture to feel its own imperative and to believe in the uniqueness of its worth. In doing so, it has to reject others which are "objectively" just as good, yet for it irrelevant. Syncretistic cultures like syncretistic religions have always proved relatively powerless to create and to influence; there is no weight of authentic history behind them. The very concept of eclectic religion and eclectic culture derives from an inappropriate analogy which suggests that a plurality can be greater than one. Culture derives its very desire to continue from its unitariness. Perhaps some deep force which explains our liking for figures of repetition is here involved; we feel confirmed through seeing things repeated in the same way, and departures from the form are viewed as laxity or ignorance.

Evidently this is the reason that every culture in the course of its formation sets up directions from which the members are constrained not to depart. Penalties for violation may be no more than cultural, although sometimes they have been moral and legal. The truth is that if the culture is to assume form and to bring the satisfactions for which cultures are created, it is not culturally feasible for everyone to do everything "any way he wants to." There is at the heart of every culture a center of authority from which there proceed subtle and pervasive pressures upon us to conform and to repel the unlike as disruptive. So culture too is faced with the metaphysical problem of freedom and organization, which rules out the possibility of uncircumscribed liberty. Like all forces which shape and direct, it must insist on a pattern of inclusion and exclusion. This is a necessity of integral being and a fundamental fact to deal with in any plan for its protection.

At this center there lies a "tyrannizing image," which draws everything toward itself. This image is the ideal of its excellence. The forms that it can take and the particular manifestations that it can find are various. In some instances it has been a religious ritual; in others a sacred scripture; in others a literature which everyone is expected to know; codes of conduct (and even of warfare) may be the highest embodied form. But examine them as we will, we find this inward facing toward some high representation. This is the sacred well of the culture from which inspiring waters like magnetic lines of force flow out and hold the various activities in a subservience of acknowledgment. Not to feel this magnetic pull toward identification and assimilation is to be outside the culture.

Such centripetalism is the essence of culture's power to cohere and to endure. There is a center which commands all things, and this center is open to imaginative but not logical discovery. It is a focus of value, a law of relationships, an inspiriting vision. By its very nature it sets up rankings and orders; to be near it is to be higher; to be far from it in the sense of not feeling its attraction is to be lower. Culture is thus by nature aristocratic, for it is a means of discriminating between what counts for much and what counts for little; this no doubt explains the necessity man feels to create it. It is his protest against the uniformity and dead level of simple succession. He *will* establish a center of value and see to it that the group is oriented toward it. This is his rejection of any merely naturalistic ordering of his life, his declaration of independence from mere environment. Discrimination, selection, and preference with regard to the tyrannizing image are its constitutives.

For this reason it is the very nature of culture to be exclusive. Without the power to reject that which does not understand or acknowledge its center of force, it would disintegrate. We might say that a culture continues by attracting and attracts by continuing. In this way it maintains its identity. There can be no such thing as a "democratic" culture in the sense of one open to everybody at all times on equal terms. To *know* the right thing, without mediating thoughts as to what and when, is to be native born to the culture. An individual absorbs his native culture as he acquires his native tongue, with the most subtle shades of intonation; again, like the idioms of a language the ways of a culture are rooted too deep in immemorial bias and feeling to be analyzed. If a culture appears arbitrary in the preferences it makes and the lines it draws, this is because it is a willed creation.

The truth most important for us to recognize in our present crisis is this principle of integration and exclusiveness. There is for all things, as Aristotle pointed out, an entelechy, a binding, type-determining factor, which gives to a thing its specific form and property of coherence. The fact that a culture is a spiritual and imaginative creation does not mean that it is any less bound by this pervading law. Just as the skin of a sound fruit protects it from dispersion or evaporation, so the form of a culture keeps it from ceasing to exist through a miscellaneous commingling. Form is intellectual and negative; it sets boundaries which affirm in the very process of denying. The form of a culture is its style, which it asserts against the world of meaningless "democratic" existence. In a highly developed culture this sense of style permeates everything; it is in dress and manners, in art and institutions, in architecture and cookery. It imparts tone to the whole of society by keeping before its members a standard of the right and not right. But this form depends upon the centripetal image of an ideal of perfection and goodness and upon confidence in ruling out what is unlike or fortuitous.

The task in our time of the conservative is to defend this concentration and to expose as erroneous attempts to break down the discriminations of a culture. For once the inward-looking vision and the impulse to resist the alien are lost, disruption must ensue. What was a whole ceases to feel its reason for being a whole, and the different parts may suffer a random distortion—random just because there is no longer a unifying idea to prescribe fitness and size. Parts then get out of line and begin to usurp the places and roles belonging to other parts. This is the chaos that the true friend of culture beholds with deepest apprehension, not only because it deprives him of so much but because in the masses it can induce monstrous outbursts of irrationality. All men, and not merely the sensitive and the gifted, need the integrating service of this vision, although not all realize that they need it. Lancelot Law Whyte in his *Next Development in Man* has vividly expressed the power of this urge:

> Man abhors the absence of integration. He demands integration, and will create religions, achieve heroic self-sacrifice, pursue mad ambitions, or follow the ecstasy of danger rather than live without. If society refuses him this satisfaction in constructive form, he will seize a destructive principle to which he can devote himself and will take revenge on the society which thought his only demand was pleasure. Vice, in this sense, shows the integrating power of virtue, of which it is merely the negative form. The mass-man readily rejected the utilitarian philosophy which had created him and accepted in its place the new mass religion of national suicide.[3]

The final sentence, written with reference to the fascist movements of Europe, reminds us that if no reasonable cultural unification is offered, an unreasonable one may be invented and carried to frightful lengths.

The greatest perversion of culture in our time is a misconception of the role of democracy. As the preceding definition makes clear, a culture integrates a people qualitatively. Under the widely current misconception, it is supposed that democracy can integrate them as quantitative units—that is, as units without relation to the value structure of the ideal. The most pressing duty of the believer in culture today is to define democracy and keep it within its place, in doing which he not only will preserve it as a viable form but also will protect those other areas of activity which are essential to supply a different kind of need.

Democracy is not a pattern for all existence any more than a form of economic activity is a substitute for the whole of living. Truly considered, democracy is nothing more than an ideal of equity among men in their political relationships. Its roots are in the truth that every individual has an inviolable personality, a private experience, and an authentic voice. Every individual is a reporter of what affects him, and he offers motions, as it were, concerning the general political welfare. To make this possible, a democratic state decrees a certain limited equality among its citizens. Even so, this equality is more theoretical than actual. But theories of this kind may have their practical usefulness as well as their noble objects. Thus in a parliamentary assembly we might give each speaker ten minutes to express his views, although we know that one man can say more in ten minutes than another can in an hour. Still, the equality serves the larger purpose. And so with democracy in its consulting of opinions and its counting of votes.

But democracy has to do with citizenship, and as Ortega has pointed out in one of his trenchant essays, our citizenship is the most insipid of our qualities. It concerns the things we have to get done in order to be in position to do things higher in the scale. It is account keeping or household management, an essentially low order of practical activity. It is better to do this well than ill, and it should be done with equity to the individuals involved. But it is senseless to say that dutiful household management is the highest commission of man and that whatever proves instrumental in this must be our principle of ordering all social and cultural life. In our present confusion over the role of culture, this is what is being done with the limited concept "democracy."

When democracy is taken from its proper place and is allowed to fill the entire horizon, it produces an envious hatred not only of all distinction but even of all difference. The ensuing distortion conceals its very purpose, which is to keep natural inequalities from obtruding in the one area where equality has intelligible function. The reason we consent to treat men as equals in this area of activity is that we know they are not equals in other areas. The fanatical democrat insists upon making them equal in all departments, regardless of the type of activity and vocation. It is of course the essence of fanaticism to seize upon some fragment of truth or value and to regard it as the exclusive object of man's striving. So democracy, a valuable but limited political concept, has been elevated by some into a creed as comprehensive as a religion or a philosophy, already at the cost of widespread subversion.

Ortega has wisely pointed out that this is not the spirit of true democracy, but of plebeianism. It exalts the very things that democracy was hopefully inaugurated to combat in the ranks of the people.

> The initial result is the wounding of the very sentiment which gave rise to democracy: for the concept of democracy springs from the desire to save the plebs from their low condition. But the doctrinaire democrat, who has converted a technique, democracy, into an end, soon finds himself sympathizing with the plebs precisely because of their plebeianism—their customs, manners, and intellectual tone. An example of this is the socialist creed (for we are dealing here with a creed, a secular religion) which has for one article of faith the dogma that only a proletarian head is fit for true science and reformed morality.[4]

Today we are being asked to accept "democratic living." The eulogistic tone with which this phrase is pronounced invites the question of whether this could be the "tyrannizing image" of some new culture. The answer is "no," if by democracy one means simple communism. Now there are in fact some places where a large measure of equality is in effect among the members without prejudice to the cultural life which they support. Such is true of the communities of some religious orders, where, for example, no outward discrimination is made between those who carry on the work of teaching and those who look after maintenance. It is true also of some educational institutions where the students do a large part of the work; no real distinction is made between those who hold "white collar" jobs and those who labor in the cow barns. Anyone who has visited such a community knows that the social atmosphere there is most agreeable and relaxing. But when one studies the impulse that sustains them, one realizes that the democracy is made possible by a consecration to and a hierarchy of purpose. In the religious communities it is of course the service of the religion; in the schools it is the furtherance of education. Nobody pretends that in these areas all are equal. There is selection according to ability, vocation, and dedication. This structure of purpose and calling is really the insurer of the democracy that exists; equality is maintained where it is useful because there is an overriding aim to be served. If this overriding aim were conceivably withdrawn, it is easy to picture even such communities breaking up into competitive pressure groups among "unequals." It is the authority of the mission which they carry on that keeps inequalities of service in a manageable and pleasing order. Thus the cohesiveness of such communities lies in the idea that informs and possesses them.

What I have here spoken of as true of small associations bears analogy with peoples and nations: a culture is a means of uniting society by making provision for differences. Differences do not create resentment unless the seed of resentment has been otherwise planted. A just man finds satisfaction in the knowledge that society has various roles for various kinds of people and that they in the performance of these roles create a kind of symphony of labor, play, and social life. There arises in fact a distinct pleasure from knowing that society is structured, diversified, balanced, and complex. Blind levelers do not realize that people can enjoy seeing things above them as well as on a plane with them. Societies with differentiation afford pleasure to the moral imagination as an aesthetic design affords rest to the eye. The propaganda of egalitarianism encourages belief that any society embodying distinctions must necessarily be torn with envy and hatred. But theory does not show and empirical observation does not discover that societies having a proper internal differentiation are unhappy. On the contrary, they may be reposeful and content. Of a number of examples which could be used to support this, I choose one described by Goethe in *Poetry and Truth*. Commenting on the Germany in which he had grown up, this great poet and philosopher of life—"Europe's wisest head"—had this to say:

> The tranquillized condition of Germany, of which my native town had formed a part for more than a century, had remained intact in spite of many wars and convulsions. The existence of the most varied social grades, including as they did the highest as well as the lowest, the Emperor as well as the Jew, instead of separating the various members, seemed rather to unite them; and this condition of things was conducive to a feeling of contentment.[5]

Goethe, whose insight told him the true nature of the French Revolution while many of the romantics and rationalists were still befooled, was not deceived by the effect of classes.

> In Germany it had hardly occurred to anyone yet to look with envy on this vast privileged class, or to grudge its obviously worldly advantages. The middle classes had quietly devoted themselves to com-

> merce and the sciences, and by these pursuits, as well as by the practice of the mechanical arts, had raised themselves to a position of importance which fully compensated their political inferiority; the free or partially free cities encouraged their activities, so that members of these classes were able to lead lives of peace and comfort. The man who increased his wealth or enhanced his intellectual influence, especially in matters of law or state, could always be sure of both respect and authority. In the Supreme Court of the Empire and elsewhere, the bench of nobles was faced by one of learned lawyers; the freer, less restricted outlook of the one worked in friendly harmony with the other, and not a trace of rivalry could be detected between them in everyday life. The noble felt secure in his exclusive and time-hallowed privileges, and the burgher felt it beneath his dignity to pretend to their possession by adding a prefix to his name.[6]

This was the Germany of poets, musicians, and philosophers. The classes thrived on a mutual dependence, and the principle of distinction, far from being felt as invidious, was the cement that held the whole together. One senses the kind of satisfaction that was felt in seeing different kinds of people to the right and left of one and, since it is in the nature of things, above and below. Not to be overlooked is the fact that a "lowest" class often finds satisfaction in knowing itself "superior" to other classes in certain respects—in hardihood, in industry, or in religiousness.

A society which is cohesive in this way through classes which have developed naturally out of civic and cultural vocation is in point of fact stronger than one which is undifferentiated. The latter tends to be inflexible and brittle; it does not have the internal give and take of the former. The inner organizations of a structural society act as struts and braces and enable it to withstand a blow which would shatter the other. The whole is sustained by its parts, which afford, as it were, a protection in depth. Nations composed of such societies have proved themselves very tough in international encounters. English society, despite a high degree of classness, has displayed intense patriotism and great power of endurance in crises. The society of the American South, which is formed somewhat upon the English model, has stood up under strong attacks and pressures from the outside through its sense of being organized. All the evidence shows that differentiation which is not fragmentation is a source of strength. But such differentiation is possible only if there is a center toward which the parts look for their meaning and validation. One of the functions of cultural activity is to objectify this center so that it will exist as an ever-present reminder of one's place and one's vocation. A high degree of cultural orientation is, accordingly, a symptom of a healthy society.

In brief, culture is an exclusive, which is to say, self-defining creation, which satisfies needs arising from man's feeling and imagination. Every culture has a kind of ontological basis in social life, and this social life does not express itself in equality, but in a common participation from different levels and through different vocations.

Because of these facts and because of the political contentiousness of our time the question has actually been raised as to whether culture is "reactionary." The question itself reveals a confusion of categories which should never have been permitted. But we know from the words and deeds of Communists and their sympathizers that they make much of this subject and that they are prone to condemn artistic or cultural expression which deviates from their harsh political line. Now it is true, if one takes a very narrow and false view of progress, that much which the world has valued as culture could be condemned as "reactionary." For one thing, the very concept of culture runs counter to blind progressivism, by which I mean that state of mind which cannot measure anything except by number and linear extension. Since culture operates in the realm of quality and offers not greater magnitudes but more refined and intense sentiments, it is an engagement of the spirit lying beyond the thinking of those who have allowed their minds to be dominated by material categories. Speed and mass, virtually the slogans of contemporary Western civilization, are the antithesis of culture. The pointless series of "new developments" and expansions which the modern barbarian delights in look poor and hollow when placed beside authentic creations of the spirit. Since the two impulses move in opposite directions, the one does recede from the other. The barbarian, were he capable of a critical vocabulary, might brand what frustrates his kind of pleasure as "reaction." The possession of culture by historical elites gives some edge to this as a political weapon, but the charge of course mistakes the true gift brought by this creation of the spirit.

Under another aspect culture can be viewed as "reactionary" because it involves a good deal of ceremonial waste, which cannot be explained to those whose vision of life is merely economic and sensate.

This brings up the supremely important matter of style. All culture incorporates the idea of style, which is an homage to an intangible but felt need of the spirit. We hear references to "the modern style" in buildings and other creations where man customarily expresses his desire to impose order and design, yet this seems really to be a negation of style, relieved a little perhaps by imaginative attempts to suggest mass.

True style displays itself in elaboration, rhythm, and distance, which demand activity of the imagination and play of the spirit. Elaboration means going beyond what is useful to produce what is engaging to contemplation. Rhythm is a marking of beginnings and endings. In place of a meaningless continuum, rhythm provides intelligibility and the sense that the material has been handled in a subjective interest. It is human to dislike mere lapse. When one sees things in rhythmical configuration, he feels that they have been brought into the realm of the spirit. Rhythm is thus a way of breaking up nihilistic monotony and of proclaiming that there is a world of value. Distance is what preserves us from the vulgarity of immediacy. Extension and proportion in space, as in architecture, and extension in time, as in manners and deportment, help to give gratifying form to these creations. All style has in it an element of ritual, which signifies steps which cannot be passed over.

Today these factors of style, which is of the essence of culture, are regarded as if they were mere persiflage. Elaboration is suspected of spending too much on nonutilitarian needs, and the limited ends of engineering efficiency take precedence. Rhythm suffers because one cannot wait for the period to come around. In regard to distance, it is felt that there *should* be nothing between man and what he wants; distance is a kind of prohibition; and the new man sees no sanction in arrangements that stand in the way of immediate gratification. He has not been taught the subtlety to perceive that what one gains by immediate seizure one pays for by more serious losses. Impatience with space and time seems to be driving the modern to an increasing surrender of all ideas of order. Everywhere there is reversion to the plain and the casual, and style itself takes on an obsolescent look, as if it belonged to some era destined never again to appear.

It may be thought negligent that in this exposition I have made no reference to the now extensive studies of various cultures by anthropologists. The reason is that anthropological relativism is the chief quandary to be avoided in the kind of search that is undertaken here. The method of the anthropologists is descriptive, as everyone who has looked at their type of study knows. Essentially geographers and cataloguers of cultures, they are interested in a wide collection of particulars, so that their object could be summed up as *polymathein* rather than *polynoein:* to know much rather than to understand much. I may do some of them less than justice by this charge, yet it is by and large true. What I am certain of is that their practice constitutes a distraction for the one whose interest is in the value of culture and especially of his own culture.

For him the main object is to seize the formal *Innigkeit* of cultural expression and then to decide in what way his own is being menaced or vitiated. Thereafter he is in position to be both doctor and preacher and indeed it is hard to conceive of a man's being thus interested in culture without feeling moved to proceed against its enemies.

I have pointed to the fact that a culture comes into being under the influence of a "tyrannizing" image or vision. I use the word "tyrannizing" hoping that it will be excused its sinister connotations and understood as meaning unifying and compelling. A culture then is a complex of values polarized by an image or idea. It cannot be perfectly tolerant or even tolerant to any large extent because it lives by homogeneity. It therefore has to exclude on grounds which are cultural and not "rational" what does not comport with its driving impulse.

A grave danger arises when this principle is challenged by rationalistic thinkers, as is happening today. In speaking of a culture's power to influence and to bind I have more than once used the word "integrate," since a culture is something unitary gathered about the dominating idea. But "integration" and "segregation" are two sides of the same operation. A culture integrates by segregating its forms of activity and its members from those not belonging. The right to self-segregate then is an indispensable ground of its being. Enough has been said to show that our culture today is faced with very serious threats in the form of rationalistic drives to prohibit in the name of equality cultural segregation. The effect of this would be to break up the natural cultural cohesion and to try to replace it with artificial politically dictated integration. Such "integration" would of course be a failure because where deep inner impulse is lacking cohesiveness for any length of time is impossible. This crisis has been brought to our attention most spectacularly in the attempt to "integrate" culturally distinct elements by court action. It is, however, only the most publicized of the moves; others are taking place in areas not in the spotlight, but all originate in ignorance, if not in a suicidal determination to write an end to the heritage of Western culture.

1. T. S. Eliot, *Notes Toward the Definition of Culture* (New York, 1949), 17.
2. An example of this is often seen in the relation of the academic person to the culture in which he lives. He may be and often is learned in it, but he is not exactly of it. I have felt more than once that this fact is proved by the peculiar explicitness of the speech of college professors. They are usually at great pains to draw

out the meaning of their phrases and to verbalize all the connections of thought. Some of this may result from the habit of simplifying things for youthful learners, but this is not the whole account of it. In the speech of a culture maintained by a traditional society, there will occur many elisions and ellipses of meaning. It is not necessary to state them, because anyone can supply the omissions; it is rather the awkwardness of pedantry to put them into words. But the man who is outside the tradition, or who is self-consciously halfway between the tradition and something else, goes about it in a different way: its beliefs, values, and institutions are "objects" to him, and he refers to them with something of the objective completeness of the technical description. This is why professors "sound so funny" when they talk of something that is an everyday subject to the ordinary man. This ordinary man wonders why the professor, instead of using lumbering phrases to designate the obvious, cannot assume more. It may also explain why professors as a class are suspected of dissidence. Their speech does not sound like the speech of a person who is perfectly solid with his tradition, which is oftentimes the case.

3. Lancelot Law Whyte, *The Next Development in Man* (New York, 1948), 188.
4. José Ortega y Gasset, "Morbid Democracy," *Modern Age: A Conservative Review* (Summer, 1957), 54.
5. Goethe, *Poetry and Truth From My Life* (2 vols.; London, 1913), II, 240.
6. *Ibid.*, II, 241.

Letter from Birmingham Jail*

Martin Luther King

April 16, 1963

MY DEAR FELLOW CLERGYMEN:

While confined here in the Birmingham city jail, I came across your recent statement calling my present activities "unwise and untimely." Seldom do I pause to answer criticism of my work and ideas. If I sought to answer all the criticisms that cross my desk, my secretaries would

---

* AUTHOR'S NOTE: This response to a published statement by eight fellow clergymen from Alabama (Bishop C. C. J. Carpenter, Bishop Joseph A. Durick, Rabbi Hilton L. Grafman, Bishop Paul Hardin, Bishop Holan B. Harmon, the Reverend George M. Murray, the Reverend Edward V. Ramage and the Reverend Earl Stallings) was composed under somewhat constricting circumstances. Begun on the margins of the newspaper in which the statement appeared while I was in jail, the letter was continued on scraps of writing paper supplied by a friendly Negro trusty, and concluded on a pad my attorneys were eventually permitted to leave me. Although the text remains in substance unaltered, I have indulged in the author's prerogative of polishing it for publication.

have little time for anything other than such correspondence in the course of the day, and I would have no time for constructive work. But since I feel that you are men of genuine good will and that your criticisms are sincerely set forth, I want to try to answer your statement in what I hope will be patient and reasonable terms.

I think I should indicate why I am here in Birmingham, since you have been influenced by the view which argues against "outsiders coming in." I have the honor of serving as president of the Southern Christian Leadership Conference, an organization operating in every southern state, with headquarters in Atlanta, Georgia. We have some eighty-five affiliated organizations across the South, and one of them is the Alabama Christian Movement for Human Rights. Frequently we share staff, educational and financial resources with our affiliates. Several months ago the affiliate here in Birmingham asked us to be on call to engage in a nonviolent direct-action program if such were deemed necessary. We readily consented, and when the hour came we lived up to our promise. So I, along with several members of my staff, am here because I was invited here. I am here because I have organizational ties here.

But more basically, I am in Birmingham because injustice is here. Just as the prophets of the eighth century B.C. left their villages and carried their "thus saith the Lord" far beyond the boundaries of their home towns, and just as the Apostle Paul left his village of Tarsus and carried the gospel of Jesus Christ to the far corners of the Greco-Roman world, so am I compelled to carry the gospel of freedom beyond my own home town. Like Paul, I must constantly respond to the Macedonian call for aid.

Moreover, I am cognizant of the interrelatedness of all communities and states. I cannot sit idly by in Atlanta and not be concerned about what happens in Birmingham. Injustice anywhere is a threat to justice everywhere. We are caught in an inescapable network of mutuality, tied in a single garment of destiny. Whatever affects one directly, affects all indirectly. Never again can we afford to live with the narrow, provincial "outside agitator" idea. Anyone who lives inside the United States can never be considered an outsider anywhere within its bounds.

You deplore the demonstrations taking place in Birmingham. But your statement, I am sorry to say, fails to express a similar concern for the conditions that brought about the demonstrations. I am sure that none of you would want to rest content with the superficial kind of social analysis that deals merely with effects and does not grapple with underlying causes. It is unfortunate that demonstrations are taking place in Birmingham, but it is even more unfortunate that the city's white power structure left the Negro community with no alternative.

In any nonviolent campaign there are four basic steps: collection of the facts to determine whether injustices exist; negotiation; self-purification; and direct action. We have gone through all these steps in Birmingham. There can be no gainsaying the fact that racial injustice engulfs this community. Birmingham is probably the most thoroughly segregated city in the United States. Its ugly record of brutality is widely known. Negroes have experienced grossly unjust treatment in the courts. There have been more unsolved bombings of Negro homes and churches in Birmingham than in any other city in the nation. These are the hard, brutal facts of the case. On the basis of these conditions, Negro leaders sought to negotiate with the city fathers. But the latter consistently refused to engage in good-faith negotiation.

Then, last September, came the opportunity to talk with leaders of Birmingham's economic community. In the course of the negotiations, certain promises were made by the merchants—for example, to remove the stores' humiliating racial signs. On the basis of these promises, the Reverend Fred Shuttlesworth and the leaders of the Alabama Christian Movement for Human Rights agreed to a moratorium on all demonstrations. As the weeks and months went by, we realized that we were the victims of a broken promise. A few signs, briefly removed, returned; the others remained.

As in so many past experiences, our hopes had been blasted, and the shadow of deep disappointment settled upon us. We had no alternative except to prepare for direct action, whereby we would present our very bodies as a means of laying our case before the conscience of the local and the national community. Mindful of the difficulties involved, we decided to undertake a process of self-purification. We began a series of workshops on nonviolence, and we repeatedly asked ourselves: "Are you able to accept blows without retaliating?" "Are you able to endure the ordeal of jail?" We decided to schedule our direct-action program for the Easter season, realizing that except for Christmas, this is the main shopping period of the year. Knowing that a strong economic-withdrawal program would be the by-product of direct action, we felt that this would be the best time to bring pressure to bear on the merchants for the needed change.

Then it occurred to us that Birmingham's mayoral election was coming up in March, and we speedily decided to postpone action until after election day. When we discovered that the Commissioner of Public Safety, Eugene "Bull" Connor, had piled up enough votes to be in the run-off, we decided again to postpone action until the day after the run-off so that the demonstrations could not be used to cloud the issues. Like many others, we waited to see Mr. Connor defeated, and to this end we endured postponement after postponement. Having aided in this community need, we felt that our direct-action program could be delayed no longer.

You may well ask: "Why direct action? Why sit-ins, marches and so forth? Isn't negotiation a better path?" You are quite right in calling for negotiation. Indeed, this is the very purpose of direct action. Nonviolent direct action seeks to create such a crisis and foster such a tension that a community which has constantly refused to negotiate is forced to confront the issue. It seeks so to dramatize the issue that it can no longer be ignored. My citing the creation of tension as part of the work of the nonviolent-resister may sound rather shocking. But I must confess that I am not afraid of the word "tension." I have earnestly opposed violent tension, but there is a type of constructive, nonviolent tension which is necessary for growth. Just as Socrates felt that it was necessary to create a tension in the mind so that individuals could rise from the bondage of myths and half-truths to the unfettered realm of creative analysis and objective appraisal, so must we see the need for nonviolent gadflies to create the kind of tension in society that will help men rise from the dark depths of prejudice and racism to the majestic heights of understanding and brotherhood.

The purpose of our direct-action program is to create a situation so crisis-packed that it will inevitably open the door to negotiation. I therefore concur with you in your call for negotiation. Too long has our beloved Southland been bogged down in a tragic effort to live in monologue rather than dialogue.

One of the basic points in your statement is that the action that I and my associates have taken in Birmingham is untimely. Some have asked: "Why didn't you give the new city administration time to act?" The only answer that I can give to this query is that the new Birmingham administration must be prodded about as much as the outgoing one, before it will act. We are sadly mistaken if we feel that the election of Albert Boutwell as mayor will bring the millennium to Birmingham. While Mr. Boutwell is a much more gentle person than Mr. Connor, they are both segregationists, dedicated to maintenance of the status quo. I have hope that Mr. Boutwell will be reasonable enough to see the futility of massive resistance to desegregation. But he will not see this without pressure from devotees of civil rights. My friends, I must say to you that we have not made a single gain in civil rights without determined legal and nonviolent pressure. Lamentably, it is an historical fact that privileged groups seldom give up their privileges voluntarily. Individuals may see the moral light and voluntarily give up their unjust posture; but, as Reinhold Niebuhr has reminded us, groups tend to be more immoral than individuals.

We know through painful experience that freedom is never voluntarily given by the oppressor; it must be demanded by the oppressed. Frankly, I have yet to engage in a direct-action campaign that was "well timed" in the view of those who have not suffered unduly from the disease of segregation. For years now I have heard the word "Wait!" It rings in the ear of every Negro with piercing familiarity. This "Wait" has almost always meant "Never." We must come to see, with one of our distinguished jurists, that "justice too long delayed is justice denied."

We have waited for more than 340 years for our constitutional and God-given rights. The nations of Asia and Africa are moving with jetlike speed toward gaining political independence, but we still creep at horse-and-buggy pace toward gaining a cup of coffee at a lunch counter. Perhaps it is easy for those who have never felt the stinging darts of segregation to say, "Wait." But when you have seen vicious mobs lynch your mothers and fathers at will and drown your sisters and brothers at whim; when you have seen hate-filled policemen curse, kick and even kill your black brothers and sisters; when you see the vast majority of your twenty million Negro brothers smothering in an airtight cage of poverty in the midst of an affluent society; when you suddenly find your tongue twisted and your speech stammering as you seek to explain to your six-year-old daughter why she can't go to the public amusement park that has just been advertised on television, and see tears welling up in her eyes when she is told that Funtown is closed to colored children, and see ominous clouds of inferiority beginning to form in her little mental sky, and see her beginning to distort her personality by developing an unconscious bitterness toward white people; when you have to concoct an answer for a five-year-old son who is asking: "Daddy, why do white people treat colored people so mean?"; when you take a cross-country drive and find it necessary to sleep night after night in the uncomfortable corners of your automobile because no motel will accept you; when you are humiliated day in and day out by nagging signs reading "white" and "colored"; when your first name becomes "nigger," your middle name becomes "boy" (however old you are) and your last name becomes "John," and your wife and mother are never given the respected title "Mrs."; when you are harried by day and haunted by night by the fact that you are a Negro, living constantly at tiptoe stance, never quite knowing what to expect next, and are plagued with inner fears and outer resentments; when you are forever fighting a degenerating sense of "nobodiness"—then you will understand why we find it difficult to wait. There comes a time when the cup of endurance runs over, and men are no longer willing to be plunged into the abyss of despair. I hope, sirs, you can understand our legitimate and unavoidable impatience.

You express a great deal of anxiety over our willingness to break laws. This is certainly a legitimate concern. Since we so diligently urge people to obey the Supreme Court's decision of 1954 outlawing segregation in the public schools, at first glance it may seem rather paradoxical for us consciously to break laws. One may well ask: "How can you advocate breaking some laws and obeying others?" The answer lies in the fact that there are two types of laws: just and unjust. I would be the first to advocate obeying just laws. One has not only a legal but a moral responsibility to obey just laws. Conversely, one has a moral responsibility to disobey unjust laws. I would agree with St. Augustine that "an unjust law is no law at all."

Now, what is the difference between the two? How does one determine whether a law is just or unjust? A just law is a man-made code that squares with the moral law or the law of God. An unjust law is a code that is out of harmony with the moral law. To put it in the terms of St. Thomas Aquinas: An unjust law is a human law that is not rooted in eternal law and natural law. Any law that uplifts human personality is just. Any law that degrades human personality is unjust. All segregation statutes are unjust because segregation distorts the soul and damages the personality. It gives the segregator a false sense of superiority and the segregated a false sense of inferiority. Segregation, to use the terminology of the Jewish philosopher Martin Buber, substitutes an "I–it" relationship for an "I–thou" relationship and ends up relegating persons to the status of things. Hence segregation is not only politically, economically and sociologically unsound, it is morally wrong and sinful. Paul Tillich has said that sin is separation. Is not segregation an existential expression of man's tragic separation, his awful estrangement, his terrible sinfulness? Thus it is that I can urge men to obey the 1954 decision of the Supreme Court, for it is morally right; and I can urge them to disobey segregation ordinances, for they are morally wrong.

Let us consider a more concrete example of just and unjust laws. An unjust law is a code that a numerical or power majority group compels a minority group to obey but does not make binding on itself.

This is *difference* made legal. By the same token, a just law is a code that a majority compels a minority to follow and that it is willing to follow itself. This is *sameness* made legal.

Let me give another explanation. A law is unjust if it is inflicted on a minority that, as a result of being denied the right to vote, had no part in enacting or devising the law. Who can say that the legislature of Alabama which set up that state's segregation laws was democratically elected? Throughout Alabama all sorts of devious methods are used to prevent Negroes from becoming registered voters, and there are some counties in which, even though Negroes constitute a majority of the population, not a single Negro is registered. Can any law enacted under such circumstances be considered democratically structured?

Sometimes a law is just on its face and unjust in its application. For instance, I have been arrested on a charge of parading without a permit. Now, there is nothing wrong in having an ordinance which requires a permit for a parade. But such an ordinance becomes unjust when it is used to maintain segregation and to deny citizens the First-Amendment privilege of peaceful assembly and protest.

I hope you are able to see the distinction I am trying to point out. In no sense do I advocate evading or defying the law, as would the rabid segregationist. That would lead to anarchy. One who breaks an unjust law must do so openly, lovingly, and with a willingness to accept the penalty. I submit that an individual who breaks a law that conscience tells him is unjust, and who willingly accepts the penalty of imprisonment in order to arouse the conscience of the community over its injustice, is in reality expressing the highest respect for law.

Of course, there is nothing new about this kind of civil disobedience. It was evidenced sublimely in the refusal of Shadrach, Meshach and Abednego to obey the laws of Nebuchadnezzar, on the ground that a higher moral law was at stake. It was practiced superbly by the early Christians, who were willing to face hungry lions and the excruciating pain of chopping blocks rather than submit to certain unjust laws of the Roman Empire. To a degree, academic freedom is a reality today because Socrates practiced civil disobedience. In our own nation, the Boston Tea Party represented a massive act of civil disobedience.

We should never forget that everything Adolf Hitler did in Germany was "legal" and everything the Hungarian freedom fighters did in Hungary was "illegal." It was "illegal" to aid and comfort a Jew in Hitler's Germany. Even so, I am sure that, had I lived in Germany at the time, I would have aided and comforted my Jewish brothers. If today I lived in a Communist country where certain principles dear to the Christian faith are suppressed, I would openly advocate disobeying that country's antireligious laws.

I must make two honest confessions to you, my Christian and Jewish brothers. First, I must confess that over the past few years I have been gravely disappointed with the white moderate. I have almost reached the regrettable conclusion that the Negro's great stumbling block in his stride toward freedom is not the White Citizen's Counciler or the Ku Klux Klanner, but the white moderate, who is more devoted to "order" than to justice; who prefers a negative peace which is the absence of tension to a positive peace which is the presence of justice; who constantly says: "I agree with you in the goal you seek, but I cannot agree with your methods of direct action"; who paternalistically believes he can set the timetable for another man's freedom; who lives by a mythical concept of time and who constantly advises the Negro to wait for a "more convenient season." Shallow understanding from people of good will is more frustrating than absolute misunderstanding from people of ill will. Lukewarm acceptance is much more bewildering than outright rejection.

I had hoped that the white moderate would understand that law and order exist for the purpose of establishing justice and that when they fail in this purpose they become the dangerously structured dams that block the flow of social progress. I had hoped that the white moderate would understand that the present tension in the South is a necessary phase of the transition from an obnoxious negative peace, in which the Negro passively accepted his unjust plight, to a substantive and positive peace, in which all men will respect the dignity and worth of human personality. Actually, we who engage in nonviolent direct action are not the creators of tension. We merely bring to the surface the hidden tension that is already alive. We bring it out in the open, where it can be seen and dealt with. Like a boil that can never be cured so long as it is covered up but must be opened with all its ugliness to the natural medicines of air and light, injustice must be exposed, with all the tension its exposure creates, to the light of human conscience and the air of national opinion before it can be cured.

In your statement you assert that our actions, even though peaceful, must be condemned because they precipitate violence. But is this a logical assertion? Isn't this like condemning a robbed man because his possession of money precipitated the evil act of robbery? Isn't this like condemning Socrates because his unswerving commitment to truth and his philosophical inquiries precipitated the act by the misguided populace in which they made him drink hemlock? Isn't this like condemning Jesus because his unique God-consciousness and never-ceasing devotion to God's will precipitated the evil act of crucifixion? We must come to see that, as the federal courts have consistently affirmed, it is wrong to urge an individual to cease his efforts to gain his basic constitutional rights because the quest may precipitate violence. Society must protect the robbed and punish the robber.

I had also hoped that the white moderate would reject the myth concerning time in relation to the struggle for freedom. I have just received a letter from a white brother in Texas. He writes: "All Christians know that the colored people will receive equal rights eventually, but it is possible that you are in too great a religious hurry. It has taken Christianity almost two thousand years to accomplish what it has. The teachings of Christ take time to come to earth." Such an attitude stems from a tragic misconception of time, from the strangely irrational notion that there is something in the very flow of time that will inevitably cure all ills. Actually, time itself is neutral; it can be used either destructively or constructively. More and more I feel that the people of ill will have used time much more effectively than have the people of good will. We will have to repent in this generation not merely for the hateful words and actions of the bad people but for the appalling silence of the good people. Human progress never rolls in on wheels of inevitability; it comes through the tireless efforts of men willing to be co-workers with God, and without this hard work, time itself becomes an ally of the forces of social stagnation. We must use time creatively, in the knowledge that the time is always ripe to do right. Now is the time to make real the promise of democracy and transform our pending national elegy into a creative psalm of brotherhood. Now is the time to lift our national policy from the quicksand of racial injustice to the solid rock of human dignity.

You speak of our activity in Birmingham as extreme. At first I was rather disappointed that fellow clergymen would see my nonviolent efforts as those of an extremist. I began thinking about the fact that I stand in the middle of two opposing forces in the Negro community. One is a force of complacency, made up in part of Negroes who, as a result of long years of oppression, are so drained of self-respect and a sense of "somebodiness" that they have adjusted to segregation; and in part of a few middle-class Negroes who, because of a degree of academic and economic security and because in some ways they profit by segregation, have become insensitive to the problems of the masses. The other force is one of bitterness and hatred, and it comes perilously close to advocating violence. It is expressed in the various black nationalist groups that are springing up across the nation, the largest and best-known being Elijah Muhammad's Muslim movement.

Nourished by the Negro's frustration over the continued existence of racial discrimination, this movement is made up of people who have lost faith in America, who have absolutely repudiated Christianity, and who have concluded that the white man is an incorrigible "devil."

I have tried to stand between these two forces, saying that we need emulate neither the "do-nothingism" of the complacent nor the hatred and despair of the black nationalist. For there is the more excellent way of love and nonviolent protest. I am grateful to God that, through the influence of the Negro church, the way of nonviolence became an integral part of our struggle.

If this philosophy had not emerged, by now many streets of the South would, I am convinced, be flowing with blood. And I am further convinced that if our white brothers dismiss as "rabble-rousers" and "outside agitators" those of us who employ nonviolent direct action, and if they refuse to support our nonviolent efforts, millions of Negroes will, out of frustration and despair, seek solace and security in black-nationalist ideologies—a development that would inevitably lead to a frightening racial nightmare.

Oppressed people cannot remain oppressed forever. The yearning for freedom eventually manifests itself, and that is what has happened to the American Negro. Something within has reminded him of his birthright of freedom, and something without has reminded him that it can be gained. Consciously or unconsciously, he has been caught up by the *Zeitgeist*, and with his black brothers of Africa and his brown and yellow brothers of Asia, South America and the Caribbean, the United States Negro is moving with a sense of great urgency toward the promised land of racial justice. If one recognizes this vital urge that has engulfed the Negro community, one should readily understand why public demonstrations are taking place. The Negro has many pent-up resentments and latent frustrations, and he must release them. So let him march; let him make prayer pilgrimages to the city hall; let him go on freedom rides—and try to understand why he must do so. If his repressed emotions are not released in nonviolent ways, they will seek expression through violence; this is not a threat but a fact of history. So I have not said to my people: "Get rid of your discontent." Rather, I have tried to say that this normal and healthy discontent can be channeled into the creative outlet of nonviolent direct action. And now this approach is being termed extremist.

But though I was initially disappointed at being categorized as an extremist, as I continued to think about the matter I gradually gained a measure of satisfaction from the label. Was not Jesus an extremist for love: "Love your enemies, bless them that curse you, do good to them that hate you, and pray for them which despitefully use you, and persecute you." Was not Amos an extremist for justice: "Let justice roll down like waters and righteousness like an ever-flowing stream." Was not Paul an extremist for the Christian gospel: "I bear in my body the marks of the Lord Jesus." Was not Martin Luther an extremist: "Here I stand; I cannot do otherwise, so help me God." And John Bunyan: "I will stay in jail to the end of my days before I make a butchery of my conscience." And Abraham Lincoln: "This nation cannot survive half slave and half free." And Thomas Jefferson: "We hold these truths to be self-evident, that all men are created equal . . ." So the question is not whether we will be extremists, but what kind of extremists we will be. Will we be extremists for hate or for love? Will we be extremists for the preservation of injustice or for the extension of justice? In that dramatic scene on Calvary's hill three men were crucified. We must never forget that all three were crucified for the same crime—the crime of extremism. Two were extremists for immorality, and thus fell below their environment. The other, Jesus Christ, was an extremist for love, truth and goodness, and thereby rose above his environment. Perhaps the South, the nation and the world are in dire need of creative extremists.

I had hoped that the white moderate would see this need. Perhaps I was too optimistic; perhaps I expected too much. I suppose I should have realized that few members of the oppressor race can understand the deep groans and passionate yearnings of the oppressed race, and still fewer have the vision to see that injustice must be rooted out by strong, persistent and determined action. I am thankful, however, that some of our white brothers in the South have grasped the meaning of this social revolution and committed themselves to it. They are still all too few in quantity, but they are big in quality. Some—such as Ralph McGill, Lillian Smith, Harry Golden, James McBride Dabbs, Ann Braden and Sarah Patton Boyle—have written about our struggle in eloquent and prophetic terms. Others have marched with us down nameless streets of the South. They have languished in filthy, roach-infested jails, suffering the abuse and brutality of policemen who view them as "dirty nigger-lovers." Unlike so many of their moderate brothers and sisters, they have recognized the urgency of the moment and sensed the need for powerful "action" antidotes to combat the disease of segregation.

Let me take note of my other major disappointment. I have been so greatly disappointed with the white church and its leadership. Of course, there are some notable exceptions. I am not unmindful of the fact that each of you has taken some significant stands on this issue. I commend you, Reverend Stallings, for your Christian stand on this past Sunday, in welcoming Negroes to your worship service on a nonsegregated basis. I commend the Catholic leaders of this state for integrating Spring Hill College several years ago.

But despite these notable exceptions, I must honestly reiterate that I have been disappointed with the church. I do not say this as one of those negative critics who can always find something wrong with the church. I say this as a minister of the gospel, who loves the church; who was nurtured in its bosom; who has been sustained by its spiritual blessings and who will remain true to it as long as the cord of life shall lengthen.

When I was suddenly catapulted into the leadership of the bus protest in Montgomery, Alabama, a few years ago, I felt we would be supported by the white church. I felt that the white ministers, priests and rabbis of the South would be among our strongest allies. Instead, some have been outright opponents, refusing to understand the freedom movement and misrepresenting its leaders; all too many others have been more cautious than courageous and have remained silent behind the anesthetizing security of stained-glass windows.

In spite of my shattered dreams, I came to Birmingham with the hope that the white religious leadership of this community would see the justice of our cause and, with deep moral concern, would serve as the channel through which our just grievances could reach the power structure. I had hoped that each of you would understand. But again I have been disappointed.

I have heard numerous southern religious leaders admonish their worshipers to comply with a desegregation decision because it is the law, but I have longed to hear white ministers declare: "Follow this decree because integration is morally right and because the Negro is your brother." In the midst of blatant injustices inflicted upon the Negro, I have watched white churchmen stand on the sideline and mouth pious irrelevancies and sanctimonious trivialities. In the midst of a mighty struggle to rid our nation of racial and economic injustice, I have heard many ministers say: "Those are social issues, with which the gospel has no real concern." And I have watched many churches commit themselves to a completely otherworldly religion which makes a strange, un-Biblical distinction between body and soul, between the sacred and the secular.

I have traveled the length and breadth of Alabama, Mississippi and all the other southern states. On sweltering summer days and crisp autumn mornings I have looked at the South's beautiful churches with their lofty spires pointing heavenward. I have beheld the impressive outlines of her massive religious-education buildings. Over and over I have found myself asking: "What kind of people worship here? Who is their God? Where were their voices when the lips of Governor Barnett dripped with words of interposition and nullification? Where were they when Governor Wallace gave a clarion call for defiance and hatred? Where were their voices of support when bruised and weary Negro men and women decided to rise from the dark dungeons of complacency to the bright hills of creative protest?"

Yes, these questions are still in my mind. In deep disappointment I have wept over the laxity of the church. But be assured that my tears have been tears of love. There can be no deep disappointment where there is not deep love. Yes, I love the church. How could I do otherwise? I am in the rather unique position of being the son, the grandson and the great-grandson of preachers. Yes, I see the church as the body of Christ. But, oh! How we have blemished and scarred that body through social neglect and through fear of being nonconformists.

There was a time when the church was very powerful—in the time when the early Christians rejoiced at being deemed worthy to suffer for what they believed. In those days the church was not merely a thermometer that recorded the ideas and principles of popular opinion; it was a thermostat that transformed the mores of society. Whenever the early Christians entered a town, the people in power became disturbed and immediately sought to convict the Christians for being "disturbers of the peace" and "outside agitators." But the Christians pressed on, in the conviction that they were "a colony of heaven," called to obey God rather than man. Small in number, they were big in commitment. They were too God-intoxicatd to be "astronomically intimidated." By their effort and example they brought an end to such ancient evils as infanticide and gladiatorial contests.

Things are different now. So often the contemporary church is a weak, ineffectual voice with an uncertain sound. So often it is an archdefender of the status quo. Far from being disturbed by the presence of the church, the power structure of the average community is consoled by the church's silent—and often even vocal—sanction of things as they are.

But the judgment of God is upon the church as never before. If today's church does not recapture the sacrificial spirit of the early church, it will lose its authenticity, forfeit the loyalty of millions, and be dismissed as an irrelevant social club with no meaning for the twentieth century. Every day I meet young people whose disappointment with the church has turned into outright disgust.

Perhaps I have once again been too optimistic. Is organized religion too inextricably bound to the status quo to save our nation and the world? Perhaps I must turn my faith to the inner spiritual church, the church within the church, as the true *ekklesia* and the hope of the world. But again I am thankful to God that some noble souls from the ranks of organized religion have broken loose from the paralyzing chains of conformity and joined us as active partners in the struggle for freedom. They have left their secure congregations and walked the streets of Albany, Georgia, with us. They have gone down the highways of the South on tortuous rides for freedom. Yes, they have gone to jail with us. Some have been dismissed from their churches, have lost the support of their bishops and fellow ministers. But they have acted in the faith that right defeated is stronger than evil triumphant. Their witness has been the spiritual salt that has preserved the true meaning of the gospel in these troubled times. They have carved a tunnel of hope through the dark mountain of disappointment.

I hope the church as a whole will meet the challenge of this decisive hour. But even if the church does not come to the aid of justice, I have no despair about the future. I have no fear about the outcome of our struggle in Birmingham, even if our motives are at present misunderstood. We will reach the goal of freedom in Birmingham and all over the nation, because the goal of America is freedom. Abused and scorned though we may be, our destiny is tied up with America's destiny. Before the pilgrims landed at Plymouth, we were here. Before the pen of Jefferson etched the majestic words of the Declaration of Independence across the pages of history, we were here. For more than two centuries our forebears labored in this country without wages; they made cotton king; they built the homes of their masters while suffering gross injustice and shameful humiliation—and yet out of a bottomless vitality they continued to thrive and develop. If the inexpressible cruelties of slavery could not stop us, the opposition we now face will surely fail. We will win our freedom because the sacred heritage of our nation and the eternal will of God are embodied in our echoing demands.

Before closing I feel impelled to mention one other point in your statement that has troubled me profoundly. You warmly commended the Birmingham police force for keeping "order" and "preventing violence." I doubt that you would have so warmly commended the police force if you had seen its dogs sinking their teeth into unarmed, nonviolent Negroes. I doubt that you would so quickly commend the policemen if you were to observe their ugly and inhumane treatment of Negroes here in the city jail; if you were to watch them push and curse old Negro women and young Negro girls; if you were to see them slap and kick old Negro men and young boys; if you were to observe them, as they did on two occasions, refuse to give us food because we wanted to sing our grace together. I cannot join you in your praise of the Birmingham police department.

It is true that the police have exercised a degree of discipline in handling the demonstrators. In this sense they have conducted themselves rather "nonviolently" in public. But for what purpose? To preserve the evil system of segregation. Over the past few years I have consistently preached that nonviolence demands that the means we use must be as pure as the ends we seek. I have tried to make clear that it is wrong to use immoral means to attain moral ends. But now I must affirm that it is just as wrong, or perhaps even more so, to use moral means to preserve immoral ends. Perhaps Mr. Connor and his policemen have been rather nonviolent in public, as was Chief Pritchett in Albany, Georgia, but they have used the moral means of nonviolence to maintain the immoral end of racial injustice. As T. S. Eliot has said: "The last temptation is the greatest treason: To do the right deed for the wrong reason."

I wish you had commended the Negro sit-inners and demonstrators of Birmingham for their sublime courage, their willingness to suffer and their amazing discipline in the midst of great provocation. One day the South will recognize its real heroes. They will be the James Merediths, with the noble sense of purpose that enables them to face jeering and hostile mobs, and with the agonizing loneliness that characterizes the life of the pioneer. They will be old, oppressed, battered Negro women, symbolized in a seventy-two-year-old woman in Montgomery, Alabama, who rose up with a sense of dignity and with her people decided not to ride segregated buses, and who responded with ungrammatical profundity to one who inquired about her weariness: "My feets is tired, but my soul is at rest." They will be the young high school and college students, the young ministers of the gospel and a host of their elders, courageously and nonviolently sitting in at lunch counters and willingly going to jail for conscience' sake. One day the South will know that when these disinherited children of God sat down at lunch counters, they were in reality standing up for what is best in the American dream and for the most sacred values in our Judaeo-Christian heritage, thereby bringing our nation back to those great wells of democracy which were dug deep by the founding fathers in their formulation of the Constitution and the Declaration of Independence.

Never before have I written so long a letter. I'm afraid it is much too long to take your precious time. I can assure you that it would have been much shorter if I had been writing from a comfortable desk, but what else can one do when he is alone in a narrow jail cell, other than write long letters, think long thoughts and pray long prayers?

If I have said anything in this letter that overstates the truth and indicates an unreasonable impatience, I beg you to forgive me. If I have said anything that understates the truth and indicates my having a patience that allows me to settle for anything less than brotherhood, I beg God to forgive me.

I hope this letter finds you strong in the faith. I also hope that circumstances will soon make it possible for me to meet each of you, not as an integrationist or a civil-rights leader but as a fellow clergyman and a Christian brother. Let us all hope that the dark clouds of racial prejudice will soon pass away and the deep fog of misunderstanding will be lifted from our fear-drenched communities, and in some not too distant tomorrow the radiant stars of love and brotherhood will shine over our great nation with all their scintillating beauty.

Yours for the cause of Peace and Brotherhood,
MARTIN LUTHER KING, JR.

"Black" Is a Country

LeRoi Jones

To a growing list of "dirty" words that make Americans squirm add the word *Nationalism.* I would say that the word has gained almost as much infamy in some quarters of this country as that all-time anathema and ugliness, *Communism.* In fact, some journalists, commentators, and similar types have begun to use the two words interchangeably. It goes without saying that said commentators, etc., and the great masses of Americans who shudder visibly at the mention of those words cannot know what they mean. And it is certainly not my function, here, to rectify that situation completely. But I do think that unless the great majority of people in this country begin to understand just exactly what Nationalism is (or at least that variety of Nationalism which is most in evidence among the smaller, so-called uncommitted countries of the world) they will pass from the scene like the boxer who "never knew what hit him."

The concept of "acting in one's own best interests" is certainly not unknown to America or to the rest of the so-called Free World (which

---

I am told includes Portugal, South Africa, and parts of Mississippi). In fact, I would say it is just this concept which has allowed the Western peoples to remain for so long the richest and best-fed in the world. No matter what people or countries had ultimately to suffer while they were pursuing these "best interests," the pragmatic efficiency of England, France, or the United States in accomplishing such ends is almost legendary. Weird historical "music," in the so-called Opium Wars in China (Britain), the "defense" of the Suez Canal (Britain/ France), the Spanish-American and Castro-American Wars (United States)—some examples, both recent and long past, of this "best interests" doctrine as applied by the West—leaps immediately to mind. And these kinds of activities can also be included within the definition of *Nationalism.* So it seems strange at first to see Westerners squirming at the mention of a concept and/or practice they themselves have been most responsible for perfecting. There is a comic analogy in the fact that in con man language "savage" means "sucker."

The "rub," of course, is that when another people or country, who have been used or exploited because it served the best interests of a Western power, suddenly become politically and/or physically powerful enough to begin talking about *their* own best interests, which of course are usually in direct opposition to the wishes of their exploiters, it is then that *Nationalism* becomes a dirty word—one to be stricken from as many minds as possible, by whatever methods. (To my mind, it is absurd to think for a moment that the people who killed Patrice Lumumba thought he was a Communist. They understood exactly what he was.) And it seems a simple enough conclusion to me that most of the so-called "hotspots" in the world are caused by this same conflict of "nationalisms," even in our own South. (An historical aside: The Civil War in the United States was of course the victory of the industrial interests in the country over the agricultural—a kind of nationalism. For these same reasons, any white racist in the South today who suddenly, for whatever hypothetical reasons, became strong enough to convince some large part of the white South that secession was the only way to solve the South's problems would be disposed of by the tobacco people, etc., in short order. More "Nationalism." The conflict of interests.)

What I am driving at is the fact that to me the Africans, Asians, and Latin Americans who are news today because of their nationalism, *i.e.*, the militant espousal of the doctrine of serving one's own people's interests before those of a foreign country, *e.g.*, the United States, are exactly the examples the black man in this country should use in his struggle for *independence.* (And that is what the struggle remains, for independence—from the political, economic, social, spiritual, and psychological domination of the white man. Put more simply, the struggle moves to make certain that no man has the right to dictate the life of another man. The struggle is not simply for "equality," or "better jobs," or "better schools," and the rest of those half-hearted liberal clichés; it is to completely *free* the black man from the domination of the white man. Nothing else. The man who asks the question "Would You Let Your Daughter Marry One?" must realize that that question is generally outmoded. The question now for those same people becomes "What Would I do If One Turned My Daughter Down?" It is the freedom to make the choice that is my insistence, and the insistence, I hope, of most black Americans.) And it is the new nationalists everywhere who are pointing out dramatically the road our own struggle must take. In America, black *is* a country. The Cubans are attacked by this country because they refuse to let themselves be used solely to further the Industrial interests of this country. Communism is *not* the issue. Lumumba was killed because he resisted the designs of the neo-colonialists to continue to make *money* from the labors of the African. Communism, again, was not the issue.

The black man has been separated and made to live in his own country of color. If you are black the only roads into the mainland of American life are through subservience, cowardice, and loss of manhood. Those are the white man's roads. It is time we built our own. America is as much a black country as a white one. The lives and destinies of the white American are bound up inextricably with those of the black American, even though the latter has been forced for hundreds of years to inhabit the lonely country of black. It is time we impressed the white man with the nature of his ills, as well as the nature of our own. The Negro's struggle in America is only a microcosm of the struggle of the new countries all over the world.

The idea of "passive" resistance is not the answer. It is an Indian "rope trick" that cannot be applied in this scientific country. No one believes in magic anymore. The Christian church cannot help us. The new nationalists all over the world have learned to be suspicious of "Christianity." Christ and the Dollar Sign have gotten mixed up in their minds, and they *know* that the latter is their enemy. It is time black Americans got those two confused as well. The idea of the "all black society" within the superstructure of an all white society is useless as well (even if it were possible). We *are* Americans, which is our strength as well as our desperation. The struggle is for *independence,* not separation—or assimilation for that matter. Do what you want to with *your* life . . . when you can. I want to be independent of black men just as much as I want independence from the white. It is just that achieving the latter involves all black men, or at least those who have not already taken those available roads into the mainstream I mentioned earlier—subservience, cowardice and loss of manhood.

This struggle has first got to aim itself at those black men who have already taken those three roads to "success." The "rubber stamps" of our exploitation. Usually, as we know, these rubber stamps are set up as our "leaders." Official Negroes they are called. Good. Let them be official. It only means that they are as sick and useless as everything else in this country that has, of recent years, been unofficial. When we speak of the ugliness of American foreign policy, we cannot separate our disgust with that from the knowledge that these official Negroes, as such, must be the repositories of those same policies. The best interests of the black man in America cannot be furthered by these puppets and messengers. It is not in the best interests of the black man if another black man gets up in the United Nations and apologizes to that august body for the conduct of "his people." It is not in the best interests of the black American if another black American suggests to the world that the only way in which his people are going to achieve their independence is to get walked on in public places or blown out of buses. And it is strictly up to those black people who realize these things to come out and say them. Not only say them, but act upon them. And we must act now, in what I see as an extreme "nationalism," *i.e.*, in the best interests of our country, the name of which the rest of America has pounded into our heads for four hundred years, *Black*.

Project "C"

Lerone Bennett

February, 1963, was a quiet, curious month.

It was the second month of the Emancipation centennial and men looked back, in hope and in anger, to Abraham Lincoln's words and Abraham Lincoln's deed.

John Fitzgerald Kennedy, the thirty-fifth President of the United States, and Medgar Evers, an obscure NAACP official, spoke in this month of that last full measure of devotion which both would pay before the year had run its course. In Birmingham, four children who would soon be dead heard Lincoln's name spoken and his deed praised. From a thousand pulpits and a thousand lecterns came words of hope and words of freedom. Centennial orators declaimed, proclamations were read, prayers were spoken. And all went on as before. Rats scampered across the littered corridors of Harlem tenements and water bubbled from the "white" and "colored" fountains in

Reprinted from *The Negro Mood* (pp. 3-23) by permission of the Johnson Publishing Company.

the Birmingham city hall. Papers of importance were signed as before. Black men stood in lines before unemployment offices, new plays opened on Broadway and schoolboys recited the Gettysburg Address.

It was a curious business in a curious month in a curious year—Negro and white Americans marching on to danger with the words and the deeds of Lincoln on their lips and in their minds. There were no signs then of the black fury to come. But there was a stillness in the Harlems of the mind and in Arlington the white crosses stood mute and accusing in the bright February sun.

In this quiet, eerie month, a tall, thin man slipped into Birmingham, Alabama. He arrived at midday on Flight 623, Delta Airlines, and went immediately to Gaston's Motel, the modernistic glass and brick pile in the heart of the Negro ghetto.

Before unpacking, the tall man opened a brown leather attaché case and extracted a sheaf of papers. The papers were marked CONFIDENTIAL. And across the top of each page was a legend:

PROJECT "C"

Project "C" was the code name for a proposed series of racial demonstrations in Birmingham.

And what did the "C" stand for?

It was a shorthand symbol for a chillingly blunt concept: CONFRONTATION. A confrontation between Negroes and whites—not in the courts but on the steps of city hall, not at the conference table but in the streets, not by ones and twos but by hundreds and thousands.

The man behind the concept was Martin Luther King, Jr., the thirty-four-year-old president of the Southern Christian Leadership Conference (SCLC). King had emerged from the Montgomery bus boycott as the spiritual leader of a passive resistance movement that changed the contours of race relations. In the first two years of the sixties, he attracted international attention with a series of direct action thrusts in Southern cities. But none of the thrusts led to a dramatic breakthrough. As the Emancipation Proclamation Centennial drew near, King cast about for a Bastille, i.e., a key point that could yield more than a local or symbolic victory. With incredible boldness, he selected Birmingham which was widely regarded as an impregnable fortress of Jim Crow.

The detailed plans for Project "C" were hammered out in a series of meetings at SCLC's Atlanta headquarters in the summer and fall of 1962. The dominant personalities in these meetings were King and three Baptist ministers: Ralph D. Abernathy, treasurer of SCLC; Wyatt Tee Walker, executive director of SCLC; Fred L. Shuttlesworth, secretary of SCLC and president of SCLC's Alabama affiliate.

Project "C" was scheduled and postponed several times. By February, 1963, however, King was convinced that a showdown situation was necessary for racial progress in Birmingham. There was no way for him to know then, there was no way, really, for anyone to know that the project prophetically called "C" would lead Negro and white Americans to the brink of an eyeball-to-eyeball confrontation.

It was decided early in February to proceed with Project "C" on April 3, the day after Birmingham's municipal election. But SCLC was nothing if not thorough. Two months before D-day, Wyatt Tee Walker was dispatched to Birmingham to lay the formal foundations.

In Room 16 at Gaston's Motel, in the month of February, 1963, Walker, a tall Baptist minister in black horn-rimmed glasses and an Ivy League suit, sat for a long time studying the "battle plans." Then, as the sun dropped behind the hills, the Rev. Mr. Walker slipped out of his room and kept his first appointment.

By nightfall, the first stone was laid.

No one knew then that a revolution was in the offing.

February was a quiet month.

Rats scampered across the littered corridors of Harlem tenements and in Birmingham the statue of Vulcan on Red Mountain was aglow.

In the next few weeks, Walker, Shuttlesworth and other SCLC aides shuttled in and out of Birmingham, contacting key persons and laying the groundwork for the struggle to come. Secondary and tertiary targets were selected, and a code system was devised to confuse "the enemy." On the telephone SCLC aides spoke obliquely of "candidates" for the scheduled baptism.

Throughout this period, strategic plans were reviewed and refined. The best routes for mass marches were plotted and listed on a map. SCLC aides walked from the Sixteenth Street Baptist Church to city hall and noted the time on a chart. They also noted key features of the terrain and made cryptic notes on charts and pieces of paper.

All through the early months of 1963, while centennial orators postured and threatened, SCLC aides worked. Information on the ownership of business and industrial concerns in Birmingham was compiled; and wealthy whites and Negroes were lined up as potential contributors to a bail bond fund.

While these events were unfolding, local leaders made one final attempt to negotiate with Birmingham's white leaders. When this effort failed, Martin Luther King, Jr., and his top aides invaded the city and started Phase I of Project "C."

For more than a month, King and his nonviolent army struggled with the forces of Theophilus Eugene (Bull) Connor, the Birmingham commissioner of public safety. Thousands were arrested and humiliated amid scenes of incredible brutality. Some demonstrators were bitten by police dogs; others were bowled over by high-powered water hoses. The whole angry fabric of resistance and rebellion reached a peak on May 11-12, 1963, with a bombing counterattack by white segregationists. Angered by the bombings, Negroes rioted, burned the stores of white businessmen and fought with policemen, state troopers, and firemen.

The Bastille of Birmingham was a turning point in the Negro resistance movement. Sparks from the flames of Birmingham leaped from ghetto to ghetto, igniting inflammable material that had been gathering for years, welding Negroes into a great black mass of livid indignation.

Something snapped during the struggle in the streets of Birmingham. The billy clubs, the fire hoses and the contempt for Negro women and children swept away the last vestiges of credulity and millions knew themselves victims.

After Birmingham, the Negro Freedom Movement grew in intensity and scope. In 1963 alone, there were more than two thousand demonstrations (sleep-ins, sit-ins, pray-ins, wade-ins and mass marches) and more than ten thousand demonstrators were arrested.

As the year wore on, lurching to three bloody climaxes, the assassinations of President Kennedy and Medgar Evers and the bomb-murder of four children in a Birmingham church, resistance stiffened in the North. Organizations of white taxpayers, parents, and realtors came forward to agitate against open occupancy and open school enrollment. More and more people, as the year wore on, reminded the Negro of his situation: minority status maintained by the naked force of an overwhelming majority. As the North-South consensus developed, as the great tide of white concern in the North receded, Negro leaders found themselves far away from their accustomed haunts, swept up on the burning beaches of history in ridiculous poses. What did they do? Some proposed a strategic retreat to the old islands of protest and voter registration. But others, with remarkable boldness, struck out for new and higher ground.

Beginning in January, 1964, one hundred and one years after emancipation, the Freedom Movement began to inch toward the dangerous road of open and continuous self-assertion. The momentum began to build with smashing school boycotts in Northern cities, with mass confrontations in Maryland, Georgia, and Florida.

There was a new dimension in these demonstrations. The movement, before Birmingham, was largely confined to a small elite of nonviolent student professionals. In the summer of 1963, the angry men of World War II and the Korean War entered the ranks. And as 1964 began there was an involvement of the lowest strata of the Negro working class. The rent strikes of New York City and Washington and hunger marches in Chicago were reflections of the engagement of a hitherto uncommitted group.

Step by step, demonstration by demonstration, Negroes inched toward open and bitter alienation. They sprawled in the streets to stop traffic; they chained themselves to dump trucks to stop work at construction sites; they used their bodies to bar entrance to schools and boards of education.

A measure of the change in mood was the increasing harshness of Negro-white confrontations. In Maryland, Mississippi, Illinois, Florida, and New York, Negro and white Americans faced each other in 1964 in massive confrontations that resembled miniature wars.

By the summer of 1964, some of the more venturesome Negro leaders were openly calling for civil disobedience campaigns, i.e., the nonpayment of taxes, noncooperation with government agencies and massive attempts to create what Bayard Rustin, a leading philosopher of the movement, called "creative social confusion."

At the root of the current upheaval is a cataclysmic shift in the mood of Negroes, a shift mirrored in changing patterns of protest and social contention. The causes of this epochal shift lie deep in the total Negro-white situation. The current rebellion, which began February, 1960, and reached a peak in 1963-64, cannot be understood apart from the long history of preparatory work. To focus on the peak years of 1963-64 and to ignore the long history of developing protest is to miss not only the mountain but the meaning of the peak.

Bryan Edwards, the great anatomist of social upheavals, said once that it takes at least three generations to make a revolution.

The first generation, in short, submits.

The second generation protests.

The third generation acts.

One does not have to accept Edwards' theory in its entirety to recognize the core of truth it contains. Revolutions do not spring full-blown from the head of Zeus or Martin Luther King, Jr. They are products of slowly accumulating changes in the nerve plasm of individuals. Over a long period of time, discontent builds up, accumulates and strains against the dams of social habit. The explosion that follows is a product of action and a lack of action, the increasing pressure of discontent as well as the counterpressure of the dam.

The dam against which Negro discontent is focused is white power. Any realistic analysis of the Negro rebellion must begin with the Negro's situation, a situation defined by power or the lack of it.

In the beginning, insofar as the Negro is concerned, was not a word but a monstrous fact: white power.

Forty-one years ago, a group of "prominent white citizens" of Tuskegee, Alabama, defined the Negro's situation in a frank talk with Robert R. Moton, Booker T. Washington's successor as president of Tuskegee Institute. In the summer of the Negro's discontent, Mayor Allen Thompson of Jackson, Mississippi, used almost the same words in a frank talk to a group of Negro ministers. Here are the two quotes.

"You understand," the prominent white citizen said in 1923, "that we have the legislature, we make the laws, we have the judges, the sheriffs, the jails. We have the hardware stores and the arms."

"I'm not threatening you," Mayor Thompson said in the summer of 1963. "But we've got the guns, we've got the force."

Power.

Let us begin by talking about power.

White guns, white judges, white armies, white tanks, white bombs, white symbols: this is the element into which the Negro is flung and to which he must make a creative social response or die.

From birth to death, the Negro is handled, distorted and violated by the symbols and tentacles of white power, tentacles that worm their way into his neurons and invade the gray cells of his cortex. As he grows up, he makes a tentative adjustment to white power. At puberty, if he survives and if he remains outside prisons or insane asylums, he makes a separate peace—a peace of accommodation or protest. The price of this peace is high, fantastically high. The price, quite simply, is social emasculation. The Negro not only dons a mask; he becomes, in many instances, the mask he dons. Behind the public mask is a man who fears, cries, bleeds, loves, defecates, hates—a man who knows, as James Weldon Johnson knew, that "the resort to force remains and will doubtless remain the rightful recourse of oppressed peoples"—a man who knows this but rejects it, as Johnson rejected it, "because in our case it would be futile."

From a logical standpoint, of course, there can be only two basic responses to arbitrarily imposed power: open revolt or accommodation. The Negro resistance movement has moved within the confines of two contradictory imperatives: 1) the need to reject open revolt and 2) the need to reject acceptance. This is a cruel and grinding dilemma. If the Negro revolts, in other words, he loses all. But if he refuses to revolt, he also loses all. For acceptance, on whatever level, is violation.

The history of the Negro in America, then, has been a quest for a revolt that was not a revolt—a revolt, in other words, that did not seem to the white power structure to be an open revolt. Martin Luther King, Jr., and the sit-in students, as we shall see, solved the technical problems by clothing a resistance movement in the comforting garb of love and forgiveness.

Before King, almost all Negroes were enmeshed in different levels of collaboration. The overwhelming weight of the culture pushed them into "their places" and, as Ralph J. Bunche pointed out in the forties, all Negroes had "a place" in America and, in Chicago or Birmingham, they usually remained in it. Some Negroes, of course, accommodated themselves better than others. Some internalized the values of white people and imitated them. Still others adjusted to external factors and maintained—or tried to maintain—internal freedom. The latter group adjusted but protested every step of the way. But protest is not revolt. This is the point of departure for an understanding of the Negro rebellion. One sends a telegram protesting an indignity or one passes a resolution condemning it or one appeals to authority for help or protection or redress. The question of revolt arises when the request is denied and one comes hard up against the question: "What are you going to do about it?"

Faced with overwhelming power, backed up by the implacable hostility of a dominant majority, the Negro has elaborated four techniques of resistance: direct action, violent and nonviolent, black nationalism and protest, a vague, umbrella word covering a whole constellation of postures and poses revolving around litigation, lobbying and a propaganda of enlightenment. Distinct from and, in most cases, opposed to these strategies of contention is a strain of accommodation which reached its height—some would say its depth—in the submissive policy of Booker Taliaferro Washington.

The weaving and interweaving of three additional themes should also be noted: the search for an opening to the masses; the quest for the right key or instrument (ballots, bullets, Bibles, law books, dollar bills or the human body used as a weapon in strikes, boycotts, marches or other direct attacks); the quest for reliable allies (liberals or radicals, aristocrats or laborers). Hovering over all, subtly shaping and influencing all, is the harsh imperative of avoiding action that would unite all white Americans in a "holy war" against all Negro Americans.

The Negro situation spawns individual types who respond to white power with life styles corresponding to the four major techniques of resistance: militants, for example, who express themselves through protest; moderates who essay a middle course between accommodation and protest; accommodators who accept segregation and strive for various modes of individual advancement; and activists who repudiate protest, accommodation and moderation and demand action, violent or nonviolent. In a completely different category are Negro nationalists who say the civil rights struggle is useless and recommend total separation, either in America or Africa.

The dialogue of destiny in the ghetto is dominated by the militants and moderates who man the command posts of the institutions and associations of the black elite. But the hegemony of militants and moderates has never been complete. Since the thirties, there has been a continuing conversation between militants and moderates of the elite and activists and black nationalists.

The moderately militant black elite has scored impressive victories (the NAACP legal campaign and the Urban League welfare program), but it has not made an appreciable dent in the great white wall, a fact which does not, taken alone, condemn it. It may be—and only time will tell—that the wall is unbreachable. And yet it is difficult to avoid the conclusion that elite failures stem from self-imposed limitations of style and what Ralph J. Bunche called "a narrow vision of leadership."

The moderately militant black elite, from the very beginning, cut itself loose from the only element that could give it real power—the Negro masses. This was a fatal error that condemned the elite to impotence and the masses to apathy. Having forsworn mass action and risky adventures for freedom, having, in fact, committed themselves to the system, thereby losing freedom of action, elite members had, of necessity, to approach white men of power as suppliants who could not make serious threats and back them up.

Seconded by powerful voices in the white liberal establishment, tolerated and sometimes encouraged by the white power structure, the black elite created the protest movement and laid the foundation for the current Freedom Movement. Despite that fact, or perhaps because of it, elite influence is dwindling. The elite, more than anything else, is a victim of success—success that pitilessly exposed the inner contradictions of its own strategy and premises.

In the late fifties, litigation, the epitome of elite strategy, reached a point of diminishing return and it became increasingly clear that the elite had no answer to massive defiance of court orders, the spread of *de facto* segregation in the North and the widening gap between the average annual income of Negroes and whites. There may not, in fact, be any answers to these challenges within the confines of the American system. But an increasing number of Negroes are turning, in despair and in burgeoning hope, to activists who say the black elite cannot solve the problem because it is a part of the problem.

The Negro rebellion marks the coming to power of activists who are disenchanted with both the white and black power elites. It also marks a fundamental shift in Negro leadership patterns. Like all social upheavals, the Negro rebellion is not one but two revolutions—a revolution against the militant-moderate within and the reactionary without.

In the background of this shift in strategy are many elements: the root-shaking dislocations of World War II; the continuing migration to the North and West; the growth of a Negro middle class which had the foresight and ingenuity to give birth to radical children; the impact of mass media which disseminated the slogans of the "Free World"; the external pressure of a competing ideology which made an issue of humanism; and the subtle shift in America from rampant individualism to an attenuated welfare state.

These elements, and others, created the climate which made rebellion possible. But they did not create the rebellion which was a result of a parallelogram of four contextual forces:

1) The development of a new self-conception in the Negro psyche and the growth of a revolutionary will to dignity.

2) The development of a new principle of leadership which abandoned the elite concept of selected agents acting for the masses in various theaters of power.

3) The development of a social myth which provided a new script of roles and models for Negro youth.

4) The existence of a competing ideology in a world power struggle which made wholesale repression embarrassing, if not distasteful.

To understand how these four lines of force came together, to understand how they approached each other over a period of one hundred years, we must go back a few steps and examine the dominant fact in American life—broken community.

A community is a body of people sharing common expectations and common obligations. Real community is based on reciprocity of emotion and relation between individuals sharing a common vision of the possibilities and potentialities of man. The basic fact of race relations in America is that white people and Negroes do not belong to the same community. White people, with few exceptions, do not feel that they have unqualified moral obligations to Negroes—and Negroes, in self-defense, return the compliment.

The breaking of the bonds of community between Negroes and whites began in slavery and was given legal form in the Reconstruction period. In these two epochs, white power destroyed the Negro's family, annihilated his personality and consigned him to a lower order of humanity.

The seeds of the current revolution were sown in the last decade of the nineteenth century by Negro intellectuals who refused to accept the place prepared for them. In the dawn years of the twentieth century, Negro intellectuals and reform-minded whites formed an uneasy alliance. Out of this alliance came the National Association for the Advancement of Colored People and the National Urban League.

The old protest movement, as distinguished from the new Freedom Movement, was an invention of the militants and moderates of the League and the NAACP. Of crucial importance in the context of the postslavery Negro renaissance was the work of the NAACP. By organizing a bold legal campaign, the NAACP opened the eyes of Negroes to a whole new vista of struggle. But the NAACP and the Urban League were organized around a narrow principle of leadership. Both organizations were composed largely of middle- and upper-income Negroes and whites who were somewhat removed from the masses. And it was from the masses that the first revolutionary impulse came.

During the first two decades of the twentieth century, Negroes were groping in some dim, obscure way toward an understanding of their role in American life. A feeling was growing in the backwoods of the South—a feeling that life could be better, brighter and more meaningful. The mood crystallized in 1915-16 in a mass migration which has continued to this day. The great Negro Migration—the most significant population upheaval since the wagon trains rolled West—changed the shape of race relations. It nationalized the race problem, gave the Negro a base of political power in the North and set the stage for our present confrontation.

World War I, following close on the heels of the black migrants, shattered the old racial equilibrium. After that war, it was no longer possible for Negroes to avoid the issue of their place in American life. The treatment of Negro soldiers in Europe and the hostile environment to which they returned made a permanent impression on the Negro mind. So did the Red Summer of 1919, a summer of terror and blood and twenty-six race riots.

If World War I was not the beginning of Negro emancipation, it was, at least, the beginning of wisdom. The war abroad and the quiet war at home gave birth to the New Negro Revolt of the twenties which was a little miniature of the revolt of the sixties. There were three identical phases: a literary revival that focused attention on the Negro folk tradition, a student revolt that began at Fisk and spread to other colleges and a black nationalist crusade which was America's first Negro mass movement.

The lightning of the Great Depression, following the thunderclap of World War I, illuminated the precarious ledge on which the Negro existed. In the light of this event, Negroes looked at themselves and knew themselves—and they were naked. Aside from dreary statistics and sociological jargon that hides more than it reveals, the psychological fact was shattering. And it hovers somewhere in the deeps of the Negro psyche.

The first fruit of despair was a shift in strategy. The elite methods of litigation and lobbying were repudiated. Hungry youth took to the streets, picketing, boycotting and demonstrating. A harbinger of things to come, and a revelation of the depth of Negro despair, was the Harlem riot of 1935 in which Negroes blindly smashed glass—and can it be doubted?—idols.

World War II accelerated the fury. At the very beginning of that conflict, Negroes made it clear that they were tired of making the world safe for a commodity that was in short supply at home. The period between 1940 and 1943 was remarkably similar to the period between 1960 and 1963. Mass meetings were held, stores were picketed and spirituals were sung. A. Philip Randolph, the spiritual father of the current movement, electrified America with a call for a nonviolent civil disobedience movement. Randolph's call struck a responsive chord in the hearts of young Americans who were tired of petitioning and resolving. Several organizations were founded in these years to agitate for a new departure. The most significant was the Congress of Racial Equality (CORE) which staged its first sit-in in Chicago in 1942. The whole pageant of accelerated defiance reached a pitch in 1947 with a NAACP appeal to the United Nations. The audacity of activists in 1948-49 (the Peekskill riots, the Progressive party and A. Phillip Randolph's call for a civil disobedience movement against the draft) caused widespread concern. The Civil Rights Report of 1947, the Democratic party plank of 1948 and the integration of the armed forces were, in part, attempts to contain Negro discontent which was taking a dangerous and unpredictable turn.

Although it apparently failed, the revolt of the forties was, in effect, a huge dress rehearsal for the upheaval that came a decade later. The experiences of the forties roused the Negro masses from their lethargy and taught them lessons they would never forget.

The thirties and the forties: these were the truly decisive years in the Negro odyssey. The epoch from 1930 to 1945 shook the Negro ghetto to its foundation, giving rise to estrangement, alienation and thought.

The Negro emerged in this period as a questing social being with an awareness of his strength and his situation. Everything in Negro life marked the change—the publication of *Native Son*, the radical alteration in the texture of modern jazz, the militant posture of Negro youth and the mushroom growth of nationalist movements.

All these changes occurred between 1930 and 1945. In that fifteen-year period, there was a greater change in the Negro psyche than in the whole period between 1860 and 1930. By the end of the forties, it was apparent to almost everyone that the Negro had moved within himself. Myrdal put his finger on the inner emigration early in the war. Said he: "America can never more regard its Negroes as a patient, submissive minority. Negroes will continually become less well accommodated. They will organize for defense and offense. They will be more vociferous. They will watch their opportunities ever more keenly."

The new mood in the ghetto was a function of many variables, some external and some internal. In the great world beyond the Atlantic and the Pacific, there was a shrinkage of the white ego which reached the limits of its four-hundred-year expansion. There was, contrariwise, an expansion of the Negro ghetto at home, an expansion expressed most vividly in the lava-like march of Negro ghettos to the city limits of a hundred municipalities.

These two movements, external contraction and internal distension, changed race relations forever. Negroes and whites began to look at each other in different ways. And they began, each in his own way, to prepare for the confrontation to come.

There was, in sum, a radical new conception at work in the ghetto, a conception that reflected an equally radical alteration in the Negro mood. The Big Change in Negro life occurred not in the sixties but in the forties. The only things wanting were a voice to give tongue to it, an instrument to contain it and a detonating spark. The detonating spark was the Supreme Court decision of 1954 which was the result of a long and brilliant legal campaign by the NAACP. This decision reopened the national compromise of 1877 and essayed a new definition of the Negro's status in American life. It was followed the next year by the Montgomery bus boycott, out of which came a new ideology and a remarkable fisher of men, Martin Luther King, Jr.

Montgomery was a great myth, in the best sense of the word. It was a womb from which emerged a corpus of models and images to which growth could aspire.

Montgomery and the Supreme Court decisions were key elements in the growth cycle of a new generation, a generation, it should be noted, that had never known the white man when he was not hard pressed, a generation born and raised in the fateful break between two epochs.

This generation came to seed in an era of bad faith. It became apparent soon after 1954 that the Supreme Court decision was not going to be obeyed. There began the whole dreary ritual of September sickness, of skirmishes in schoolyards, of troops and tanks and despair. A certain hope died in these years. A certain faith. There was a convulsion of the collective mind.

To make matters worse, the economic situation became menacing. With the beginning of a series of "economic downturns," the Negro was pushed back toward the well-remembered days of the thirties. More ominous was the day-to-day aggression of automation.

Another milestone on the road to Birmingham, a cause and an effect of the mood of despair and desperation, was the rise of the Black Muslims. Not many Negroes were impressed by the Muslims' call for total separation. But almost all Negroes were touched by their savage indictment of hypocrisy and their delicious acceptance of the fact of being black.

In this climate, four young men sat down in Greensboro, North Carolina, and a whole generation began the long and painful process of standing up. The sit-in movement raced across the South, scoring unheard-of successes. More importantly, three organizations—the Student Nonviolent Coordinating Committee (SNCC), the Congress of Racial Equality and the Southern Christian Leadership Conference—came forward to give tone and direction to the agony and the fervor of the most significant youth movement in American history.

In 1960-61, the rivulets of hope and ambition began to descend from their secret places in the high mountains of Negro despair. Then it was that myth, self-conception, leadership, and external pressure mated.

From Martin Luther King, Jr., came the nonviolent ideology (based not so much on Gandhi as the Baptist church) and the idea that every man was responsible for his own freedom and that he could not discharge that responsibility by contributing two dollars to an organization and voting on resolutions once a year. SNCC contributed the concept of the professional rebel, of the man or woman or child who abandoned place, position and prestige to fight on the front lines for a subsistence wage. From SNCC also came the concept of "going to the people" and living with them in order to organize and create indigenous leadership. CORE brought a long history of direct action to the marriage and a tough-talking, tough-acting stance.

The struggle moved now from courtrooms to the streets, from litigation to demonstrations. One phase followed another: the sit-ins leading to the Freedom Rides and the Freedom Rides leading to Albany, Georgia, which led to Birmingham and confrontation.

The movement grew on what it fed on, escalating goals and making them seem higher. The more the activists gained, the more they wanted. The more they protested, the more they wanted to protest. The more they won, the more they wanted to win.

Negroes of all ranks were swept along by the dancing waves of discontent. Like a sensitizing symbol, like a grandiose myth, the Freedom Movement set up a lively exchange of influences, the first effect of which was to create a mood, a *Stimmung*, a collective state of mind, to which each individual contributed and by which each was moulded.

In the crucible of collective excitement, the bony structure of Negro belief and habit became soft and was pushed into new and more aggressive shapes. Under the impact of the mood, Negroes became more suggestible, more malleable and more responsive to new stimulation and new ideas. Their circle of claims on society widened and a new racial self arose to supplement and include individual racial selves. Movement and mood sustained and reinforced each other, creating new roles and self-conceptions by which individual Negroes could measure themselves.

To the immense influence of the new mood must be added the factor of success. As the movement moved from success to success, there was a progressive widening of the circle of combatants and an increasing audacity of vision.

Propelled by these psychic dynamisms, the movement leaped in 1963-64 from crisis to crisis, escalating the racial problems to new frontiers of strife and controversy.

The leaping waves of discontent and direct action pose large problems of analysis. Is the Freedom Movement, for example, a revolution?

There can be no neat and categorical answer to this question. Every revolution creates its own path and demands judgment on its own terms. This is particularly true of a nonviolent revolution on the part of an oppressed minority which does not intend to take over a government but to fulfill it—a distinction, to be sure, that gives small comfort to defenders of the status quo. For the black rebels are demanding not a token but a complete change in things as they are.

A revolution, in essence, is a rapid but not necessarily violent social change through which the power relations of social groups are changed and a new order established. The main criterion of a revolution is a desire and a will on the part of a group to force a fundamental change in the social order.

Judged by these standards, the Freedom Movement assumes a different face. Almost all active members of the movement desire a basic change in the social order. Not all, however, have a revolutionary will. Whether this will crystallizes or not depends to a great extent on our responses. For the main goal of the movement is a basic change in the power relations between Negro and white Americans.

It is not noted often enough that power relations between Negroes and whites have already changed. The Negro today is the dominant social fact in almost every metropolitan community of any size. He elects scores of mayors from Nashville and Atlanta to Chicago and Detroit; he provides the margin of profit for thousands of businesses; and his voice is often decisive in American Presidential elections.

These are surface manifestations of a basic shift in the real position of American Negroes. The Negro upheaval, like most revolutions, is an attempt to force recognition of a change which has already occurred, a change which is stymied by obsolescent social arrangements and outmoded institutions.

The Freedom Movement has already forced a minor realignment in Negro-white power relations. Since the beginning of the sit-in age, there has been a shift in the relations between Negro and white Americans. More concessions have been made to *Negro power* since 1960 than in any comparable period in the history of America.

The 1960-64 convulsion, to sum up, meets some of the basic tests of a classic upheaval: the direct intervention of the masses, for example, and the reliance on direct action which is, to the Freedom Movement, what Clausewitz called war: a continuation of politics by other means.

Tactics, strategy, objectives: all point to a petit revolution straining on the ledge of an open confrontation. But the movement, so far, has not solved the two basic problems that would make it a real revolution: the organization of a sustained national resistance movement and the mobilization of the so-called under-class in the great concrete ghettos. For this reason and others, primarily the limitations of the Negro situation, it would be more accurate to call the upheaval a rebellion, a turning away from, a going out of—a becoming.

Semantics apart, the cataclysm in the streets is real enough, and it proceeds from revolutionary premises. The fundamental premise is that old forms and old ways are no longer adequate and that the social system, as organized, is incapable of solving, through normal channels, the urgent problem presented to it by history. The second major premise is allied to the first: that the social system, as organized, is part of the problem and cannot be appealed to or relied upon as an independent arbiter in power conflicts of which it is a part. The third major premise is that white Americans, generally speaking, lack the will, the courage, and the intelligence to voluntarily grant

Negroes their civil rights and that they must be forced to do it by pressure.

Here are the minor premises:

1) That people do not discriminate for the fun of it, that the function of prejudice is to defend interests (social, economic, political and psychological interests) and that appeals to the fair play of prejudiced people are prayers said to the wind.

2) That communities will change discriminatory patterns if they are forced to make a clear-cut choice between bias and another highly cherished value—economic gain, education or civic peace.

3) That struggle and conflict are necessary for social change, that showdown situations are desirable because they throw the whole range of race relations into the arena of public discussion.

4) That the constitutional rights of live human beings are at stake and that these rights are neither ballotable nor negotiable; that negotiation, to be meaningful, must take place between equals acting in good faith and that the issues here are precisely equality and the good faith, if not the good sense, of white Americans.

5) That peace is the presence of community and not the absence of conflict; and that demonstrations against Jim Crow are attempts to establish peace and not breaches of the peace which, according to black rebels, has never existed anywhere and at anytime between black and white Americans.

We may or may not agree with these premises. It doesn't matter, really. For what we must realize now is that the burden of proof is on us. The face of the Commonwealth gives abundant testimony of the total failure of the politics of good intentions. What we must do now is to examine our own inarticulate premises and our own involvement or lack of involvement in a struggle that goes to the heart of our meaning as a people.

We stand now in a lull in the lurch of history. The barometer drops so low before a storm. No man wants a storm, but wishing will not sweep away the clouds. If we do not act, the storm will come—if not now, five years from now; if not then, ten years later. There has been, as we have seen, a Negro revolt in every decade of this century. Each revolt failed, only to emerge in the next decade on a higher level of development. It is not to our best interest for the current rebellion to fail. For one hesitates to speculate on the form and intensity a Negro revolt will take in the seventies and eighties when Negroes form a majority in many of our major cities.

We are heading now for a land no American has traversed. For perhaps the first time in our history, we have a thoroughly restive minority population on our hands. So far we have done our best to bring out the worst in urban Negroes who are strategically placed to cause social chaos. Negroes, for the most part, inhabit the inner cores of America's largest cities; and they hold the key to the future of the city and the future of Amerian democracy. If we do not want a black Ireland here, if we do not want our cities divided into mutually hostile casbahs, if we do not want the Negro rebellion to become a real revolution, then we must dare to flesh out the words we profess.

This is an important moment in the history of the Commonwealth. There stretch out before us two roads and two roads only. America must now become America or something else, a Fourth Reich perhaps, or a Fourth Reich of the spirit. To put the matter bluntly, we must become what we say we are or give in to the secret dream that blights our hearts.

Let us not deceive ourselves. The problem before us now is not the Negro but ourselves; not civil rights but the city; not love but the creation of that America which could have been and should have been and never was.

6
Man and Machine

The First Megamachine

Lewis Mumford

1. The Design of the Human Machine

Until the nineteenth century, history was largely a chronicle of the deeds and misdeeds of kings, nobles, and armies. In revolt against a general obliviousness to the daily life and affairs of ordinary people, democratic historians swung to the opposite extreme: so the part actually played by kings has, during the last half century, been grossly under-rated, even though most of the attributes of kingship are now exercised, or a larger scale than ever before, by the all-powerful sovereign state.

From the earliest records, we know that the king incarnated the whole community and by divine right arrogated to himself the functions and offices of communal life. Only one aspect of kingship has been left out of this traditional account: strangely, the king's greatest and most lasting achievement has passed unnoticed, despite the fact that all his other public activities rested upon it. For though the

Reprinted from *Diogenes* 55, Fall 1966, by permission of *Diogenes, Revue Internationale des Sciences Humaines.*

myth of royal power claimed divine sanction, its rise and spread would have been impossible without the invention of the human machine. That was the supreme feat of kingship: a technological exploit that was transmitted in one form or another through purely human agents for some five thousands years before it was finally embodied in an equally totalitarian but impersonal form in modern technology.

To understand the point of origin and the line of descent is to have a fresh insight into the fate and destiny of modern man: for unless our own civilization learns to control the processes and the purposes that have so long been automatically—that is unconsciously—at work, the social abberations that have accompanied the perfection of a machine technology, threaten even worse consequences than they did in the Pyramid Age.

Though the collective human machine came into existence roughly during the same period as the first industrial use of copper, it was an independent innovation, and did not at first utilize any new mechanical aids. But the royal machine, once conceived, was assembled within a short period; and it spread rapidly, not by being imitated, but by being forcefully imposed by kings, acting as only gods or the anointed representatives of gods could act. Wherever it was successfully put together the new machine commanded power and performed labor on a scale that was never even conceivable before. With this ability to concentrate immense mechanical forces, a new dynamism came into play, which overcame, by the magic of success, the sluggish routines, the petty inhibitions, the dull repetitive routines of the basic neolithic village culture, once the scene of so many fresh experiments in horticulture and breeding.

With the energies available through the royal machine—let us call it the megamachine—the very dimensions of space and time were enlarged. Operations that once could hardly be finished in centuries were now accomplished in less than a generation. If whole mountains were not moved, large portions of them were, sometimes in blocks far bigger than any ordinary motor truck could now handle; while, on the level plains, man-made mountains of stone or baked clay, pyramids and ziggurats, arose in response to royal command. No power machines at all comparable to this mechanism were utilized on any scale until watermills and windmills swept over Western Europe from the fourteenth century of our era.

Why did this new mechanism remain invisible to the archaeologist and the historian? Because it was composed solely of human parts; and it possessed a definite functional structure only as long as the magical abracadabra and the royal command that put it together were accepted as beyond human challenge by all the members of society. Once the polarizing force of kingship was weakened, whether by death or defeat, by skepticism or by brute resistance, the whole machine would collapse and its parts would either regroup in smaller units (feudal or urban) or completely disappear, much in the way that a routed army does when the chain of command is broken. These first collective machines were as frail, as vulnerable, as the theological and magical conceptions that were essential to their performance.

From the beginning, this human machine presented two aspects: one negative and coercive, the other positive and constructive. In fact, the second factors, could not function unless the first were present. Though the military machine probably came before the labor machine, it was the latter that first achieved an incomparable perfection of performance, not alone in quantity of work done, but in quality. To call these collective entities machines is no idle play on words. If a machine be defined more or less in accord with the classic definition of Reuleaux, as a combination of resistant parts, each specialized in function, operating under human control, to transmit motion and to perform work, then the labor machine was a real machine: all the more because its component parts, though composed of human bone, nerve, and muscle, were reduced to their bare mechanical elements and rigidly restricted to the performance of their mechanical tasks.

Such machines, of immense power and practical utility, had already been invented by kings in the early part of the Pyramid Age, from the end of the fourth millennium on. Just because of their detachment from any external structure, they had paradoxically much fuller capacities for change and adaptation than the more rigid metallic counterparts of a modern assembly line. In fact, it is in the building of the pyramids that we find the first indubitable evidence of the machine's existence, and the first proof of its astonishing efficiency. Wherever kingship spread, the human machine, in its destructive if not its constructive form, always went with it. This holds as true for Mesopotamia, India, China, or Peru, as for Egypt.

2. The Archetypal Machine

Let us examine the human machine in its archetypal original form. As so often happens, there was a certain clarity in this first demonstration that was lost when the machine was diffused and worked into the more complex patterns of later societies, mingling with more familiar but humbler forms. And if it never achieved a higher peak of performance, this is perhaps not only because of the singular human talents that designed and operated these early machines, but also perhaps because the myth that held the human part of the machine together could never again exert such a massive attractive power, unstained as it was in Egypt, until the sixth dynasty by letdowns and failures, its inherent perversities still unexposed.

The pyramid took form as a tomb to hold the embalmed body of the Pharaoh and secure his safe passage into the after-life: though he alone, at first, had the prospect of such a godlike extension of his existence, the very idea of being able to fabricate personal immortality shows an alteration in all the dimension of existence.

Between the first small pyramid, built in the step form we find later in Central America, and the mighty pyramid of Cheops at Giza, the first and the most enduring of the Seven Wonders of the Ancient World, lies the short span of three hundred years. On the ancient time-scale for inventions the most primitive form and the final one, never again to be equalled, were practically contemporary. The swiftness of this development indicates a concentration of physical power and technical imagination: for it took far more than faith to move the mountain of stone that composed this ultimate monument. That transformation is all the more striking because the Pharaohs' tombs did not stand alone: they were part of a whole city of the dead, with buildings that housed the priests who conducted the elaborate rituals deemed necessary to ensure a happy fate for the departed divinity.

The Great Pyramid is one of the most colossal and perfect examples of the engineer's art at any period or in any culture. Considering the state of all the other arts in the third millennium, no construction of our own day surpasses this in either technical virtuosity or human audacity. This great enterprise was undertaken by a culture that was just emerging from the Stone Age, and was long to continue using stone tools, though copper was available for the chisels and saws that shaped building stones for the new monuments.

The actual operations were performed by specialized handicraft workers, aided by an army of unskilled or semi-skilled laborers, drafted at quarterly intervals from agriculture. The whole job was done with no other material aids than the "simple machines" of classical mechanics: the inclined plane and the lever, for neither wheel nor pulley nor screw had yet been invented. We know from graphic representations that large stones were hauled on sledges, by battalions of men, across the desert sands. Yet the single stone slab that covers the inner chamber of the Great Pyramid where the Pharaoh lies weighed fifty tons. An architect today would think twice before calling for such a mechanical exploit.

Now the Great Pyramid is more than a formidable mountain of stone, 755 feet square at the base, rising to a height of 481.4 feet. It is a structure with a complex interior, consisting of a series of passages at different levels that lead into the final burial chamber. Yet every part of it was built with a kind of precision that, as J. H. Breasted emphasized, belong to the optician's art rather than that of the modern bridge builder or skyscraper constructor. Blocks of stone were set together with seams of considerable length, showing joints of one-ten-thousandth of an inch; while the dimensions of the sides at the base differ by only 7.9 inches, in a structure that covers acres. In short, what we now characterize as flawless machine precision and machine perfection first manifested itself in the building of this great tomb: at once a symbol of the mountain of creation that emerged out of the primeval waters and a visible effort, so far remarkably successful, by purely human measure, to solidify both time and the human body in an eternal form. No ordinary human hands, no ordinary human effort, no ordinary kind of human collaboration such as was available in the building of village huts and the planting of fields, could muster such a superhuman force, or achieve an almost supernatural result. Only a divine king could accomplish such an act of the human will and such a large-scale material transformation.

Was it possible to create such a structure without the aid of a machine? Emphatically not. I repeat, the product itself showed that it was not only the work of a machine, but of an instrument of precision. Though the technological equipment of dynastic Egypt was still crude, the patient workmanship and disciplined method made good these shortcomings. The social organization had leaped ahead five thousand years to create the first large-scale power machine: a machine of a hundred thousand manpower, that is, the equivalent, roughly, of 10,000 horsepower: a machine composed of a multitude of uniform, specialized, interchangeable, but functionally differentiated parts, rigorously marshalled together and co-ordinated in a process centrally organized and centrally directed: each part behaving as a mechanical component of the mechanized whole: unmoved by any internal impulse that would interfere with the working of the mechanism.

In less than three centuries, this collective human machine was perfected. Once organized and set in motion by the Pharaoh through his chief architect, *the technical competence* and imagination that envisaged the entire design was passed on, by word of mouth, and written instruction, to the component parts: the skilled workers, the overseers and taskmasters, the dumb hands. The kind of mind that designed the Pyramid was a new human type, capable of abstraction of a high order, using astronomical observations for the siting of the structure, so that each side was oriented exactly in line with true points of the compass: since at inundation the Pyramid site is only one quarter of a mile from the river, a rock foundation—which demanded the removal of sand—was needed. In the Great Pyramid the perimeter of that bed deviates from true level by little more than one-half an inch.

But the workers who carried out the design also had minds of a new order: trained in obedience to the letter, limited in response to the word of command descending from the king through a bureaucratic hierarchy, forfeiting during the period of service any trace of autonomy of initiative; slavishly undeviating in performance. Their leaders could read written orders; for the men employed left their names in red ochre, Edwards tells us, on the blocks of the Medium Pyramid: "Boat Gang," "Vigorous Gang." They themselves would have felt at home today on an assembly line. Only the naked pin-up girl was lacking.

Alike in organization, in mode of work, and in product, there is no doubt that the machines that built the pyramids, and that performed all the other great constructive works of "civilization" in other provinces and cultures, were true machines. In their basic operations, they collectively performed the equivalent of a whole corps of power shovels, bulldozers, tractors, mechanical saws, and pneumatic drills, with an exactitude of measurement, a refinement of skill, and even an output of work that would still be a theme for boasting today.

This extension of magnitude in every direction, this raising of the ceiling of human effort, this subordination of individual aptitudes and interests to the mechanical job in hand, and this unification of a multitude of subordinates to a single end that derived from the divine power exercised by the king, in turn, by the success of the result, confirmed that power.

For note: it was the king who uttered the original commands: it was the king who demanded absolute obedience and punished disobedience with torture, mutilation or death: it was the king who alone had the godlike power of turning live men into dead mechanical objects: and finally it was the king who assembled the parts to form the machine and imposed the new discipline of mechanical organization, with the same regularity that moved the heavenly bodies on their undeviating course.

No vegetation god, no fertility myth, could produce this kind of cold abstract order, this detachment of power from life. Only one empowered by the Sun God could remove all hitherto respected norms or limits of human endeavour. The king figures, in early accounts, as being of heroic mold: he alone slays lions singlehanded, builds great city walls, or like Menes turns the course of rivers. That straining ambition, that defiant effort belongs only to the king and the machine that he set in motion.

3. The Transmission Gear

To understand the structure or the performance of the human machine, one must do more than center attention upon the point where it materializes. Even our present technology, with its vast reticulation of visible machines, cannot be understood on those terms alone. In order to put together a collective machine composed solely of human parts, one needed a complex transmission mechanism, to ensure that commands issued at the top would be swiftly and accurately conveyed to every member of the unit, so that the parts would interlock to form a single operating whole.

Two collective devices were essential, to make the machine work: a reliable organization of knowledge, natural and supernatural: and an elaborate structure for giving and carrying out orders. The first was incorporated in the priesthood, without whose active aid divine kingship could not have come into existence: the second in a bureaucracy: both hierarchical organizations at whose apex stood the temple and the palace. Without them the power complex could not operate. This condition remains true today, even though the existence of automated factories and computer-regulated units conceals the human components essential even to automation.

What would now be called science was an integral part of the new machine system from the beginning. This science, based on cosmic regularities, flourished with the cult of the sun: record-keeping, timekeeping, star-watching, calendar-making, coincide with and support the institution of kingship, even though no small part of the efforts of the priesthood were, in addition, devoted to interpreting the meaning of singular events, such as the appearance of comets or eclipses of the sun or moon, or natural irregularities, such as the flight of birds or the state of a sacrificed animal's entrails.

No king could move safely or effectively without the support of such organized higher knowledge, any more than the Pentagon can move today without consulting scientists, "games theorists," and computers, a new hierarchy supposedly less fallible than entrail-diviners, but to judge by their repeated miscalculations, not notably so. To be effective, this kind of knowledge must remain a priestly monopoly: if everyone had equal access to the sources of knowledge and to the system of interpretation, no one would believe in infallibility, since its errors could not be concealed. Hence the shocked protest of Ipuwer against the revolutionaries who overthrew the Old Kingdom was that the "secrets of the temple lay unbared;" that is, they had made "classified information" public. Secret knowledge belongs to any system of total control. Until printing was invented, this remained a class monopoly.

Not the least affiliation of kingship with the worship of the sun is the fact that the king, like the sun, exerts force at a distance. For the first time in history, power became effective outside the immediate range of hearing and vision and the arm's reach. No military weapon by itself sufficed to convey such power: what was needed was a special form of transmission gear: an army of scribes, messengers, stewards, super-intendents, gang bosses, and major and minor executives, whose very existence depended upon their carrying out the king's orders, or those of his powerful ministers and generals, to the letter. In other words, a bureaucracy: a group of men, capable of transmitting and executing a command, with the ritualistic punctilio of a priest, the mindless obedience of a soldier.

To fancy that bureaucracy is a relatively recent institution is to ignore the annals of ancient history. The first documents that attest the existence of bureaucracy belong to the Pyramid Age. In a cenotaph description at Abydos, a career official under Pepi I, in the Sixth Dynasty, c. 2375 B.C., reported "His majesty sent me at the head of this army, while the counts, while the Seal-bearers of the King of Lower Egypt, while the sole companions of the Palace, while the nomarchs (governors) and *mayors* of Upper and Lower Egypt, the companions and chief dragomans, the chief prophets of Upper and Lower Egypt, and the Chief bureaucrats were (each) at the head of a troop of Upper or Lower Egypt, or of the villages and towns which they might rule."

Not merely does this text establish a bureaucracy: it shows that the division of labor and specialization of functions necessary for efficient mechanical operation, had already taken place in the organization that, as executors of the sovereign's will, already controlled the operations of both the military and the labor machine. This development had begun at least three dynasties before: not by accident, with the building of the great stone pyramid of Djoser at Sakkara. Wilson observes, in *City Invincible* that "we credit Djoser, not only with the beginnings of monumental architecture in stone in Egypt, but also with the setting up of a new monster, the bureaucracy." This was no mere coincidence. And W. F. Albright, commenting upon this, pointed out that "the greater number of titles found in sealings of the First Dynasty . . . certainly pre-supposes an elaborate officialdom of some kind."

Once the heirarchic structure of the human machine was established, there was no limit to the number of hands it might control or the power it might exert. The removal of human dimensions and organic limits is indeed the chief boast of the authoritarian machine. Part of its productivity is due to its use of unstinted physical coercion to overcome human laziness or bodily fatigue. Occupational specialization was a necessary step in the assemblage of the human machine: only by intense specialization at every part of the process could the super-human accuracy and perfection of the product have been achieved. The large scale division of labor throughout industrial society begins at this point.

The Roman maxim, that the law does not concern itself with trifles, applies likewise to the human machine. The great forces that were set in motion by the king demanded collective enterprises of a commensurate order. These human machines were by nature impersonal, if not deliberately dehumanized; they had to operate on a big scale or they could not work at all; for no bureaucracy, however well organized, could govern a thousand little workshops, each with its own traditions, its own craft skills, its own wilful personal pride and sense of responsibility. So the form of control imposed by kingship was confined to great collective enterprises.

The importance of this bureaucratic link between the source of power, the divine king, and the actual human machines that performed the works of construction or destruction can hardly be exaggerated: all the more because it was the bureaucracy that collected the annual taxes and tributes that supported the new social pyramid and forcibly assembled the manpower that formed the new mechanical fabric. The bureaucracy was, in fact, the third type of "invisible machine," co-existing with the military and labor machines, and an integral part of the total structure.

Now the important part about the functioning of a classic bureaucracy is that it originates nothing: its function is to transmit, without alteration or deviation, the orders that come from above. No merely local information or human considerations must alter this inflexible transmission process—except by corruption. This administrative method ideally requires a studious repression of all the autonomous functions of the personality, and a readiness to perform the daily task with ritual exactitude. Not for the first time does such ritual exactitude enter into the process of work: indeed, it is highly unlikely that submission to colorless repetition would have been possible without the millennial discipline of religious ritual.

Bureaucratic regimentation was in fact part of the larger regimentation of life, introduced by this power-centered culture. Nothing emerges more clearly from the Pyramid texts themselves, with their wearisome repetitions of formulae, than a colossal capacity for enduring monotony: a capacity that anticipates the universal boredom achieved in our own day. Even the poetry of both early Egypt and Babylonia reveal this iterative hypnosis: the same words, in the same order, with no gain in meaning, repeated a dozen times—or a hundred times. This verbal compulsiveness is the psychical side of the systematic compulsion that brought the labor machine into existence. Only those who were sufficiently docile to endure this regimen at every stage from command to execution could become an effective unit in the human machine.

4. The Magnification of Power

Though the human machine was powerful, it was likewise extremely fragile: once the royal power was switched off, it "went dead." The royal machine reached the limit of its capabilities, without doubt, in the construction of the Great Pyramids. Soon after this came a revolt so shattering, so profound, that centuries passed before the severed regions of Egypt could be assembled once more under a single divine ruler. Never was power to be raised to such heights of absolute command again until our own day. But the institutional forces set in motion by this first effort continued to operate. Wherever the army, the bureaucracy, and the priesthood worked together under unified royal command, the technics of unqualified power would resume operation.

The marks of this new mechanical order can be easily recognized: and first, there is a change of scale. The habit of "thinking big" was introduced with the first human machines: a superhuman scale in the individual structure magnifies the sovereign authority and reduces the size and importance of all the necessary human components, except the central figure, the king himself. Both in practice and even more in fantasy, this magnification applied to time and to space. Kramer notes that in the early dynasties reigns of incredible length are attributed to legendary kings: a total of close to a quarter of a million years for the eight kings before the flood and a total of twenty-five thousand years for the first two dynasties after the flood: this tallies with similar periods that Egyptian priests were still assigning to ancient history when Herodotus and Plato visited them.

But this multiplication of years was only the secular side of the new conception of immortality: at first, in Egypt, solely the attribute of the divine king, though there, as one notes in Sumer where a whole court was massacred in the Royal Tomb at Ur to accompany the ruler to the next world, the king's servants and ministers might also participate in this imputed extension of life. In the Sumerian deluge myth Ziusudra the king (Noah's counterpart) is rewarded by the gods An and Enlil, not by a symbolic rainbow, but by being given "life like a god." The desire for life without limits was part of the general lifting of limits which the first great assemblage of power, by means of the machine, brought about.

But if death mocks at the infantile fantasy of absolute power, which the human machine promised to actualize, life mocks at it even more. The notion of eternal life, with neither conception, growth, fruition, or decay: an existence as fixed, as sterilized, as unchanging as that of the royal mummy, is only death in another form: a return to the state of arrest and fixation exhibited by the stable chemical elements that have not yet combined in sufficiently complex molecules to promote novelty and continued creativity. The old fertility gods did not shrink from the fact of death: they sought no infantile evasion, but promised rebirth and renewal, by prolongation of power. If the gods of power had not triumphed, if kingship had not found a negative mode of increasing the scope of the human machine and therewith bolstering up the royal claim to absolute obedience, the whole further course of civilization might have been radically different.

But along with the desire for eternal life, kings and their gods nourished other ambitions that have become part of the mythology of our own age. Etana, in the Sumerian fable, mounts an eagle to go in search of a curative herb for his sheep when they are stricken with sterility. At this moment, the dream of human flight was born, or at least became visible, though that dream still seemed so presumptuous that Etana, like Daedalus, was hurled to death as he neared his goal. Soon, however, kings were represented as winged bulls; and they had at their command heavenly messengers who conquered space and time in order to bring commands to their earthly subjects. Rockets and television sets were already beginning to germinate in this royal myth. The Genii of the *Arabian Nights* are only popular continuations of these earlier forms of power-magic.

Within the span of early civilization, 3000 to 1000 B.C., the formative impulse to exercise absolute control over both nature and man shifted back and forth between gods and kings. Joshua commanded the sun to stand still and destroyed the walls of Jericho by martial music:

but Yahweh himself, at an earlier moment, anticipated the Nuclear Age by destroying Sodom and Gomorrah with a single visitation of fire and brim-stone; and a while later He even resorted to germ warfare in order to demoralize the Egyptians and aid in the escape of the Jews.

In short, none of the destructive fantasies that have taken possession of leaders in our own age, from Hitler to Stalin, from the khans of the Kremlin to the khans of the Pentagon, were foreign to the souls of the divinely appointed founders of the first machine civilization. With every increase of effective power, extravagantly sadistic and murderous impulses emerged out of the unconscious: not radically different from those sanctioned, not only by Hitler's extermination of six million Jews and uncounted millions of other people, but the extermination by United States Air Force of 200,000 civilians in Tokyo in a single night by roasting alive. When a distinguished Mesopotamian scholar proclaimed that "civilization begins at Sumer" he innocently overlooked how much must be forgotten before this can be looked upon as a laudable achievement. Mass production and mass destruction are the positive and negative poles, historically, of the myth of the megamachine.

The other great prerogative of this royal technic is speed; for speed itself, in any operation, is a function of power and in turn becomes one of the chief means of displaying it. So deeply has this part of the myth of the machine become one of the uncriticized basic assumptions of our own technology that most of us have lost sight of its point of origin. But royal commands, like urgent commands in the army, are performed "on the double."

Nothing better illustrates this acceleration of pace than the fact that in Egypt, and later in Persia, each new monarch in the Pyramid Age built a new capital for use in his own lifetime. (Compare this with the centuries needed to build a medieval cathedral without royal resources for assembling power). On the practical side, roadbuilding and canal-building, which were the chief means for hastening transportation, have been all through history the favored form of royal public works: a form that reached its technological consummation in the Iron Age, with the building of the Corinth Canal through eighty feet or so of solid rock.

Only an economy of abundance, at a time when there were at most four or five million people in the Nile Valley, could have afforded to drain off the labor of a hundred thousand men annually, and provide them with sufficient food to perform their colossal task; for on the scale these works were executed, that was the most sterile possible use of man power. Though many Egyptologists cannot bring themselves to accept the implications, John Maynard Keynes' notion of Pyramid Building, as a necessary device for coping with the surplus labor force in an affluent society without resorting to social equalization, was not an inept metaphor. This was an archetypal example of simulated productivity. Rocket-building is our modern equivalent.

But the most lasting economic contribution of the first myth of the machine was the separation between those that worked and those that lived in idleness on the surplus extracted from the worker by reducing his standard of living to penury. According to Akkadian and Babylonian scriptures, no less than those of Sumer, the gods created men in order to free themselves from the hard necessity of work. Here, as in so many other places, the gods prefigure in fantasy what kings actually do. In times of peace, kings and nobles live by the pleasure principle; eating, drinking, hunting, playing games, and copulating endlessly. So at the very period when the myth of the machine was taking place, the problems of an economy of abundance first became visible in the behavior and the fantasies of the ruling classes.

If we watch the aberrations of the ruling classes throughout history, we shall see how far most of them were from understanding the limitations of power, or of a life that centered upon an effortless consumption: the reduced life of the parasite on a tolerant host. The boredom of satiety dogged this economy of surplus power and surplus food from the very beginning: it led to insensate personal luxury and even more insensate acts of collective delinquency and destruction.

One early example of this dilemma of affluence must suffice. An Egyptian story, translated by Flinders Petrie reveals the emptiness of a Pharaoh's life, in which every desire was too easily satisfied, and time hung with unbearable heaviness on his hands. Desperate, he appeals to his counsellors for some relief from his boredom; and one of them has a classic suggestion: that he fill a boat with thinly veiled, almost naked girls, who will paddle over the water and sing songs for him. For the hour, tedium, to the Pharaoh's great delight, was overcome; for, as Petrie aptly remarks, the vizier had invented the first Musical Revue: that solace of the "tired business man."

In short, at its earliest point of development under the myth of divine kingship, the amorality and the purposelessness of unlimited power were revealed in both religious legend and recorded history. Though the whole panoply of modern inventions lay beyond the scope of the collective machine, which could provide only partial and clumsy substitutes, the fundamental animus behind these inventions—the effort to conquer space and time, to expand human energy through the use of cosmic forces and to establish absolute human control over both nature and man, all had been planted and nurtured in the soil of fantasy.

Some of these seeds sprouted immediately: others which needed for their execution a far higher degree of technical skill, a higher capacity for logical and mathematical abstractions, required five thousand years before they were ready to sprout. When that happened, the divine king would appear again in a new form.

Man and Magic: First Encounters with the Machine

Oscar Handlin

Man confronts the machine with trepidation. Mechanization serves humans and also threatens them. Complex contrivances do the work of hundreds of laborers and also create profound social displacements. Enormous power that can send a craft into outer space can, misused, destroy life. What we admire, we therefore also dread.

These ambivalent attitudes have a long history that antedates by a good deal the period of high industrialization. The hopes and fears now attached to the machine, long ago also moved men whose wildest imaginings did not conceive the ingenious apparatus that became commonplace in the twentieth century.

In 1854 Herman Melville was living in Berkshire County, Massachusetts. Bitterly disappointed at the failure of *Moby Dick* and *Pierre*, he had tried unsuccessfully to secure a consular appointment. A somber mood undoubtedly influenced his work of this period. He wrote

From *The American Scholar*, Vol. 33, Summer, 1964.

comparatively little—only a few short stories and those not among his best. Yet one among them was a significant social document.

In it Melville described a paper factory, such as existed in his vicinity. The whole setting was dismal, and in accord with the gloom of the author. The Devil's Dungeon Paper Mill occupied a large whitewashed building "like some great white sepulchre." Passing though it, the narrator saw the "blank-looking" girls "pale with work," each a "tame minister" tending an "iron animal." "Machinery—that vaunted slave of humanity—here stood menially served by human beings."

At last the narrator stood before a great new $12,000 machine. "Something of awe now stole over me, as I gazed upon this *inflexible* iron animal. . . . What made the thing I saw so specially terrible to me was the metallic necessity, the unbudging fatality which governed it." The dismay and foreboding of this account were far removed from the idyllic descriptions, common at the time, of the wonders of Lowell and of its cheerful ladies of the loom. Melville's personal sense of depression made him more acutely sensitive to some human problems than his contemporaries and gave his observations special value.

The Massachusetts paper mills were neither very large nor particularly harsh in their treatment of employees. They were depressing because they harnessed those who labored there to a routine. The rows of girls stood before the machines like "so many mares haltered to the rack." They were totally controlled; and it was not right they should be so bound.

Underlying that protest was an unexpressed grievance against the machine as such. Routine was not necessarily an undesirable circumstance of human life. In other contexts, it stood for order and regularity. For the husbandman bound to the cycle of his crops, for the sailor who stood his appointed order of watches, routine was not debasing, as the mechanical pattern was. The routine established by the machine differed from that established by the seasons or by the orbit of the sun because it took no account of human considerations, because it operated in an uncongenial setting, and because it detached man from the natural forces that should regulate his life.

The iron animal enslaved those who served it. It went its own way, while the people bound to it ceased to be free. It limited man's will; and since it took no cognizance of moral consideration, it also limited his ability to make choices of good over evil.

The mechanical monster was particularly frightening because it was installed in the factory, in which labor was organized in a novel manner. The factory brought together workers in numbers that theretofore had only been managed through some form of servitude. An entrepreneur in 1800 who tried to conceive of how a hundred people should be mobilized and brought to act in coordination with the machine could fasten on but few precedents. He could imagine a military company or a ship's crew, a monastery or a poorhouse or a gaol. In each of these agglomerations, the essential element that permitted the coordination of many persons was a rigid code of discipline that curtailed the individual's freedom. It was no coincidence that the architecture of the early factories had much in common with that of the barracks, the military camp and the prison. Hence the foreboding that the power of the machine in this setting would constrict personal liberties.

In the factories, the machine exerted an unnatural effect upon the people who tended it. The routine of the farmer had been coordinate with the forces of the visible world around him, or at least it seemed so. The alterations of the seasons told him when to plant and when to reap; the rising and the setting sun told him when to begin his labors and when to rest. The machine disregarded all such considerations and operated at its own pace, winter and summer, day and night.

The new regime detached work from the other aspects of life. Melville's narrator asked why the operatives of whatever age were "indiscriminately called girls, never women." The answer was: "the fact of their being generally unmarried—that's the reason. . . . For our factory here, we will have no married women; they are apt to be off-and-on too much. We want none but steady workers: twelve hours to the day, day after day, through the three hundred and sixty-five days." They were all maidens and would remain so.

In time, the machine would be tended also by married women, as well as by men, boys and girls. But the situation Melville found was nevertheless symbolic. The early efforts at paternalism in some places quickly faded; and the workers confronted the enterprise alone in a relationship that was purely economic. All those who entered the factory did so as detached individuals. Within its gates, they were not members of families or of groups but isolated integers, each with his own line on the payroll; nothing extraneous counted. During the working hours, the laborers had no other identity than that established by the job. From being people who were parts of households, known by a whole community, they had been reduced to being servants of the machine. Hence the shock of such men as Melville in the initial encounter with what was to come.

Through most of the nineteenth century, however, these doubts agitated few but the intellectuals. Now and then the artisans displaced by the machines expressed their resentment in Luddite riots and in political hostility to the great corporations. But the masses actually employed in the factories accepted their new situation with surprising equanimity. Often they suffered from difficult conditions of labor and from even more difficult conditions of life. But their trials were tempered by a sense of confidence in the human capacity to master the devices that humans had fabricated. They were sure that man could control and use the enormous power of the machines.

They were encouraged in that belief by the fact that the experience of factory labor was not altogether as discontinuous with their past as it seemed to outsiders. The physical setting, for example, was not totally different. The earliest factories appeared in the rural countryside, not far removed from the familiar landscape of open fields, streams and woods. They used waterpower for a long time and thus gave the appearance of mills more complex than those familiar to every man, but essentially the same. Nor were the machines, whether of wood or iron, totally strange. The waterwheels, the great drive shafts and pulleys that dominated these plants embodied no essential new principles. To onlookers they were impressive in their ingenuity and power, but the manner of their operation was clearly visible and seemed but to extend and improve devices with which men had long been acquainted.

The nineteenth-century factory could be understood in terms of widespread attitudes, particularly strong in the United States, but also characteristic of Western society as a whole. Modern man was a tinkerer; he continually sought to avoid labor and to spare himself excessive strain. For generation after generation, he had searched for improvements toward that end; and the first machines of the nineteenth century were simply extensions of familiar techniques. It was characteristic, for instance, that one of the earliest American utopian works to conceive of invention as a way of liberating man from labor had a thoroughly rural setting. In Mary Griffith's *Three Hundred Years Hence* (1836), great machines, moved by some internal power, did all the work of agriculture.

Therefore, the machine could also be regarded as man's liberator, as Étienne Cabet had suggested it would be in *Voyage en Icarie*. In the series of great expositions that began at the Crystal Palace in London in 1851 and ran down through the end of the nineteenth century, the focal point was often the array of new machinery treated as symbolic of the age. The American commissioners to the Paris Universal Exposition of 1867 published six volumes of observations on the inventions exhibited there. In the introduction to their report, Secretary of State William H. Seward explained that it was "through the universal language of the products of labor" that "the artisans of all countries hold communication." Industrialization was "in the interests of the mass of the people" for it promoted "an appreciation of the true dignity of labor, and its paramount claims to consideration as the basis of national wealth and power." Far from fearing that the machine would debase man, Seward was confident that it would elevate him to new dignity.

By and large, the nineteenth century clung to its optimism. Edward Bellamy, John Macnie and the utopian novelists of the 1880's and 1890's had no doubt that the machine would liberate mankind through the abundance it created. They did not deny that it would also harness man to its service. But they welcomed the consequent routine, the regularity and the order. Bellamy explained that the idea of *Looking Backward* came to him when he "recognized in the modern military system" the prototype of the Industrial Army that manned his utopia. The men of the year 2000 had "simply applied the principle of universal military service . . . to the labor question." The gains in efficiency and affluence that followed solved all the problems of freedom raised by doing so.

H. G. Wells supplied a perfect encyclopedia of these hopes for the future. Beginning with his *Anticipations* (1902), a succession of roseate works showed the machine transforming and improving human life, which would evolve toward ever more centralized control. One state, one language, one ruling will would organize all men into efficient productive units. Indeed there would be no need at all for human labor as a source of energy. "Were our political and social and moral devices only as well contrived to their ends as a linotype machine . . . or an electric tram-car, there need now . . . be no appreciable toil in the world." Despite the anticipatory fears of those concerned with the future of man's spirit, in the last analysis there was faith that the machine remained a product of man and would obey his command.

Both the hopes and the fears persisted on beyond the turn of the century. Men continued to expect that the machine would compensate for the deficiencies of their own society and would resolve in the future the problems with which they could not deal in the present. *The Shape of Things to Come,* as H. G. Wells saw it, was dominated by industrial plenitude that was a product of invention. Self-consciously the engineers assumed that they could not only make the machines run but manage society as well; and the technocrats envisioned a mechanical order, efficient, antiseptic and capable of dealing with any contingency.

Yet doubts always offset the confidence. Karel Capek's *R.U.R.* in the 1920's created a sensation in its nightmare vision of a robot's universal which completely dominated humanity. The greatest of the popular artists, René Clair and Charlie Chaplin, in *À nous la liberté* and *Modern Times,* expressed an identical protest: the assembly line made man its slave, repressed his emotions and crushed his individuality. He could escape to freedom only by revolting against the machine. In *Brave New World* and *1984,* Aldous Huxley and George Orwell stood utopia on its head. The necessity for mobilizing large groups along military lines, which provided Bellamy with his Industrial Army, to these writers established a terrifying engine of oppression.

Much in these protests had a familiar ring; to a considerable degree these artists repeated the criticisms Melville had already made much earlier; to some extent their revulsion was the general response of the artist for the machine. Yet, there were indications that the threat after 1900 was increasingly menacing, the machine more dangerous to humanity than ever before.

The numbers involved were much larger than in any previous era. The factory no longer counted its employees in the scores, but in the thousands; and that increased the impersonality and rigid discipline of the plant. The analogy to the army became closer and more frightening as individual identity diminished in importance. The hordes that passed through the gates each morning had to be accounted for and their time put to a precise, measured, profitable use. Before the turn of the century, Frederick W. Taylor had already outlined the principles of industrial management; and the demands of efficiency were served with increasing severity as the decades passed. Technological innovation became not only an end in itself but also a means of establishing greater control over the labor force. The more enlightened enterprises recognized the importance of human relations; but they did so as a means of increasing their efficiency, and the devices they used had the further effect of manipulating the lives of their employees.

An altered environment increased the external pressures upon personality. In the second half of the nineteenth century the factories had become urban, either through the growth in the size of the towns in which they had been located or through the shift to metropolitan centers. All the difficulties of industrial experience were therefore compounded. The machine, the factory and the city became identified as a single entity oppressive of man.

Finally, toward the end of the nineteenth century, the machine itself changed. Regarded from the perspective of the onlooker, the first indication of the transformation was visual. In the factories built in 1900, the drive shafts and the pulleys were no longer visible. Power was transmitted through wires and tubes—often hidden—and the whole was covered up and shielded so that the machine gave the appearance of being self-contained and autonomous. The onlooker no longer saw a comprehensible apparatus; he saw an enclosed shape actuated by a hidden source of power from which the products flowed by an occult process.

Some of the changes in design were incidental to other purposes. The demands of safety, for instance, often produced the shields that concealed the mechanism of operation. Other modifications were aesthetic, although even those were related to the meaning the machine held for men. An unbroken sheet of black metal seemed more pleasing to the eye than a complex of belting and gears because it conformed to the idea of the machine as self-contained.

The application to the machine and to industry of electricity was an even more important break with past human experience. Men had been experimenting with various manifestations of electricity for two hundred years, but it remained a mysterious force, somehow confused with galvanic magnetism, somehow related to the secret of life, but not popularly understood, not as comprehensible as water and steam power had been. Even after a multitude of appliances had brought it into every home, few men could grasp how a current passing through a wire created light and sound or turned the wheels of great machines.

The growing gap between the machines and their users widened steadily. In the twentieth century it was no longer the tinkerer who was inventor. The innovations were less likely to be products of industrial experience than of a science that stood quite apart from the rest of life; the people who operated the machines understood neither the instruments they served nor the technical fund of knowledge that shaped the industrial process. The old fear that the "iron animals" would deprive man of his humanity was intensified by the fact that the machines were the products of a science that had itself become increasingly alien to the mass of men.

In Melville's day, there had still been no sharp distinction between the scientist and other men or between science and other kinds of learning. All knowledge was continuous and essentially of one sort; and it was accessible to anyone who had the wit to seek it. Higher education was then somewhat more formally organized than it had been in Franklin's Philadelphia, where a printer studied electricity, or a glazier, mathematics or a politician, philosophy or a farmer, botany. But the structural changes that isolated science from modern life had only just begun.

In the second half of the nineteenth century they proceeded rapidly and radically. Knowledge became specialized, professionalized and institutionalized. The three tendencies were interrelated and each had the effect of creating a closed body of skills and information not accessible to the uninitiated.

Specialization was the product of forces inside and outside science. The mere accumulation of data stored up in libraries and journals made it increasingly difficult for any individual to master more than a limited sector of any field. It seemed to follow that the more limited the field the more readily could it be mastered; and that, in itself, further encouraged specialization. In addition, the emphasis upon classification as the first step in all inductive learning induced scientists to mark out, and concentrate in, a distinctive and circumscribed field of research. Finally, the growing rigor of the tests for validation required constantly improved techniques; and it was a rare individual who commanded more than one set. Science became the province of the expert who excelled in the one subject he knew thoroughly.

The result was a high degree of compartmentalization. C. P. Snow's discussion of the "Two Cultures" has obscured the genuine issue. The problem was not so much the existence of two distinct—literary and scientific—cultures, but rather the fragmentation of all knowledge into a multitude of different disciplines, each familiar only to its own initiates. A chemist was not much more able to discourse with an astronomer than with a sociologist, or an economist with an anthropologist than with a physicist. The overlapping of techniques, language and subject matter kept some lines of communication open, but each field was really known only to those who specialized in it.

The tendency toward specialization certainly contributed to the great advances of modern science. But it also demanded such a high degree of competence that it, in fact, excluded the amateur and made the practice of science entirely professional. Learning now required a prescribed course of preparation; it imposed defined canons of judgment and validation; and it developed the *esprit de corps* of a coherent and united group.

Finally, specialization and professionalization tended to institutionalize science. Not only did research become so expensive that no individual could buy his own telescope, computer or cyclotron, but the organization of scientific enterprise increasingly fell into forms established by government, business, universities and foundations. These features facilitated the great achievements of the past century. They were also responsible for the developing gulf that set scientists off from other men.

Science, as a body of defined knowledge, had its own needs and set its own standards. But the population not served by science had needs of its own which it satisfied through its own ways of knowing. Side by side with the official defined science there appeared a popular science, vague, undisciplined, unordered and yet extremely influential. It touched upon the official science, but did not accept its limits. And it more adequately met the immediate requirements of the people.

The popular science was not always less correct, by our own standards, than the official science. It would be hard to assert with confidence, for instance, that the faith healing, nature cures and patent medicines of the 1890's were less effective than the ministrations of the graduates of recognized medical schools; or that the vision of the universe exposed in the Sunday supplement was less accurate than that of the physics textbook. By the tests of practice—of whether it worked—popular science did as well as the official science.

The deficiencies of popular science were of quite another order. It formed part of no canon that marked out its boundaries or established order among its various parts. It consisted rather of discontinuous observations, often the projection of fantasy and wish fulfillment, and generally lacking in coherence and consistency. Above all it embraced no test of validity save experience. It was as easy to believe that there was another world within the crust of the earth as that there were other worlds in outer space. One took the little pills; the pain went away. One heard the knocking; the spirits were there. The observable connections between cause and result were explanation enough. It was unnecessary to seek an understanding of the links in the chain between the two.

Popular science, in other words, was magic. The men and women who moved into the highly complex and technically elaborate industrial society of our times simply assimilated the phenomena about them in terms of the one comprehensible category they already knew, that of magic. And it was thus too that they understood the defined science of the laboratory and the university. The man who pressed a button and saw the light appear, who turned a switch and set the machine in motion felt no need to understand electricity or mechanics; the operations he performed made the limited kind of sense that the other mysterious events of life did.

The machine, which was a product of science, was also magic, understandable only in terms of *how* it worked, not of why. Hence the lack of comprehension or of control; hence also the mixture of dread and anticipation as in the past.

The complex relationships among man, magic and the machine, were foreshadowed in a modern version of one of the seminal human myths. Frankenstein is a dedicated young man who seeks knowledge to help mankind. He is a scientist who discovers the secret of life through the study of electricity, galvanism and chemistry, and applies his formula to create a machine-monster.

The monster quickly proves himself superior in power to the man. In the confrontation, the machine gives the orders: "Slave, I before reasoned with you, but you have proved yourself unworthy of my condescension. Remember that I have power. . . . I can make you so wretched that the light of day will be hateful to you. You are my creator, but I am your master;—obey!" It is no coincidence that the machine will seem the master to many men in modern society.

Within the limits of the story, the question properly rises: why does the monster become the oppressive master of men? It was not evil to begin with or created out of deliberate malice.

The machine speaks once more: "Once my fancy was soothed with dreams of virtue, of fame and of enjoyment. Once I falsely hoped to meet with beings who pardoning my outward form would love me for the excellent qualities I was capable of unfolding. . . . I cannot believe that I am the same creature whose thoughts were once filled with sublime and transcendent visions of the beauty and majesty of goodness. But it is even so; the fallen angel becomes a malignant devil." And it is even so that modern men will continue to think of the machine and of science—potentially good yet capable of perpetrating a frightful catalogue of sins.

The question remains: why this ominous foreboding, which antedated industrialization and was confirmed by it?

Mary Shelley later recalled the circumstances under which the idea came to her, in 1816, while she listened to her husband and Lord Byron pass the long evenings in talk by the shores of Lake Leman. Often their conversation turned to science and particularly to the mystery of electricity and to experiments in creating life through galvanism. And a vision suddenly came to her of the dreadful "effect of any human endeavour to mock the stupendous mechanism of the Creator of the world." The impiety inherent in the magic of which they spoke invited retribution.

Mary Shelley gave her novel a subtitle, *The Modern Prometheus.* She was thus aware of the connection of her theme with the ancient myth of the punishment visited upon the being who robbed heaven of fire for the benefit of man. It was a theme that her husband had also treated and that had recurred for centuries and would continue to recur in Western imaginative writing.

Even the most optimistic imaginations long continue to shudder with that primeval fear. "This accursed science, " exclaims H. G. Wells, "is the very Devil. You tamper with it—and it offers you gifts. And directly you take them it knocks you to pieces in some unexpected way. Old passions and new weapons—now it upsets your religion, now it upsets your social ideas, now it whirls you off to desolation and misery!" The ability to work miracles leaves the world "smashed and utterly destroyed."

In their first encounters with the machine some men, like Melville, already recognized it as a monstrous defiance of natural order and shuddered at the possible consequences. Their nineteenth-century contemporaries, however, were mostly dazzled by the enormous utility of the machine. But when it later lost its familiarity and became identified with the magic of science, the old terror welled up; they would be punished for the use of that forbidden fire that was of such great service to them. The trepidation wells up in us still.

Our Industrial Culture

Gerard Piel

One of our national assets at a critical hour in the Second World War was four thick volumes containing nothing but pages and pages of numbers. These pages of numbers had the same forbidding opacity as the logarithm tables with which most of us terminated our unhappy exposure to mathematics in our second year of high school. But they were significant, because, like those in the logarithm tables, these numbers expressed functions; that is, the numerical relationships between variables in a system of equations. The functions in this case, called Bessel functions, after the nineteenth-century astronomer Friedrich Wilhelm Bessel, expressed relationships between variables at a somewhat more advanced stage than trigonometry. The possession of these tables saved precious hours of computation at many centers engaged in the urgent business of developing new weapons for the fighting of the Second World War. In the laboratory at Los Alamos, for example, the Bessel functions helped to facilitate calculations involved in the development of the most horrendous weapon of all.

For the existence of these tables, the war effort was indebted to a less enthralling period of our nation's history. They were, in fact, a boondoggle of the Works Progress Administration. They recalled a time when the nation had too many engineers and too many scientists and when even some of our 1,100 Ph.D.'s in the field of mathematics were to be found on W.P.A. In those days, before the giant mechanical brains had put in their appearance, the forbidding labor of computation blocked the application of advanced mathematical methods in many fields of engineering. With a surplus of ordinary human brains available—unemployed clerks and accountants and the like—the mathematicians on W.P.A. put them to work compiling tables of Bessel functions and many other much needed numbers.

Today, with billions of dollars in public and private funds available each year for research and development, all kinds of urgent projects go begging for lack of engineers and scientists. The shortage of talent is advertised in all of our major cities by pages of display copy in the help-wanted sections of the Sunday newspapers. One corporation president has declared his readiness to hire the entire class of 1955, from engineers on up through Ph.D.'s in physics. Today there are no unemployed mathematicians. Nearly a fourth of them have left the campus to go to work for industry, where they command a median salary of $9,100 a year.

It may seem surprising then, in this seller's market for their talents, that there are scientists and mathematicians who sigh for the old days. Physicists recall the times when "sealing wax and string and love" were all they needed to do their work. Some mathematicians have even been heard to say that they wish they were back on W.P.A.

The discontent among the scientists arises from their feeling that the work for which they are now so well paid is not the work of science. The billions available for expenditure on research and development, in the view of many scientists, are not going toward the improvement of the situation of science in America. On the contrary, these expenditures are using up irreplaceable resources. The money and the talent that it buys are going not into the advance of science and the lofty, long-range goals it sets for human capacity, but the lowly, short-term gains of practical advantage in weapons, productive machinery, and consumer goods. For the future welfare of our technology and our science alike, they fear that irreversible damage is being done to our scientific resources.

It is a confession often made by American engineers and scientists that the United States has made less than its proportionate contribution to the advance of basic scientific knowledge. In the words of one distinguished chemical engineer, Crawford Greenewalt, president of Du Pont Company, "We have been fortunate in the past in having available to us the results of basic science from the world at large. This has permitted us to indulge our industrial genius without at the same time contributing our fair share to the world's fund of basic knowledge."

Among the few Americans who are credited with major achievements in the advance of basic understanding is Benjamin Franklin. His investigations of the nature of lightning—according to the Latin inscription on a famous portrait: "He snatched lightning from the sky and the scepter from the hand of the tyrant"—establish him as an experimenter of the first rank; it is less well known that Franklin made fundamental contributions to the theory of electricity—represented by such terms as "charge," "plus" and "minus," "current," and "pressure"—which are still used in the textbooks of today. We have to skip more than a century of American history before we come to Josiah Willard Gibbs, whose contributions to the theory of thermodynamics pervade all of the disciplines in industry and in science that deal with the behavior of matter.

It is difficult, of course, to measure a nation's attainments in any branch of culture, even science, by objective standards. If we take the admittedly special record of the annual award of Nobel Prizes for such a standard, however, we see that it is not until the present generation that American scientists begin to win these prizes in proportion to our possession of the world's wealth and technological power.

Our industrial system rests upon discoveries of fundamental new knowledge and basic scientific principles which were made in Europe. It was there that scientists formulated the laws governing the play of natural forces, the transformations of energy and the nature and behavior of matter and energy, the chemical behavior of matter, that underlie the giant achievements of American industry. Even in our own day, we have seen the technology of nuclear energy arise from the work of scientists who came to our country from abroad.

In the realm of applied science as well, we must credit Europe with such basic developments as the machine tool, the steam engine, the steam turbine, the dynamo, and the internal combustion engine. Like the Soviet Union today, America was able to import a largely full-grown and mature technology from abroad to accomplish its industrial revolution. As recently as the First World War, the American economy was dependent upon Germany for its supply of critical organic chemicals. Only with the seizure of the German patents did American industrial enterprise enter this field.

Thus, the primary technological distinction of the United States lies neither in fundamental science nor even in engineering. America's pre-eminence rests upon the national capacity to organize technology on a grand scale. For the evocation of this capacity, Americans have been fortunate in the possession of the resources of a continent and a political system that made the continent the market for its own abundance. American industry could take advantage, as could no other national industrial establishment, of the efficiencies made possible by capital investment. The result is the giantism that characterizes American technology. The efficient unit of production in America is larger than in any other country. Our steel industry can build an entire plant around a high-speed, continuous-strip mill that rolls a ribbon of steel ten feet wide. The only reason for rolling such a wide strip is the convenience and economy of the one-piece automobile roof, drawn with one stroke of a giant press; the widest sheet rolled abroad is eighty inches. Similarly, it is only in the United States that an automobile manufacturer can tool an engine plant for the production of ten million identical units and thereby achieve a degree of automatization that is the envy of engineers abroad. The resultant reduction in the labor cost of American manufactured products prices them within the means of the mass market.

Science did not begin to receive the encouragement of significant patronage in this country until the turn of the century. It was then that the first giant fortunes accumulated in the American industrial revolution became available for such nonutilitarian enterprises as the advancement of learning. In testimony to the patrons' aspiration to disassociate their philanthropy from the harsh world of industry and commerce, the largest sums went to astronomy and medical research. Consequently, it was in these fields that American science first established claim to world eminence. No other nation's scientific establishment approaches the American in the magnificence of its observatories, and the United States excels all other nations in the number of first-rate medical research institutions per unit of population.

Other departments of science in our universities came in for their share of funds during the first half of this century, through the swelling of university endowments. A decisive role in the broadening and diversification of support was played by the Rockefeller fortune. It financed the reconstruction of the entire system of medical education and set the system on the path of self-sustained progress, with teaching fructified by research. The list of Rockefeller fellows contains, among others, the names of the first generation of American nuclear physicists

—Rabi, Oppenheimer, Lawrence, Allison, Smyth, and others—whose fellowships took them to the great centers in Europe for their training in this new field. In big sums, Rockefeller money went to the creation of new centers of scientific enterprise, at the Rockefeller Institute in New York City, at Vanderbilt University, and at Washington University in St. Louis. In smaller sums, in accord with the strategy devised by Warren Weaver, the Rockefeller Foundation laid "greatly increasing emphasis on biology and psychology, and on those special developments in mathematics, physics and chemistry which are themselves fundamental to biology." There is no doubt that this strategy contributed heavily to the great distinction of American science in genetics, biochemistry, biophysics, and the other growing points in the life sciences where physics and chemistry have been brought to bear. When the first generation of American nuclear physicists was ready with original work of its own, it was Rockefeller money that staked them in the building of the first giant accelerator, the Berkeley cyclotron, completed in 1940, just in time to make its contribution to the Manhattan Project. That the Rockefeller influence was considerable may be judged from the calculation that the total Rockefeller outlay at least equaled the total endowment income available to science in our universities through the first four decades of this century.

On a dollar basis, however, the most impressive development in this period was the initiation and the expansion of industrial research, starting in those industries that were dependent upon the most recent advances in science, first the communications and electrical industries and then, after the First World War, the chemical industry. By 1940 the nation's total annual investment in research and development had climbed to $350 million. This was a little less than 0.5 per cent of our gross national product and compared unfavorably with the 1 per cent or more that was maintained in England and Germany. Characteristically, the bulk of these funds, $240 million, came from industry. Some $70 million was provided by the federal treasury, and only $35 million, a tenth of the total, came from other sources, including university endowments.

It is a commonplace that money has strings tied to it. Given the fact that most of the money for science was supplied by taxpayers and stockholders, we must conclude that the bulk of it was directed to applied science—or science as means to an end—rather than science as an end in itself. On the most favorable basis, it has been calculated that not more than one dollar out of every six was then going to the support of basic research.

Of course, the dollar figure may not be the most reliable index of the division of effort. It costs a great deal more to do industrial research than to equip a pure mathematician with his blackboard and chalk. But in England, where the development of industrial research was admittedly retarded, the corresponding ratio of support for applied research was estimated to be about fifty-fifty.

It was at the outbreak of the Second World War that the United States first came to recognize science as an essential element of national strength, to be ranked equal in importance to the industrial and military establishments. From the outset, the scientific community was the most thoroughly mobilized of all of the elements in our population. Thanks to the indiscriminate policies of our draft act, teaching as well as basic research was suspended for the duration. The nation's scientists became engineers for the duration, engineers in the all-embracing discipline of scientific warfare.

The mobilization of science for the Second World War makes a memorable chapter in our history. Whereas the industrial might and the manpower of the nation were mobilized under draft, the scientists of the country came forward on their own initiative to press their services upon the government. Long before Pearl Harbor, the "uranium committee" assembled the few score workers in the new science of nuclear physics. They rounded up their own funds, set up their own security system, and conducted the first fateful and conclusive experiments before they persuaded the federal government to back them in the Manhattan Project. Less well known is the story of the research in biological warfare, which originated in a masterful two-hundred-page monograph prepared by two Columbia University biologists and submitted by them in secret to the War Department.

These and other volunteer efforts were co-ordinated by the organization of the Office of Scientific Research and Development as a formal government agency. Headed by leaders of the scientific community, this agency not only deployed its own substantial budget but guided the expenditure of a tenfold increase in the annual federal outlay for research. The concerting of money and talent reduced years of development to months and brought such spectacular new arts and devices as radar and sonar, the proximity fuse, and servo-mechanism control of gunfire from the laboratory to the battlefield in time to play a decisive part in victory. With equal dispatch, it brought penicillin and blood plasma into mass production to reduce battlefield deaths to less than 2 per cent of the wounded delivered to battalion aid stations on the battlefield. The applied Mathematics Panel of the O.S.R.D.

brought radically new and powerful methods to the task of quality control in the factories and to the rationalization of the technology and tactics of aerial warfare. But no development so completely symbolizes the role that science played in the fighting of the war as the double thunderclap at Hiroshima and Nagasaki.

In the demobilization, there was no cutting of expenditures for research and development comparable to the slashing of budgets in other departments of the federal government. Government and industry were now committed to support science on the same grand scale to which it had become so uncomfortably accustomed in the war. The nation's annual outlay for science has mounted from $350 million in 1940 to more than $3 billion in 1955.

In the universal euphoria the one note of dissent was sounded by the scientists themselves. Their mood is best expressed in a mournful ballad sung by the atomic scientists at one of their first professional meetings at the end of the war. The last verse goes:

> Take away your billion dollars, take away your tainted gold,
> You can keep your damn ten billion volts, my soul will not be sold.
> Take away your Army generals; their kiss is death, I'm sure.
> Everything I build is mine, and every volt I make is pure.
> Oh, dammit! Engineering isn't physics, is that plain?
> Take, oh take, your billion dollars, let's be physicists again.

The sentiments of the atomic scientists were shared by the scientific community at large. With equal eloquence, in prose, other scientists urged all who would listen to take account of the important distinction between engineering and science. They presented their brief to the public in an impressive series of hearings before the Kilgore Committee of the U.S. Senate and in the Bush and the Steelman reports, prepared at the direction of Presidents Roosevelt and Truman.

Things like atomic bombs and penicillin, they said, show us what we can do with knowledge we have already won. This application of existing knowledge to practical ends is the business of applied science, or engineering. Science, in contrast, is concerned with increasing our knowledge through the investigation of the unknown. The continued progress of applied science requires sustained advance in pure science. As the Bush Report declared: "Basic research leads to new knowledge. It provides scientific capital. It creates the fund from which the practical applications of knowledge must be drawn. New products and new processes do not appear fullgrown. They are founded on new principles and new conceptions, which in turn are painstakingly developed by research in the purest realms of science."

With pure science suspended for the duration, the wartime developments had eaten heavily into the accumulated capital of scientific knowledge. Vannevar Bush said: "We have been living on our fat." The Steelman Report pointed out that "our country has made less than its proportionate contribution to basic science" and that, in such projects as the atomic bomb, our scientists were merely exploiting basic knowledge that had been established abroad, by German, French, English, Russian, and Italian investigators. The destruction of the ancient centers of learning abroad portended the drying up of the traditional springs of new knowledge. With the continued neglect of science threatening to bring the advance of engineering to a halt, our industrial system faced the prospect of intellectual bankruptcy.

The reports were unanimous in prescription as well as diagnosis. It was clear that pure science could no longer depend on private philanthropy to offset the overriding demand by government and industry for applied science. The future of science was now dependent upon the taxpayer. Through their government citizens must now open up the endless frontier of science. Just as, in the past, the opening of the public domain had fostered the rise of our industrial prosperity, so the expanding public domain of scientific knowledge would guarantee its future.

Specifically, the reports urged the establishment of a National Science Foundation. This agency would be devoted exclusively to the financing of pure research. It would become the agency through which public funds, in tens of millions of dollars, could redress the balance in emphasis between pure and applied science.

Today, after a decade, the vision of an expanding public domain of pure science financed by the taxpayer is far short of realization. For lack of public interest, it took five years to get the National Science Foundation through Congress. In the interim, thanks to statesmanlike management, the Office of Naval Research served as a kind of under-the-table National Science Foundation, finding seagoing justification for such unnaval studies as the behavior of army ants and the navigation of bats. This year the National Science Foundation has $15 million to spend. But this outlay must support its entire program, including the financing of scholarships and fellowships as well as the backing of research. Meanwhile the total research and development budget of the federal government has mounted to $2 billion. The weight with which these huge expenditures fall upon the side of applied science is indicated by the fact that 75 per cent of the total is laid out by the Department of Defense and another 10 per cent by the Atomic Energy Commission.

Industry has meanwhile increased its expenditures nearly five times to more than $1 billion a year. The current directory of industrial research laboratories lists nearly 30,000 of these institutions. Their glass-brick façades and green lawns have become a familiar feature of the suburban landscape and the four-color covers of corporate annual reports.

As against the total $3 billion expenditure by industry and government, the income from endowments and philanthropy adds up to no more than $90 million, compared with $35 million before the war. If we enter the inflation discount, the free funds available to science for research in our universities are not much greater than in 1940. They constitute a minority interest even in the financing of the work of scientists within our universities. More than $500 million of the outlays of the federal government and industry is expended through contracts in universities and other non-profit laboratories. To put themselves in the way of these funds, our universities have been developing a new corporate device. This is the off-campus research institute, which undertakes applied research and development projects under contract to industry and government. By means of this device some insulation is provided for the university's own research laboratories against the stigma of commercialism and the nuisance of the security system surrounding military research. On the other hand, many institutions are conducting these extracurricular activities under their own roof.

It is difficult, of course, to determine in any exact way what proportion of the total national budget of somewhat more than $3 billion is expended on applied as against pure research. In the laboratory itself, there can be no hard and fast distinction. The most hopeful estimate of the National Science Foundation is that one out of every fifteen dollars of the government's expenditures goes to pure science. Given the even stronger practical bias that corporate management must lay upon the expenditure of its stockholders' funds, the emphasis in industrial expenditures must go more heavily to applied science. The truth, therefore, is that we are spending about one dollar on pure science for every twenty dollars available for applied science, as against the ratio of one to six which prevailed before the war.

The important point is that both kinds of money seek the time and talent of the same finite number of qualified investigators who constitute our country's primary scientific capital. A ratio of twenty to one in favor of applied science sets up a powerful and all-pervading pressure that subtly modifies the aims of a career in science, brings competing and inappropriate values into the university laboratory, and subverts the character of the scientific enterprise. The scientist who stays on the campus does so at the personal cost of a large differential in income and under the professional hazard of having to promote the largest portion of support for his work from external souces. In weaker institutions a professorship has come to be little more than a "hunting license," and even in strong institutions the standard of performance is to multiply "hard" money three times over in "soft," or short-term support. Industrial consultantships and research salaries attached to government contracts help to ease the personal-income differential; soft money comes most easily from sources interested in the project rather than the man. Quick solutions and the heady sense of participation in large events carry more immediate satisfactions than the lonely gamble on a lifelong work. These are the poignant circumstances expressed by the gross statistics of expenditure on science. They have prompted more than one honorable scientist to cry out for peace and quiet on the campus.

Meanwhile, in the big world outside of the academy, science continues to ascend in influence and prestige. Along with 400,000 engineers, industry now employs nearly 100,000 scientists. On the average, the technical personnel of industry represent one out of every forty employees. Some industries employ as few as ten workers for every engineer or scientist, and some companies, including some very big ones, have as few as five. The office of director of research has attained top-managerial status, and Ph.D.'s are moving thence with ease into full command—three of the seven largest chemical companies are headed by Ph.D.'s.

The arrival of the scientist in industry has had an almost equally remarkable effect upon the strategy of industrial management. With industry spending $30 billion a year on new plant and equipment, it is the initiative and judgment of the director of research that heavily determine what business his company will be in five years from now. The Du Pont Company reports that half of its sales and more than 75 per cent of its profits come from products that were in the research laboratory only ten years ago. The security analyst of today must consult the scientific journals as well as the balance sheet in forecasting the growth of corporations.

The acceleration in the tempo of technological progress continues itself to accelerate. Whereas it took one hundred years for the steam engine to make its arrival felt in economic and social history, and fifty years for electricity to have its impact, the present interval between a discovery in the basic sciences and its application in technology seems to have shrunk to a decade. Applied science has been brought into the closest liaison with current progress in the pure sciences.

The gigantic industrial installations of nuclear technology embody ideas and concepts that existed in the heads of only a few physicists just a few years ago. In some industries, notably communications, electronics, aircraft, and chemicals, the progress of technology presses on the limits of knowledge. The prospect of power from the fusion reactions has brought the even more remote discipline of astrophysics into engineering. It is for assistance in these realms that industry and government now bring their hundreds of millions of dollars to the university laboratories and the off-campus research institutes.

There is much, therefore, to support the view that the continued progress of technology is confronted with an impasse. In our eagerness to exploit the possibilities of applied science, we have neglected the claims of pure science. As we use up the accumulated capital of basic knowledge, the progress of technology must slow down and come eventually to a halt.

Some of the questions confronting applied research are fundamental in the deepest sense and open new pathways in basic research. They would never have occurred to an investigator working in isolation from technology; they are generated by the high complexity of the industrial system. But the problems raised by technology tend to become the only fundamental ones, because they are advanced with the most compelling insistence by the system itself. Increasingly, the existing order of technology tends to assert the priorities of research and give direction to the work of science. Progress may therefore continue. But, as in organic evolution, the increasing intricacy and specialization of the system must set corresponding restrictions upon the possibilities for further growth.

It may be that we are already surfeited with technology—although that is a statement one hears only from citizens of the world's more fortunate nations. It may even be argued that existing technology is adequate to the satisfaction of the material wants of mankind, even with allowance for the present steep increase in world population. If the advance of technology supplied the sole motive for work in science, then the book might be closed without regret.

But, of course, this is not the case, and the work of science is not yet done. To bring the work to a stop, men must be made to stop asking questions. The brave new world that takes up this task will need all of the crushing and insidious power that a highly advanced technology can place in willful hands.

We still have many questions to ask; we have just begun, in fact, to ask the right ones. Our concern to be answered engages larger aspects of our existence than the utilitarian ends, vital as these are, that are served by technology. The appeal to utility, which helped to sell Congress on the National Science Foundation, must not be permitted to obscure the public's true interest in the public domain of science. That interest is identical with the true interest of the scientist; it is the need to understand. Paul Sears, a botanist and student of human ecology, has defined this interest: "It is the great destiny of science not to ease man's labors or prolong his life, noble as these aims may be, nor to serve the ends of power, but to enable man to walk upright without fear in a world which he at length will understand and which is his home.

If the scientific enterprise is to flourish under public patronage, it must be supported for the right reasons. The taxpayer, who has succeeded the philanthropist as the patron of science, must advance those reasons. He must do so against the claims of special interests in government and industry that press forward with the wrong motives today.

What this implies is public support of higher education as well as of research, for the two functions of the university are inextricably involved with each other. Curiously, while university presidents set up new departments in their cabinets to promote public funds, they continue to debate the propriety of public support. The bogey of political control of our universities fades, however, by comparison with the consequences of the present traffic with selfish interests. Peace and quiet must be restored to the campus. Our universities must be reconstituted as autonomous centers of initiative, independent of their sources of income and beyond intimidation in their service as primary springs of innovation and change in the life of society.

Man's Conquest of Space

Hannah Arendt

Has man's conquest of space increased or diminished his stature? The question raised is addressed to the layman, not the scientist, and it is inspired by the humanist's concern with man, as distinguished from the physicist's concern with the reality of the physical world. To understand physical reality seems to demand not only the renunciation of an anthropocentric or geocentric world view, but also a radical elimination of all anthropomorphic elements and principles, as they arise either from the world given to the five human senses or from the categories inherent in the human mind. The question assumes that man is the highest being we know of, an assumption which we have inherited from the Romans, whose *humanitas* was so alien to the Greek frame of mind that they had not even a word for it. (The reason for the absence of the word *humanitas* from Greek language and thought was that the Greeks, in contrast to the Romans, never thought that man is the highest being there is. Aristotle calls this belief *atopos,* "absurd.") This view of man is even more alien to the scientist, to whom man is no more than a special case of organic life, and to whom man's habitat—the earth, together with earthbound laws—is no more than a special borderline case of absolute, universal laws, that is, laws that rule the immensity of the universe. Surely, the scientist cannot permit himself to ask: What consequences will the result of my investigations have for the stature (or, for that matter, for the future) of man? It has been the glory of modern science that it has been able to emancipate itself completely from all such truly humanistic concerns.

The question propounded here, insofar as it is addressed to the layman, must be answered in terms of common sense and in everyday language (if it can be answered at all). The answer is not likely to convince the scientist, because he has been forced, under the compulsion of facts and experiments, to renounce sense perception and hence common sense, by which we coordinate the perception of our five senses into the total awareness of reality. He has also been forced to renounce normal language, which even in its most sophisticated conceptual refinements remains inextricably bound to the world of the senses and to our common sense. For the scientist, man is no more than an observer of the universe in its manifold manifestations. The progress of modern science has demonstrated very forcefully to what an extent this observed universe, the infinitely small no less than the infinitely large, escapes not only the coarseness of human sense perception but even the enormously ingenious instruments that have been built for its refinement. The phenomena with which modern physical research is concerned turn up like "mysterious messengers from the real world," according to Max Planck in *The Universe in the Light of Modern Physics,* and we know no more about them than that they affect our measuring instruments in a certain way, suspecting all the while with Eddington that "the former have as much resemblance to the latter as a telephone number has to a subscriber."

The goal of modern science, which eventually and quite literally has led us to the moon, is no longer "to augment and order" human experiences (as Niels Bohr, still tied to a vocabulary that his own work has helped to make obsolete, described it); it is much rather to discover what lies *behind* natural phenomena as they reveal themselves to the senses and the mind of man. Had the scientist reflected upon the nature of the human sensory and mental apparatus, had he raised questions such as *What is the nature of man and what should be his stature? What is the goal of science and why does man pursue knowl-*

edge? or even *What is life and what distinguishes human from animal life?*, he would never have arrived where modern science stands today. The answers to these questions would have acted as definitions and hence as limitations of his efforts. In the words of Niels Bohr, "Only by renouncing an explanation of life in the ordinary sense do we gain a possibility of taking into account its characteristics."

That the question proposed here makes no sense to the scientist *qua* scientist is no argument against it. The question challenges the layman and the humanist to sit in judgment over what the scientist is doing, and this debate must of course be joined by the scientists themselves insofar as they are fellow citizens. But all answers given in this debate, whether they come from laymen or philosophers or scientists, are nonscientific (although not antiscientific); they can never be demonstrably true or false. Their truth resembles rather the validity of agreements than the compelling validity of scientific statements. Even when the answers are given by philosophers whose way of life is solitude, they are arrived at by an exchange of opinions among many men, most of whom may no longer be among the living. Such truth can never command general agreement, but it frequently outlasts the compellingly and demonstrably true statements of the sciences which, especially in recent times, have the uncomfortable inclination never to stay put, although at any given moment they are, and must be, valid for all. In other words, notions such as life, or man, or science, or knowledge are prescientific by definition, and the question is whether or not the actual development of science which has led to the conquest of terrestrial space and to the invasion of the space of the universe has changed these notions to such an extent that they no longer make sense. For the point of the matter is, of course, that modern science—no matter what its origins and original goals—has changed and reconstructed the world we live in so radically that it could be argued that the layman and the humanist, still trusting their common sense and communicating in everyday language are out of touch with reality, and that their questions and anxieties have become irrelevant. Who cares about the stature of man when he can go to the moon? This sort of bypassing the question would be very tempting indeed if it were true that we have come to live in a world that only the scientists "understand." They would then be in a position of the "few" whose superior knowledge entitles them to rule the "many," namely, the laymen and the humanists and the philosophers, or all those who raise prescientific questions because of ignorance.

This division between the scientist and the layman, however, is very far from the truth. The fact is not merely that the scientist spends more than half of his life in the same world of sense perception, of common sense, and of everyday language as his fellow citizens, but that he has come in his own privileged field of activity to a point where the naïve questions and anxieties of the layman have made themselves felt very forcefully, albeit in a different manner. The scientist has not only left behind the layman with his limited understanding, he has left behind himself and his own power of understanding, which is still human understanding, when he goes to work in the laboratory and begins to communicate in mathematical language. Max Planck was right, and the miracle of modern science is indeed that this science could be purged "of all anthropomorphic elements," because the purging itself was done by men. The theoretical perplexities that have confronted the new nonanthropocentric and nongeocentric (or heliocentric) science because its data refuse to be ordered by any of the natural mental categories of the human brain are well enough known. In the words of Erwin Schrödinger, the new universe that we try to "conquer" is not only "practically inaccessible, but not even thinkable," for "however we think it, it is wrong; not perhaps quite as meaningless as a 'triangular circle,' but much more so than a 'winged lion.'"

Even these perplexities, since they are of a theoretical nature and perhaps concern only the few, are nothing compared to such paradoxes existing in our everyday world as electronic "brains," devised and constructed by men, which can not only do man's brain work incomparably better and more swiftly (this, after all, is the outstanding characteristic of all machines), but can do "what a human brain cannot *comprehend*," as George Gamow recently put it in a very interesting essay on the "Physical Sciences and Technology," in *The Great Ideas Today 1962.* the often mentioned "lag" of the social sciences with respect to the natural sciences or of man's political development with respect to his technical and scientific know-how is no more than a red herring drawn into this debate, and can only divert attention from the main problem, which is that man can *do,* and successfully do, what he cannot comprehend and cannot express in everyday human language.

It may be noteworthy that among the scientists it was primarily the older generation, men like Einstein and Planck, Niels Bohr and Schrödinger, who were most acutely worried about this state of affairs which their own work had chiefly brought about. They were still firmly rooted in a tradition that demanded that scientific theories fulfill certain definitely humanistic requirements such as simplicity, beauty and harmony. A theory was still supposed to be "satisfactory," namely, satisfactory to human reason in that it served to "save the phenomena," to explain all observed facts. Even today, we still hear that "modern physicists are inclined to believe in the validity of general relativity for aesthetic reasons, because it is mathematically so elegant and philosophically so satisfying" (Sergio de Benedetti). Einstein's extreme reluctance to sacrifice the principle of causality as Planck's Quantum Theory demanded is well known; his main objection was of course that with it all lawfulness was about to depart from the universe, that it was as though God ruled the world by "playing dice." And since his own discoveries, according to Niels Bohr, had come about through a "remolding and generalizing [of] the whole edifice of classical physics . . . lending to our world picture a unity surpassing all previous expectations," it seems only natural that Einstein tried to come to terms with the new theories of his colleagues and his successors through "the search for a more complete conception," through a new and surpassing generalization. Thus Max Planck could call the Theory of Relativity "the completion and culmination of the structure of classical physics," its very "crowning point." But Planck himself, although fully aware that the Quantum Theory, in contrast to the Theory of Relativity, signified a complete break with classical physical theory, held it to be "essential for the healthy development of physics that among the postulates of this science we reckon, not merely the existence of law in general, but also the strictly causal character of this law."

Niels Bohr, however, went one step further. For him, causality, determinism, and necessity of laws belonged to the categories of "our necessarily prejudiced conceptual frame," and he was no longer frightened when he met "in atomic phenomena regularities of quite a new kind, defying deterministic pictorial description." The trouble is that what defies description in terms of the "prejudices" of the human mind defies description in every conceivable way of human language; it can no longer be described at all, and it is being expressed, but not described, in mathematical processes. Bohr still hoped that, since "no experience is definable without a logical frame," these new experiences would in due time fall into place through "an appropriate widening of the conceptual framework" which would also remove all present paradoxes and "apparent disharmonies." But this hope, I am afraid, will be disappointed. The categories and ideas of human reason have their ultimate source in the human senses, and all conceptual or metaphysical language is actually and strictly metaphorical. Moreover, the human brain which supposedly does our thinking is as terrestrial, earthbound, as any other part of the human body. It was precisely by abstracting from these terrestrial conditions, by appealing to a power of imagination and abstraction that would, as it were, lift the human mind out of the gravitational field of the earth and look down upon it from some point in the universe, that modern science reached its most glorious and, at the same time, most baffling achievements.

In 1929 shortly before the arrival of the Atomic Revolution, marked by the splitting of the atom and the conquest of universal space, Planck demanded that the results obtained by mathematical processes "must be translated back into the language of the world of our senses if they are to be of any use to us." The three decades that have passed since these words were written have proved not only that such translation seems less and less possible, and that the loss of contact between the physical world view and the sense world has become even more conspicuous, but also—and in our context this is even more alarming—that this has by no means meant that results of this new science are of no practical use, or that the new world view, as Planck had predicted in case the translation back into ordinary language should fail, "would be no better than a bubble ready to burst at the first puff of wind." On the contrary, one is tempted to say that it is much more likely that the planet we inhabit will go up in smoke as a consequence of theories that are entirely unrelated to the world of the senses, and defy all description in human language, than that even a *hurricane* will cause the theories to burst like a bubble.

It is, I think, safe to say that nothing was more alien to the minds of the scientists, who brought about the most radical and the most rapid revolutionary process the world has ever seen, than any will to power. Nothing was more remote than any wish to "conquer space" and to go to the moon. Nor were they prompted by an unseemly curiosity in the sense of a *temptatio oculorum.* It was indeed their search for "true reality" that led them to lose confidence in appearances, in the phenomena as they reveal themselves of their own accord to human sense and reason. They were inspired by an extraordinary love of harmony and lawfulness which taught them that they would have to step outside any merely given sequence or series of occurrences if they wanted to discover the overall beauty and order of the whole, that is, the universe. (This may explain why they seem to have been less distressed by the fact that their discoveries served the invention of the most murderous gadgets than they have been disturbed by the shattering of all their most cherished ideals of necessity and lawfulness. These ideals were lost when the scientists discovered that there is nothing indivisible in matter, no *a-tomos,* that we live in an expanding, nonlimited universe, and that chance seems to rule supreme wherever this "true reality," the physical world, has receded entirely from the range of human senses and from the range of all instruments by which their coarseness was refined.)

The modern scientific enterprise began with thoughts never thought before (Copernicus, we are told by J. Bronowski in *Science and Human Values,* imagined he was "standing in the sun . . . overlooking the planets") and with things never seen before (Galileo's telescope pierced the distance between earth and sky and in his own words delivered the secrets of the stars to human cognition "with all the certainty of sense evidence"). It reached its classic expression with Newton's law of gravitation, in which the same equation covers the movements of the heavenly bodies and the motion of terrestrial things on earth. Einstein indeed only generalized this science of the modern age when he introduced an "observer who is poised freely in space," and not just at one definite point like the sun, and he proved that not only Copernicus but also Newton still required "that the universe should have a kind of center" although this center of course was no longer the earth. It is in fact quite obvious that the scientists' strongest intellectual motivation was Einstein's "striving after generalization," and that if they appealed to power at all, it was the interconnected formidable power of abstraction and imagination. Even today, when billions of dollars are spent year in and year out for highly "useful" projects that are the immediate results of the development of pure, theoretical science, and when the actual power of countries and governments depends upon the performance of many thousands of researchers, the physicist is still likely to look down upon all these space scientists as mere "plumbers."

The sad truth of the matter, however, is that the lost contact between the world of the senses and appearances and the physical world view has been reestablished not by the pure scientist but by the "plumber." The technicians, who account today for the overwhelming majority of all "researchers," have brought the results of the scientists down to earth. And even though the scientist is still beset by paradoxes and the most bewildering perplexities, the very fact that a whole technology could develop out of his results demonstrates the "soundness" of his theories and hypotheses more convincingly than any merely scientific observation or experiment ever could. It is perfectly true that the scientist himself does not want to go to the moon; he knows that for his purposes unmanned spaceships carrying the best instruments human ingenuity can invent will do the job of exploring the moon's surface much better than dozens of astronauts. And yet, an actual change of the human world, the conquest of space or whatever we may wish to call it, is achieved only when manned space carriers are shot into the universe, so that man himself can go where up to now only human imagination and its power of abstraction, or human ingenuity and its power of fabrication, could reach. To be sure, all we plan to do now is to explore our own immediate surroundings in the universe, the infinitely small place that the human race could reach even if it were to travel with the velocity of light. In view of man's life span—the only absolute limitation left at the present moment—it is quite unlikely that he will ever go much farther. But even for this limited job, we have to leave the world of our senses and of our bodies, not only in imagination but in reality.

It is as though Einstein's imagined "observer poised in free space"—surely the creation of the human mind and its power of abstraction—is being followed by a bodily observer who must behave as though he were a mere child of abstraction and imagination. It is at this point that all the theoretical perplexities of the new physical world view intrude as realities upon man's everyday world and throw out of gear his "natural," that is, earthbound, common sense. He would, for instance, be confronted in reality with Einstein's famous "twin paradox," which hypothetically assumes that "a twin brother who takes off on a space journey in which he travels at a sizeable fraction of the speed of light would return to find his earthbound twin either older than he or little more than a dim recollection in the memory of his descendants." For although many physicists had found this paradox difficult to swallow, the "clock paradox," on which it is based, seems to have been verified experimentally, so that the only alternative to it would be the assumption that earthborn life under all circumstances remains bound to a time concept that demonstrably does not belong among "true realities," but among mere appearances. We have reached the stage where the Cartesian radical doubt of reality as such, the first philosophical answer to the discoveries of science in the modern age, may become subject to physical experiments that would make short shrift of Descartes's famous consolation, *I doubt therefore I am,* and of his conviction that, whatever the state of reality and of truth as they are given to the senses and to reason, you cannot "doubt of your doubt and remain uncertain whether you doubt or not."

The magnitude of the space enterprise seems to me beyond dispute, and all objections raised against it on the purely utilitarian level—that it is too expensive, that the money were better spent on education and the improvement of the citizens, on the fight against poverty and disease, or whatever other worthy purposes may come to mind—sound to me slightly absurd, out of tune with the things that are at stake and whose consequences today appear still quite unpredictable. There is, moreover, another reason why I think these arguments are beside the point. They are singularly inapplicable because the enterprise itself could come about only through an amazing development of man's scientific capabilities. The very integrity of science demands that not only utilitarian considerations but even the reflection upon the stature of man be left in abeyance. Has not each of the advances of science, since the time of Copernicus, almost automatically resulted in a decrease in his stature? Man, insofar as he is a scientist, does not care about his own stature in the universe or about his position on the evolutionary ladder of animal life; this "carelessness" is his pride and his glory. The simple fact that physicists split the atom without any hesitations the very moment they knew how to do it, although they realized full well the enormous destructive potentialities of their operation, demonstrates that the scientist *qua* scientist does not even care about the survival of the human race on earth or, for that matter, about the survival of the planet itself. All associations for "Atoms for Peace," all warnings not to use the new power unwisely, and even the pangs of conscience many scientists felt when the first bombs fell on Hiroshima and Nagasaki cannot obscure this simple, elementary fact. For in all these efforts the scientists acted not as scientists but as citizens, and if their voices have more authority than the voices of laymen, they do so only because the scientists are in possession of more precise information. Valid and plausible arguments against the "conquest of space" could be raised only if they were to show that the whole enterprise might be self-defeating in its own terms.

There are a few indications that such might indeed be the case. If we leave out of account the human life span, which under no circumstances (even if biology should succeed in extending it significantly and man were able to travel with the speed of light) will permit man to explore more than his immediate surroundings in the immensity of the universe, the most significant indication that it might be self-defeating consists in Heisenberg's discovery of the uncertainty principle. Heisenberg showed conclusively that there is a definite and final limit to the accuracy of all measurements obtainable by man-devised instruments. In his own words, "We decide, by our selection of the type of observation employed, which aspects of nature are to be determined and which are to be blurred." He holds that "the most important new result of nuclear physics was the recognition of the possibility of applying quite different types of natural laws, without contradiction, to one and the same physical event. This is due to the fact that within a system of laws which are based on certain fundamental ideas only certain quite definite ways of asking questions make sense, and thus, that such a system is separated from others which allow different questions to be put." From this he concluded that the modern search for "true reality" behind mere appearances, which has brought about the world we live in and resulted in the Atomic Revolution, has led into a situation in the sciences themselves in which man has lost the very objectivity of the natural world, so that man in his hunt for "objective reality" suddenly discovered that he always "confronts himself alone."

The truth of Heisenberg's observation seems to me to transcend by far the field of strictly scientific endeavor and to gain in poignancy if it is applied to the technology that has grown out of modern science. Every progress in science in the last decades, from the moment it was absorbed into technology and thus introduced into the factual world where we live our everyday lives, has brought with it a veritable avalanche of fabulous instruments and ever more ingenious machinery. All of this makes it more unlikely every day that man will encounter anything in the world around him that is not man-made and hence is not, in the last analysis, he himself in a different disguise. The astronaut, shot into outer space and imprisoned in his instrument-ridden capsule where each actual physical encounter with his surroundings would spell immediate death, might well be taken as the symbolic incarnation of Heisenberg's man—the man who will be the less likely ever to meet anything but himself the more ardently he wishes to eliminate all anthropocentric considerations from his encounter with the nonhuman world around him.

It is at this point, it seems to me, that the humanist's concern with man and the stature of man has caught up with the scientist. It is as though the sciences had done what the humanities never could have achieved, namely, to prove demonstrably the validity of this concern. The situation, as it presents itself today, oddly resembles an elaborate verification of a remark by Franz Kafka, written at the very beginning of this development: Man, he said, "found the Archimedean point, but he used it against himself; it seems that he was permitted to find it only under this condition." For the conquest of space, the search for a point outside the earth from which it would be possible to unhinge, as it were, the planet itself, is no accidental result of the modern age's science. This was from its very beginnings not a "natural" but a universal science, it was not a physics but an astrophysics which looked upon the earth from a point in the universe. In terms of this development, the attempt to conquer space means that man hopes he will be able to journey to the Archimedean point which he anticipated by sheer force of abstraction and imagination. However, in doing so, he will necessarily lose his advantage. All he can find is the Archimedean point with respect to the earth, but once arrived there and having acquired this absolute power over his earthly habitat, he would need a new Archimedean point, and so *ad infinitum*. In other words, man can only get lost in the immensity of the universe, for the only true Archimedean point would be the absolute void behind the universe.

Yet even if man recognizes that there might be absolute limits to his search for knowledge and that it might be wise to suspect such limitations whenever it turns out that the scientist can do more than he is capable of comprehending, and even if he realizes that he cannot "conquer space," but at best make a few discoveries in our solar system, the journey into space and to the Archimedean point with respect to the earth is far from being a harmless or unequivocally triumphant enterprise. It could add to the stature of man inasmuch as man, in distinction from other living things, desires to be at home in a "territory" as large as possible. In that case, he would only take possession of what is his own, although it took him a long time to discover it. These new possessions, like all property, would have to be limited, and once the limit is reached and the limitations established, the new world view that may conceivably grow out of it is likely to be once more geocentric and anthropomorphic, although not in the old sense of the earth being the center of the universe and of man being the highest being there is. It would be geocentric in the sense that the earth, and not the universe, is the center and the home of mortal men, and it would be anthropomorphic in the sense that man would count his own factual mortality among the elementary conditions under which his scientific efforts are possible at all.

At this moment, the prospects for such an entirely beneficial development and solution of the present predicaments of modern science and technology do not look particularly good. We have come to our present capacity to "conquer space" through our new ability to handle nature from a point in the universe outside the earth. For this is what we actually do when we release energy processes that ordinarily go on only in the sun, or attempt to initiate in a test tube the processes of cosmic evolution, or build machines for the production and control of energies unkown in the household of earthly nature. Without as yet actually occupying the point where Archimedes had wished to stand, we have found a way to act on the earth as though we disposed of terrestrial nature from outside, from the point of Einstein's "observer freely poised in space." If we look down from this point upon what is going on on earth and upon the various activities of men, that is, if we apply the Archimedean point to ourselves, then these activities will indeed appear to ourselves as no more than "overt behavior," which we can study with the same methods we use to study the behavior of rats. Seen from a sufficient distance, the cars in which we travel and which we know we built ourselves will look as though they were, as Heisenberg once put it, "as inescapable a part of ourselves as the snail's shell is to its occupant." All our pride in what we can do will disappear into some kind of mutation of the human race; the whole of technology, seen from this point, in fact no longer appears "as the result of a conscious human effort to extend man's material powers, but rather as a large-scale biological process." Under these circumstances, speech and everyday language would indeed be no longer a meaningful utterance that transcends behavior even if it only expresses it, and it would much better be replaced by the extreme and in itself meaningless formalism of mathematical signs.

The conquest of space and the science that made it possible have come perilously close to this point. If they ever should reach it in earnest, the stature of man would not simply be lowered by all standards we know of, it would have been destroyed.

Some Moral and Technical Consequences of Automation

Norbert Wiener

Some 13 years ago, a book of mine was published by the name of *Cybernetics.* In it I discussed the problems of control and communication in the living organism and the machine. I made a considerable number of predictions about the development of controlled machines and about the corresponding techniques of automatization, which I foresaw as having important consequences affecting the society of the future. Now, 13 years later, it seems appropriate to take stock of the present position with respect to both cybernetic technique and the social consequences of this technique.

Before commencing on the detail of these matters, I should like to mention a certain attitude of the man in the street toward cybernetics and automatization. This attitude needs a critical discussion, and in my opinion it should be rejected in its entirety. This is the assumption that machines cannot possess any degree of originality. This frequently takes the form of a statement that nothing can come out of

Reprinted from *Science,* Vol. 131, pp. 1355-58, 6 May 1960.

the machine which has not been put into it. This is often interpreted as asserting that a machine which man has made must remain continually subject to man, so that its operation is at any time open to human interference and to a change in policy. On the basis of such an attitude, many people have pooh-poohed the dangers of machine techniques, and they have flatly contradicted the early predictions of Samuel Butler that the machine might take over the control of mankind.

It is true that in the time of Samuel Butler the available machines were far less hazardous than machines are today, for they involved only power, not a certain degree of thinking and communication. However, the machine techniques of the present day have invaded the latter fields as well, so that the actual machine of today is very different from the image that Butler held, and we cannot transfer to these new devices the assumptions which seemed axiomatic a generation ago. I find myself facing a public which has formed its attitude toward the machine on the basis of an imperfect understanding of the structure and mode of operation of modern machines.

It is my thesis that machines can and do transcend some of the limitations of their designers, and that in doing so they may be both effective and dangerous. It may well be that in principle we cannot make any machine the elements of whose behavior we cannot comprehend sooner or later. This does not mean in any way that we shall be able to comprehend these elements in substantially less time than the time required for operation of the machine, or even within any given number of years or generations.

As is now generally admitted, over a limited range of operation, machines act far more rapidly than human beings and are far more precise in performing the details of their operations. This being the case, even when machines do not in any way transcend man's intelligence, they very well may, and often do, transcend man in the performance of tasks. An intelligent understanding of their mode of performance may be delayed until long after the task which they have been set has been completed.

This means that though machines are theoretically subject to human criticism, such criticism may be ineffective until long after it is relevant. To be effective in warding off disastrous consequences, our understanding of our man-made machines should in general develop *pari passu* with the performance of the machine. By the very slowness of our human actions, our effective control of our machines may be nullified. By the time we are able to react to information conveyed by our senses and stop the car we are driving, it may already have run head on into a wall.

Game-Playing

I shall come back to this point later in this article. For the present, let me discuss the technique of machines for a very specific purpose: that of playing games. In this matter I shall deal more particularly with the game of checkers, for which the International Business Machines Corporation has developed very effective game-playing machines.

Let me say once for all that we are not concerned here with the machines which operate on a perfect closed theory of the game they play. The game theory of von Neumann and Morgenstern may be suggestive as to the operation of actual game-playing machines, but it does not actually describe them.

In a game as complicated as checkers, if each player tries to choose his play in view of the best move his opponent can make, against the best response he can give, against the best response his opponent can give, and so on, he will have taken upon himself an impossible task. Not only is this humanly impossible but there is actually no reason to suppose that it is the best policy against the opponent by whom he is faced, whose limitations are equal to his own.

The von Neumann theory of games bears no very close relation to the theory by which game-playing machines operate. The latter corresponds much more closely to the methods of play used by expert but limited human chess players against other chess players. Such players depend on certain strategic evaluations, which are in essence not complete. While the von Neumann type of play is valid for games like ticktacktoe, with a complete theory, the very interest of chess and checkers lies in the fact that they do not possess a complete theory. Neither do war, nor business competition, nor any of the other forms of competitive activity in which we are really interested.

In a game like ticktacktoe, with a small number of moves, where each player is in a position to contemplate all possibilities and to establish a defense against the best possible moves of the other player, a complete theory of the von Neumann type is valid. In such a case, the game must inevitably end in a win for the first player, a win for the second player, or a draw.

I question strongly whether this concept of the perfect game is a completely realistic one in the cases of actual, nontrivial games. Great generals like Napoleon and great admirals like Nelson have proceeded in a different manner. They have been aware not only of the limitations of their opponents in such matters as materiel and personnel but equally of their limitations in experience and in military know-how. It was by a realistic appraisal of the relative inexperience in naval operations of the continental powers as compared with the highly developed tactical and strategic competence of the British fleet that Nelson was able to display the boldness which pushed the continental forces off the seas. This he could not have done had he engaged in the long, relatively indecisive, and possibly losing conflict to which his assumption of the best possible strategy on the part of his enemy would have doomed him.

In assessing not merely the materiel and personnel of his enemies but also the degree of judgment and the amount of skill in tactics and strategy to be expected of them, Nelson acted on the basis of their record in previous combats. Similarly, an important factor in Napoleon's conduct of his combat with the Austrians in Italy was his knowledge of the rigidity and mental limitations of Würmser.

This element of experience should receive adequate recognition in any realistic theory of games. It is quite legitimate for a chess player to play, not against an ideal, nonexisting, perfect antagonist, but rather against one whose habits he has been able to determine from the record. Thus, in the theory of games, at least two different intellectual efforts must be made. One is the short-term effort of playing with a determined policy for the individual game. The other is the examination of a record of many games. This record has been set by the player himself, by his opponent, or even by players with whom he has not personally played. In terms of this record, he determines the relative advantages of different policies as proved over the past.

There is even a third stage of judgment required in a chess game. This is expressed at least in part by the length of the significant past. The development of theory in chess decreases the importance of games played at a different stage of the art. On the other hand, an astute chess theoretician may estimate in advance that a certain policy currently in fashion has become of little value, and that it may be best to return to earlier modes of play to anticipate the change in policy of the people whom he is likely to find as his opponents.

Thus, in determining policy in chess there are several different levels of consideration which correspond in a certain way to the different logical types of Bertrand Russell. There is the level of tactics, the level of strategy, the level of the general considerations which should have been weighed in determining this strategy, the level in which the length of the relevant past—the past within which these considerations may be valid—is taken into account, and so on. Each new level demands a study of a much larger past than the previous one.

I have compared these levels with the logical types of Russell concerning classes, classes of classes, classes of classes of classes, and so on. It may be noted that Russell does not consider statements involving all types as significant. He brings out the futility of such questions as that concerning the barber who shaves all persons, and only those persons, who do not shave themselves. Does he shave himself? On one type he does, on the next type he does not, and so on, indefinitely. All such questions involving an infinity of types may lead to unsolvable paradoxes. Similarly, the search for the best policy under all levels of sophistication is a futile one and must lead to nothing but confusion.

These considerations arise in the determination of policy by machines as well as in the determination of policy by persons. These are the questions which arise in the programming of programming. The lowest type of game-playing machine plays in terms of a certain rigid evaluation of plays. Quantities such as the value of pieces gained or lost, the command of the pieces, their mobility, and so on, can be given numerical weights on a certain empirical basis, and a weighting may be given on this basis to each next play conforming to the rules of the game. The play with the greatest weight may be chosen. Under these circumstances, the play of the machine will seem to its antagonist—who cannot help but evaluate the chess personality of the machine—a rigid one.

Learning Machines

The next step is for the machine to take into consideration not merely the moves as they occurred in the individual game but the record of games previously played. On this basis, the machine may stop from time to time, not to play but to consider what (linear or nonlinear) weighting of the factors which it has been given to consider would correspond best to won games as opposed to lost (or drawn) games. On this basis, it continues to play with a new weighting. Such a machine would seem to its human opponent to have a far less rigid game personality, and tricks which would defeat it at an earlier stage may now fail to deceive it.

The present level of these learning machines is that they play a fair amateur game at chess but that in checkers they can show a marked superiority to the player who has programmed them after from 10 to 20 playing hours of working and indoctrination. They thus most definitely escape from the completely effective control of the man who has made them. Rigid as the repertory of factors may be which they are in a position to take into consideration, they do unquestionably—and so say those who have played with them—show originality, not merely in their tactics, which may be quite unforeseen, but even in the detailed weighting of their strategy.

As I have said, checker-playing machines which learn have developed to the point at which they can defeat the programmer. However, they appear still to have one weakness. This lies in the end game. Here the machines are somewhat clumsy in determining the best way to give the *coup de grâce*. This is due to the fact that the existing machines have for the most part adopted a program in which the identical strategy is carried out at each stage of the game. In view of the similarity of values of pieces in checkers, this is quite natural for a large part of the play but ceases to be perfectly relevant when the board is relatively empty and the main problem is that of moving into position rather than that of direct attack. Within the frame of the methods I have described it is quite possible to have a second exploration to determine what the policy should be after the number of pieces of the opponent is so reduced that these new considerations become paramount.

Chess-playing machines have not, so far, been brought to the degree of perfection of checker-playing machines, although, as I have said, they can most certainly play a respectable amateur game. Probably the reason for this is similar to the reason for their relative efficiency in the end game of checkers. In chess, not only is the end game quite different in its proper strategy from the mid-game but the opening game is also. The difference between checkers and chess in this respect is that the initial play of the pieces in checkers is not very different in character from the play which arises in the mid-game, while in chess, pieces at the beginning have an arrangement of exceptionally low mobility, so that the problem of deploying them from this position is particularly difficult. This is the reason why opening play and development form a special branch of chess theory.

There are various ways in which the machine can take cognizance of these well-known facts and explore a separate waiting strategy for the opening. This does not mean that the type of game theory which I have here discussed is not applicable to chess but merely that it requires much more consideration before we can make a machine that can play master chess. Some of my friends who are engaged in these problems believe that this goal will be achieved in from 10 to 25 years. Not being a chess expert, I do not venture to make any such predictions on my own initiative.

It is quite in the cards that learning machines will be used to program the pushing of the button in a new pushbutton war. Here we are considering a field in which automata of a nonlearning character are probably already in use. It is quite out of the question to program these machines on the basis of an actual experience in real war. For one thing, a sufficient experience to give an adequate programming would probably see humanity already wiped out.

Moreover, the techniques of pushbutton war are bound to change so much that by the time an adequate experience could have been accumulated, the basis of the beginning would have radically changed. Therefore, the programming of such a learning machine would have to be based on some sort of war game, just as commanders and staff officials now learn an important part of the art of strategy in a similar manner. Here, however, if the rules for victory in a war game do not correspond to what we actually wish for our country, it is more than likely that such a machine may produce a policy which would win a nominal victory on points at the cost of every interest we have at heart, even that of national survival.

Man and Slave

The problem, and it is a moral problem, with which we are here faced is very close to one of the great problems of slavery. Let us grant that slavery is bad because it is cruel. It is, however, self-contradictory, and for a reason which is quite different. We wish a slave to be intelligent, to be able to assist us in the carrying out of our tasks. However, we also wish him to be subservient. Complete subservience and complete intelligence do not go together. How often in ancient times the clever Greek philosopher slave of a less intelligent Roman slaveholder must have dominated the actions of his master rather than obeyed his wishes! Similarly, if the machines become more and more efficient and operate at a higher and higher psychological level, the catastrophe foreseen by Butler of the dominance of the machine comes nearer and nearer.

The human brain is a far more efficient control apparatus than is the intelligent machine when we come to the higher areas of logic. It is a self-organizing system which depends on its capacity to modify itself into a new machine rather than on ironclad accuracy and speed in problem-solving. We have already made very successful machines of the lowest logical type, with a rigid policy. We are beginning to make machines of the second logical type, where the policy itself improves with learning. In the construction of operative machines, there is no specific foreseeable limit with respect to logical type, nor is it safe to make a pronouncement about the exact level at which the brain is superior to the machine. Yet for a long time at least there will always be some level at which the brain is better than the constructed machine, even though this level may shift upwards and upwards.

It may be seen that the result of a programming technique of automatization is to remove from the mind of the designer and operator an effective understanding of many of the stages by which the machine comes to its conclusions and of what the real tactical intentions of many of its operations may be. This is highly relevant to the problem of our being able to foresee undesired consequences outside the frame of the strategy of the game while the machine is still in action and while intervention on our part may prevent the occurrence of these consequences.

Here it is necessary to realize that human action is a feedback action. To avoid a disastrous consequence, it is not enough that some action on our part should be sufficient to change the course of the machine, because it is quite possible that we lack information on which to base consideration of such an action.

In neurophysiological language, ataxia can be quite as much of a deprivation as paralysis. A patient with locomotor ataxia may not suffer from any defect of his muscles or motor nerves, but if his muscles and tendons and organs do not tell him exactly what position he is in, and whether the tensions to which his organs are subjected will or will not lead to his falling, he will be unable to stand up. Similarly, when a machine constructed by us is capable of operating on its incoming data at a pace which we cannot keep, we may not know, until too late, when to turn it off. We all know the fable of the sorcerer's apprentice, in which the boy makes the broom carry water in his master's absence, so that it is on the point of drowning him when his master reappears. If the boy had had to seek a charm to stop the mischief in the *grimoires* of his master's library, he might have been drowned before he had discovered the relevant incantation. Similarly, if a bottle factory is programmed on the basis of maximum productivity, the owner may be made bankrupt by the enormous inventory of unsalable bottles manufactured before he learns he should have stopped production six months earlier.

The "Sorcerer's Apprentice" is only one of many tales based on the assumption that the agencies of magic are literal-minded. There is the story of the genie and the fisherman in the *Arabian Nights*, in which the fisherman breaks the seal of Solomon which has imprisoned the genie and finds the genie vowed to his own destruction; there is the tale of the "Monkey's Paw," by W. W. Jacobs, in which the sergeant major brings back from India a talisman which has the power to grant each of three people three wishes. Of the first recipient of this talisman we are told only that his third wish is for death. The sergeant major, the second person whose wishes are granted, finds his experiences too terrible to relate. His friend, who receives the talisman, wishes first for £200. Shortly thereafter, an official of the factory in which his son works comes to tell him that his son has been killed in the machinery and that, without any admission of responsibility, the company is sending him as consolation the sum of £200. His next wish is that his son should come back, and the ghost knocks at the door. His third wish is that the ghost should go away.

Disastrous results are to be expected not merely in the world of fairy tales but in the real world wherever two agencies essentially foreign to each other are coupled in the attempt to achieve a common purpose. If the communication between these two agencies as to the nature of this purpose is incomplete, it must only be expected that the results of this cooperation will be unsatisfactory. If we use, to achieve our purposes, a mechanical agency with whose operation we cannot efficiently interfere once we have started it, because the action is so fast and irrevocable that we have not the data to intervene before the action is complete, then we had better be quite sure that the purpose put into the machine is the purpose which we really desire and not merely a colorful imitation of it.

Time Scales

Up to this point I have been considering the quasi-moral problems caused by the simultaneous action of the machine and the human being in a joint enterprise. We have seen that one of the chief causes of the danger of disastrous consequences in the use of the learning machine is that man and machine operate on two distinct time scales, so that the machine is much faster than man and the two do not gear together without serious difficulties. Problems of the same sort arise whenever two control operators on very different time scales act together, irrespective of which system is the faster and which system is the slower. This leaves us the much more directly moral question: What are the moral problems when man as an individual operates in connection with the controlled process of a much slower time scale, such as a portion of political history or—our main subject of inquiry—the development of science?

Let it be noted that the development of science is a control and communication process for the long-term understanding and control of matter. In this process 50 years are as a day in the life of the individual. For this reason, the individual scientist must work as a part of a process whose time scale is so long that he himself can only contemplate a very limited sector of it. Here, too, communication between the two parts of a double machine is difficult and limited. Even when the individual believes that science contributes to the human ends which he has at heart, his belief needs a continual scanning and re-evaluation which is only partly possible. For the individual scientist, even the partial appraisal of this liaison between the man and the process requires an imaginative forward glance at history which is difficult, exacting, and only limitedly achievable. And if we adhere simply to the creed of the scientist, that an incomplete knowledge of the world and of ourselves is better than no knowledge, we can still by no means always justify the naive assumption that the faster we rush ahead to employ the new powers for action which are opened up to us, the better it will be. We must always exert the full strength of our imagination to examine where the full use of our new modalities may lead us.

Some Moral and Technical Consequences of Automation: A Refutation

Arthur Samuel

In an article entitled "Some moral and technical consequences of automation" (*1*), Norbert Wiener has stated some conclusions with which I disagree. Wiener seems to believe that machines *can* possess originality and that they *are* a threat to mankind. In ascribing a contrary opinion to the man in the street—to wit, "that nothing can come out of the machine which has not been put into it"—he overlooks or ignores the fact that there is a long history of the acceptance of this more reassuring view by scientific workers in the field, from the time of Charles Babbage to the present (*2*). Apparently Wiener shares some of the lack of understanding which he ascribes to the public, at least to the extent that he reads implications into some of the recent work which the workers themselves deny.

From *Science,* Vol. 132, pp. 741-42, 16 September 1960.

It is my conviction that machines cannot possess originality in the sense implied by Wiener and that they cannot transcend man's intelligence. I agree with Wiener in his thesis that "machines can and do transcend some of the limitations of their designers, and that in doing so they may be both effective and dangerous." The modern automobile travels faster than its designer can run, it is effective, and the records of highway fatalities attest to the dangerous consequences. However, a perusal of Wiener's article reveals that much more than this is meant, and it is to this extension of the thesis that I wish to take exception.

Wiener's reference to the "Sorcerer's Apprentice," and to the many tales based on the assumption that the agencies of magic are literal-minded, might almost lead one to think that he attributes magic to the machine. He most certainly seems to imply an equality between man and the machine when he states "disastrous results are to be expected not merely in the world of fairy tales but in the real world wherever two agencies essentially foreign to each other are coupled in the attempt to achieve a common purpose." In relationships between man and a machine the machine is an agency, but only an agency of man, entirely subservient to man and to his will. Of course, no one will deny that "we had better be quite sure that the purpose put into the machine is the purpose which we really desire and not merely a colorful imitation of it." If we want our house to be at 70°F when we get up in the morning, we had better set the thermostat at 70° and not at 32°. But once the thermostat is set at 70° we can go to sleep without fear that the genie in the furnace controls might, for some reason of his own, decide that 32° was a better figure. In exactly the same way and to the same degree we must anticipate our own inability to interfere when we instruct a modern digital computer (which works faster than we do) and when we instruct a thermostat (which works while we sleep).

Wiener's analogy between a machine and a human slave is also quite misleading. He is right in his assertion that "complete subservience and complete intelligence do not go together" in a human slave with human emotions and needs and with a will of his own. To ascribe human attributes to a machine simply because the machine can simulate some forms of human behavior is, obviously, a fallacious form of reasoning.

A machine is not a genie, it does not work by magic, it does not possess a will, and, Wiener to the contrary, nothing comes out which has not been put in, barring, of course, an infrequent case of malfunctioning. Programming techniques which we now employ to instruct the modern digital computer so as to make it into a learning machine *do not* "remove from the mind of the designer and operator an effective understanding of many of the stages by which the machine comes to its conclusions." Since the machine does not have a mind of its own, the "conclusions" are not "its." The so-called "conclusions" are only the logical consequences of the input program and input data, as revealed by the mechanistic functioning of an inanimate assemblage of mechanical and electrical parts. The "intentions" which the machine seems to manifest are the intentions of the human programmer, as specified in advance, or they are subsidiary intentions derived from these, following rules specified by the programmer. We can even anticipate higher levels of abstraction, just as Wiener does, in which the program will not only modify the subsidiary intentions but will also modify the rules which are used in their derivation, or in which it will modify the ways in which it modifies the rules, and so on, or even in which one machine will design and construct a second machine with enhanced capabilities. However, and this is important, the machine *will not* and *cannot* do any of these things until it has been instructed as to how to proceed. There is and (logically there must always remain) a complete hiatus between (i) any ultimate extension and elaboration in this process of carrying out man's wishes and (ii) the development within the machine of a will of its own. To believe otherwise is either to believe in magic or to believe that the existence of man's will is an illusion and that man's actions are as mechanical as the machine's. Perhaps Wiener's article and my rebuttal have both been mechanistically determined, but this I refuse to believe.

An apparent exception to these conclusions might be claimed for projected machines of the so-called "neural net" type. These machines were not mentioned by Wiener, and, unfortunately, they cannot be adequately discussed in the space available here. Briefly, however, one envisions a collection of simple devices which, individually, simulate the neurons of an animal's nervous system and which are interconnected by some random process simulating the organization of the nervous system. It is maintained by many serious workers that such nets can be made to exhibit purposeful activity by instruction and training with reward-and-punishment routines similar to those used with young animals. Since the internal connections would be unknown, the precise behavior of the nets would be unpredictable and, therefore, potentially dangerous. At the present time, the largest nets that can be constructed are nearer in size to the nervous system of a flatworm than to the brain of man and so hardly constitute a threat. If practical machines of this type become a reality we will have to take a much closer look at their implications than either Wiener or I have been able to do.

One final matter requires some clarification—a matter having to do with Wiener's concluding remarks to the effect that "We must always exert the full strength of our imagination to examine where the full use of our new modalities may lead us." This certainly makes good sense if we assume that Wiener means for us to include the full use of our intelligence as well as of our imagination. However, coming as it did at the end of an article which raised the spectre of man's domination by a "learning machine," this statement casts an unwarranted shadow over the learning machine and, specifically, over the modern digital computer. I would be remiss were I to close without setting the record straight in this regard.

First a word about the capabilities of the digital computer. Although I have maintained that "nothing comes out that has not gone in," this does not mean that the output does not possess value over and beyond the value to us of the input data. The utility of the computer resides in the speed and accuracy with which the computer provides the desired transformations of the input data from a form which man may not be able to use directly to one which is of direct utility. In principle, a man with a pencil and a piece of paper could always arrive at the same result. In practice, it might take so long to perform the calculation that the answer would no longer be of value, and, indeed, the answer might never be obtained because of man's faculty for making mistakes. Because of the very large disparity in speeds, of the order of 100,000 to 1, on a computer we can complete calculations which are of immense economic value with great precision and with a reliability which inspires confidence, and all this in time intervals which conform to the demands of real-life situations. The magnitude of the tasks and the speed with which they are performed are truly breath-taking, and they do tend to impress the casual observer as being a form of magic, particularly when he is unacquainted with the many, many hours of human thought which have gone into both the design of the machine and, more particularly, into the writing of the program which specifies the machine's detailed behavior.

Most uses of the computer can be explained in terms of simulation. When one computes the breaking strength of an airplane wing under conditions of turbulence, one is, in effect, simulating the behavior of an actual airplane wing which is subjected to unusual stresses, all this without danger to a human pilot, and, indeed, without ever having to build the airplane in the first place. The checker-playing program on the I.B.M. 704, to which Wiener referred, actually simulates a human checker player, and the machine learns by accumulating data from its playing experience and by using some of the logical processes which might be employed by a person under similar circumstances. The specific logical processes used are, of course, those which were specified in advance by the human programmer. In these, and in many other situations, the great speed of the computer enables us to test the outcome resulting from a variety of choices of initial actions and so to choose the course with the highest payoff before the march of human events forces us to take some inadequately considered action. This ability to look into the future, as it were, by simulation on a computer is already being widely used, and as time goes on it is sure to find application in more and more aspects of our daily lives.

Finally, as to the portents for good or evil which are contained in the use of this truly remarkable machine—most, if not all, of man's inventions are instrumentalities which may be employed by both saints and sinners. One can make a case, as one of my associates has jokingly done, for the thesis that the typewriter is an invention of the devil, since its use in the nations' war offices has made wars more horrible, and because it has enslaved the flower of our young womanhood. On the whole, however, most of us concede that the typewriter, as a labor-saving device, has been a boon, not a curse. The digital computer is something more than merely another labor-saving device, since it augments man's brain rather than his brawn, and since it allows him to look into the future. If we believe, as most scientists do, that it is to our advantage to increase the rate at which we can acquire knowledge, then we can hardly do otherwise than to assert that the modern digital computer is a modality whose value is overwhelmingly on the side of the good. I rest my case with this assertion.

REFERENCES

1. N. Wiener, *Science* 131, 1355 (1960).
2. L. F. Menebra, "Sketch of the analytical engine invented by Charles Babbage, Esq.," *Taylor's Scientific Memoirs* (London, 1842), vol. 3, pp. 666-731 (translated with editorial notes by Lady Lovelace: see, particularly, p. 722); D. R. Hartree, *Calculating Instruments and Machines* (Cambridge Univ. Press, New York, 1950); A. M. Turing, *Mind: A Quarterly Review of Psychology & Philosophy* 59, 433 (1950); B. V. Bowden, *Faster Than Thought* (Pitman, New York, 1953), chap 26; A. L. Samuel, *I.B.M. J. Research and Develop.* 3, 211 (1959).

The Computerized Intellectuals

S. P. R. Charter

Man needs a new idea of himself for himself; a new perspective to meet a new challenge and a new threat; a new faith, a faith in himself, as a warming assurance against the loneliness of the cosmic cold encroaching upon him with each impressive step of the computerized intellectuals of our time.

To these intellectuals, opinions must either emerge from cleverly designed computer programs or be capable of being verified by such data insertions and manipulations. Man—his continuation, modification, or annihilation—is to them a series of complex formulations readily convertible into electronic impulses. Conclusions drawn from mechanized manipulations with almost lecherous abandon are then considered to be objective, irrefutable, and profound.

The fallacy here is not that man designs and uses amazingly complex equipment, but that his dependence upon his mechanized extensions has become so deep-rooted that he, himself, is increasingly

---

becoming an extension of his own mechanics and is decreasingly capable of functioning as a total human being. This process is being pursued with an acceleration in the name of progress; and an evolutionary coarsening seems to be taking place. Sadly enough, the mechanistic manipulators—prophets of expediency—are highly honored by the society they dishonor.

Mechanistic-man does not here refer to those of his devices that release him from animal-toil—whether in the daily mechanics of living or in the mechanics of the pursuit of knowledge—but rather to those devices that enmesh him in electronic nets and befoul his thinking.

Actually, many tools of daily living, even when they may offer an small measure of seeming comfort, are harmful to the individual and to his community. For example, the automatic garbage-disposal units so common in rabbit-run subdivisions are being outlawed in many areas because they consume too much water and pollute the water consumed by adjacent runs.

Tools used in the pursuit of knowledge frequently hinder the acquisition of knowledge. In medicine, for example, the electrocardiograph is a relatively simple device and easy to operate; but interpretations drawn from electrocardiograms by inexperienced physicians may give doctor and patient either a false sense of well-being or generate baseless fears. Here, the clever tool distinctly hinders the acquisition of knowledge since, without it, knowledge would be pursued and perhaps found along other paths. In this regard, the mechanical tool becomes a crutch to faltering intellects.

The basic approach of the computerized intellectual is essentially defeatist, isolationist, or religionist; and often a combination of the three.

Most of them are defeatist against man himself. Deliberate or accidental nuclear-weaponry-malfunction, they believe, will destroy the world at some calculable point in time. In order to eliminate the risk of total erasure, their solution is for man, now, to eliminate such devices from his arsenal of abilities. However, since man cannot expunge knowledge from the race-memory of the species, the threat of total erasure will always be with us until the inevitable terminal accident. In the opinion of these defeatists, man is therefore doomed—if not in the Biblical sense, then in the computer sense.

Many computerized intellectuals are also isolationist in that they work for governments and the network of government-industry complexes rather than for man. For these complexes, they examine permutations and combinations of imagined possibilities and probabilities which will hopefully terminate in the theoretical vanquishment of the enemy. The enemy is another government and its network of government-industry complexes. In order to retain any sanity many of these scientists attempt to isolate government from people, trying to maintain that their scientific skills and intellectual efforts are directed not at the people of a nation or at the nation itself, but only at the governments of the theoretical enemy nations. Massive weaponry, they maintain, is intended only as a threat to isolate the enemy and will never be used except as a threat. A threat that does not carry direct execution as a highly probable progression has all of the impact of a punch thrown by a shadow-boxer; therefore, they would seem to maintain that bigger weapons are only to throw bigger shadows. Meanwhile, their scientific energies can be devoted to space-penetration. Of course, space-weaponry has an intimate relationship with Earth-weaponry, and anything related to Earth-weaponry automatically opens the coffers of government. Perhaps it is not so strange that when his mechanical extensions take off from launching-pads on their soaring paths man hides in protective bunkers and ventures out only when his instruments assure him of safe exit.

The computerized intellectual is a religionist in that he has total faith in his devices, a ritual for their use which he expresses in jargonistic incantations, and an eternal belief in scientific objectivity isolated from human need. Those who do not believe in this religion are sternly excommunicated and expedited to scientific oblivion; those who do believe may also be doomed—but only accidentally.

The quantitative accumulations of fragments of knowledge, so haphazardly gathered in seeming frenzy, have not brought qualitative changes toward wisdom or toward an appreciation of the individual as the possessor of the indivisible strength of unity. There seem to be irreversible changes in man and his inter-relationship with his environment in which acceleration for its own sake appears to be the least common denominator. It does not seem to matter where we are going so long as we go there speedily. We seem to be forced to move faster in order to keep a little ahead of ourselves. While this is a scientific absurdity, it does make for a nice sort of national goal in all parts of the world. If a project is finished a month or a year ahead of schedule, the nation exults. The possibility that in terms of man's hope and destiny, the project was silly from its inception seems unimportant.

Man, of course, has no destiny without survival. Yet is man's greatest crime the discontinuation of himself? Hardly. There are many reasons for a parent to risk, offer, and give his life for the safety of his child, a safety which neither parent nor child can truly guarantee. We are capable of many acts of bravery under stress where one life is deliberately given for the survival of another, of perhaps lesser merit. Discontinuation of self is not the great crime, nor even discontinuation of the species. Total erasure leaves no destiny and no crime. Man's greatest crime is the threat of total erasure because this threat, directed daily against all people, causes the individual to cease existing as an entity with direct meaning to himself or to anyone else.

In man's constant commitment of his greatest crime we see mass-man reaching the height of importance, while individual-man ceases to have significance—often even to himself. Our computerized intellectuals are capable of extracting their fragments of knowledge only from masses of data; the tools we now possess do not function on an individual basis, but only on a comparative basis. We are in a peculiar age of the mass, physically, culturally, ethically and morally. Mass-man has no problems; he is handed solutions which he follows with as little expenditure as possible of any sort of personal awareness.

The foster father or foster brother image of government is in opposition to the actuality of the individual, since government, of whatever complexion, represents mass-morality within which the individual is stratified and compartmentalized.

If mass-morality is the basic ingredient necessary for the survival of atomic-age-man, he will continue to live with the threat of total erasure. How can the individual who permits mass-morality to envelop him survive and flourish in such a debilitating environment? Obviously he cannot. He is prey to all sorts of virulent attacks, the most potent of which is the thickening haze of moral fallout.

If man is to survive and flourish he must find a new faith in himself as an individual and as a total human being. He must resist being coated by the protective coloration of the mass. Each thought and action each day, assumes infiinite importance to the individual in his struggle against deadening absorption.

Man has become part of a strange cycle. There was a time, even in the recent past, when the harm that could be inflicted by pestilence, war, or avarice was confined within regional boundaries, leaving the remainder of Earth free to assist the damaged parts in recovering from their wounds. Somewhere there was a sanctuary for recuperation. Today this is no longer so. Each person is now so intimately placed with another that a blast in one segment of his domicile shakes the entire structure.

Despite our daily disgorging of factual fragments we are living biologically in a parasitic and antagonistic relationship with our

Earth, and not at all in a mutually symbiotic relationship. It was not always this way.

Symbiosis generally defines the living together—sometimes in intimate relationship and close union—of two dissimilar organisms, usually for mutual benefit and sometimes because of mutual need. The relationship may be between two plants, two animals, or between an animal and a plant. Occasionally this union results in an organism entirely different from either component.

The lichen, growing in its numerous variations throughout much of the world where human encroachment has not destroyed them, is often cited as an example of true symbiosis. Lichens are composed of a fungus and an alga, living together for mutual benefit. The fungus gains nutriment from the alga, since the alga contains chlorophyll, which is the essential ingredient in photosynthesis, the food-manufacturing process of plants. The alga gains some weather and insect protection from the fungus as well as a needed and increased water supply. When they attach themselves together to rocks and trees as lichen, they help to break down these parent materials into organic and inorganic soils. They are also used as food by various animals, including man.

Another symbiotic relationship is that existing between man and his domesticated food-producing animals. A cow, when properly maintained by man, offers in return for her maintenance a substantial supply of milk which, in one form or another, is an important part of man's food supply. In her final use she offers meat, leather, and hundreds of pharmaceuticals presently extractable from slaughter-house blood and offal.

While she is alive, cow and man have a rather revealing symbiotic relationship. A milk cow, before man forced her into machine-like regularity, could forage for herself. She did not produce nearly as much milk as she presently does; neither was she so dependent upon man for her food supply and maintenance. At one time she was an earth-like chunk of animal vigor, capable of protecting herself and her young. She had food to offer man, but he struggled to secure it. Today, as a result of generations of intensive domestication, the cow can no longer take care of herself and, if left unattended, is subject to all sorts of diseases and internal malfunction. Since her calf is removed from her side shortly after birth, she does not protect her young. Her milk is removed and sold and her calf is raised mainly on various milk-substitutes. But the cow herself produces considerably more milk as a result of her domestication and her symbiotic existence with man.

It is quite foreseeable that the cow will outlive her usefulness to man at some point relatively near in time. When that happens she will not be returned to her previous undomesticated and unsymbiotic habitat, mainly because man will have more intensified need for the Earth-space the cow would use. She will become a curiosity, and the symbiotic relationship between man and cow will cease to exist. This relationship is presently in the process of major basic change in many parts of the world.

The horse, once in symbiotic relationship to man and a source of much of the energy needed by man in his eternal translation of Earth's resources into human use has, within less than fifty years, become a curiosity and a luxury.

It is difficult to think of symbiotic relationships between man and any other organism that are permanently and mutually advantageous.

In terms of agricultural land, man has been able to reclaim deserts for his use by enriching soils and by bringing in the needed water. For a number of years he lives in a productive relationship with this reclaimed land; but then, whenever he intensifies his efforts toward it, the land gradually recedes from productivity. In the reclaimed arid regions of the western United States, thousands of acres return to the desert every year as intensified water-withdrawals cause drops in water-tables and a harmful increase in water-salinity. Intensive withdrawals of liquids from the earth have, in numerous dry regions, caused the land itself to subside. In the Santa Clara Valley of our West, for example, government calculations indicate that the land has sunk more than nine feet within the last fifty years, an astonishingly rapid subsidence for such a brief geologic time.

It would appear that man's relationship with his Earth is essentially parasitic.

Parasitism is an association of organisms in which one lives on or in the body of the other. The parasite lives off the host, consuming the host's ingredients and rendering no service in return. Many parasites are actually dangerous to the host. In medicine, a vast and complex area known as medical-parasitology, is devoted to this subject.

Since the parasite renders no service in return for his nourishment, recuperation, and reproduction needs, the host usually suffers measurable depletion.

What does man return to his host, the Earth?

At one time, when our country was young, its original Americans returned to the land as much as they took from it. This mutualism, a true symbiotic relationship, became part of the ritual of the American Indian. Our land is rich, our resources great, our productivity fabulous, and our generosity in times of stress and catastrophe unquestioned. But toward our land we seem to believe that the bigness of our taking demonstrates the greatness of our comprehension.

In China, family-land used to be maintained for generations in full productivity because its people returned to the fertile land almost as much as they took from it. This mutualism was part of the ritual of the Chinese farmer.

In Holland, England, France, and in many countries of the world such symbiotic relationships existed in varying degrees between man and his Earth. This is no longer true of any nation. Can we return to that time? Nobody can return to anywhere unchanged.

We now deflower the Earth and present her with bouquets of stockpiled weaponry that can, through accident or corruption, obliterate host and parasite.

There was a time in the history of our nation when we carried our frontiers into strange lands sparsely populated with those who knew themselves as Earth-people whose daily lives and ritual were intimately related to the spirit of the land and the heavens. In their symbiotic relationship with the land these early Americans developed cultures toward which we sometimes yearn in the hidden hunger of a national malnutrition. With individual courage, purpose, and pride, our frontiersmen coursed the wilderness in search of space for the expansion of their own potentialities. They merged their cultures, brought from diverse lands and ghettos across the seas, with the culture of the American Indian. But it took a tragically short time for contempt of the prior occupants to permeate the accelerating bustle of the frontier and for bloodshed, avarice, and cheating to muddy this altered environment in the name of expedience and progress. The conscience of the nation was never aroused, except sporadically, against the immorality with which our early frontier was tamed.

Did the first white-man to land in America, by the fact of his existence, inevitably condemn to oblivion the Indian, his culture, and his symbiotic inter-relationship with his Earth?

Today in this country we have what has been called a New Frontier. As we stretch our tentacles toward the frontiers of space, Earth herself has become the jumping-off place—and the race may be to the swift but not necessarily to the wise.

If we were wise, we would explore our relationship to this New Frontier in light of our experiences with the previous one.

Our new frontier is, in reality, far more than space exploration. Eliminating for the moment all rocketry and nuclear devices, all threat of annihilation, all differences among nations, we still have massive problems of man's being replaced by his machines, of increasing populations and increasing hunger, of accelerated diseases and accompanying anguish, of resources-depletion, of water and air pollution —myriad problems, and no quiet time in which to think. A significant point here is that these problems have to do with individual well-being, while rocketry and nuclear devices have to do with government well-being. National aspirations here have little to do with the aspirations of the individual.

With the explosive birth of the atomic age man entered a heterotic existence. Heterosis is the term used to define the hybrid vigor usually found in the initial crossing of different animals or plants. A cross between a Brahma dam and a Hereford bull, for example, will result in a calf in whom the strong features of each parent will usually be combined. The same is generally true of hybrid corn or cross-bred humans.

We, too, are now cross-bred. Our sire is the basic energy never before generated by man, that never before existed as a tool; and our dam is our Mother Earth to which we are bound.

There are many pitfalls in heterosis. While the first cross between two dissimilar breeds is usually stronger than either parent, crossing the offspring with a member of either parent's breed can result in throwbacks that are even weaker than either of the grandparents. For example, the first cross of a Brahma cow and a Hereford bull results in what is sometimes called a Bramford, an animal with marked hybrid vigor. Crossing this Bramford with either a Brahma or a Hereford will result in an unspecified offspring that will usually be less vigorous than the Bramford.

But there is a method of approach that can bring continuing value from heterosis. Should the Bramford be crossed with a Black Angus or a Brown Swiss, for example, the offspring of this mating will usually continue to be strong. Only when these cross-matings have been achieved by design for several generations after a considerable and adequate blending of genes can the latest offspring be crossed back to its ancestors' breed with some assurance of no harmful effects. The Santa Gertrudis is a new and vigorous cattle breed similarly designed in recent years.

This can actually be an object lesson. We have not yet had enough cross-breeding of our basic energy and our earthbound life to allow our scientists, governments, and other segmenters to dominate. In time, after we have learned to live with our heterotic vigor, after we have had an adequate blending of our altered genetic structures, we can return to our scientists and specialists and allow them to serve the whole body of mankind. Until then they should be addressed in a manner reminiscent of the Englishman who signed all his letters to public officials: "You are, Sir, our most humble servant. . ."

It would seem that for our species to survive and flourish each individual must re-kindle faith in himself, in the totality of his own being, in the strength of his own wholeness. The whole is greater than the sum of its parts because only the whole has the strength of unity. In this sense the individual is the whole, while any government is only the sum of its parts.

Each thought and gesture, each acceptance or rejection of idea, each expression of his code of personal morality, each striving, must reflect to the individual the full strength of his unity. Anything less seems to be a violation of personal dignity.

We have become so much a part of the protective coloration of the mass that each person scarcely recognizes himself and his own value. Obviously we must re-examine our own value to ourselves. While the individual cannot avoid being a statistic within accumulations of data, he can resent and resist being nothing more than a statistic to himself.

If man has any remaining measure of free choice he could well use it to guard against encroachment by those who want to absorb him into the mass, there to become diluted beyond recognition. And he could certainly begin by questioning the wisdom of the computerized intellects of our time. He could insist that the projects of our age, so very costly in terms of the individual, be presented with simplicity and clarity for comprehension by the individual. He could continually maintain that scientific skills be directed away from accelerated man-made threat. He could demand the recognition of himself as a total human being, so to be cherished and respected. And he could be told the extent of his possessions and the true nature of man-made threat, so intimately coupled to man-made promise.

Each person is the center of his universe, and the flow of time is a personal passage to each of us. With benefit to ourselves and to our immediate society, we could frequently ponder where we are, where we have been, and where we are going.

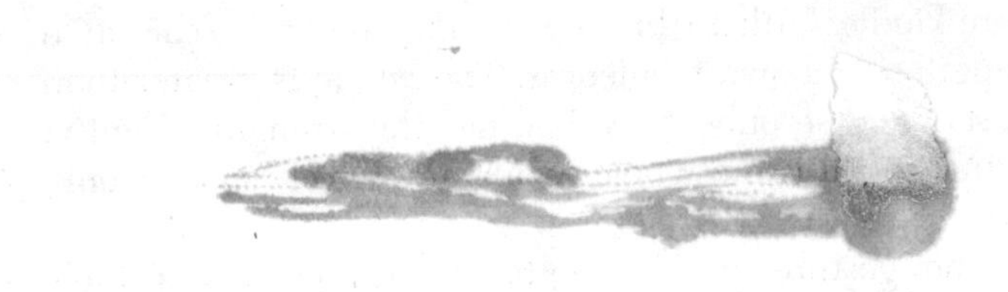